AF477802

ALEX ISRAEL

ALEX ISRAEL
SELF-PORTRAITS

KARMA

From the opening sequence of *Alfred Hitchcock Presents*, 1955–1965

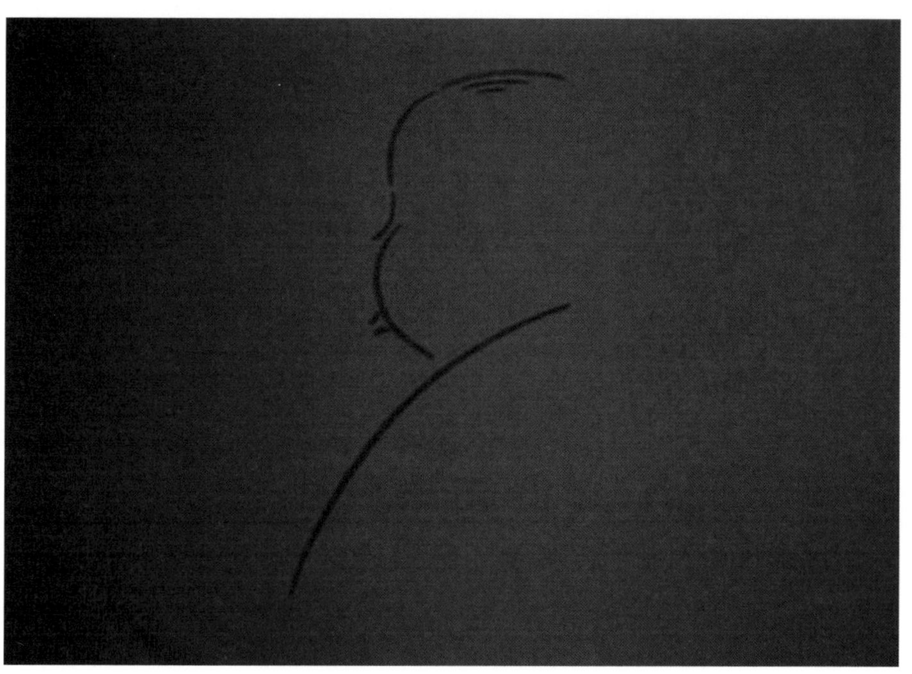

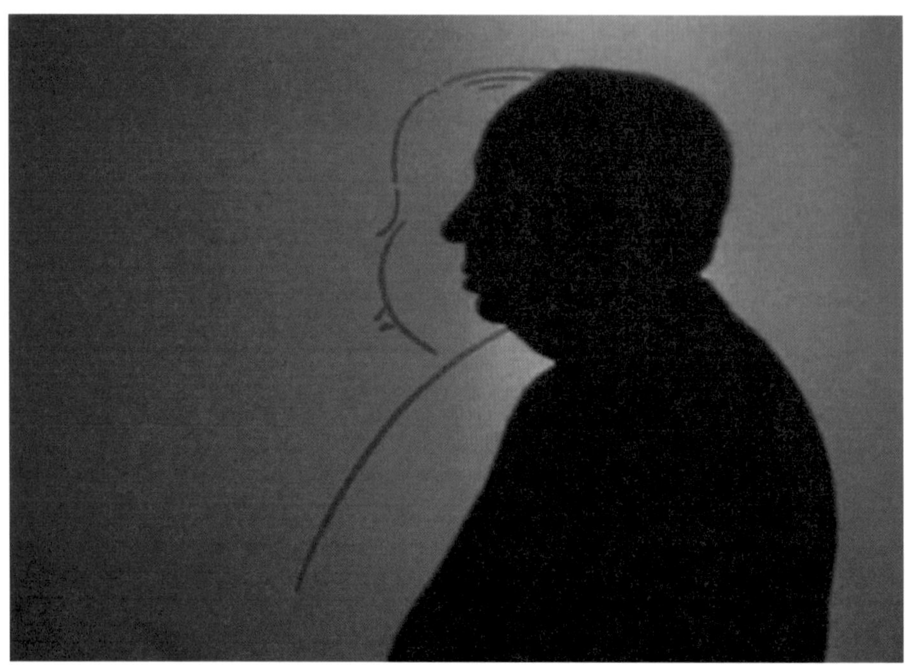

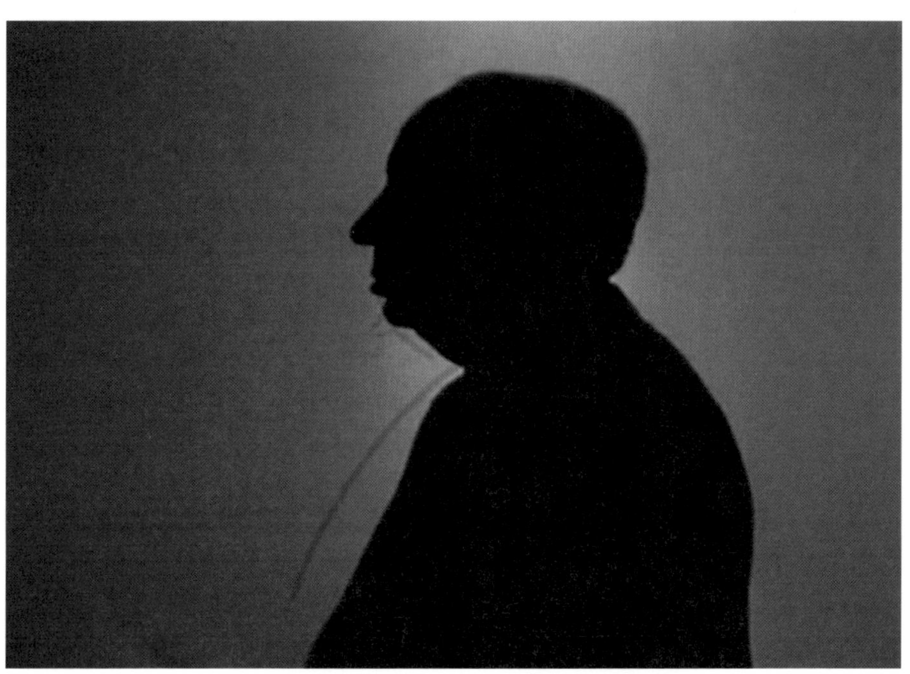

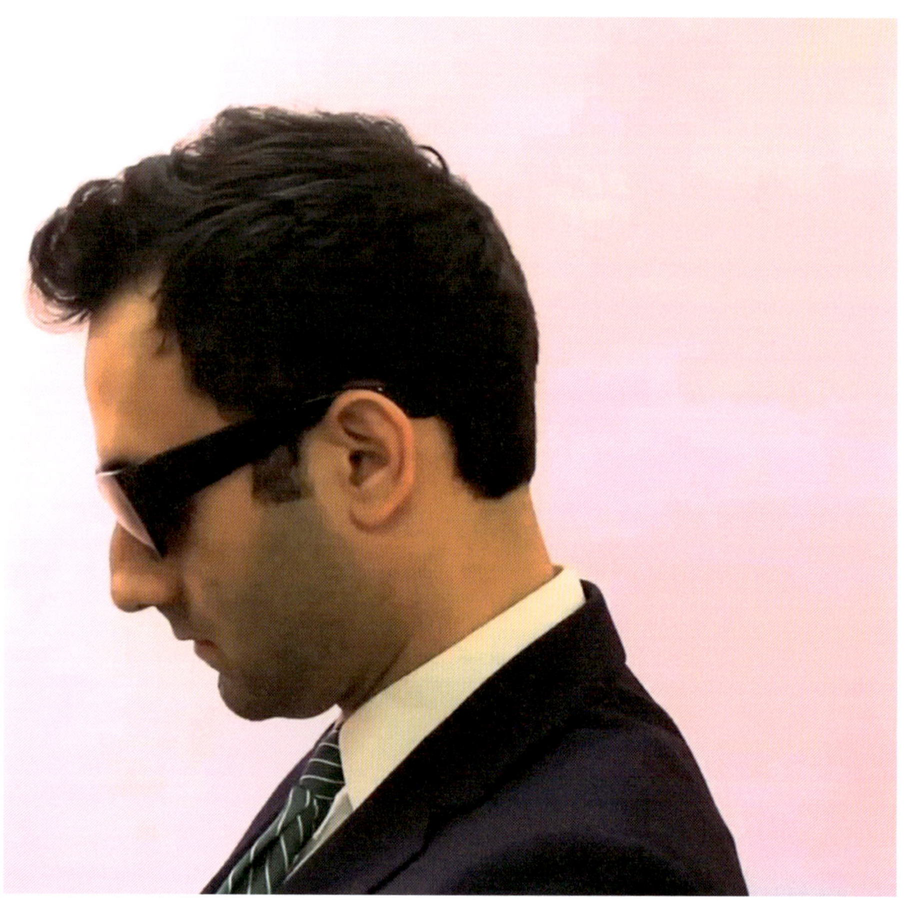

From the opening sequence of *AS IT LAYS*, 2012

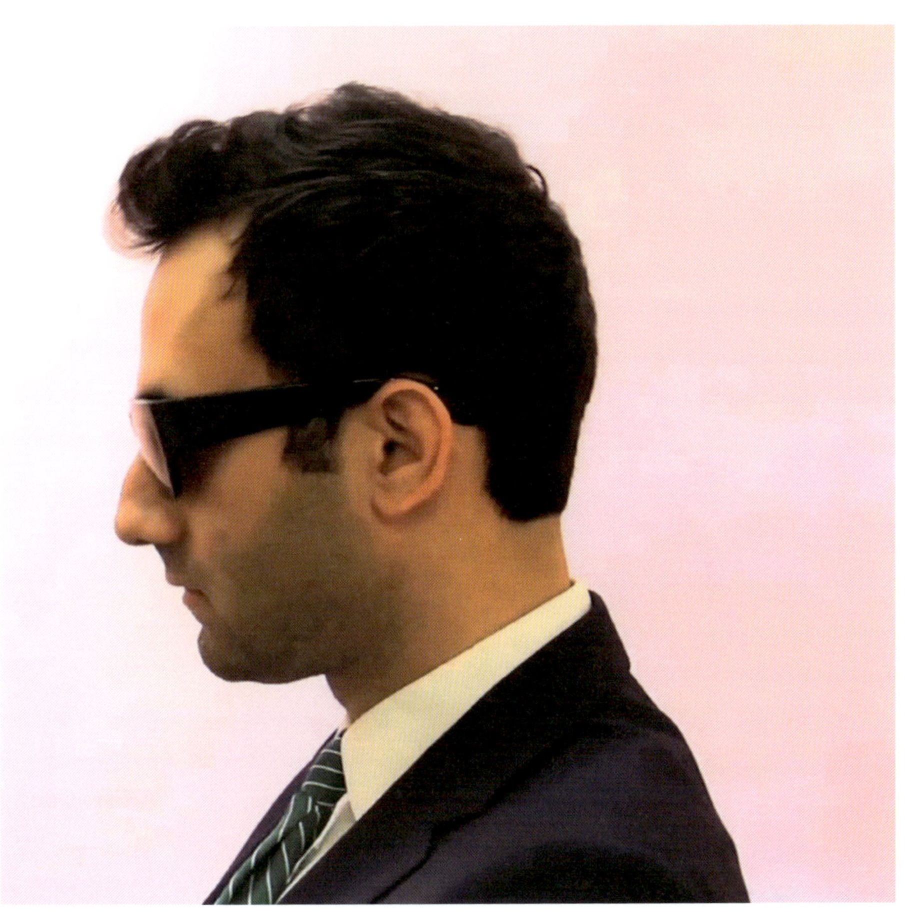

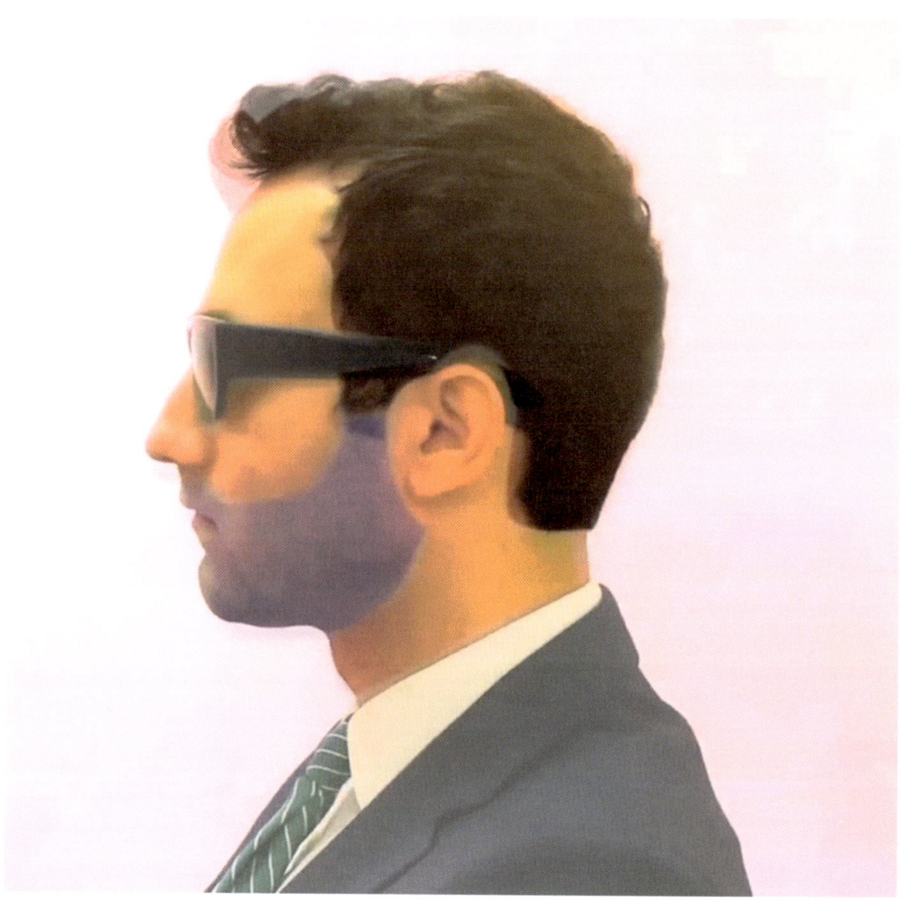

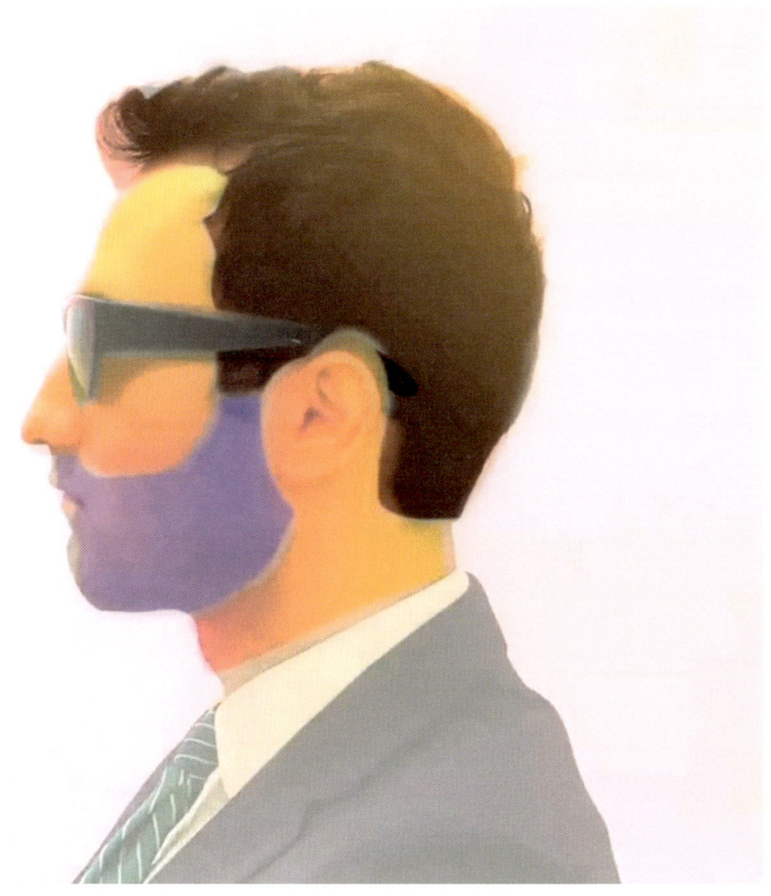

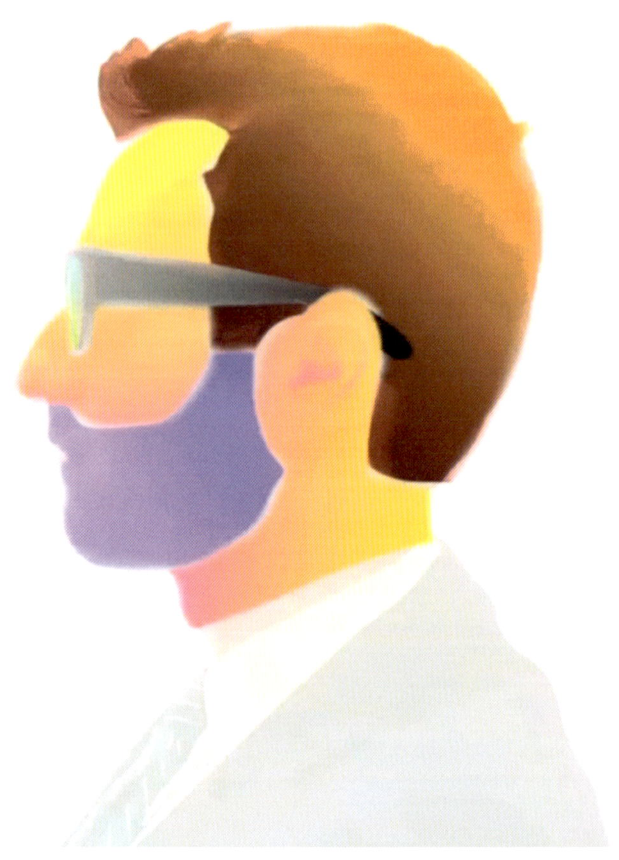

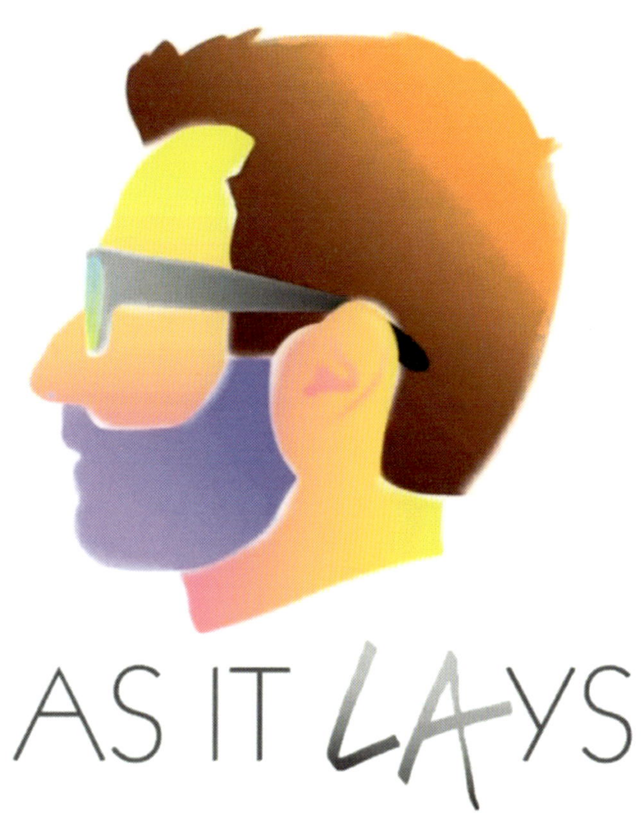

AS IT LAYS

Warner Brothers Studio, Burbank

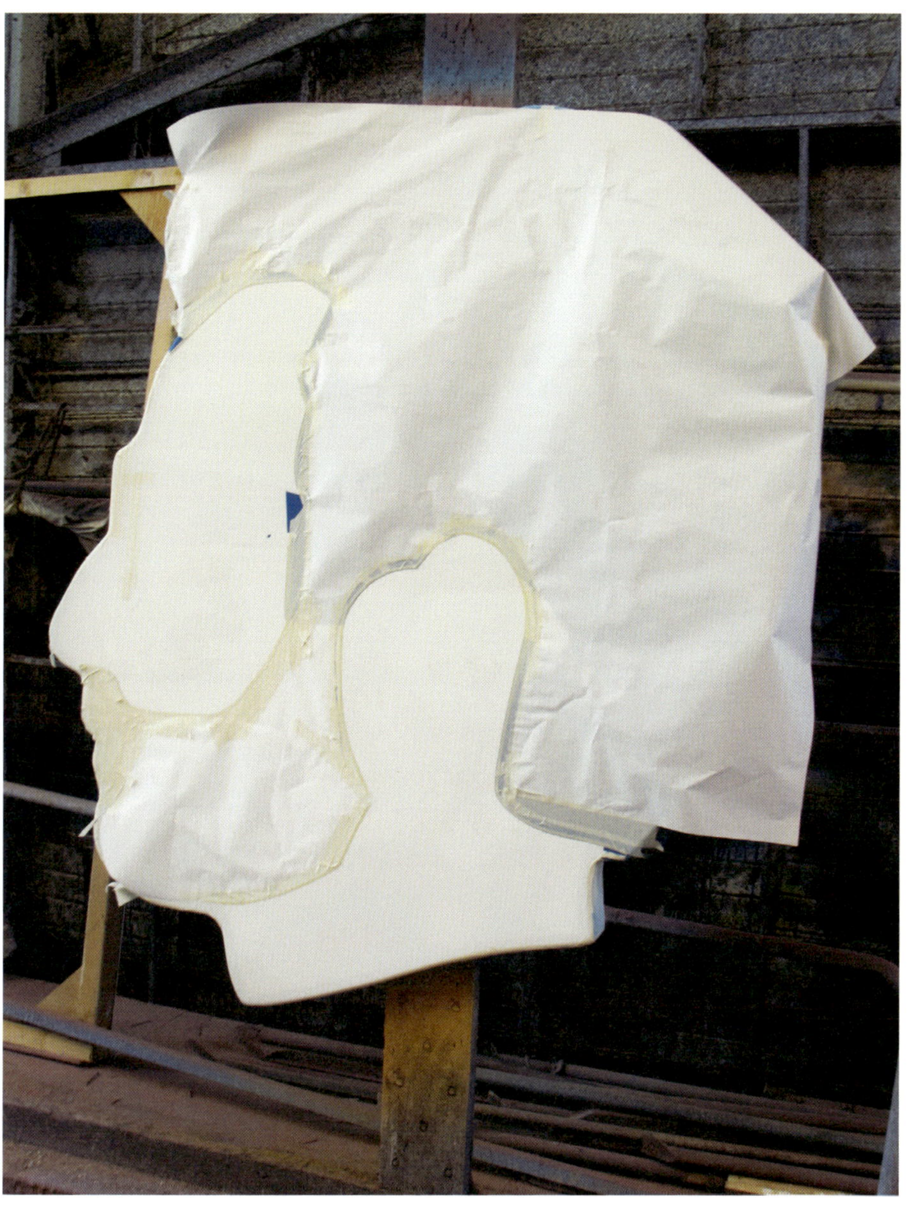

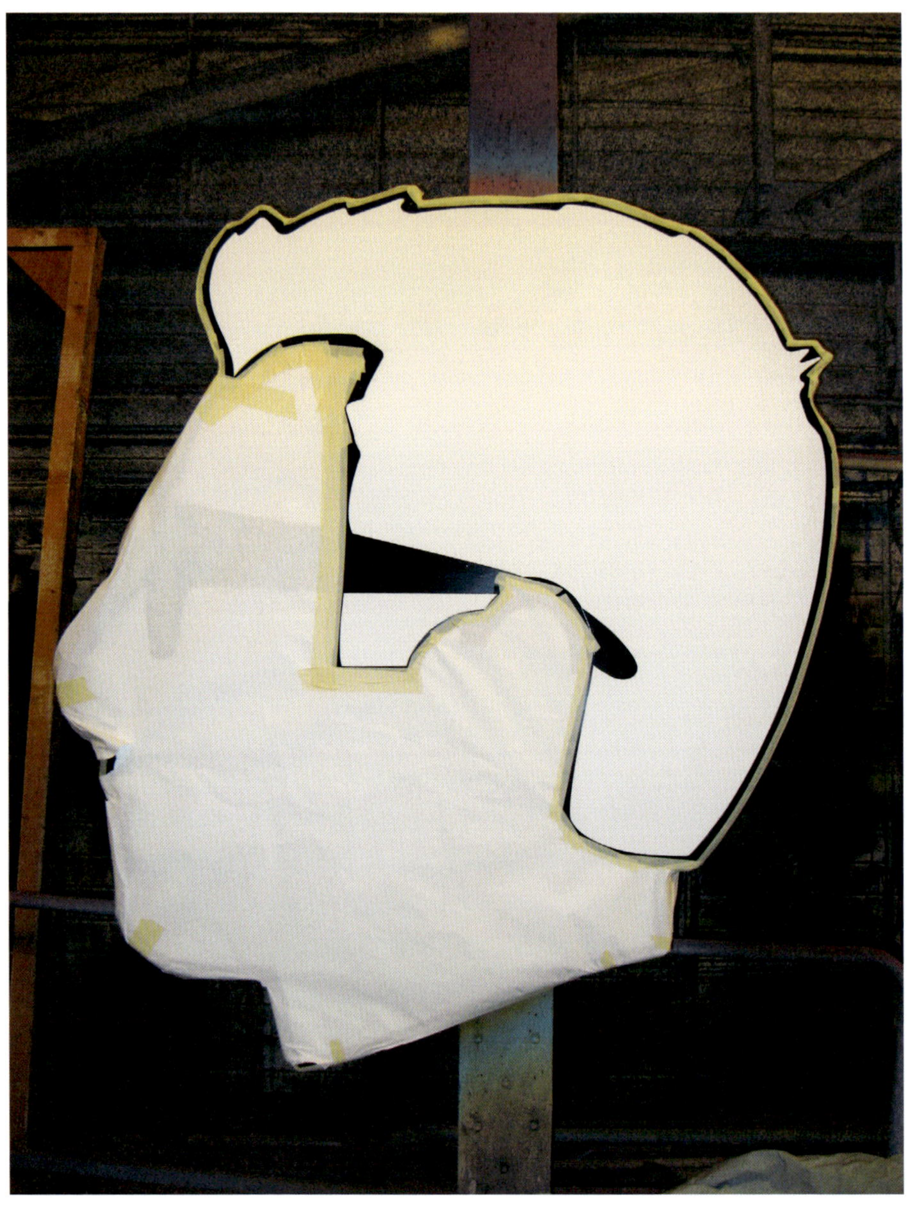

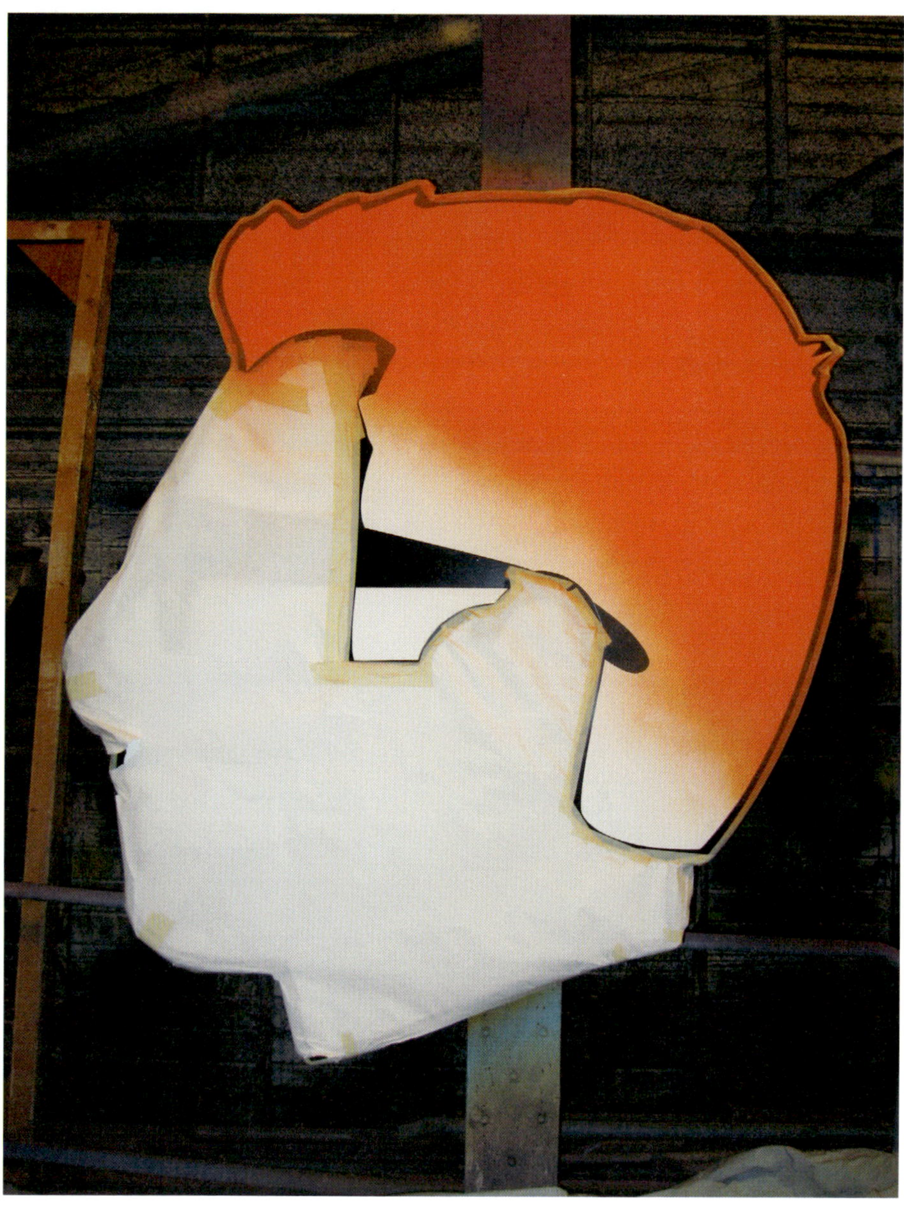

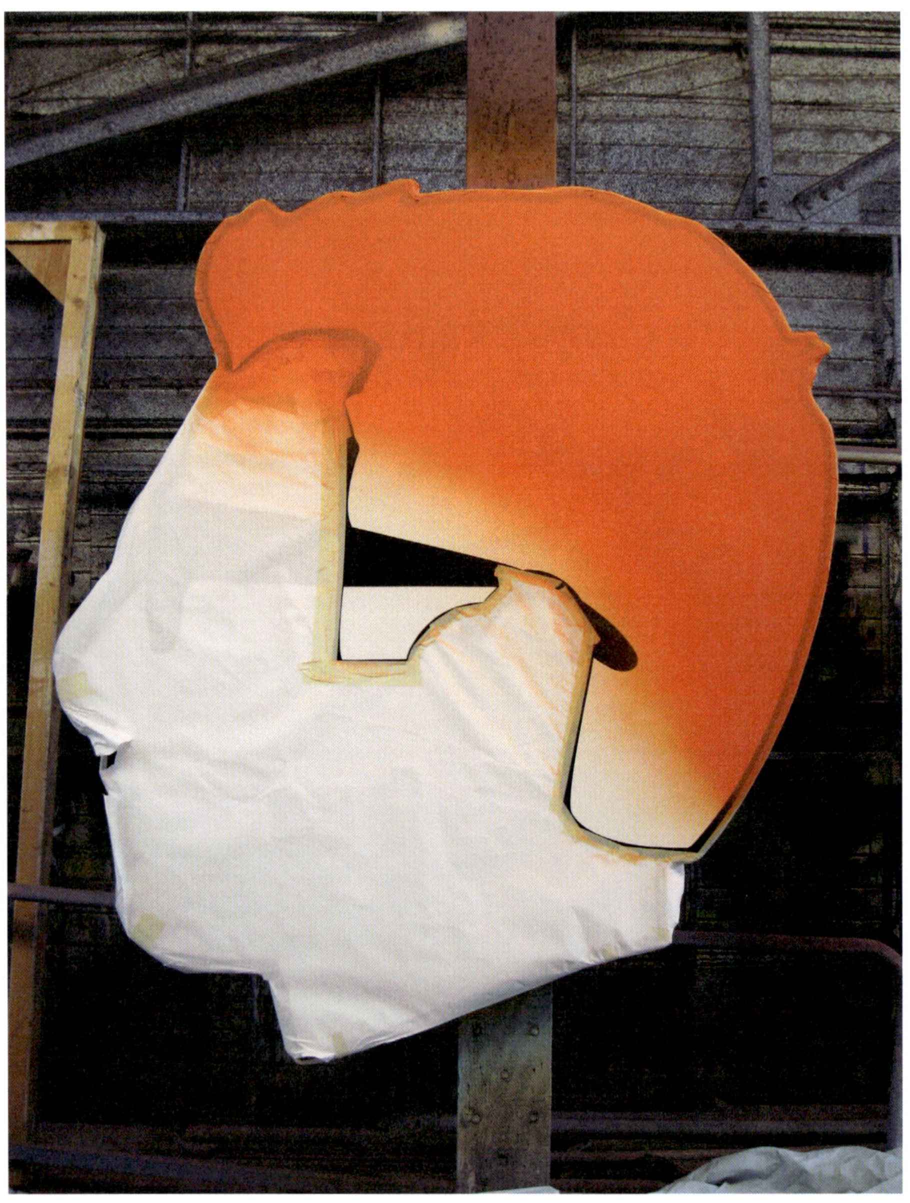

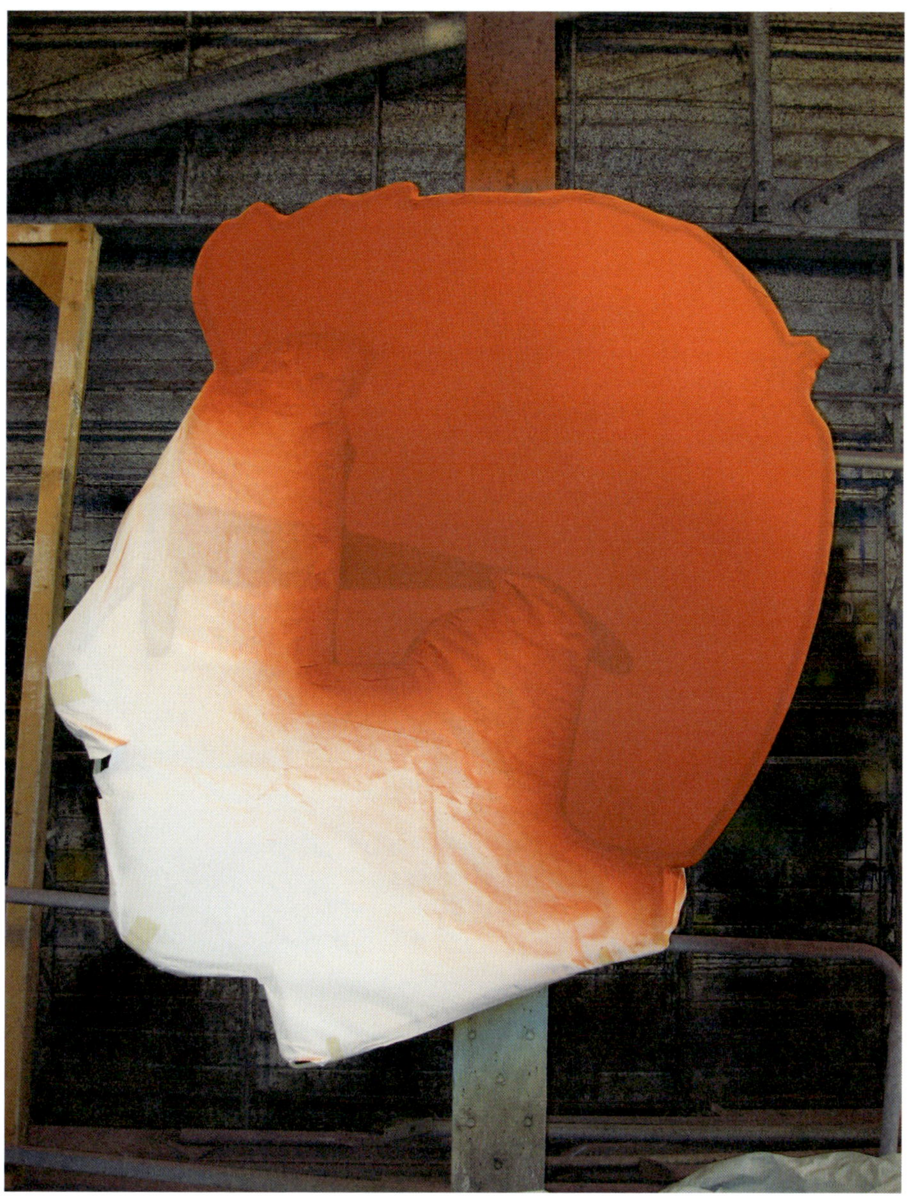

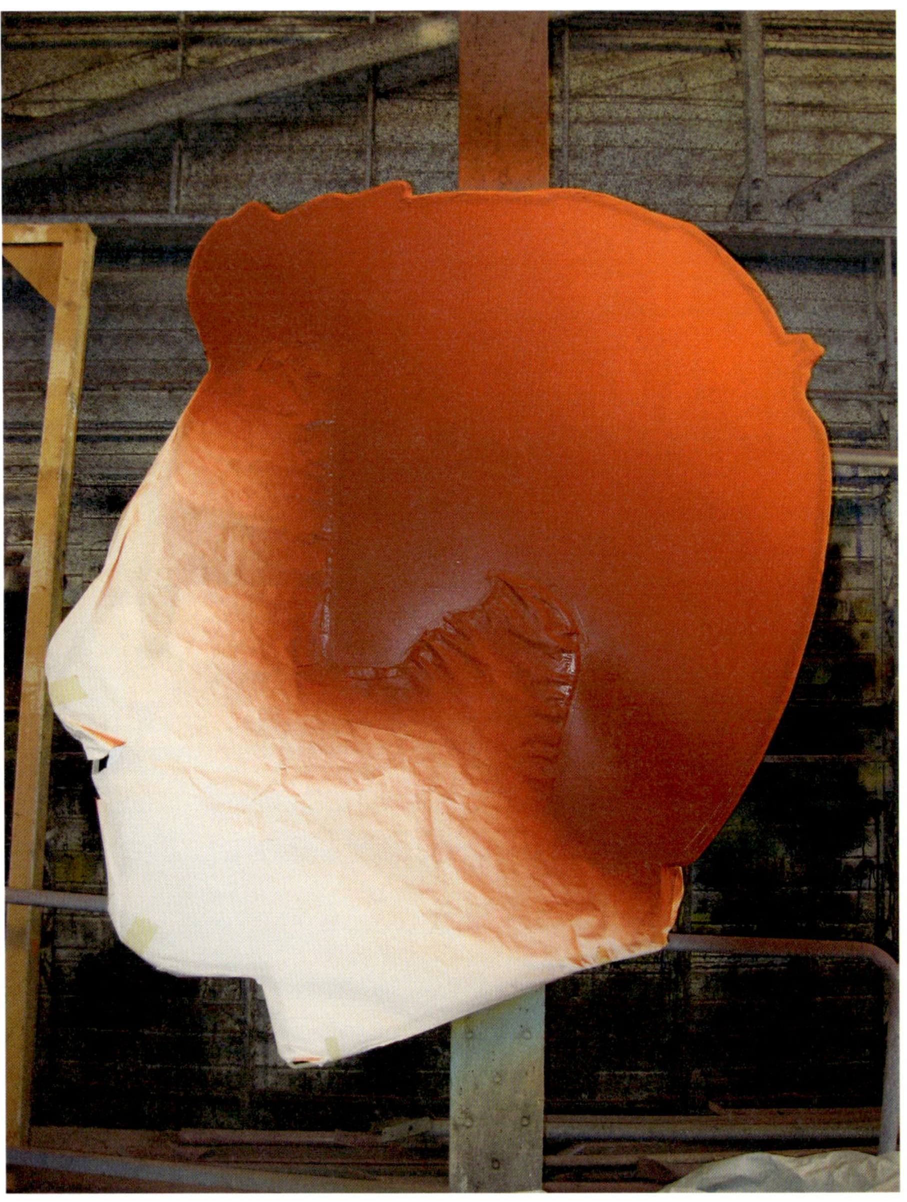

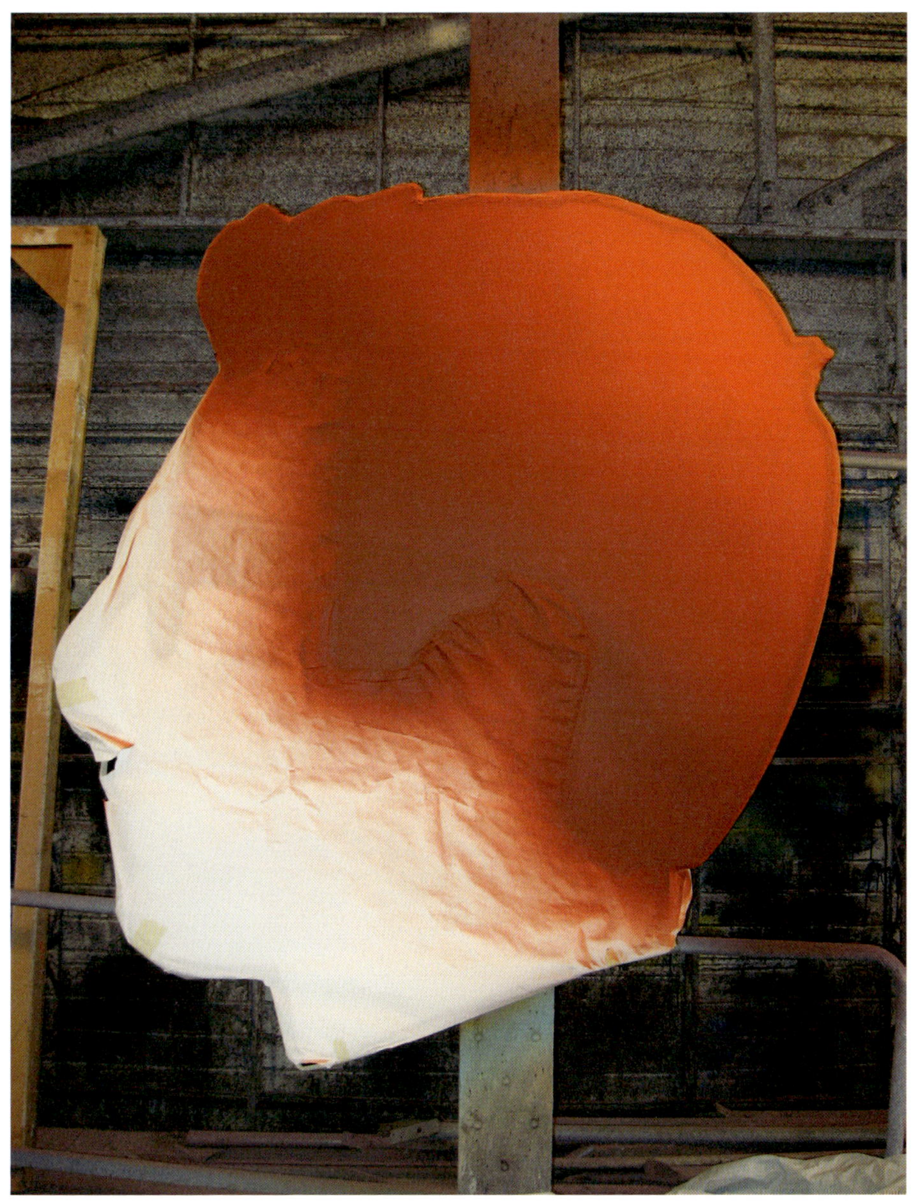

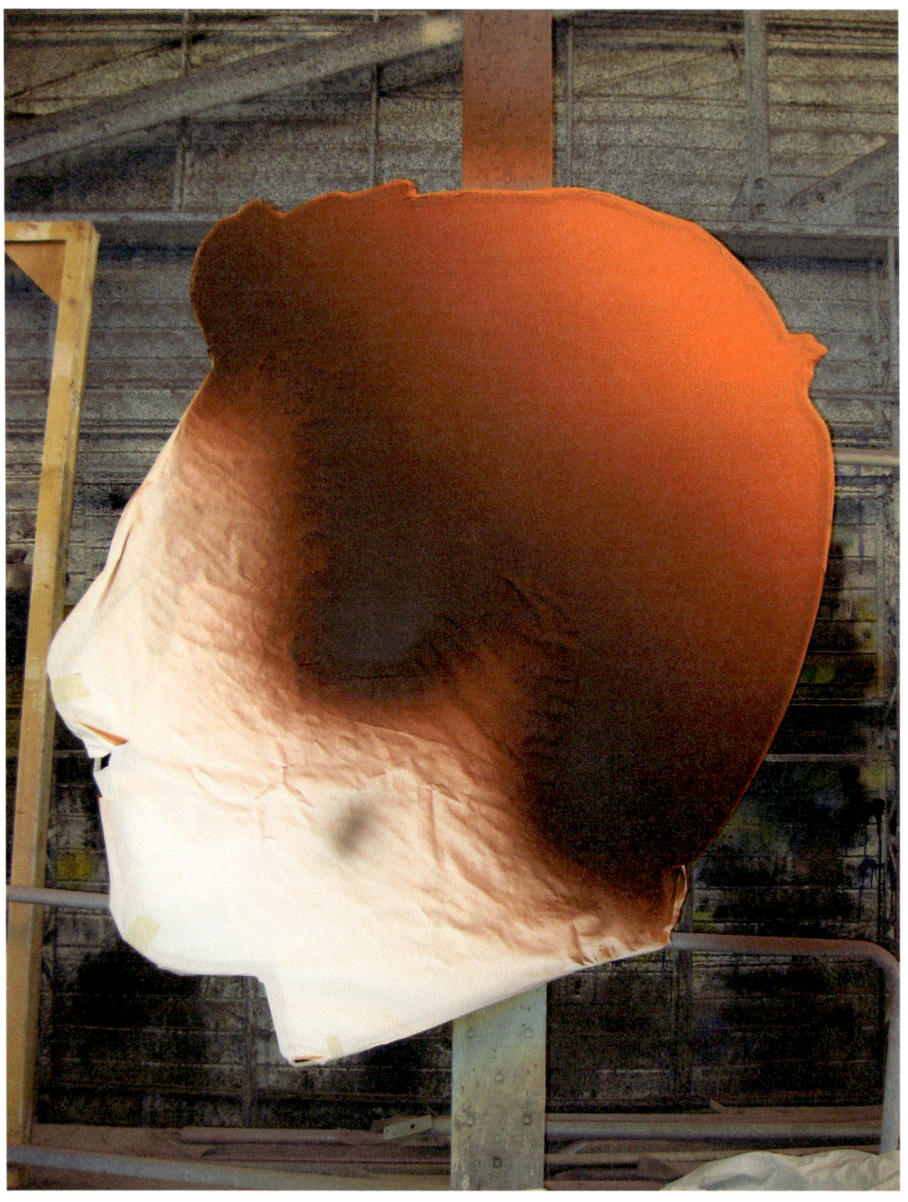

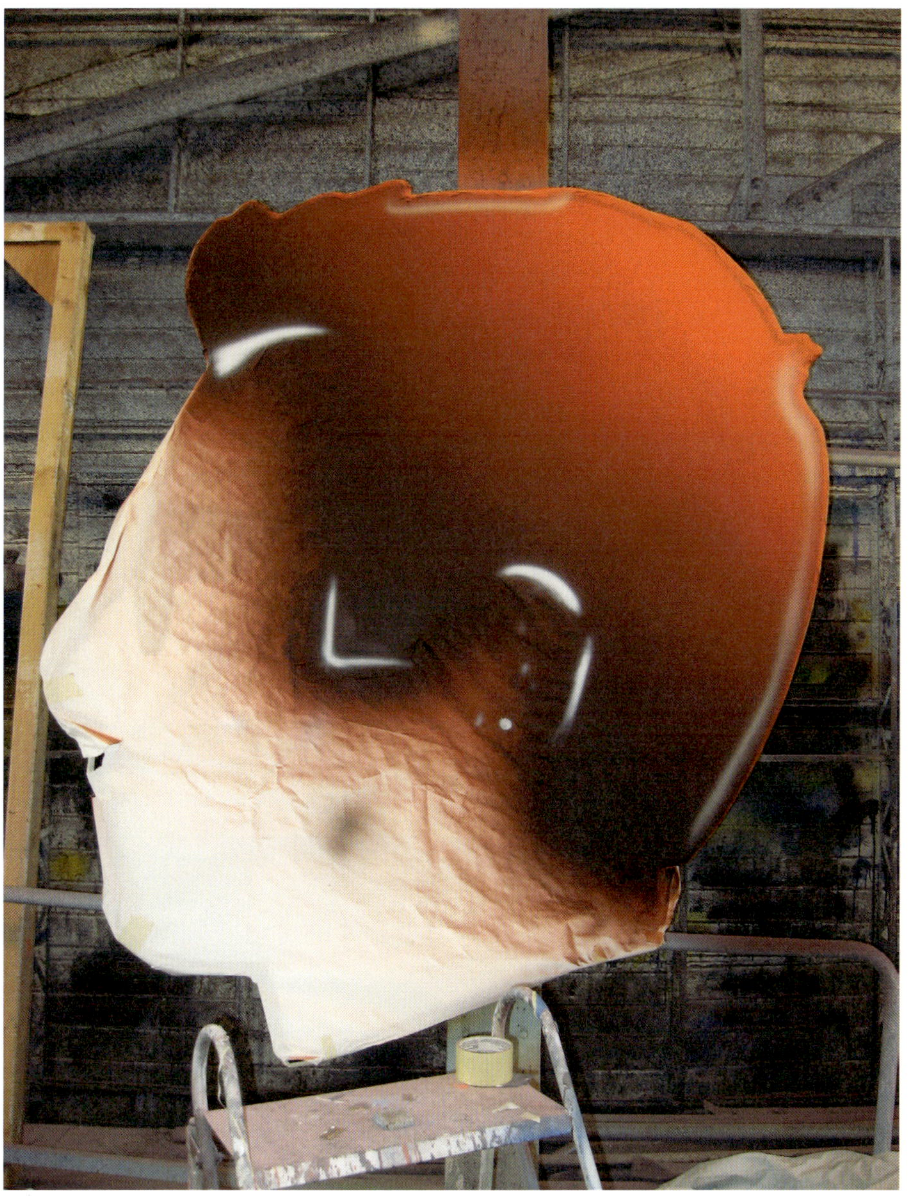

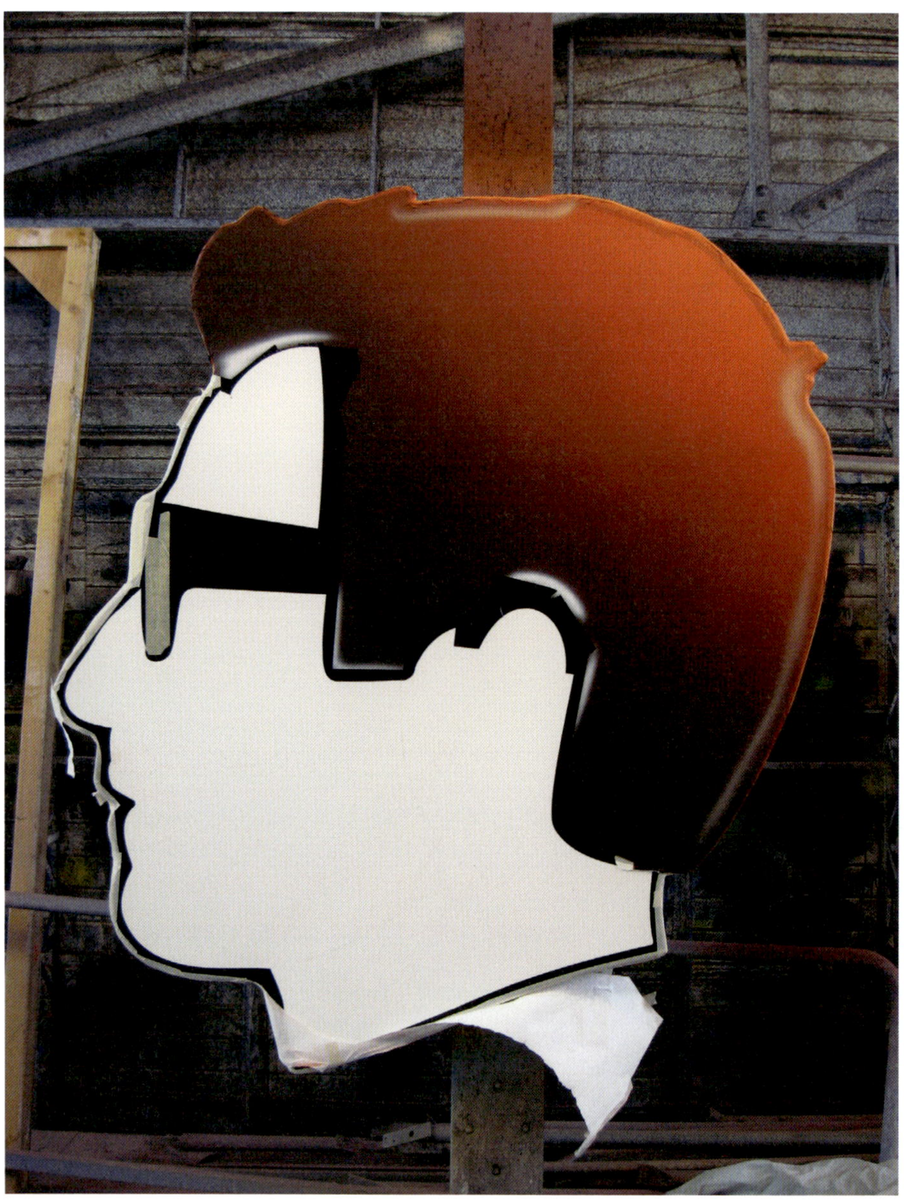

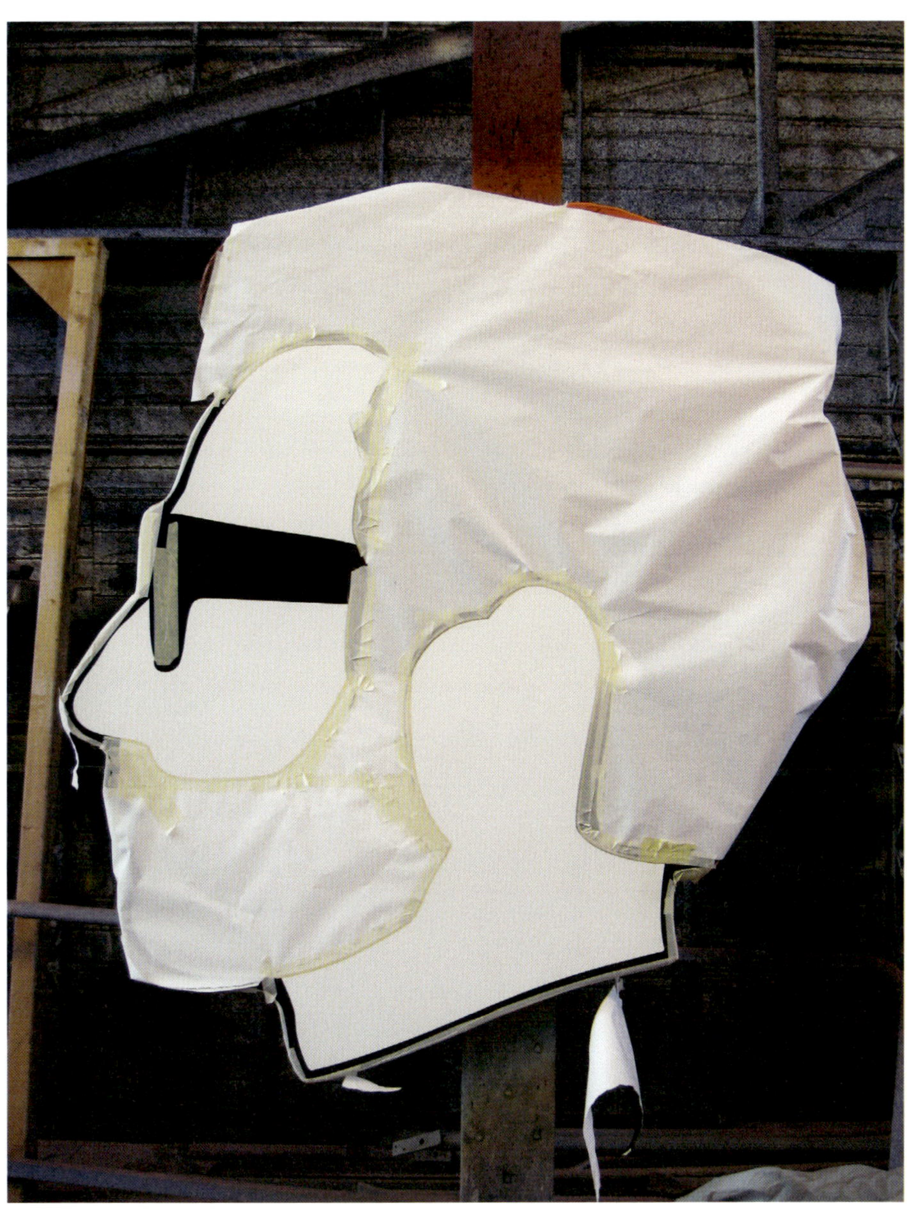

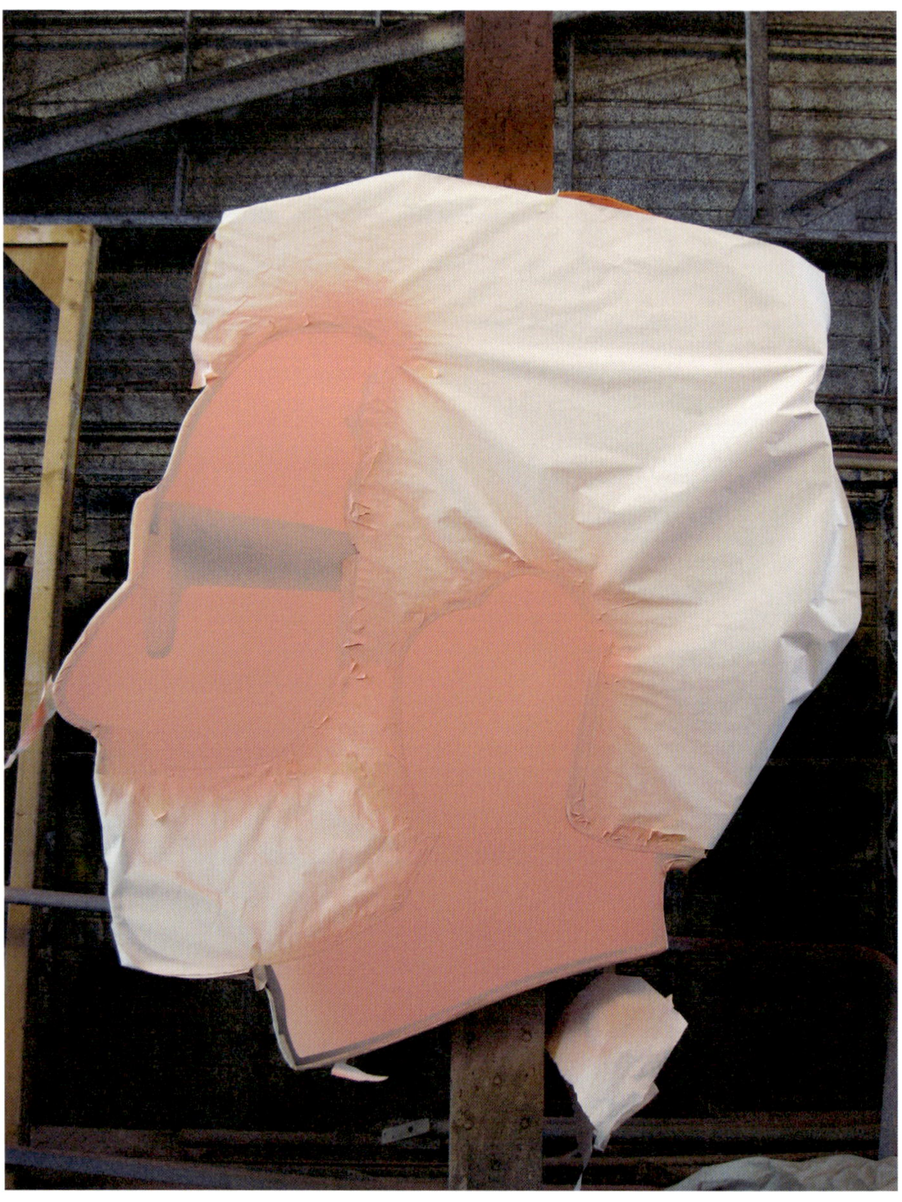

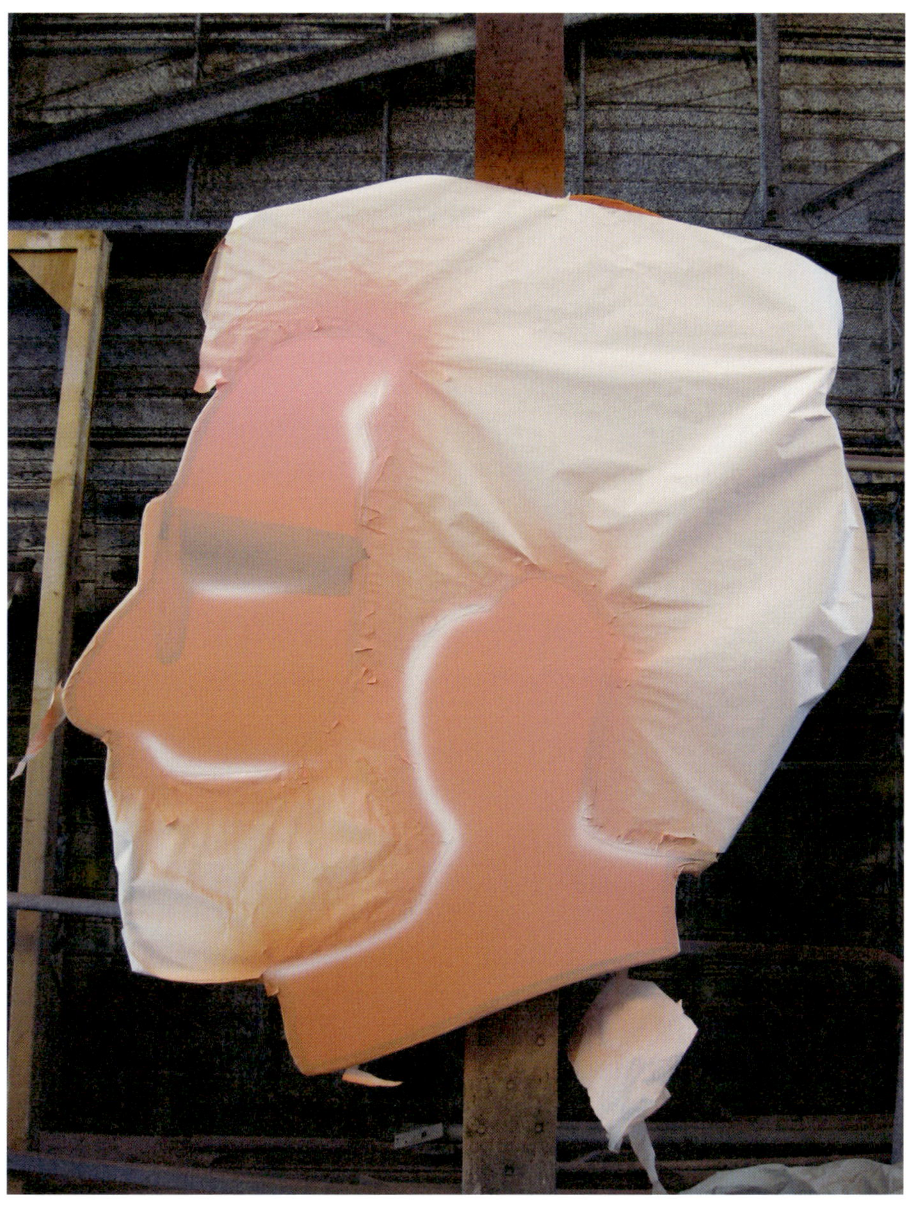

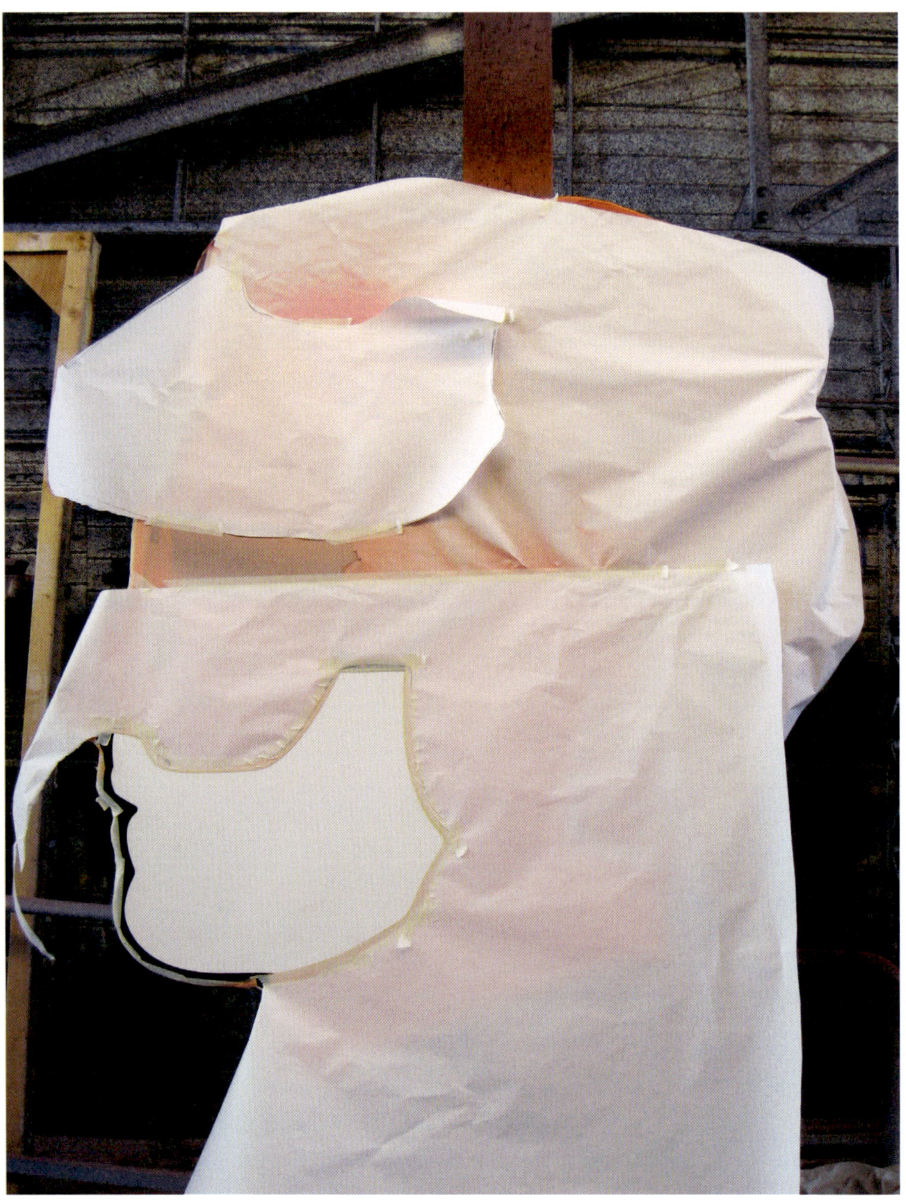

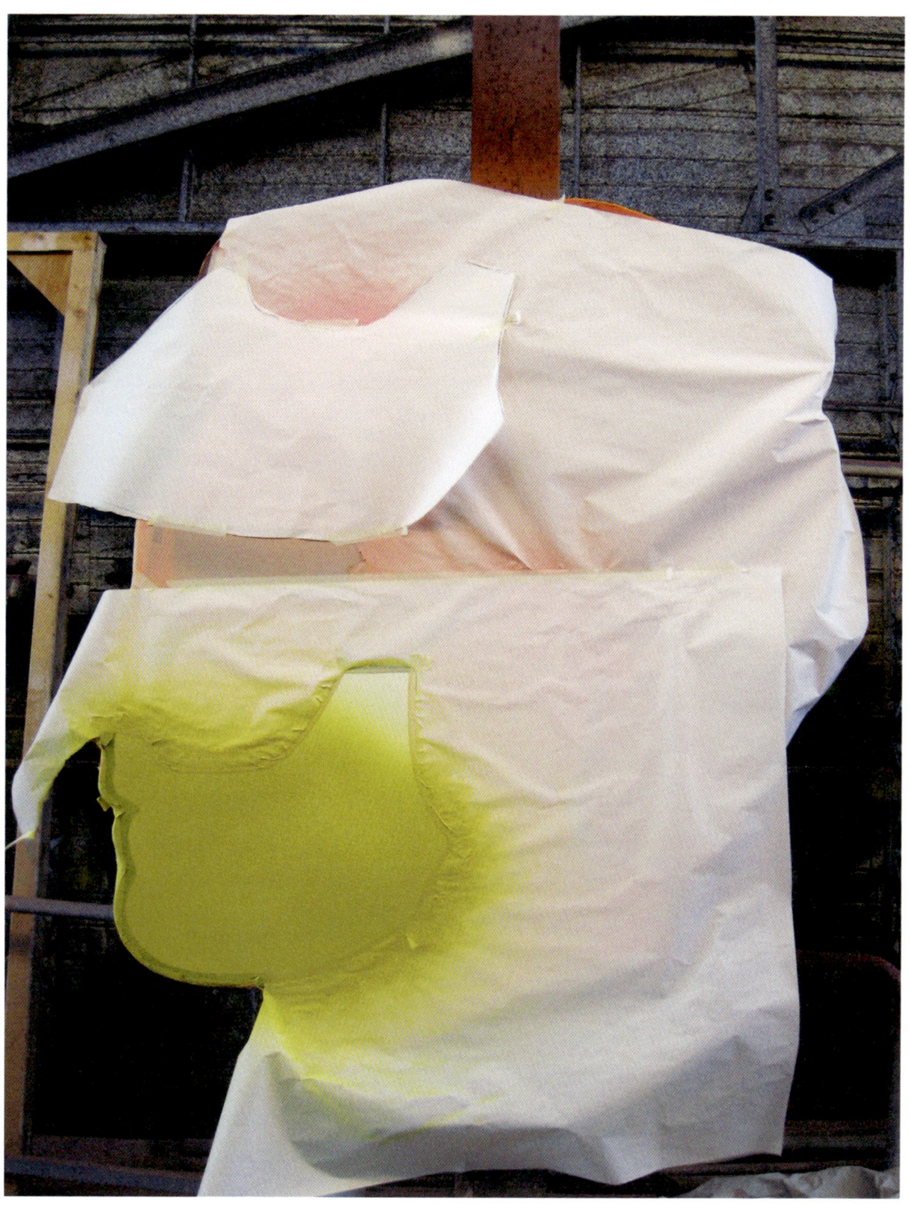

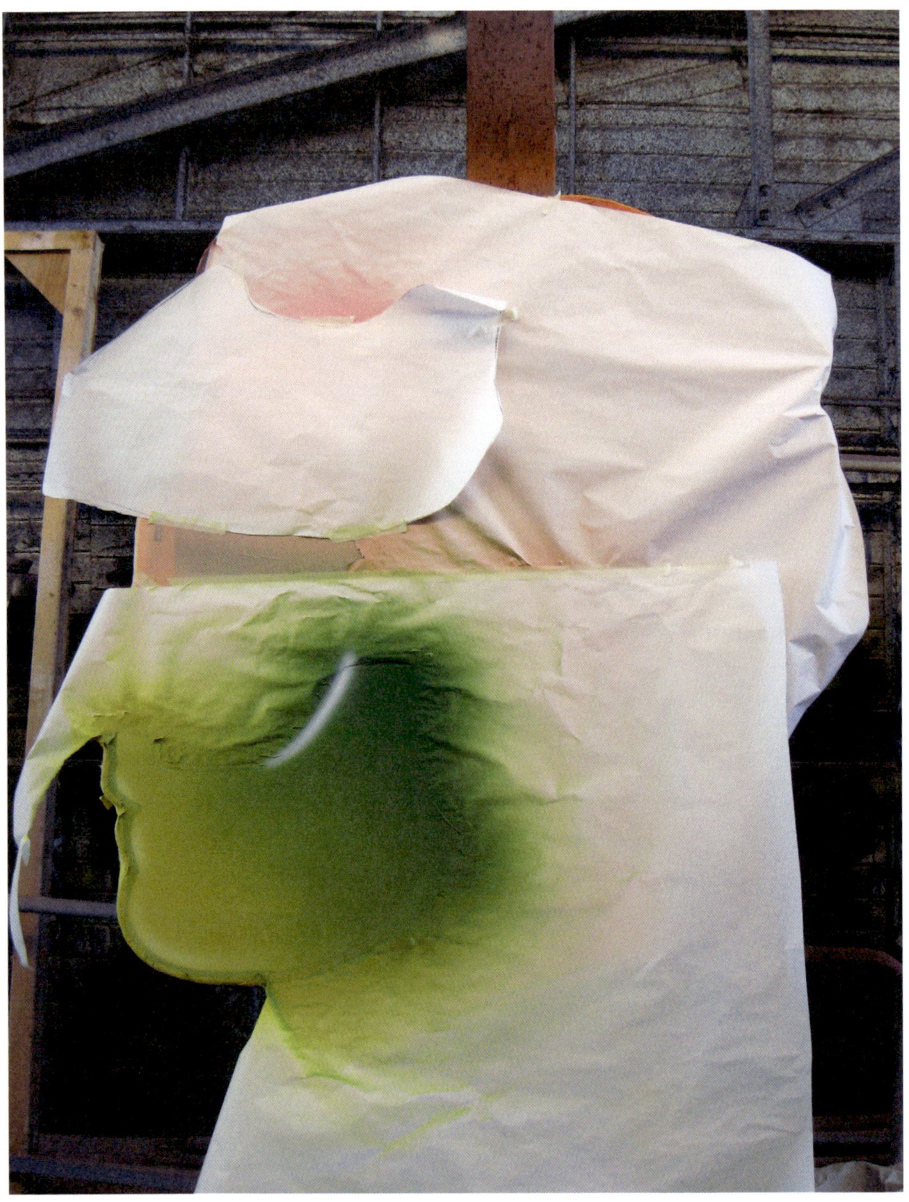

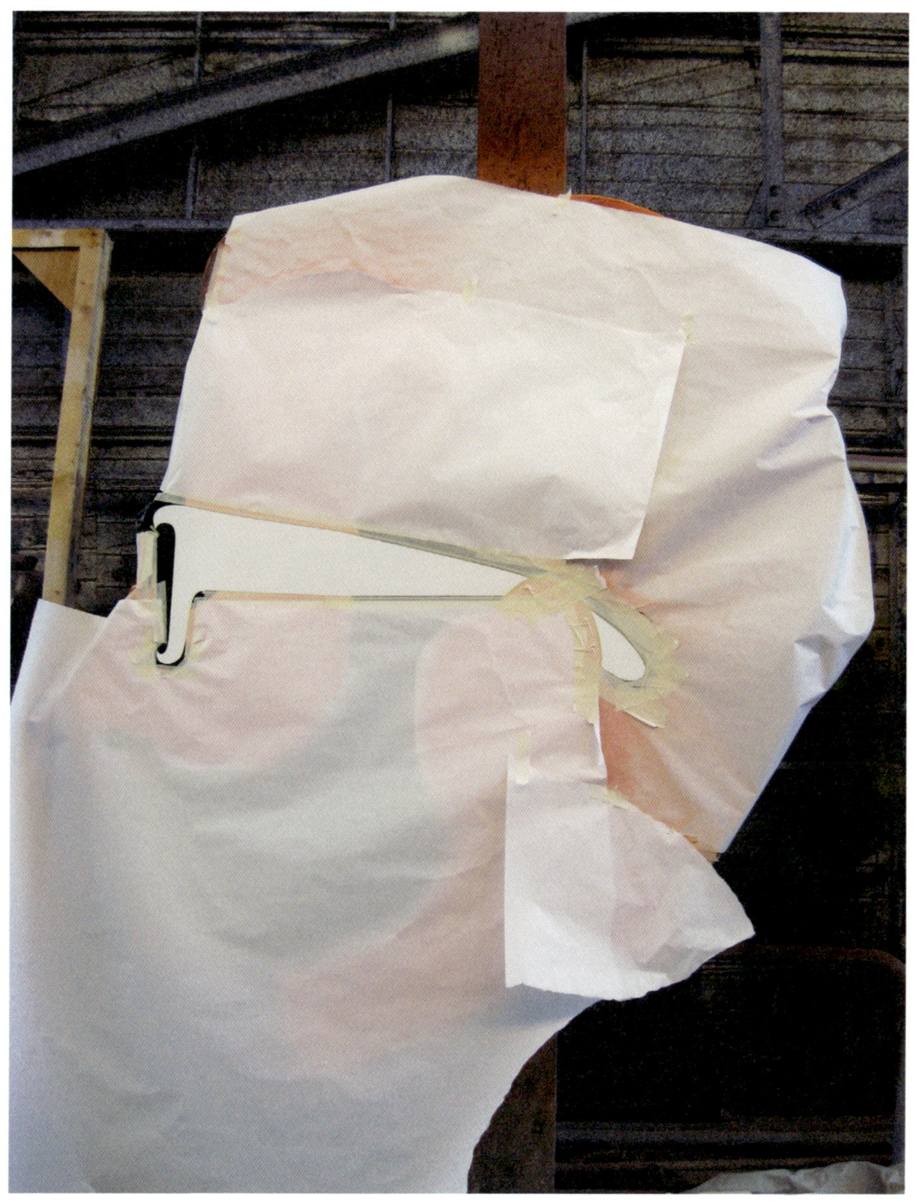

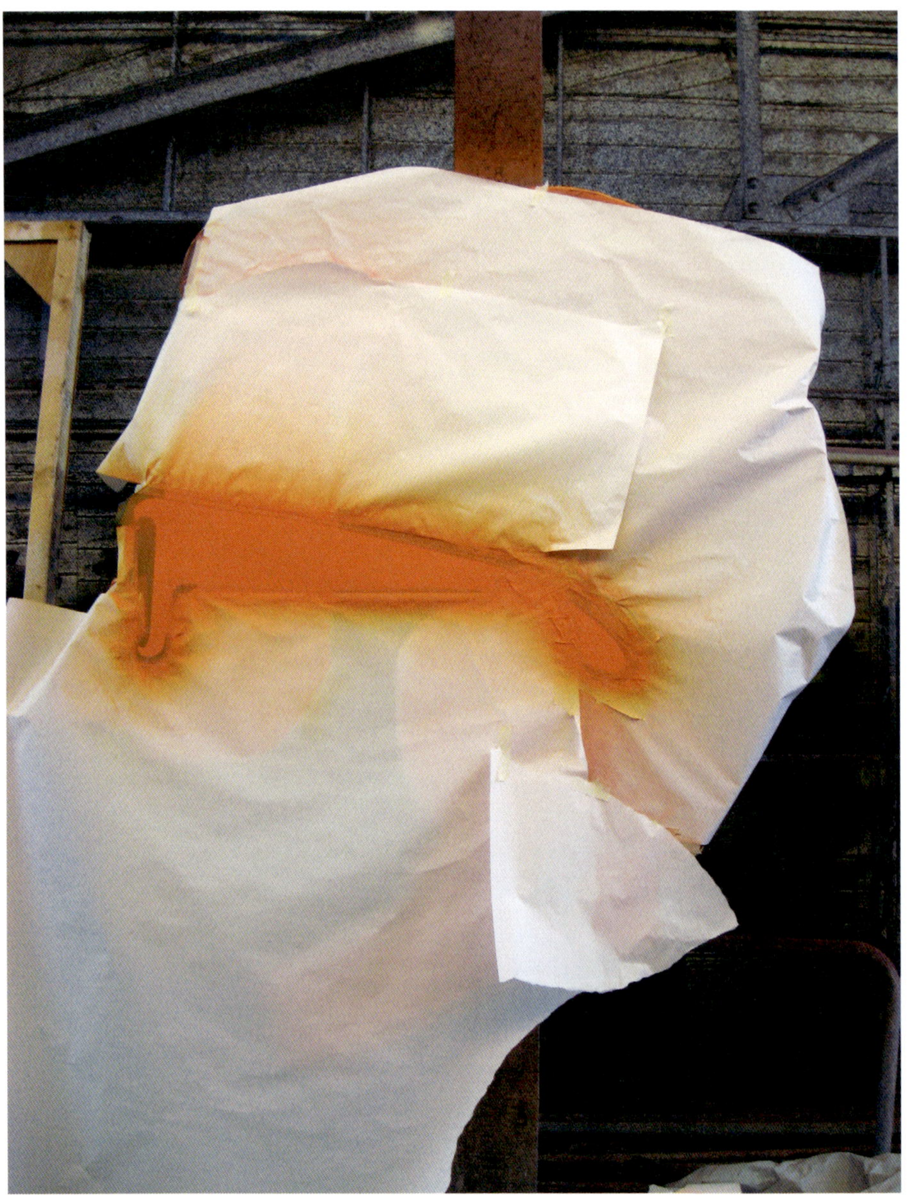

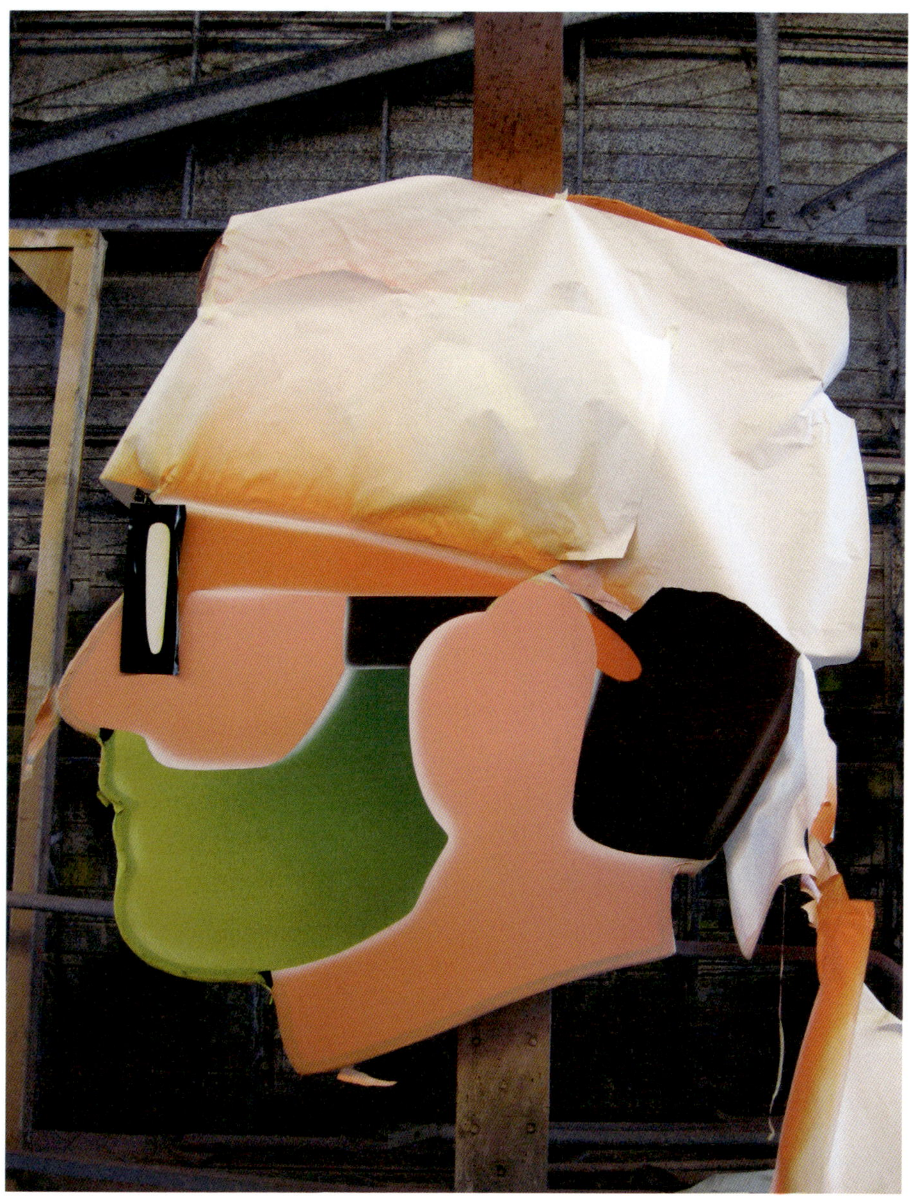

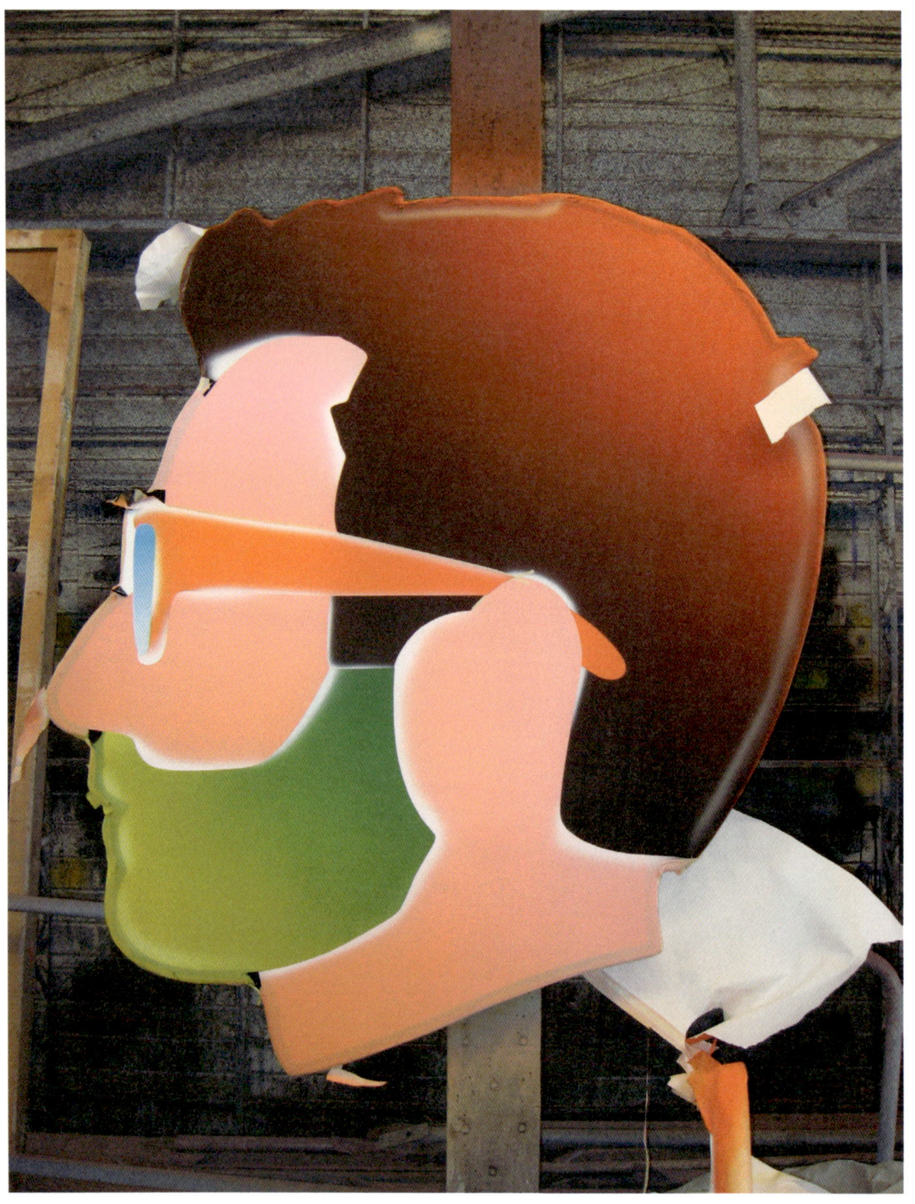

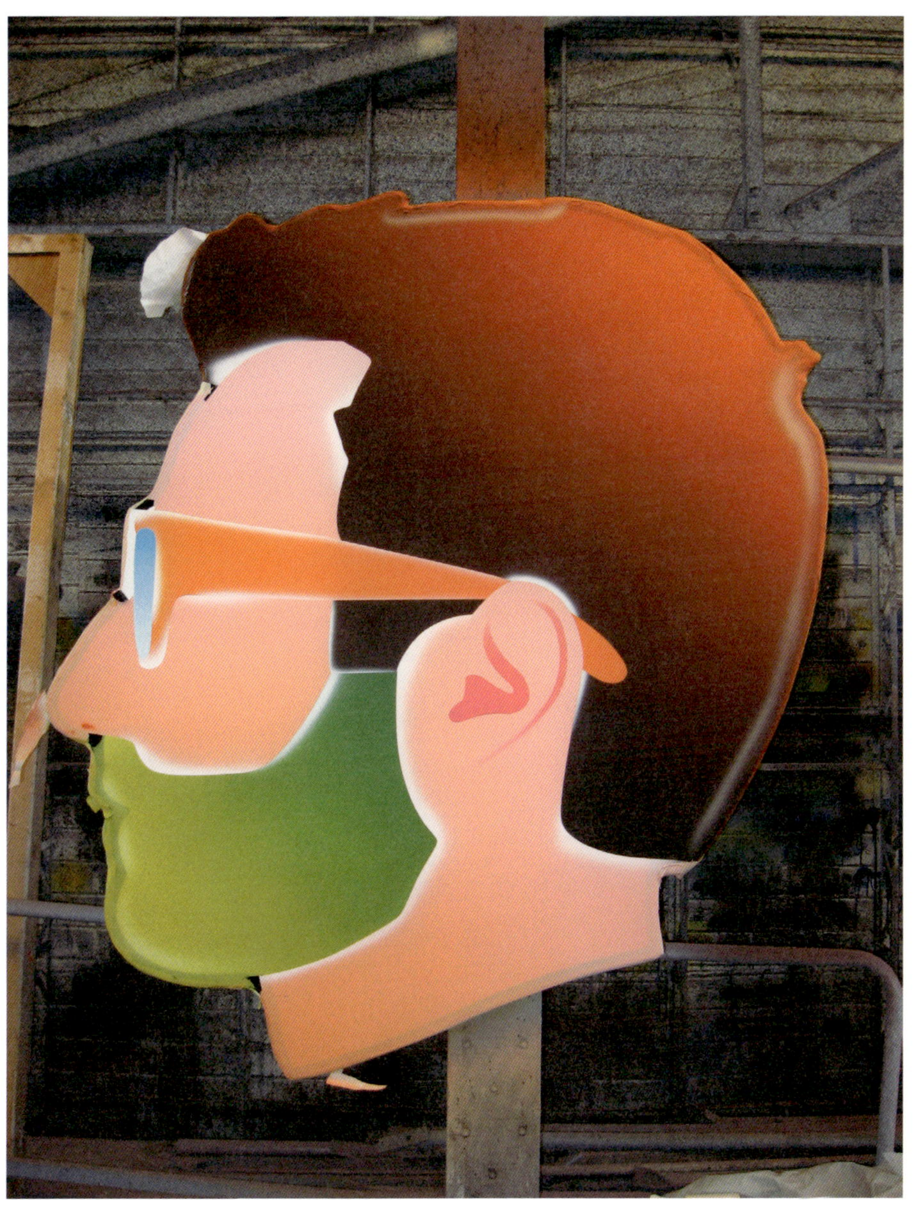

Self-Portraits
Peres Projects, Berlin
April 26–June 15, 2013

Alex Israel   Self-Portraits   Peres Projects, Berlin   April 26-June 15, 2013

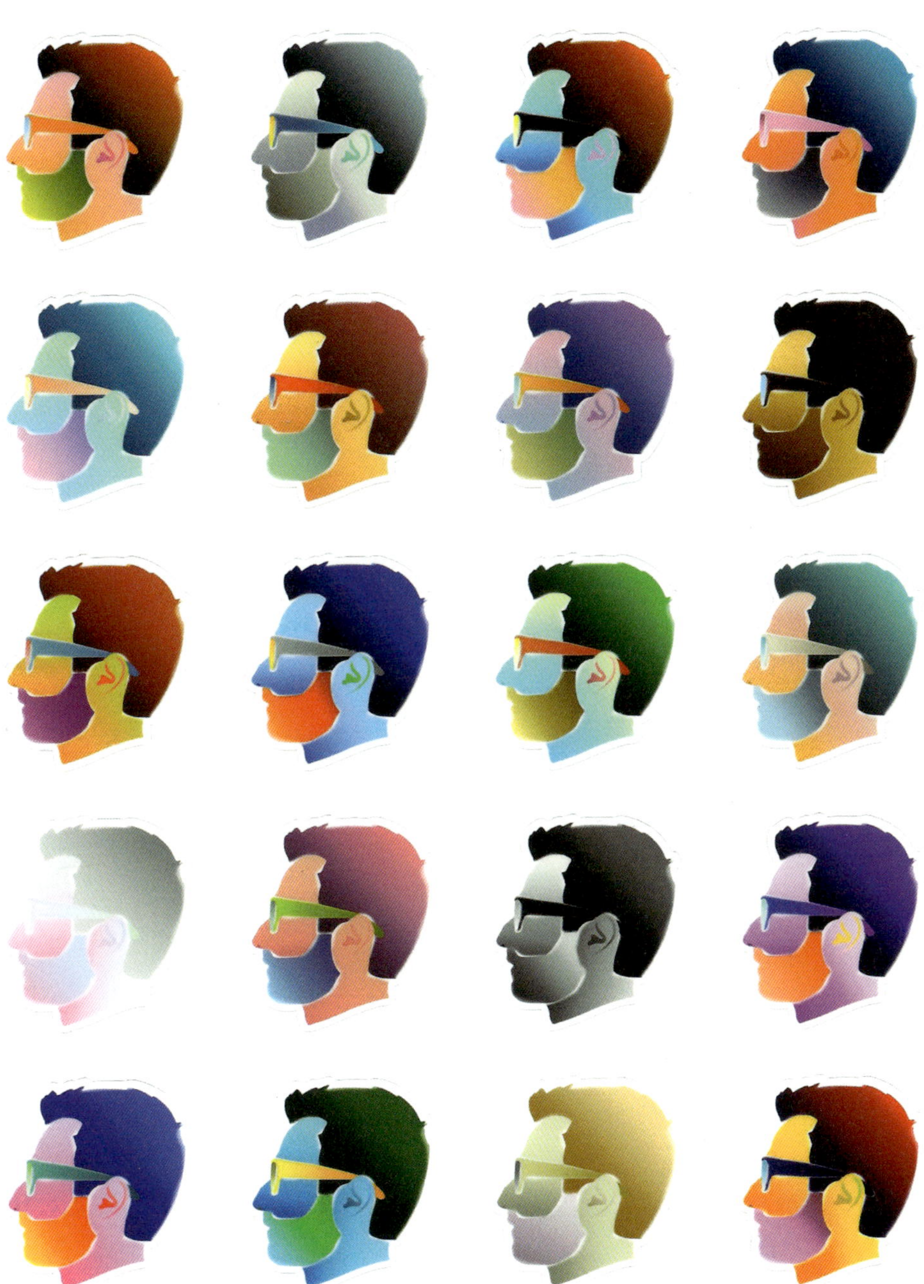

Karl-Marx-Allee 82, Tuesday – Saturday 11 am – 6 pm, www.peresprojects.com

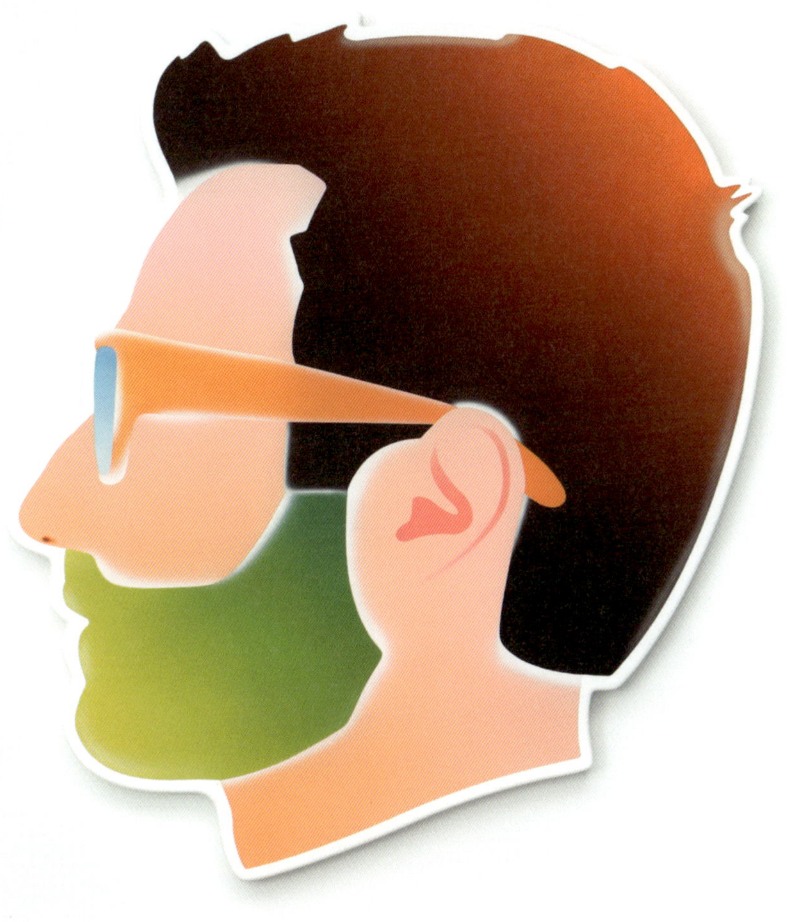

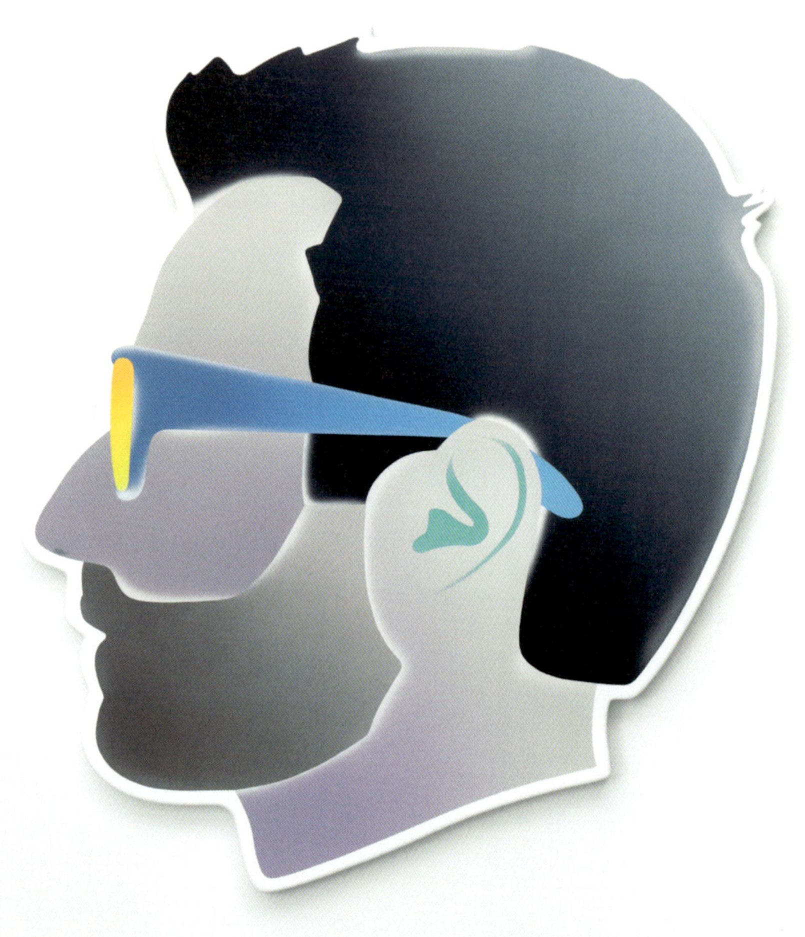

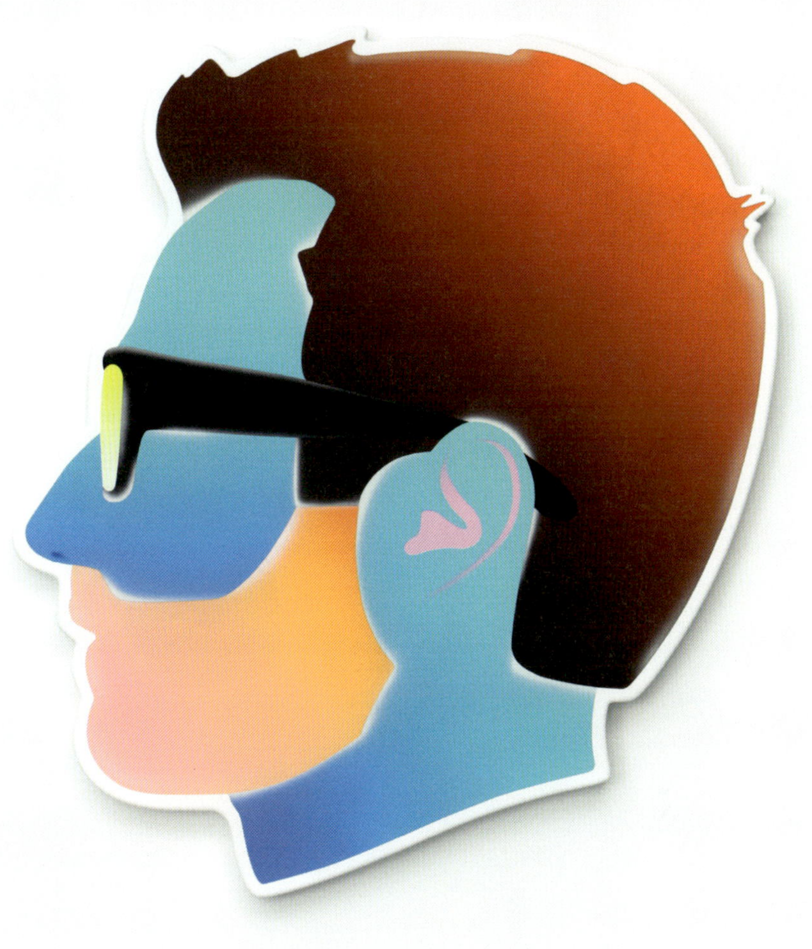

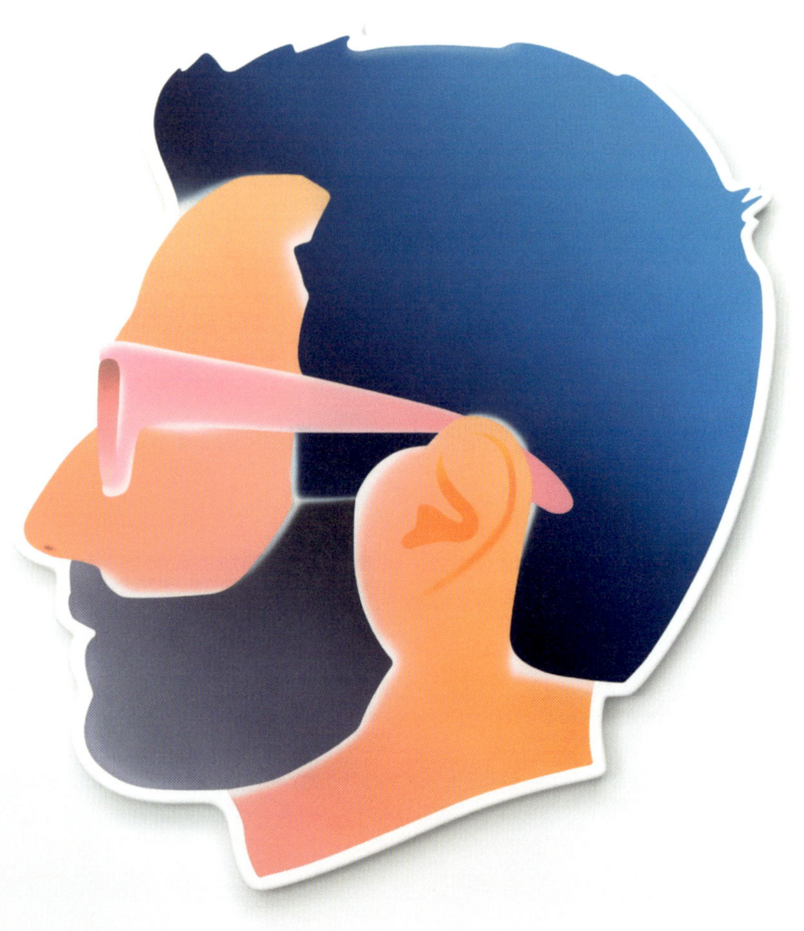

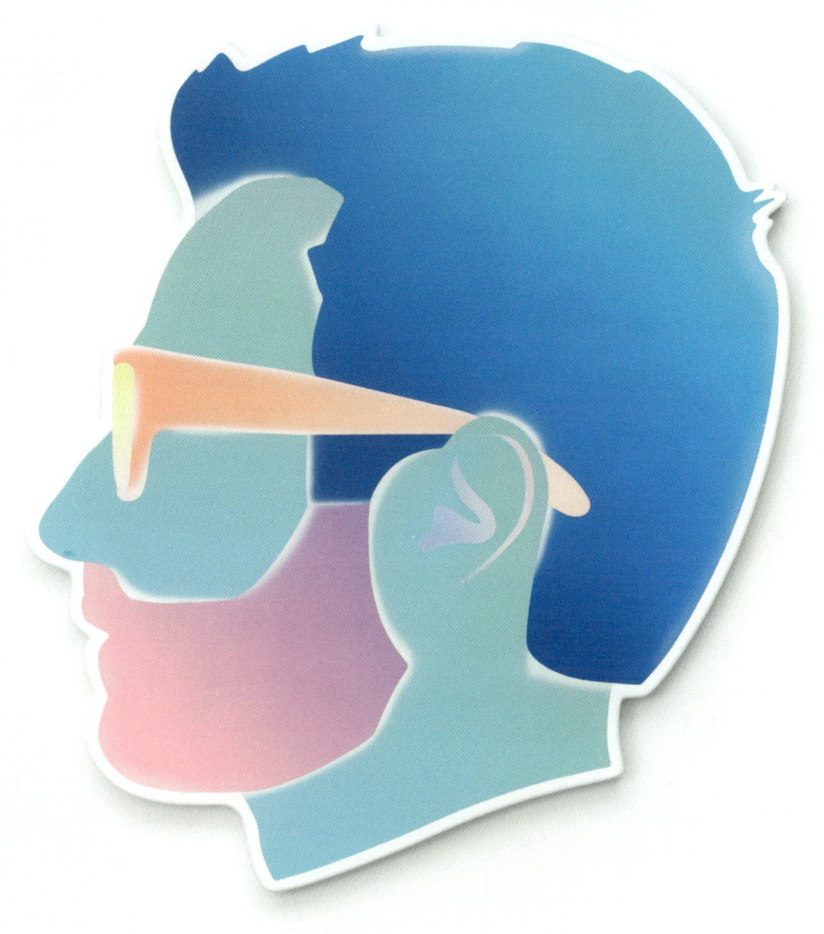

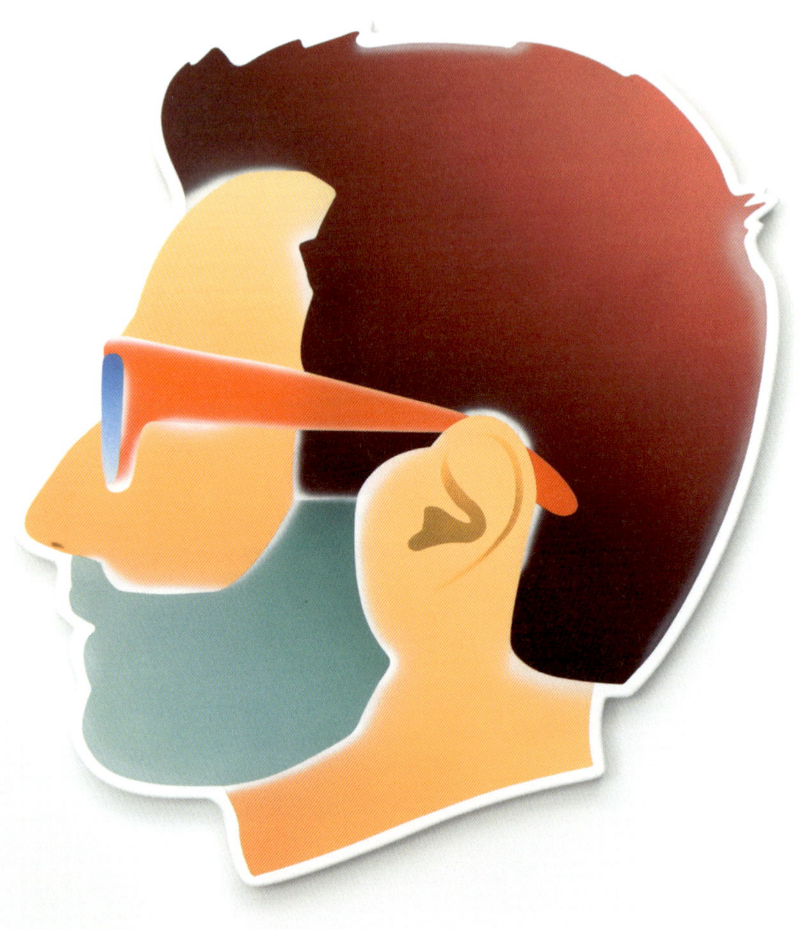

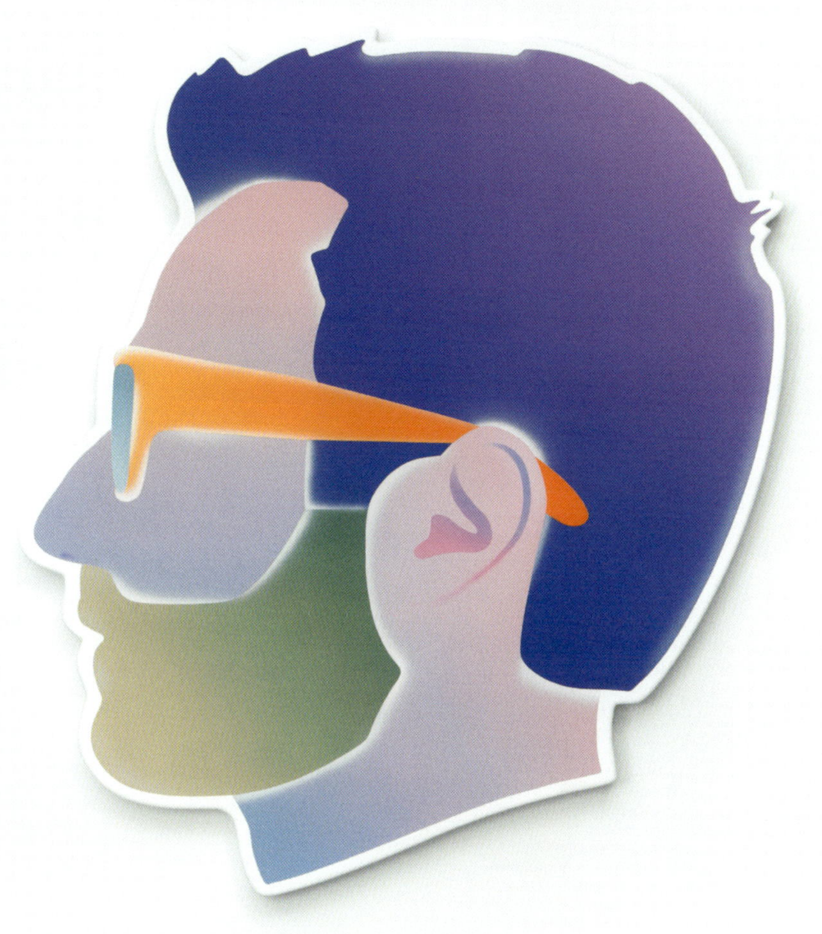

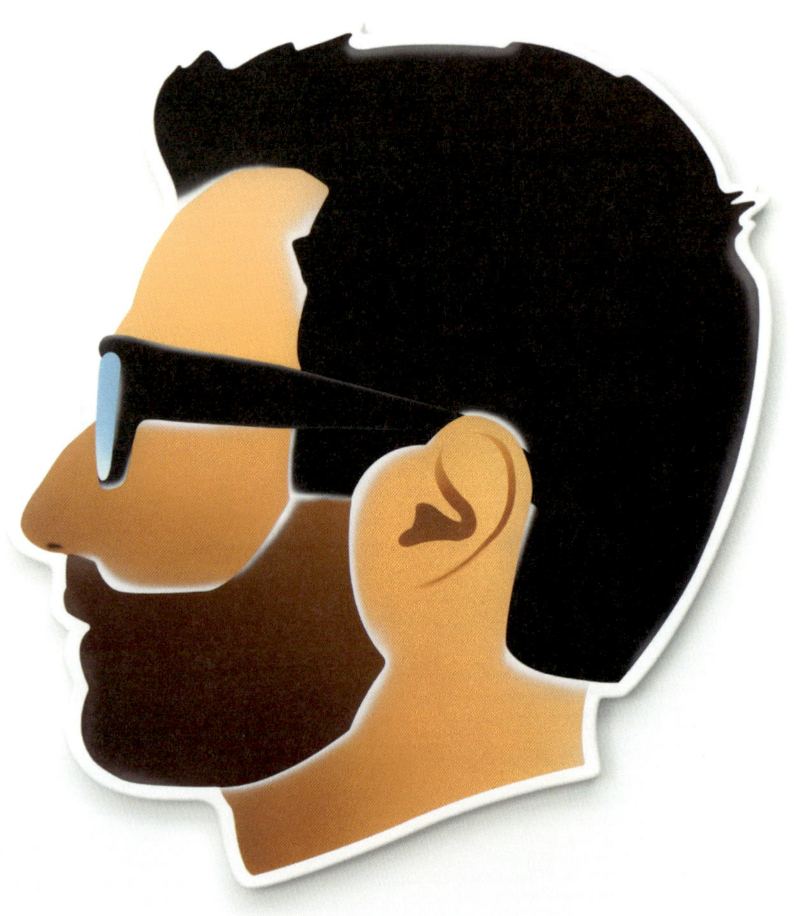

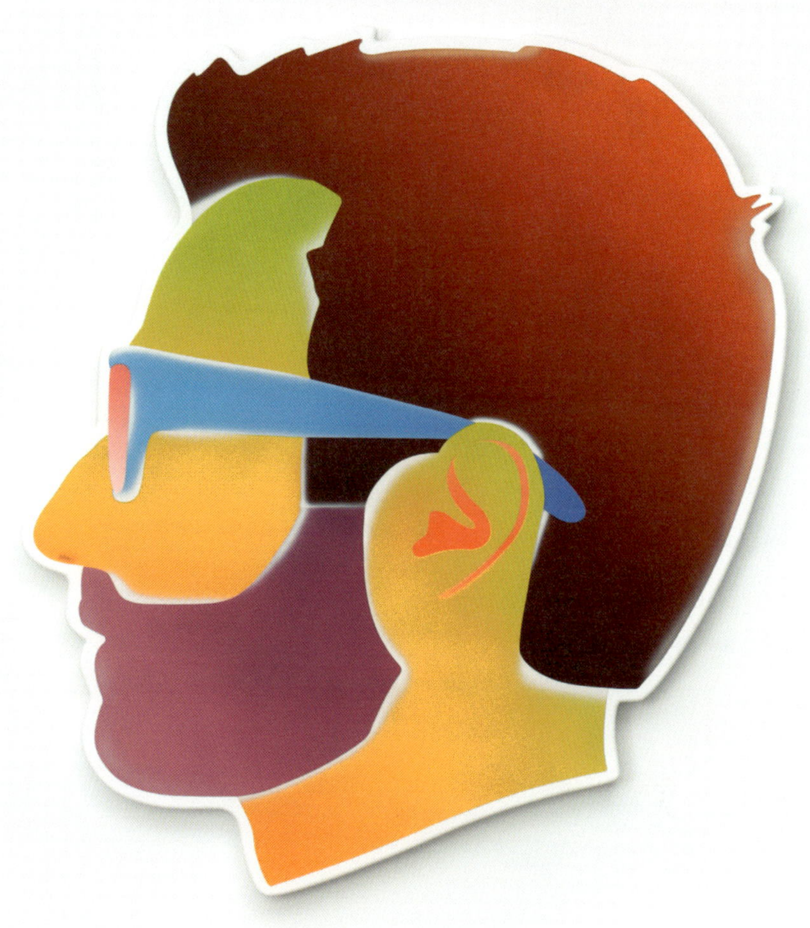

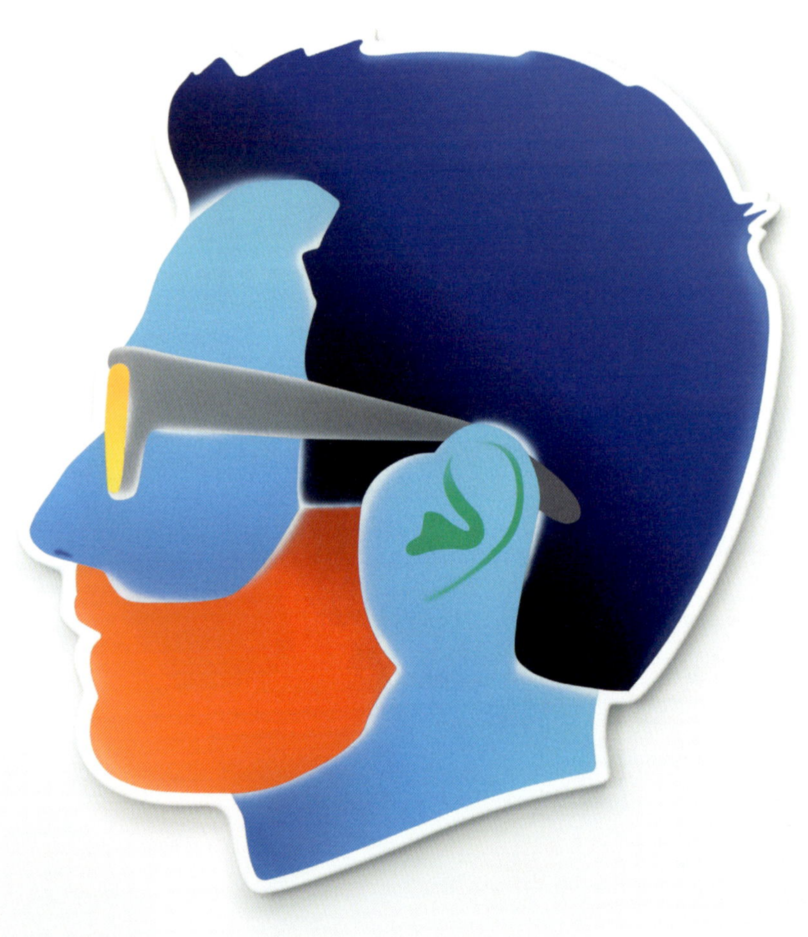

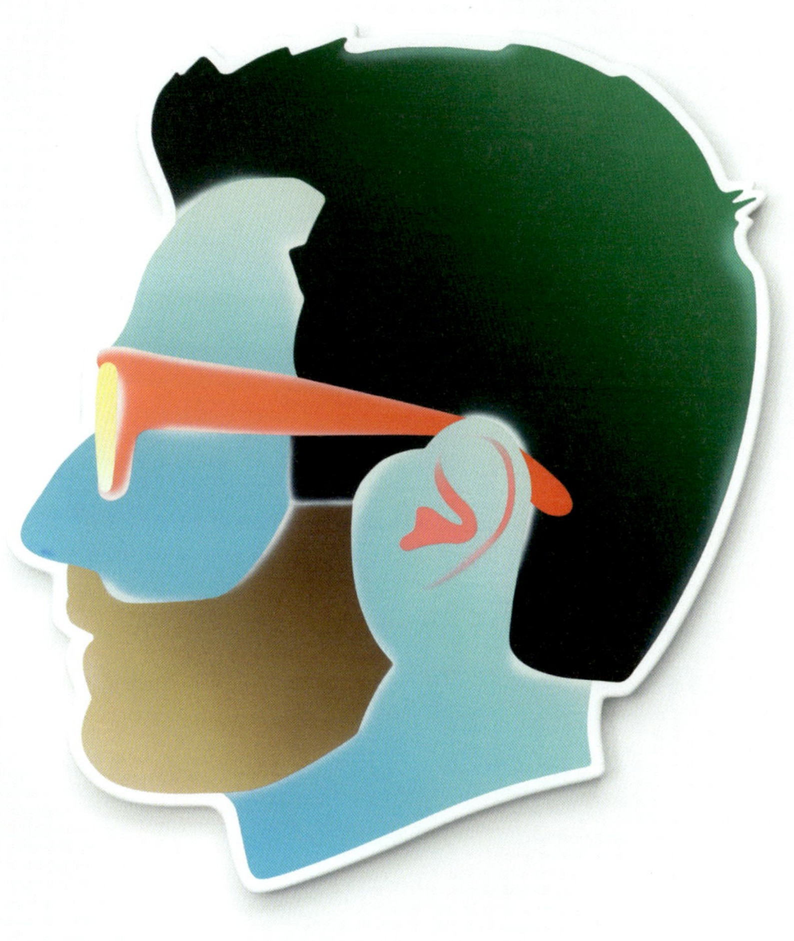

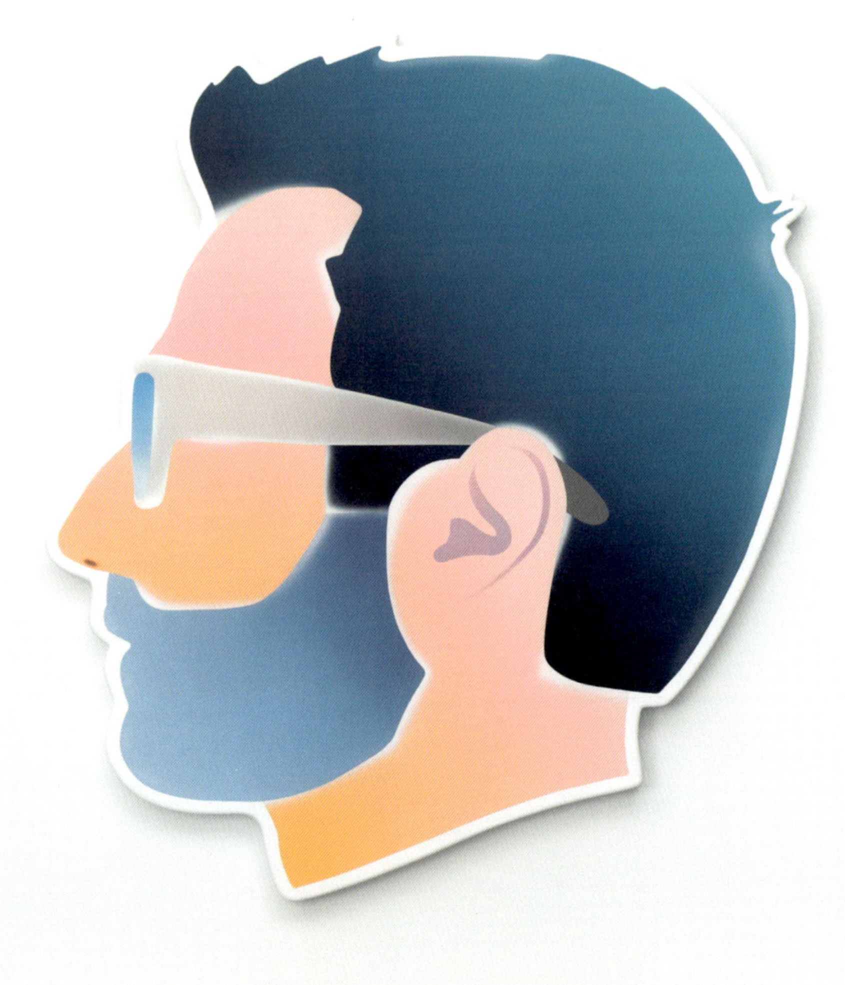

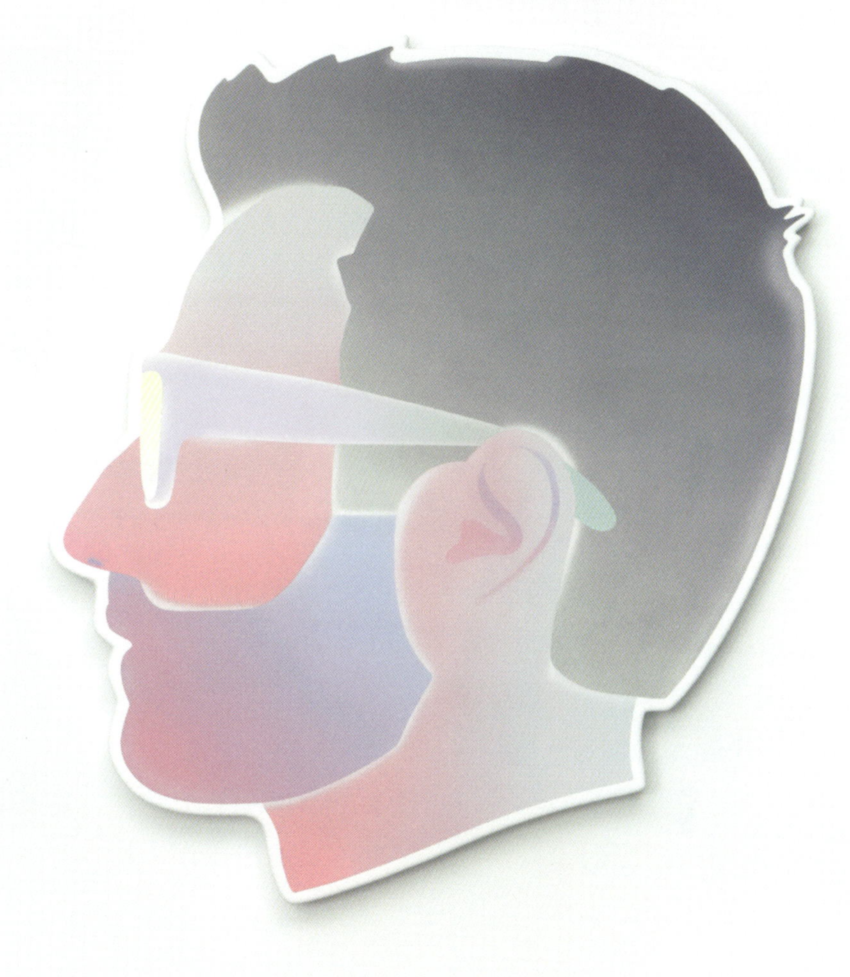

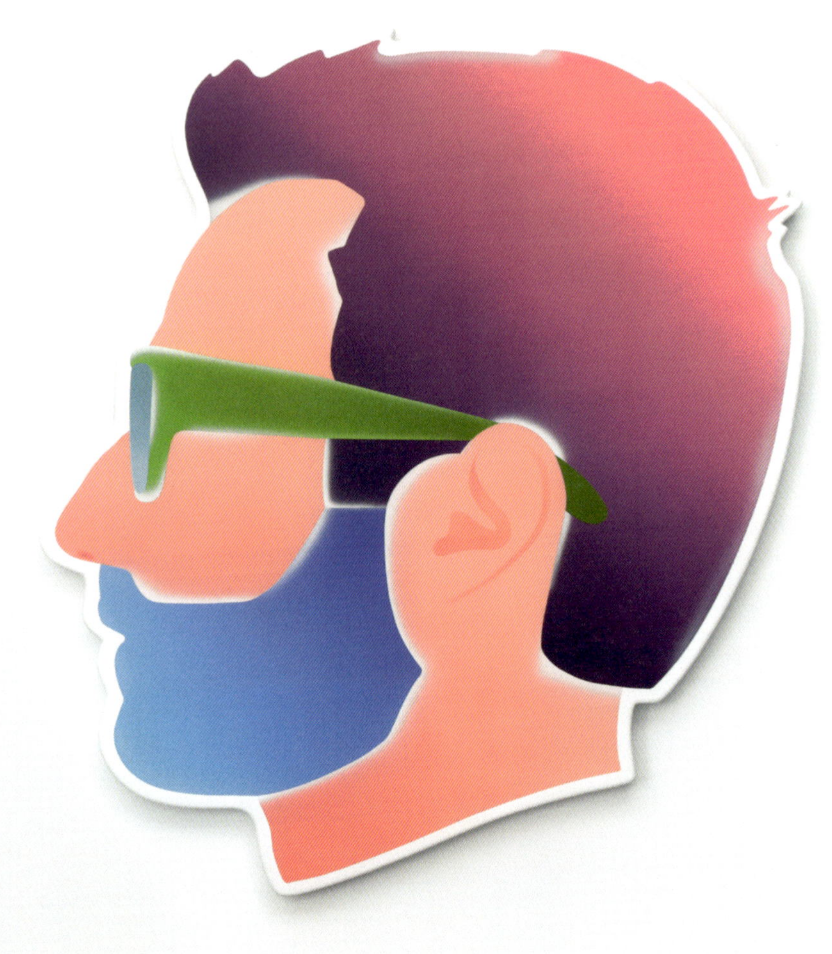

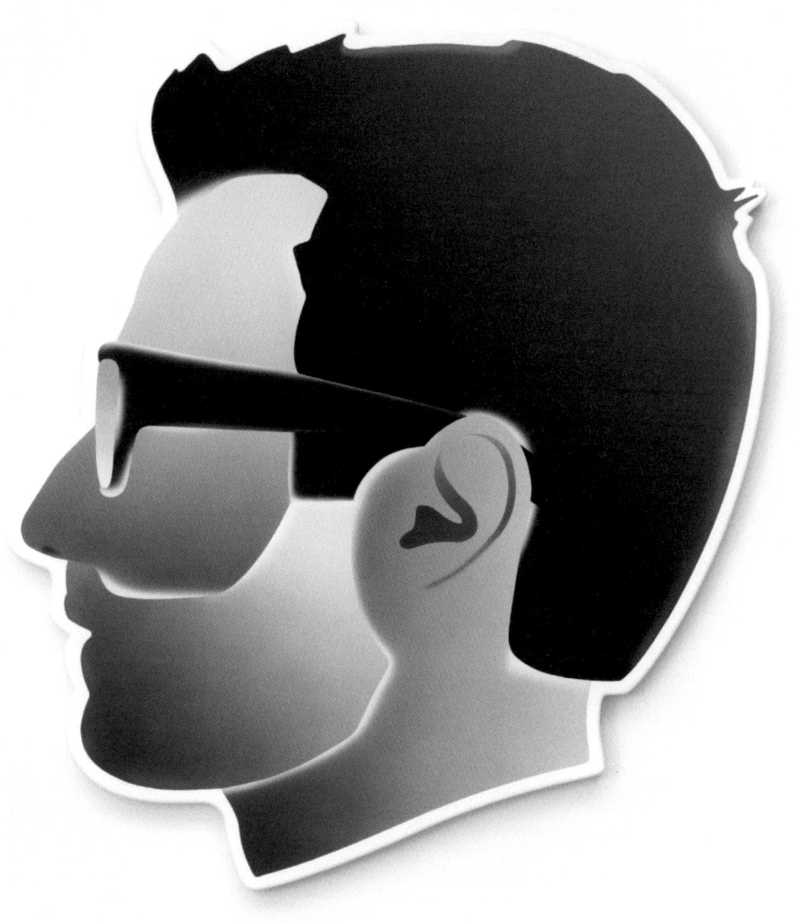

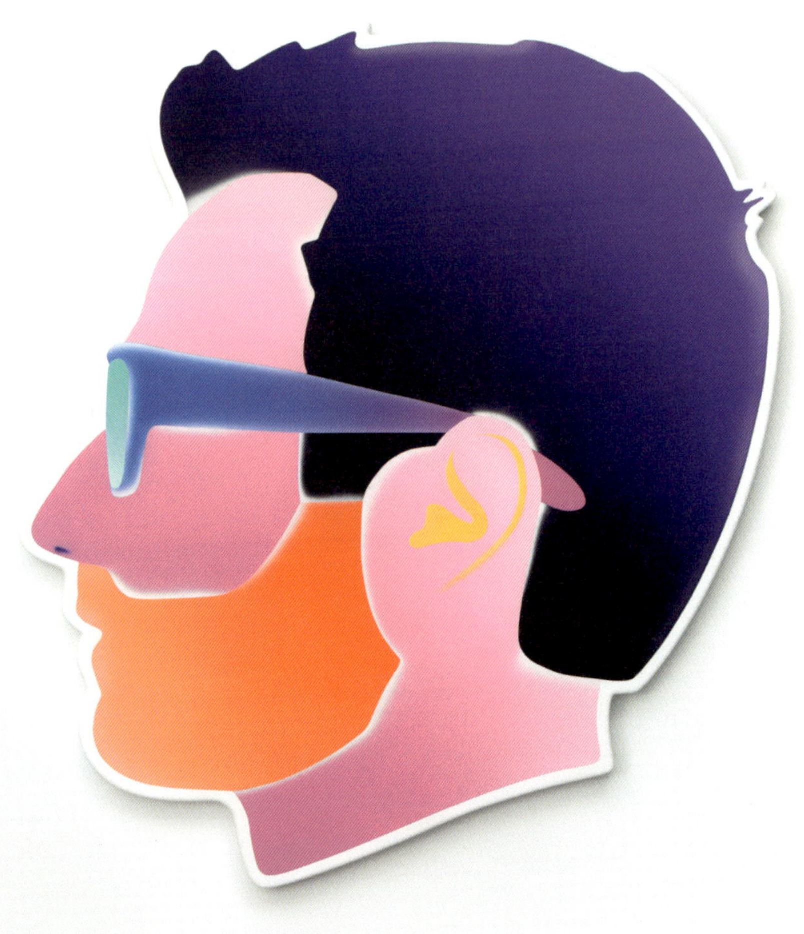

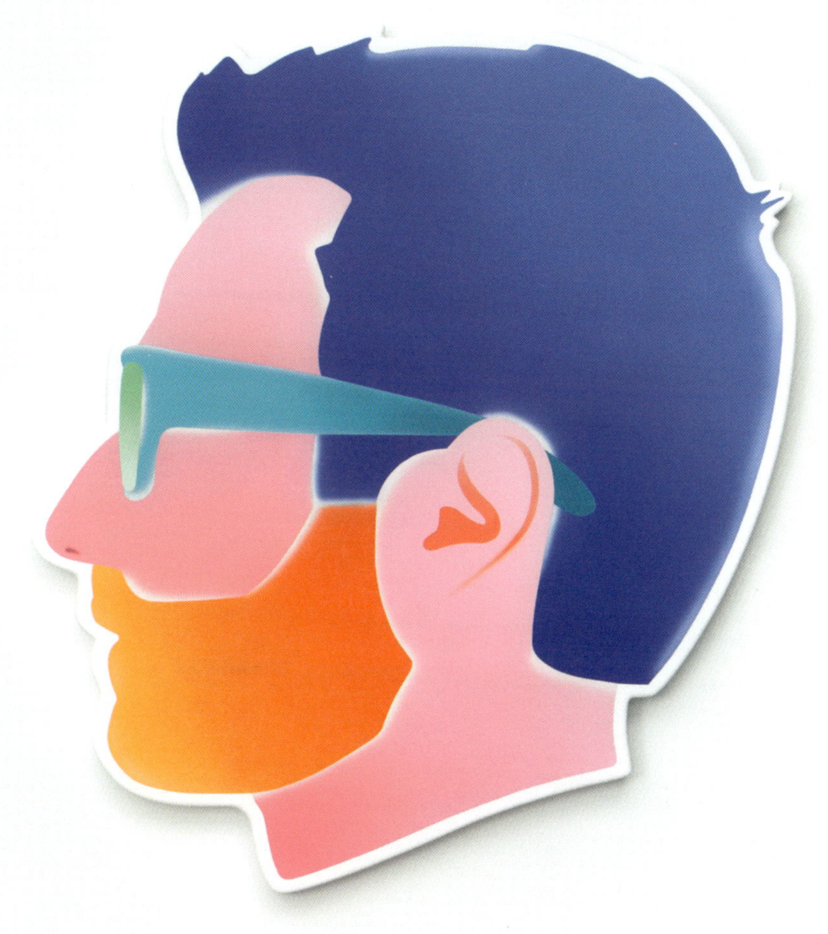

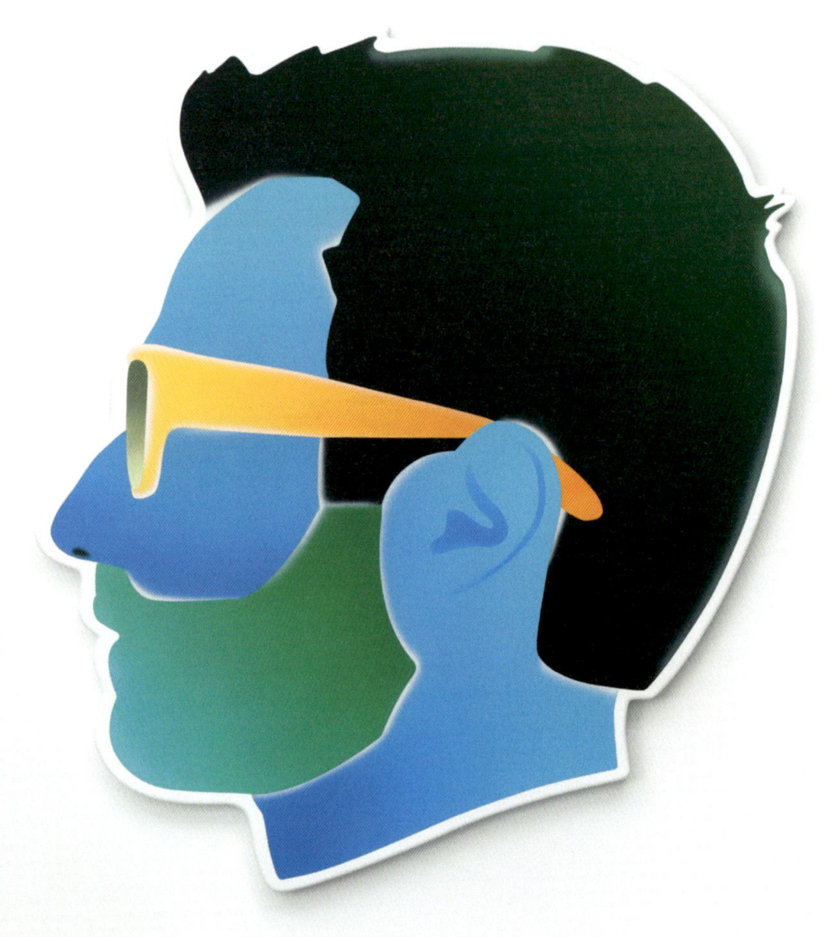

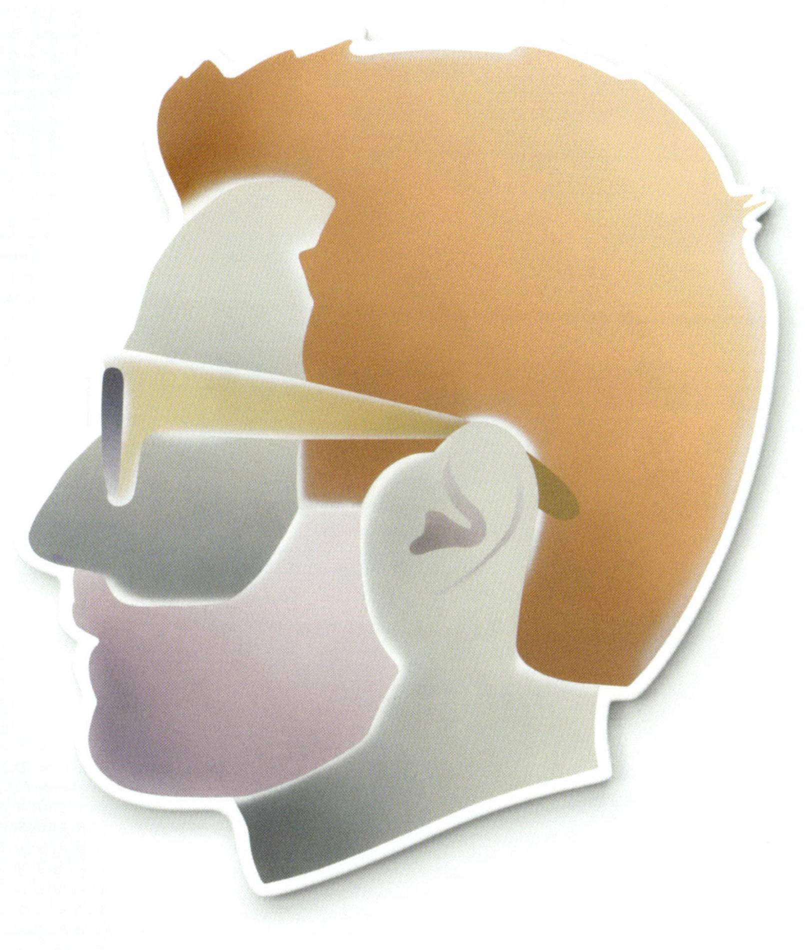

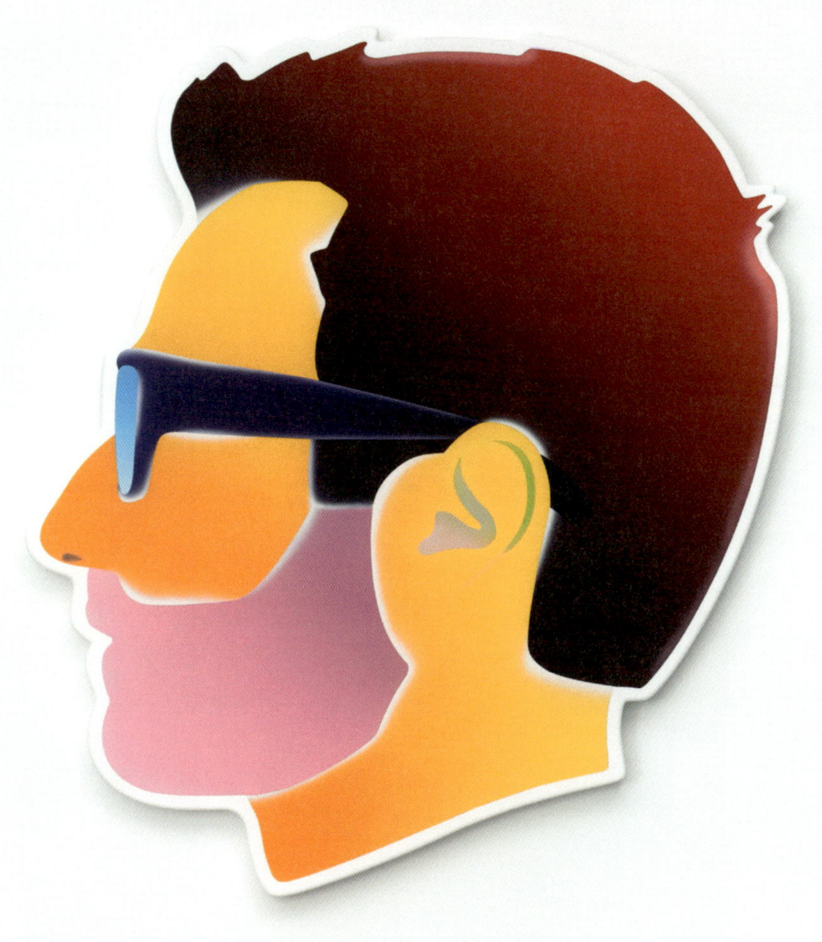

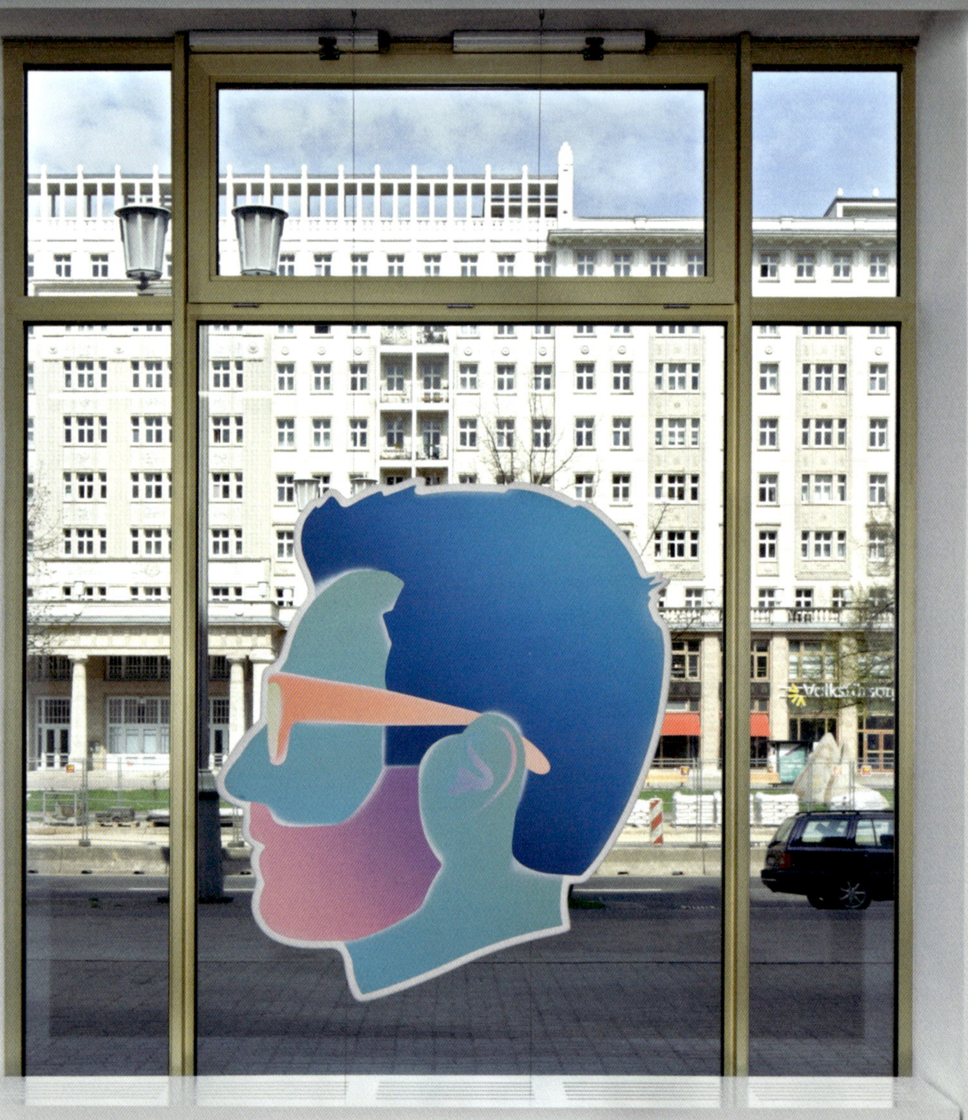

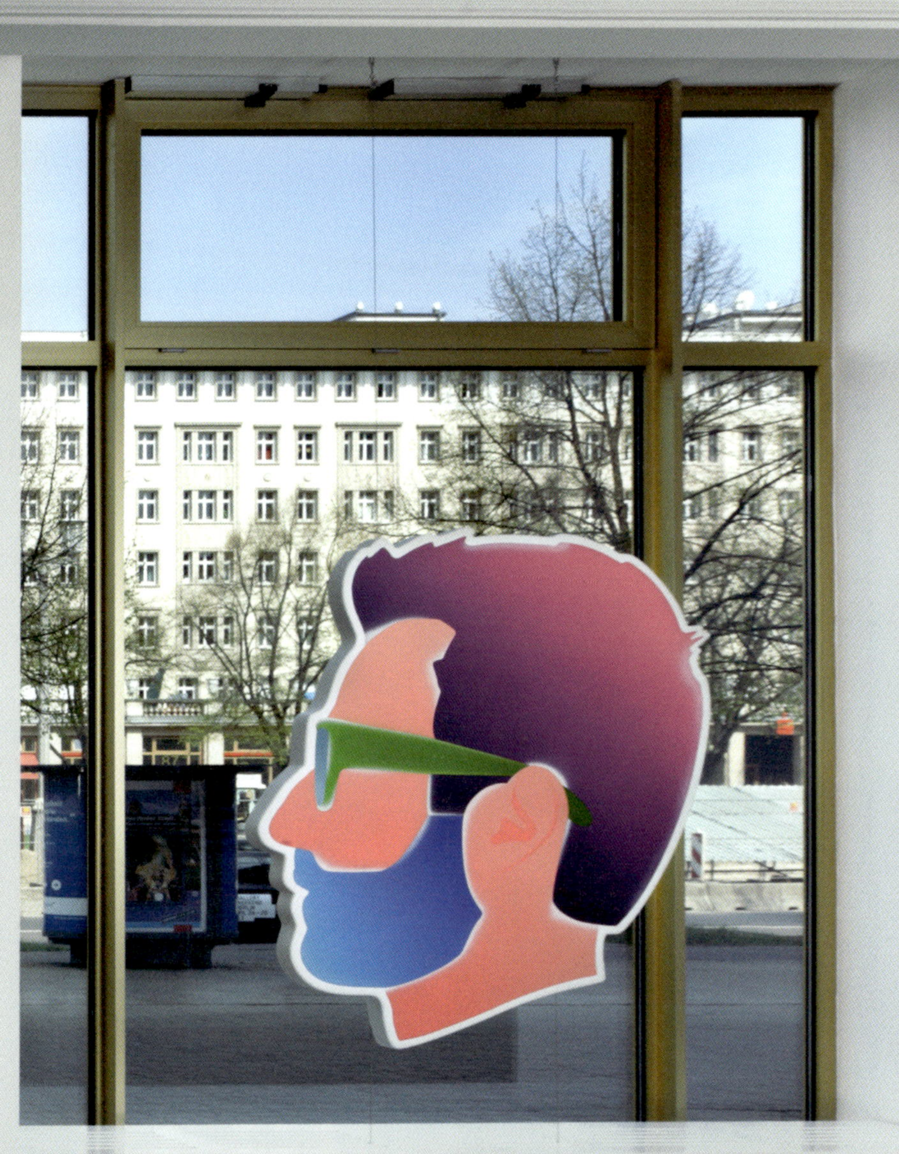

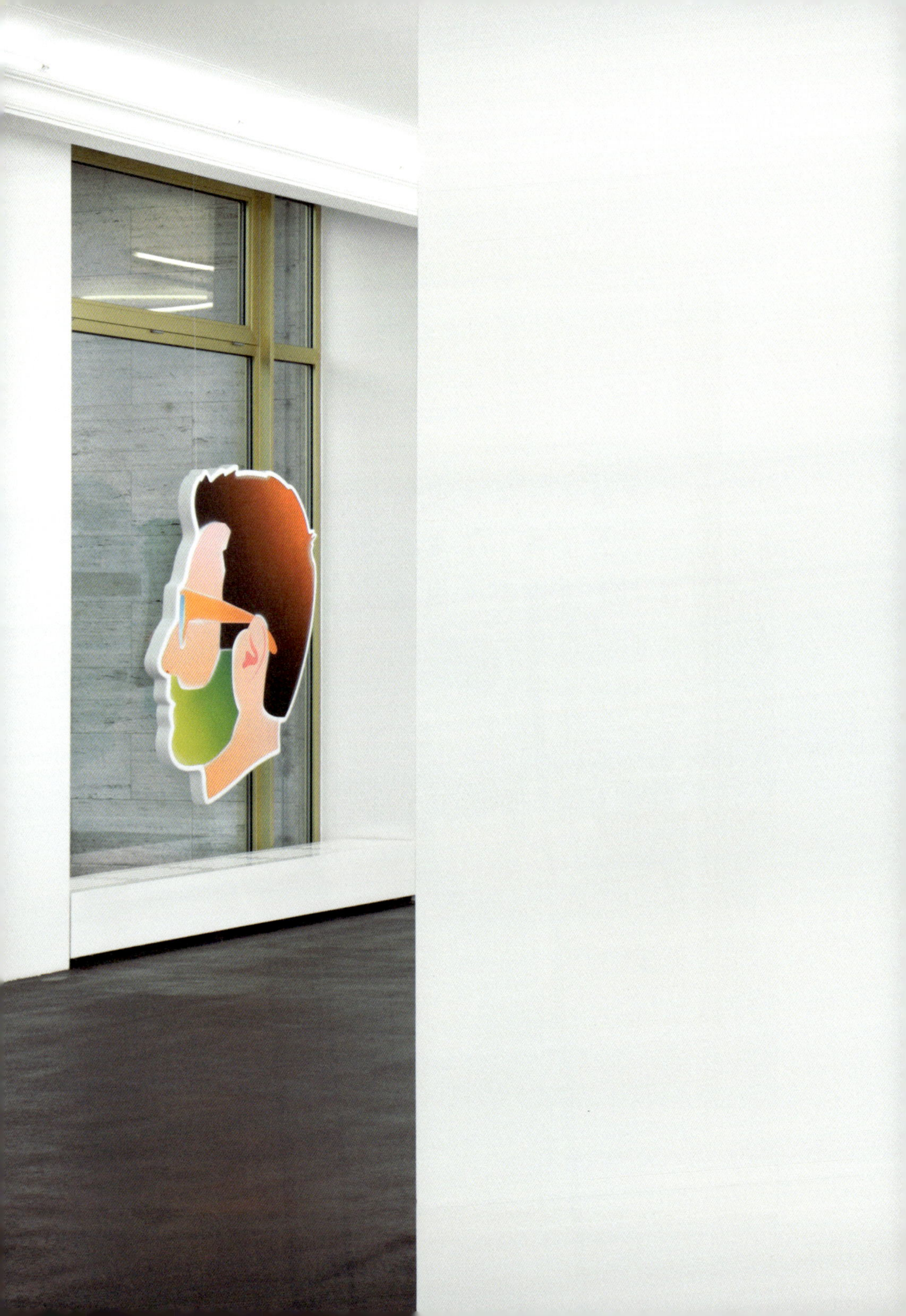

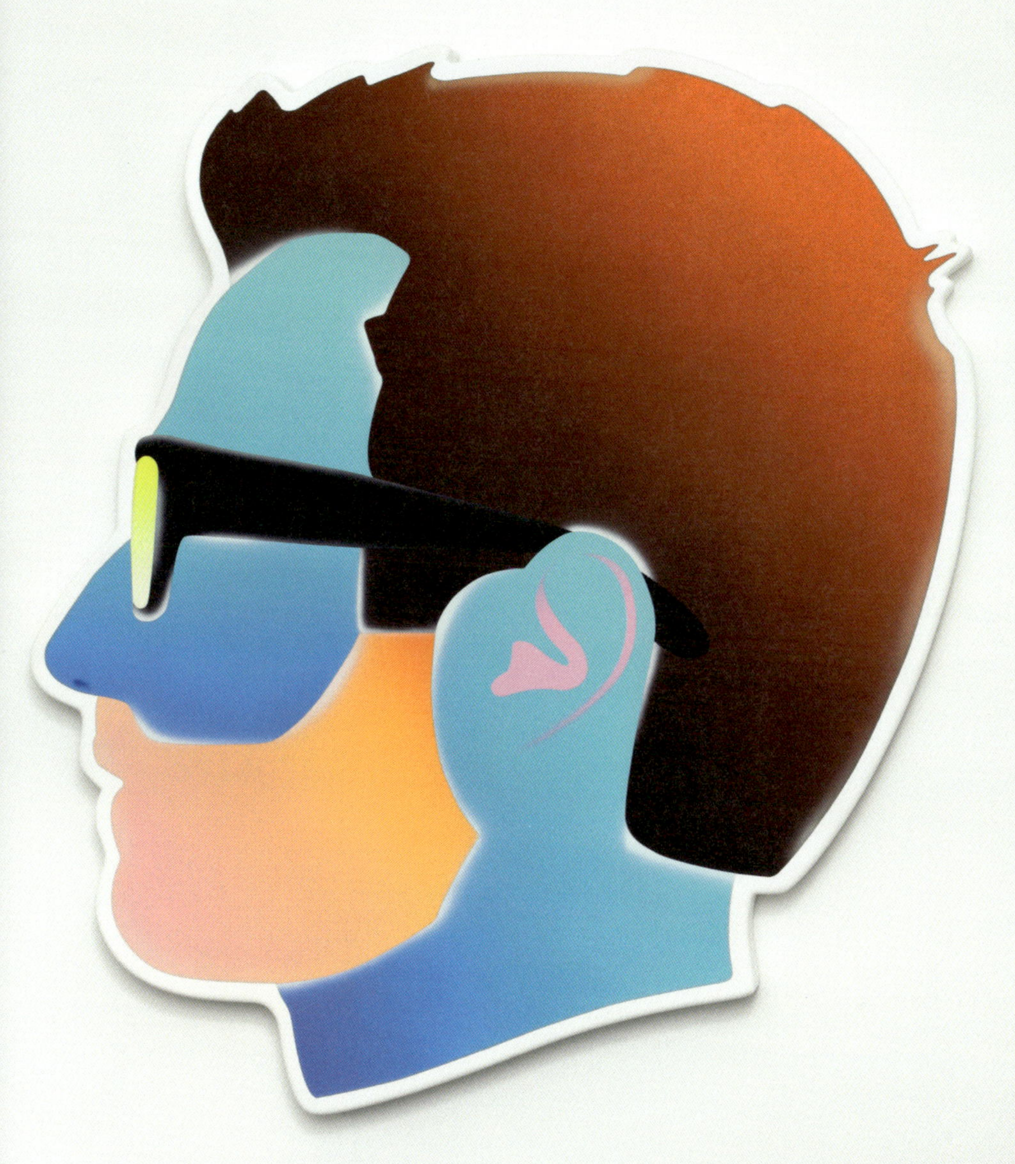

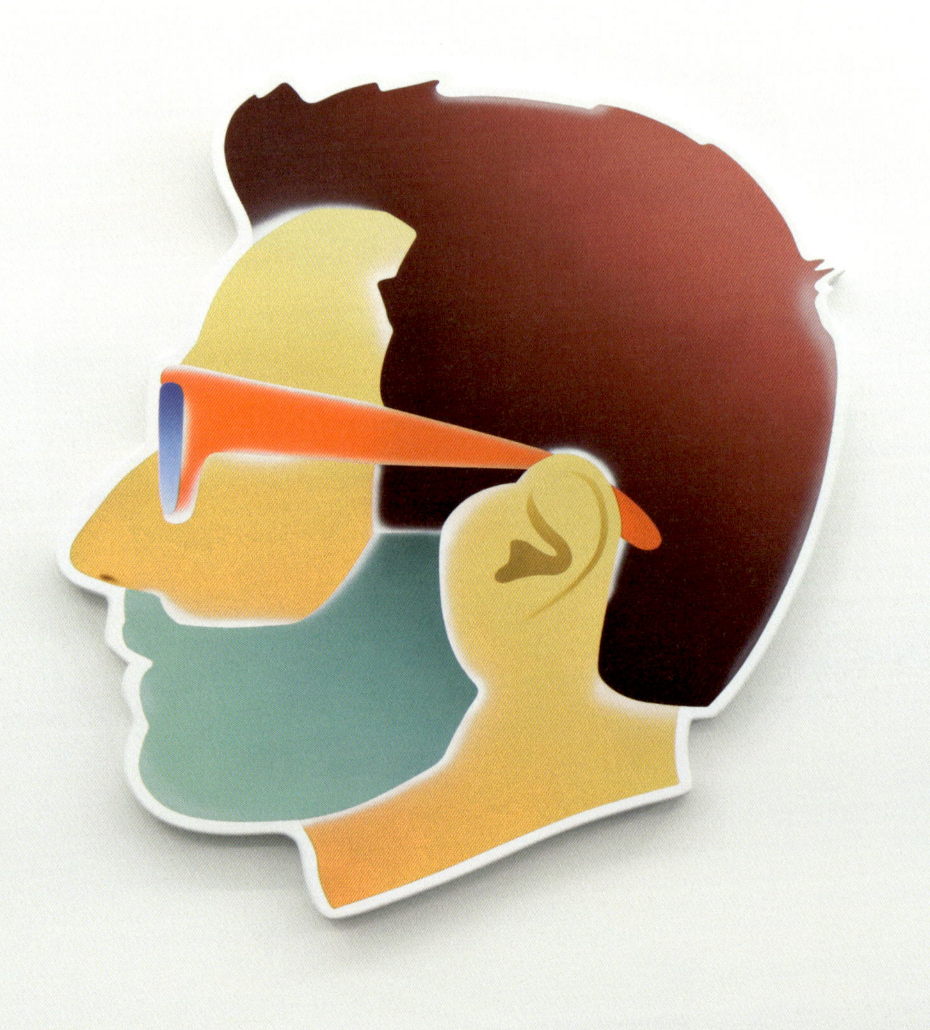

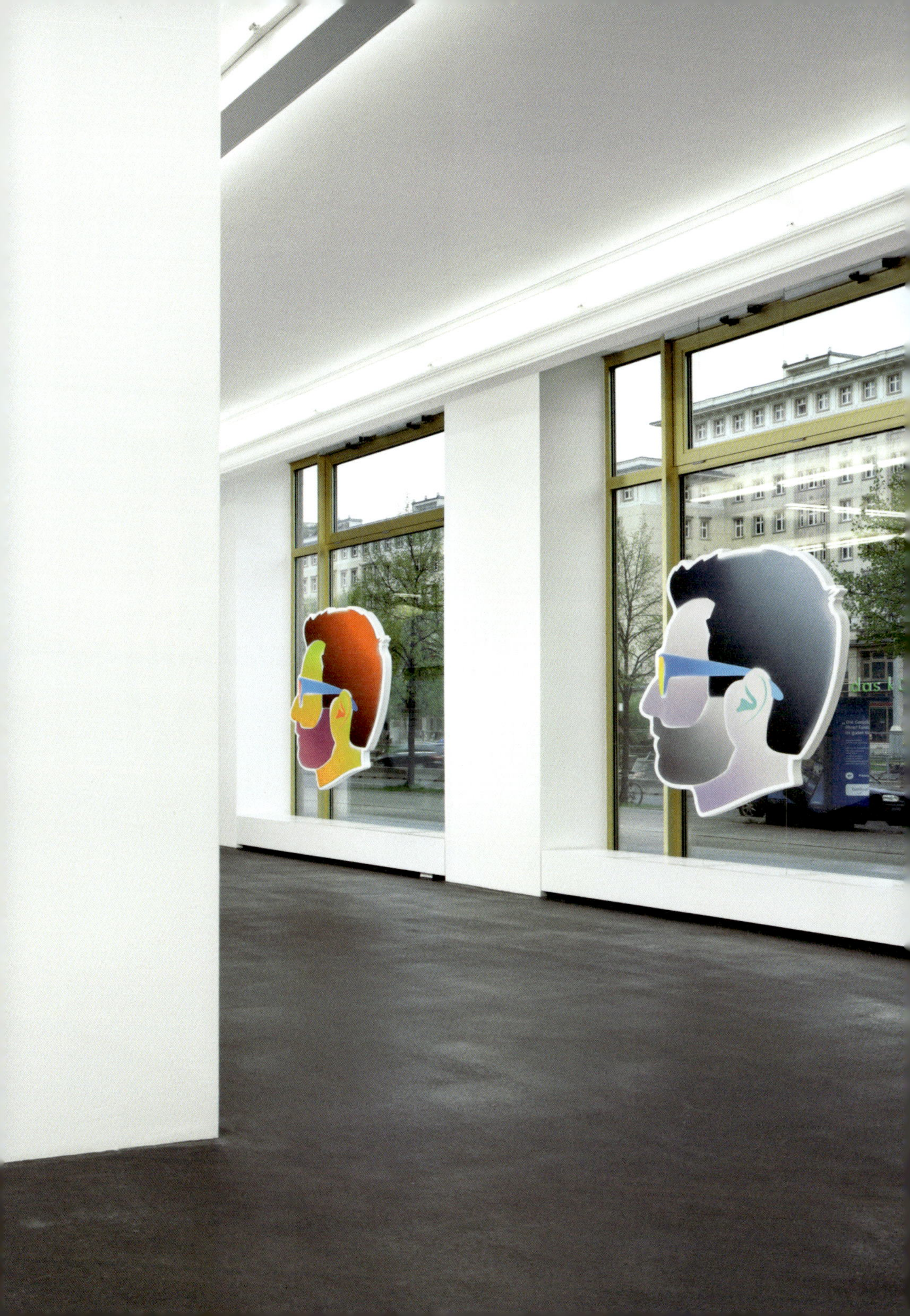

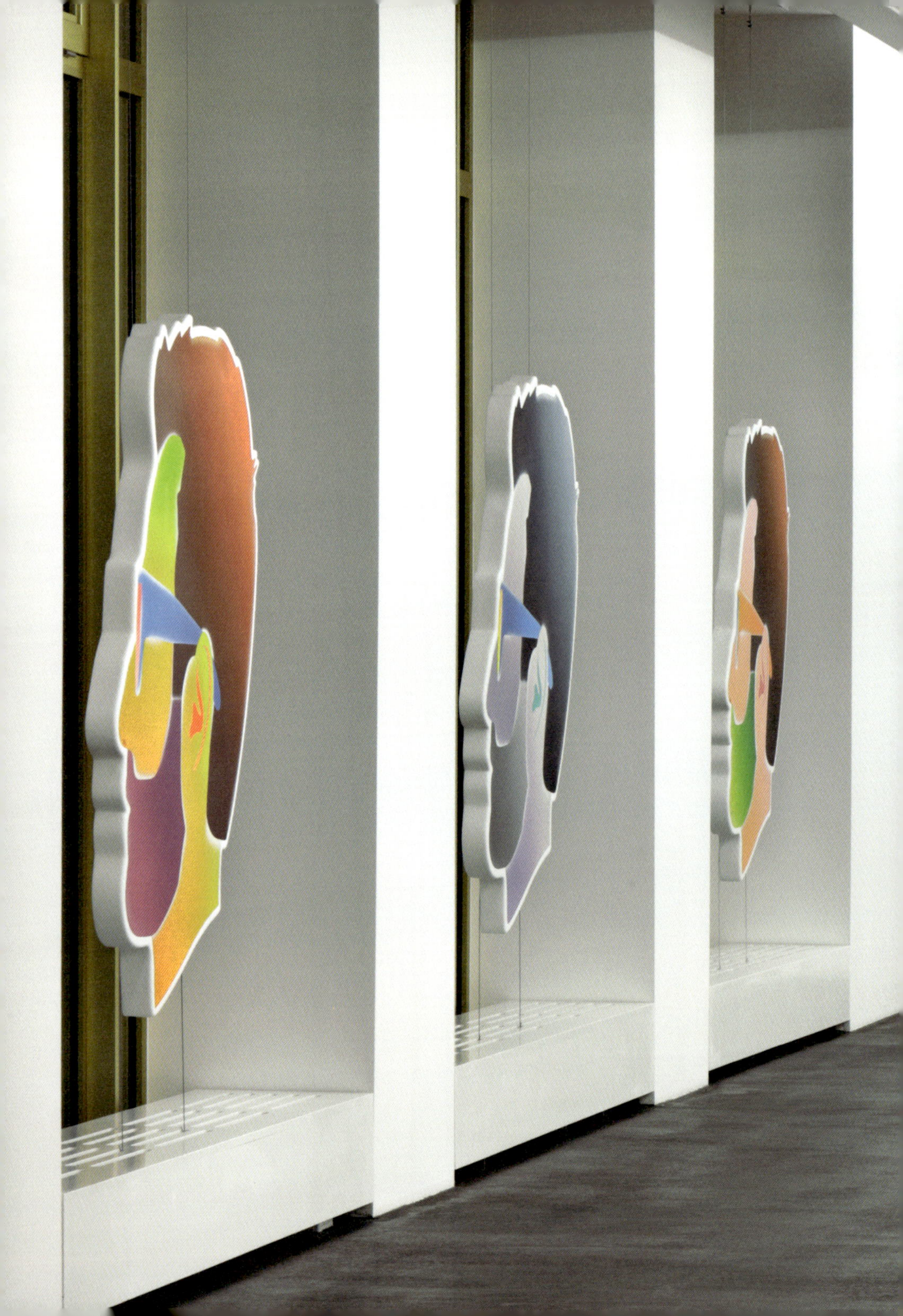

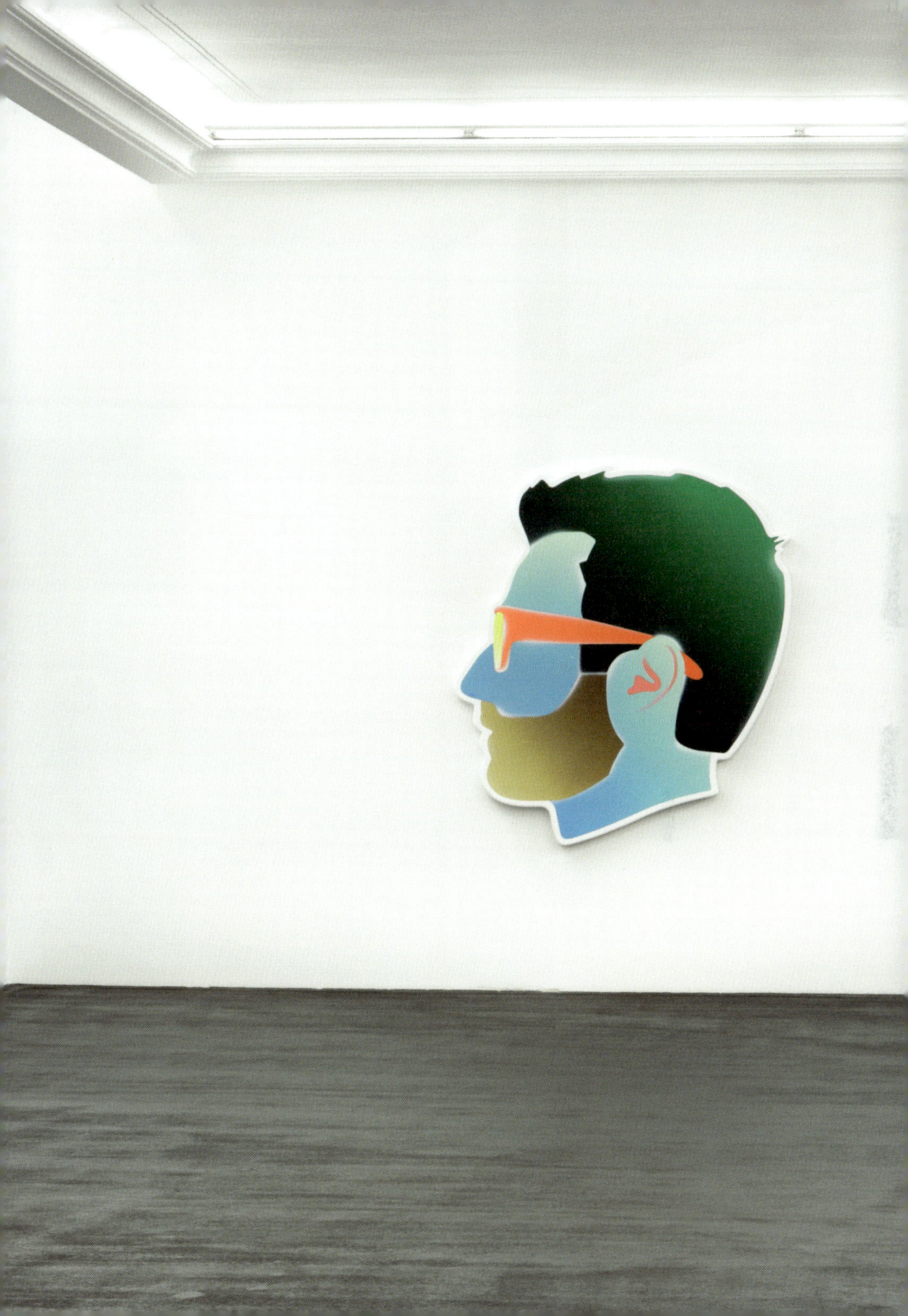

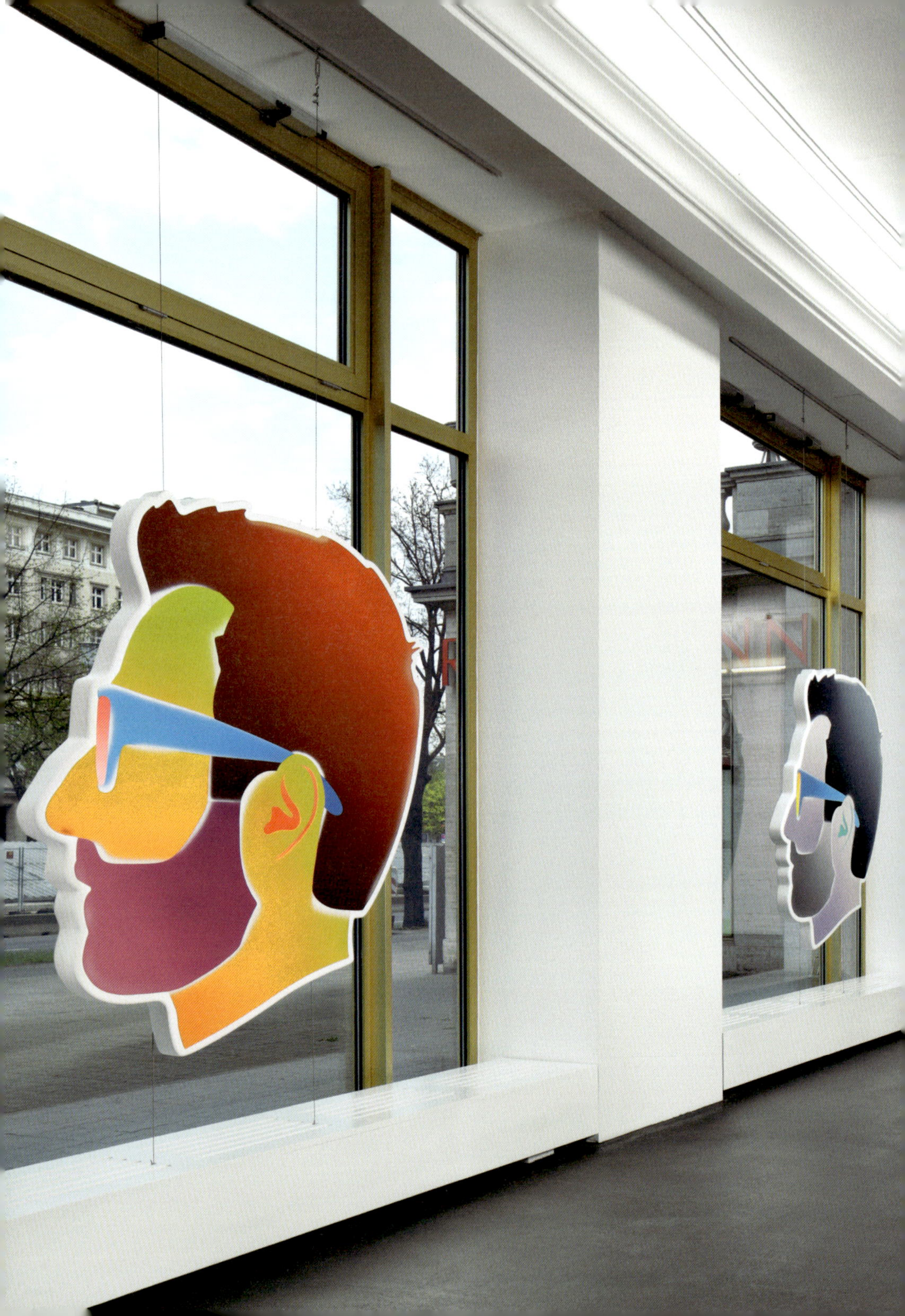

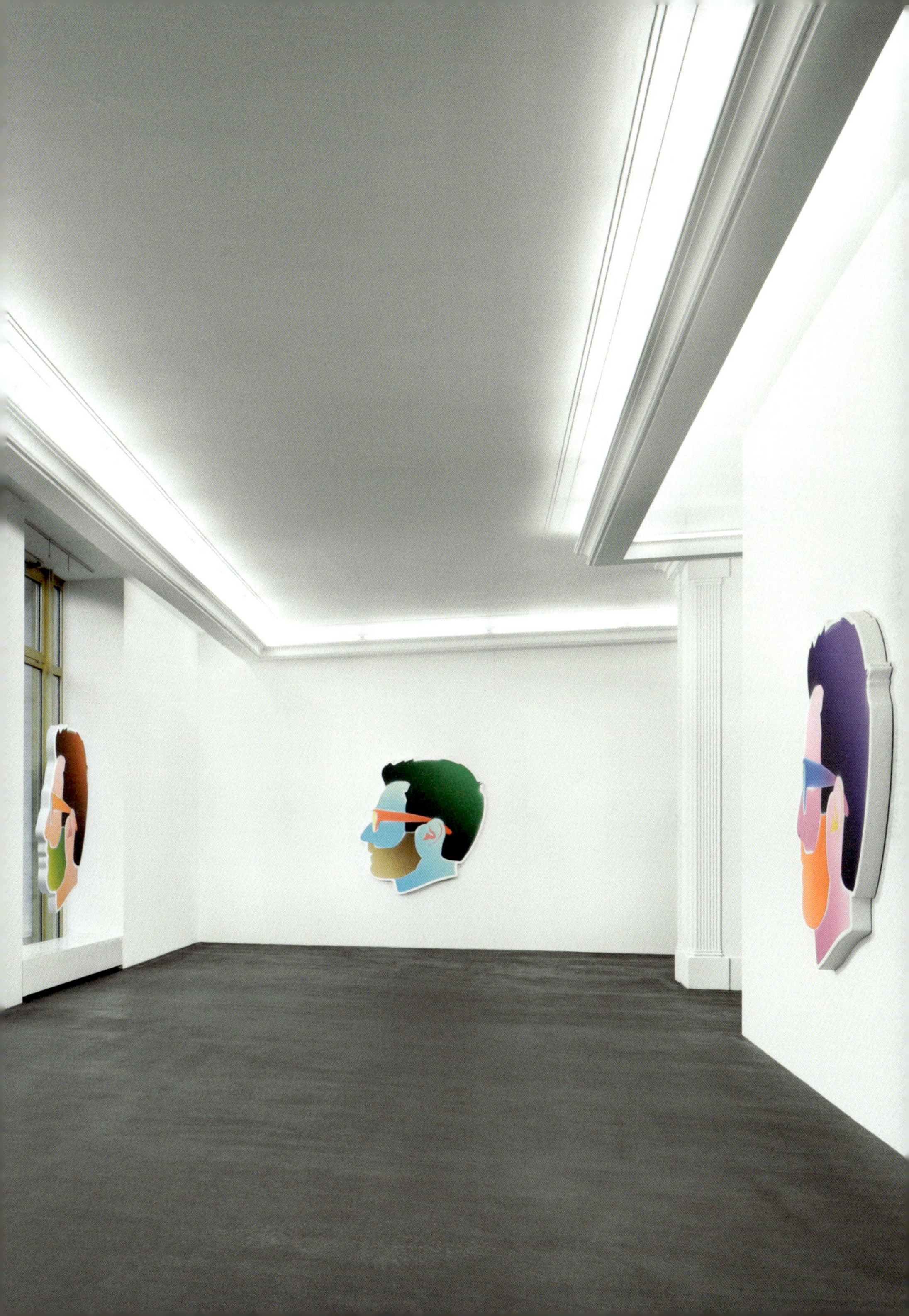

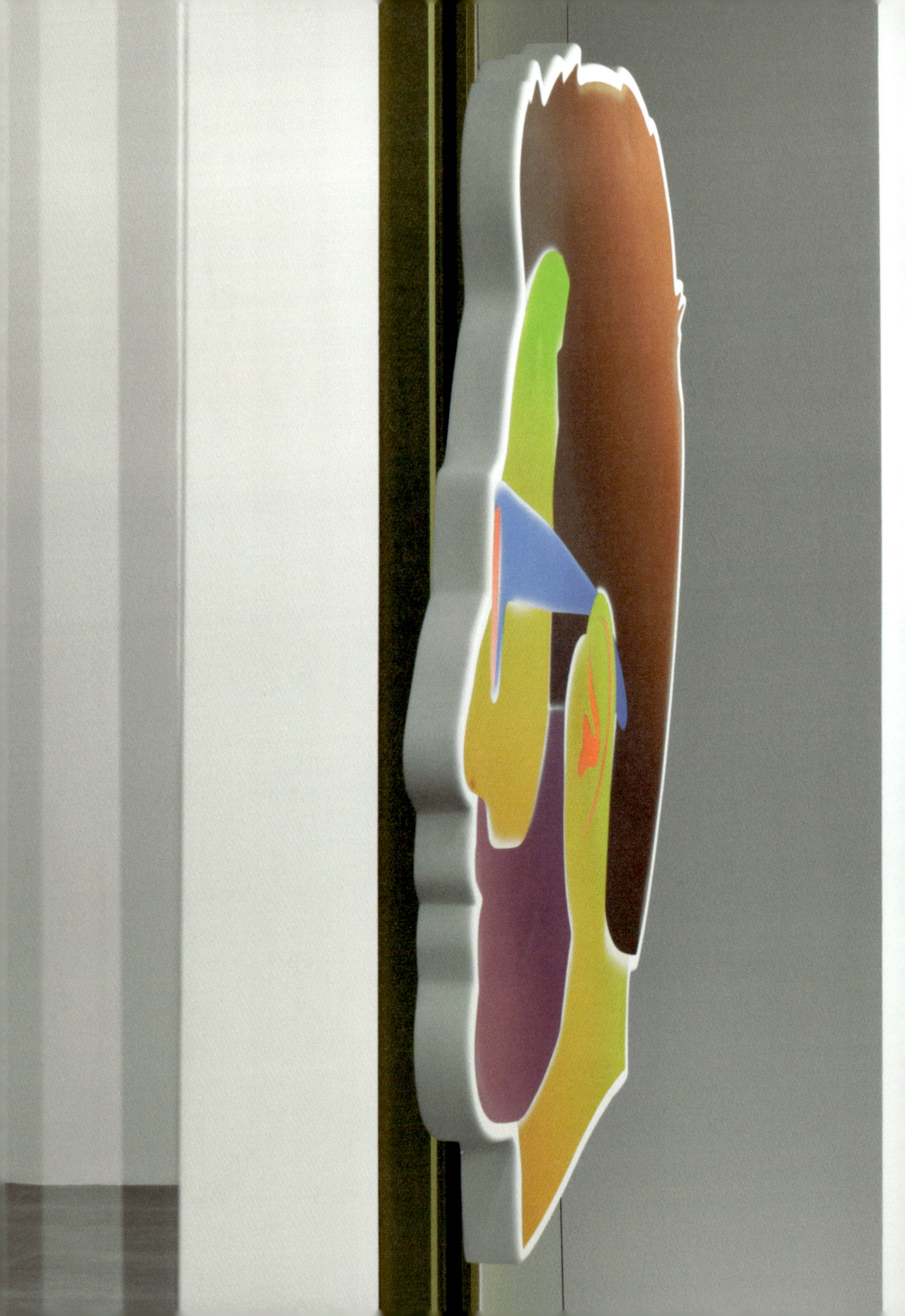

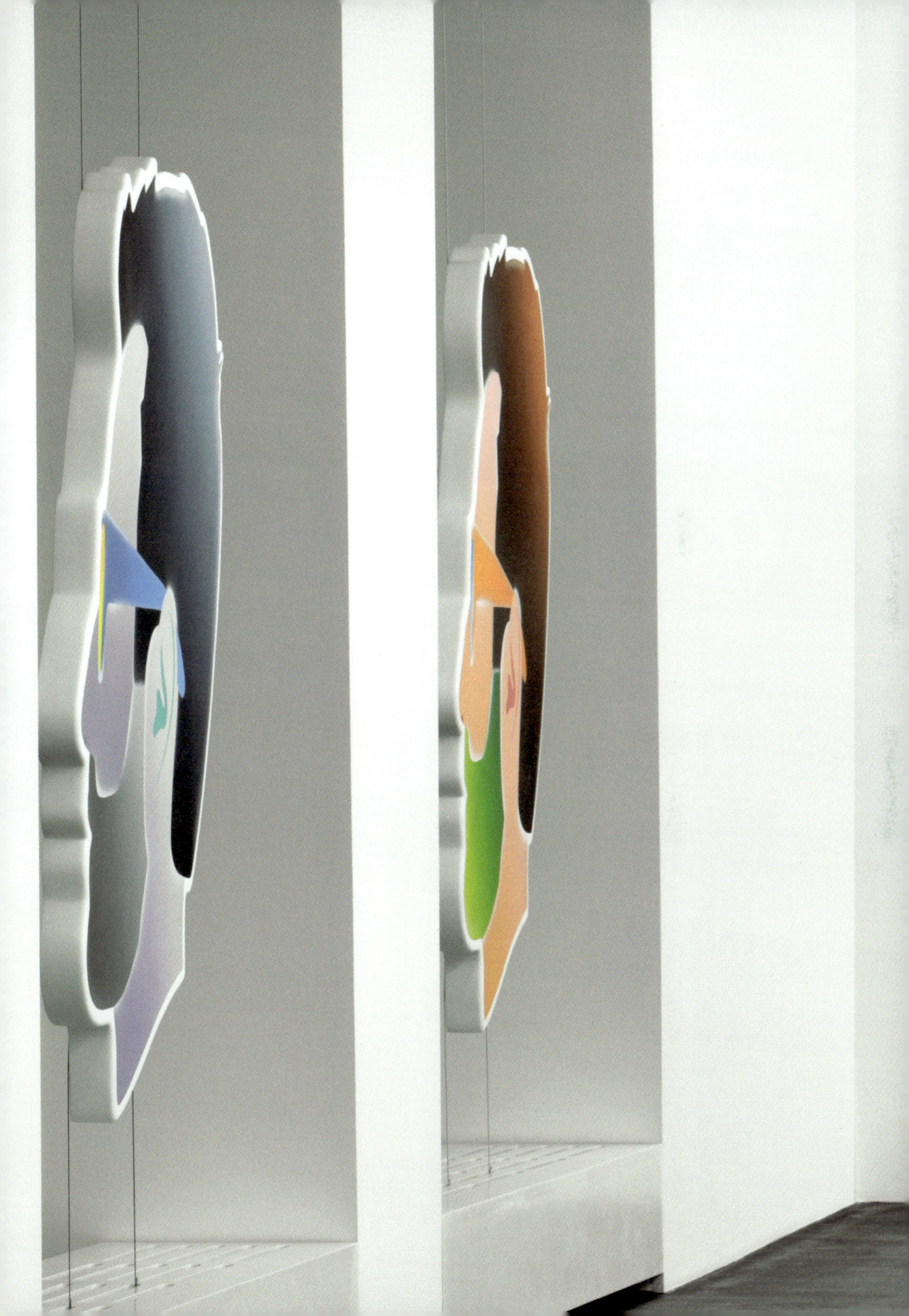

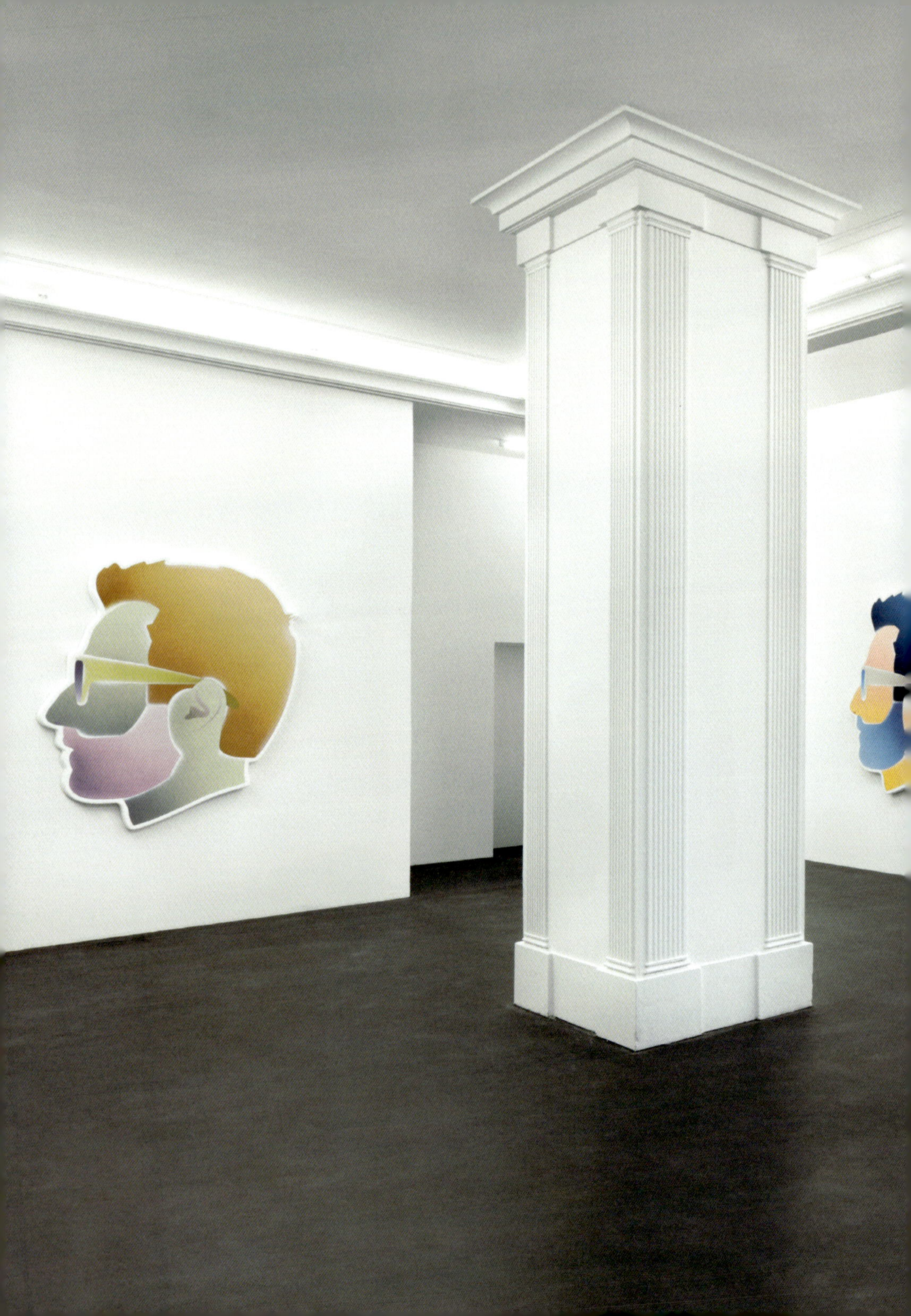

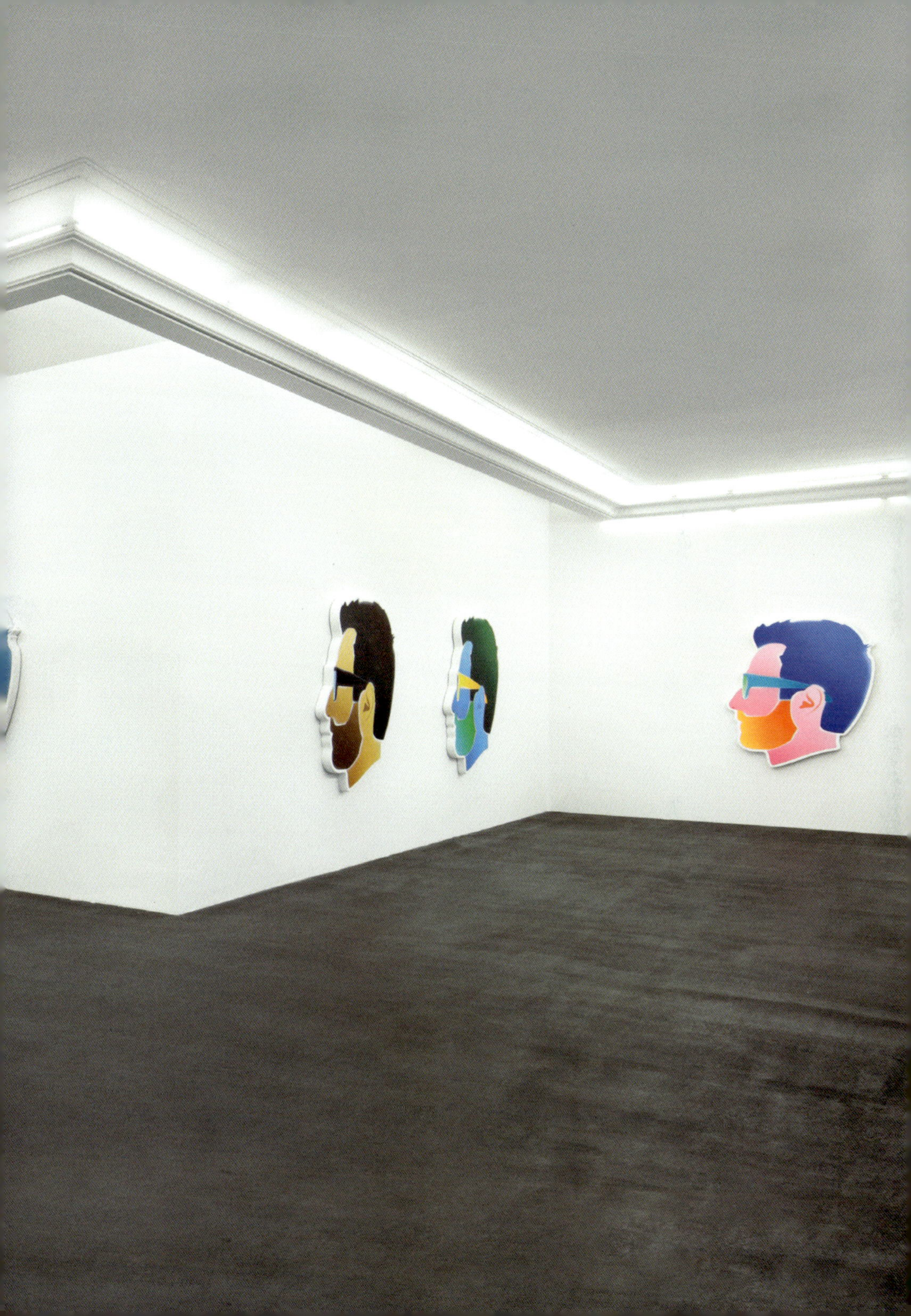

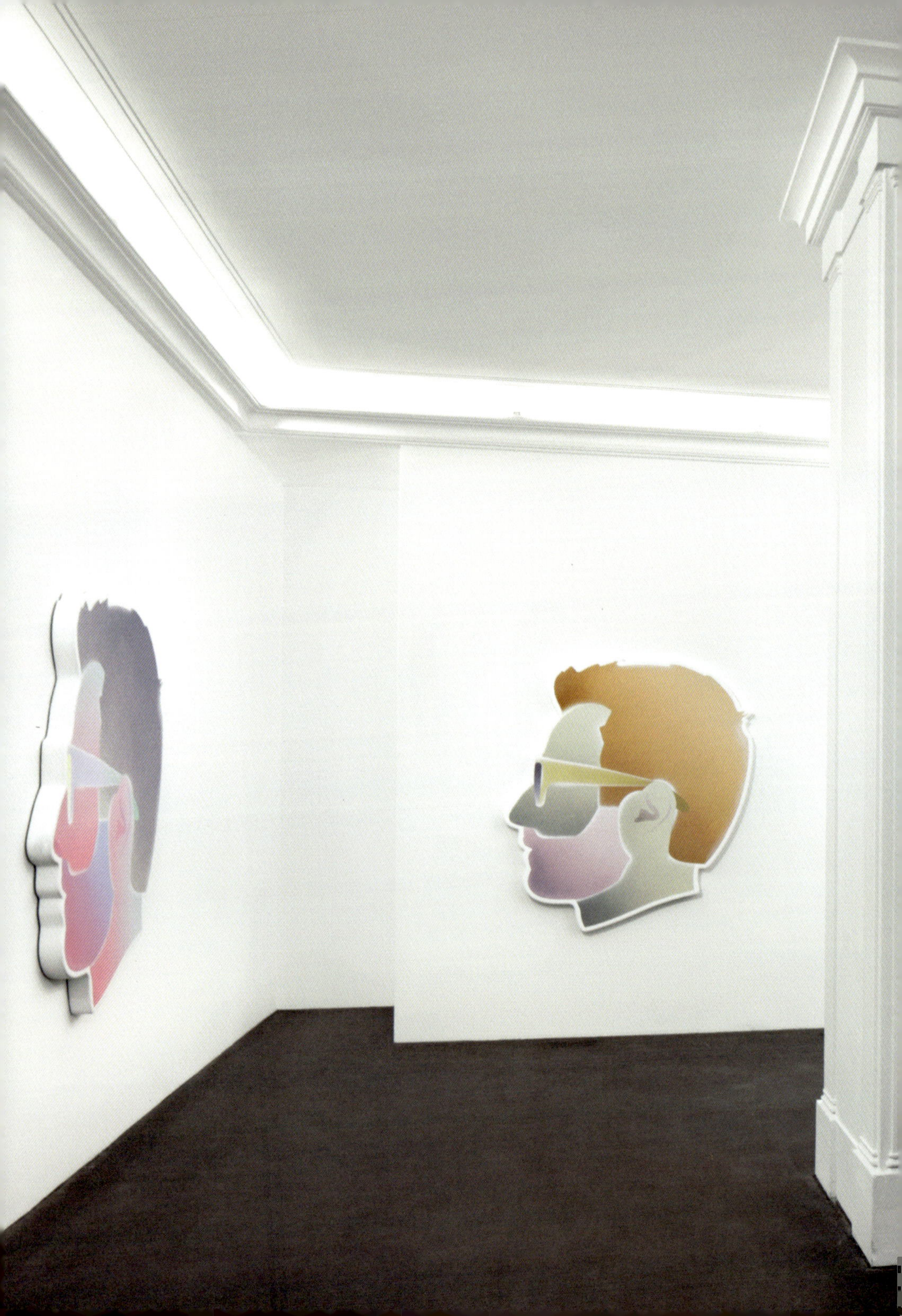

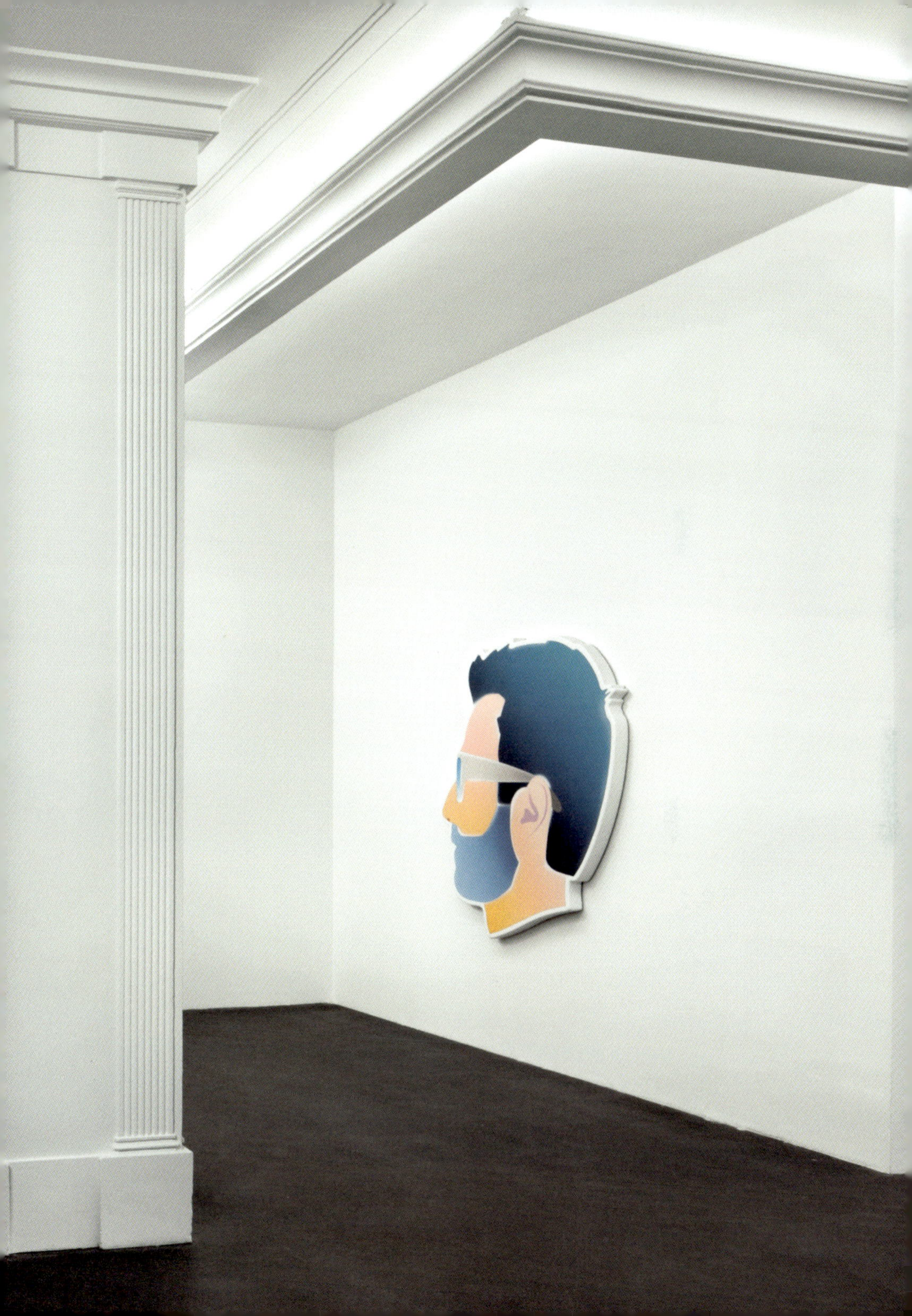

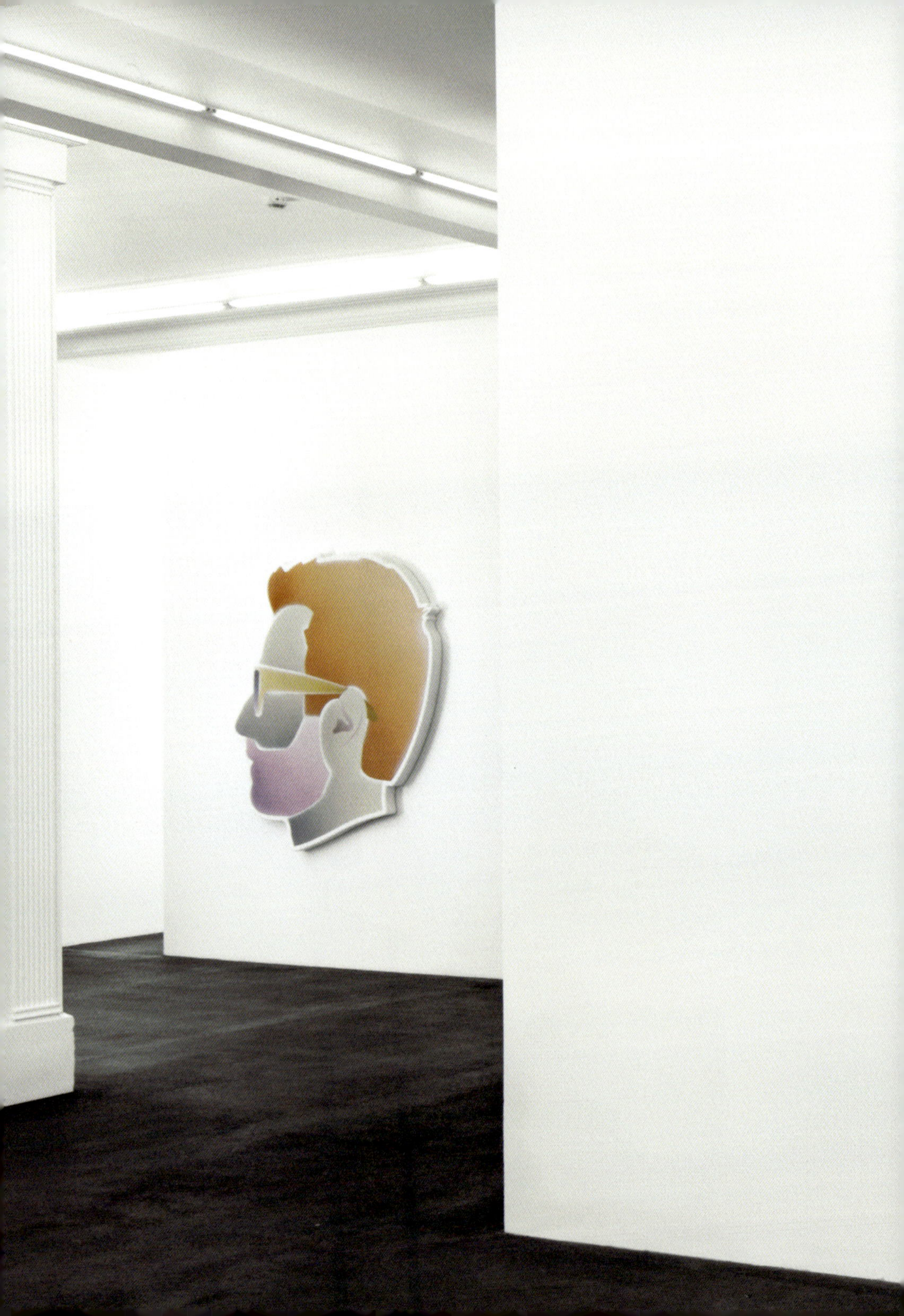

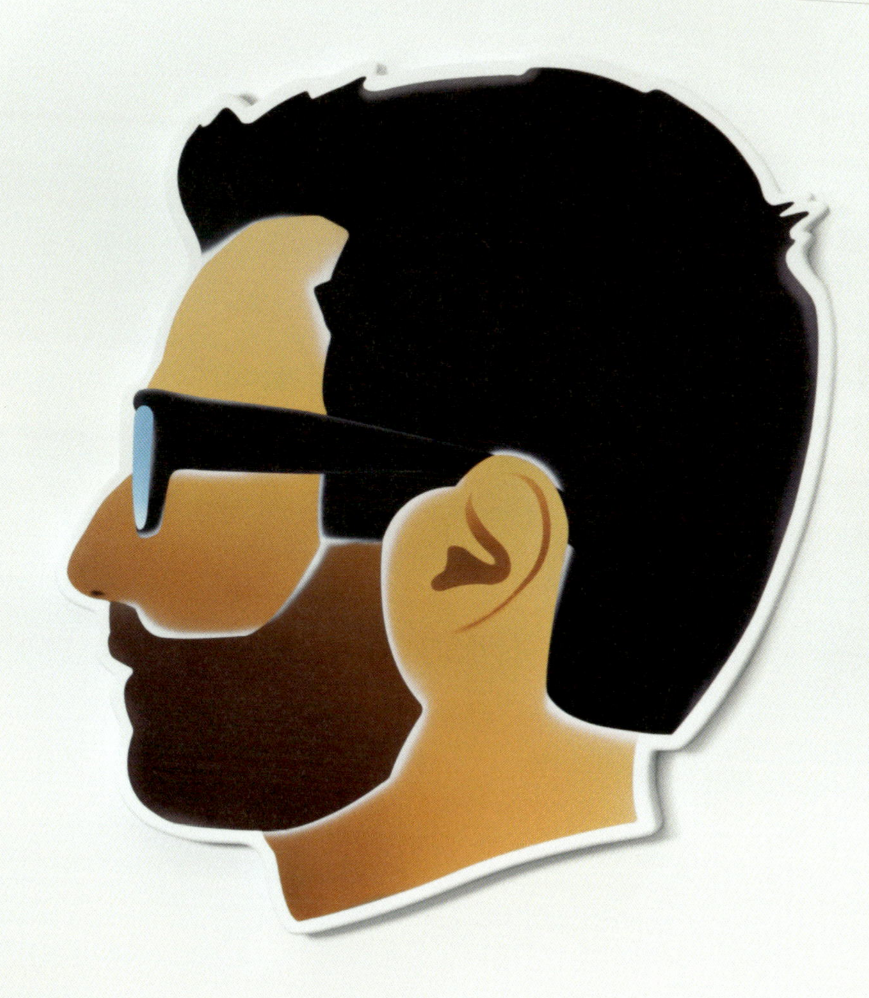

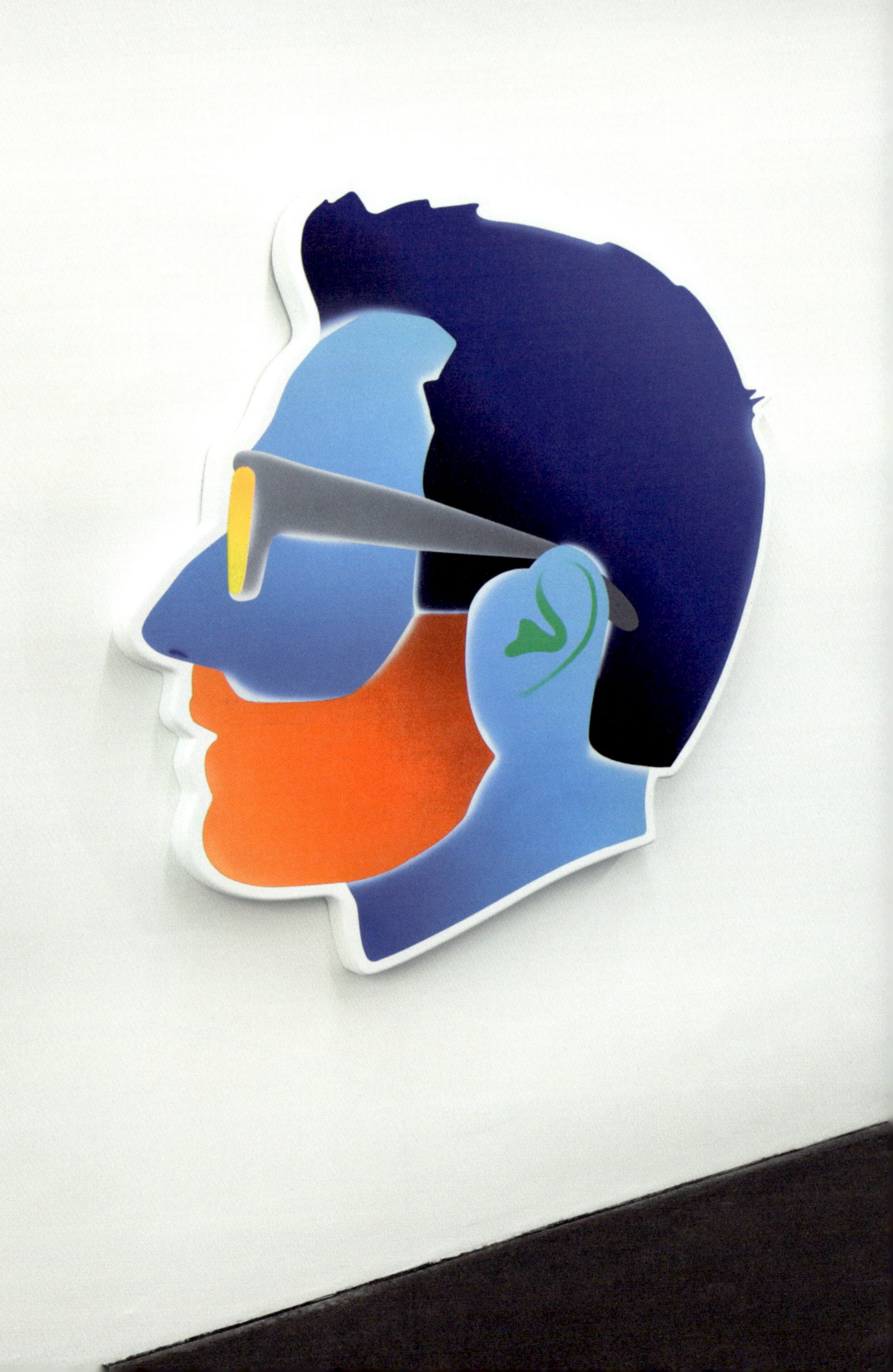

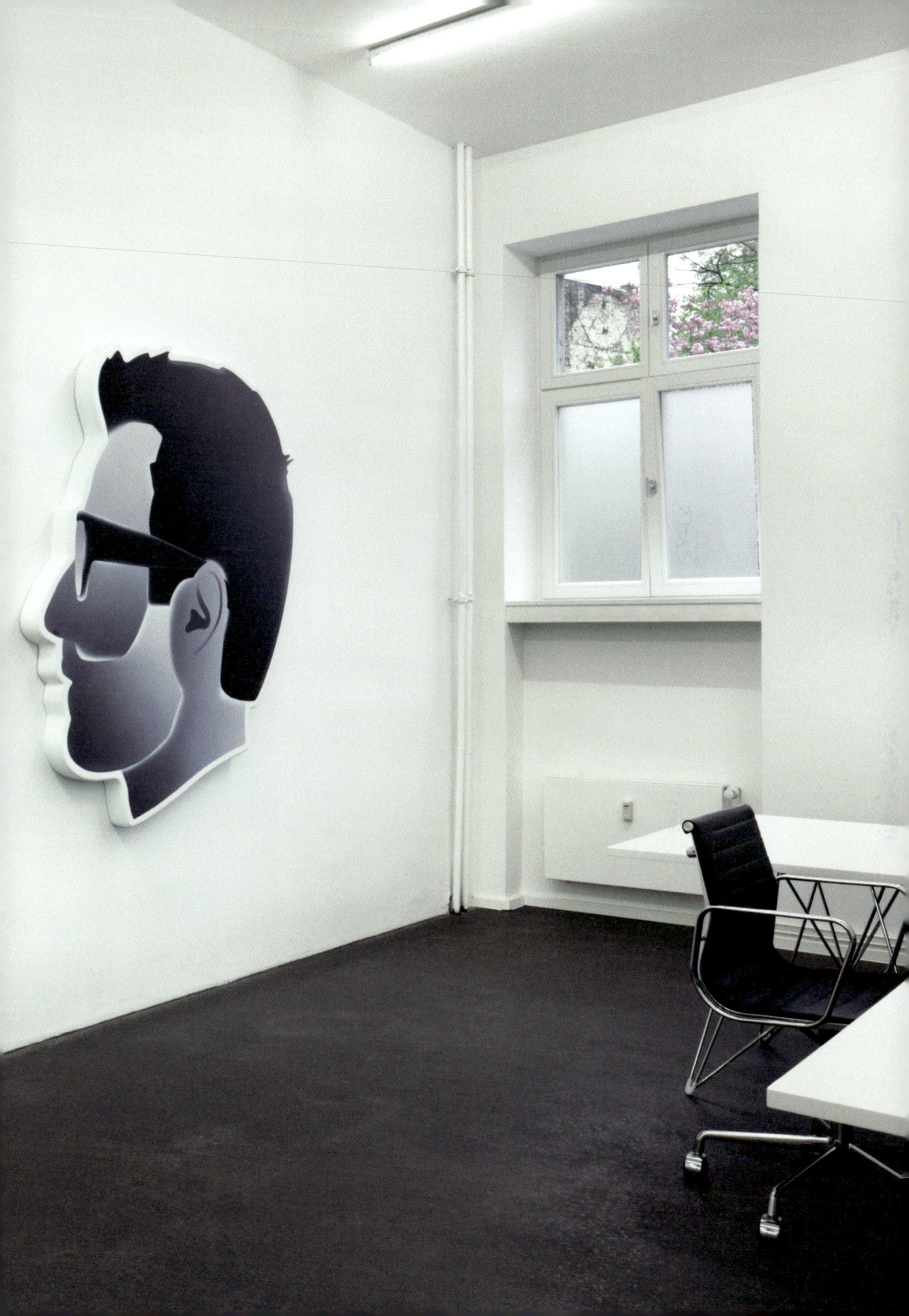

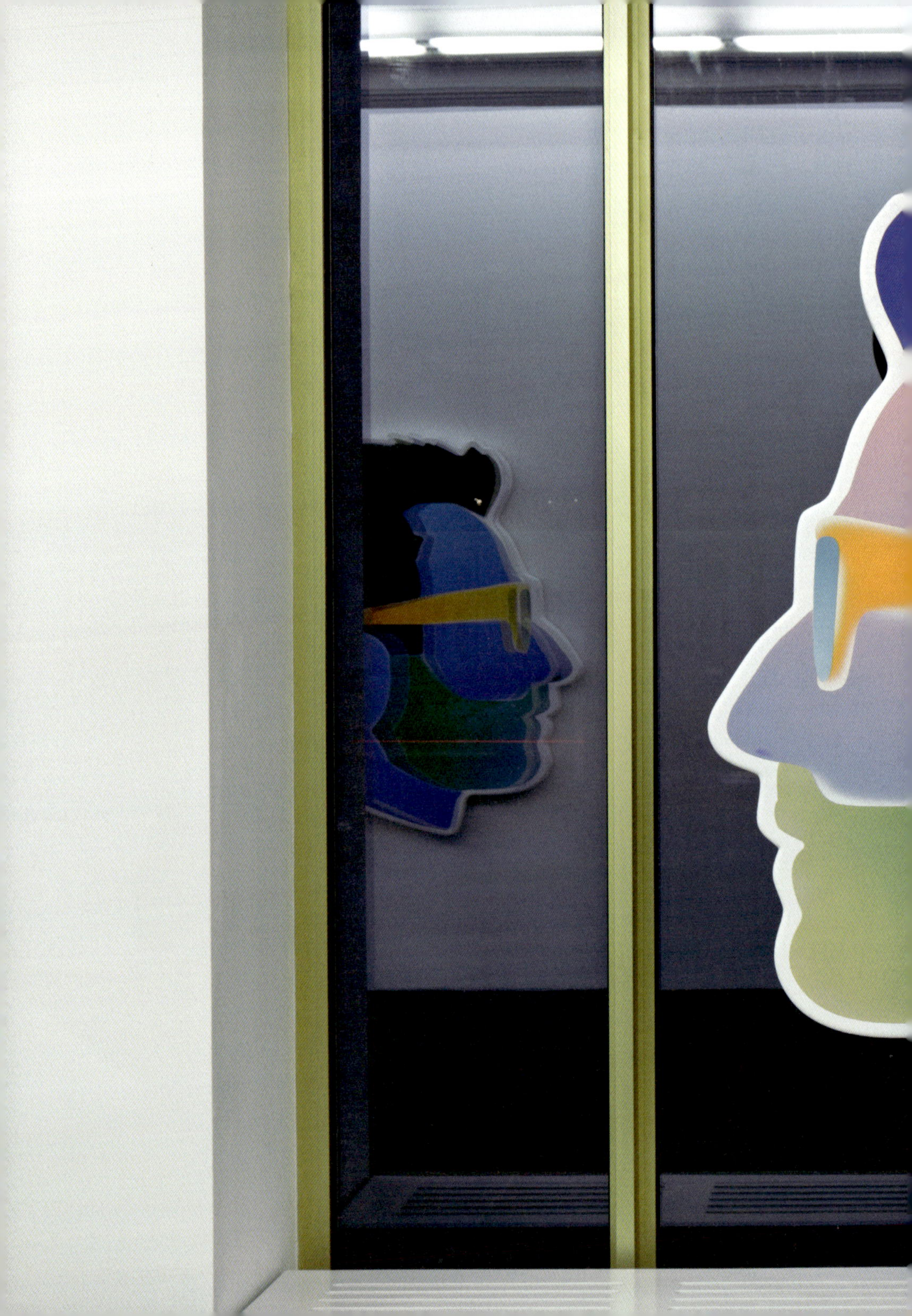

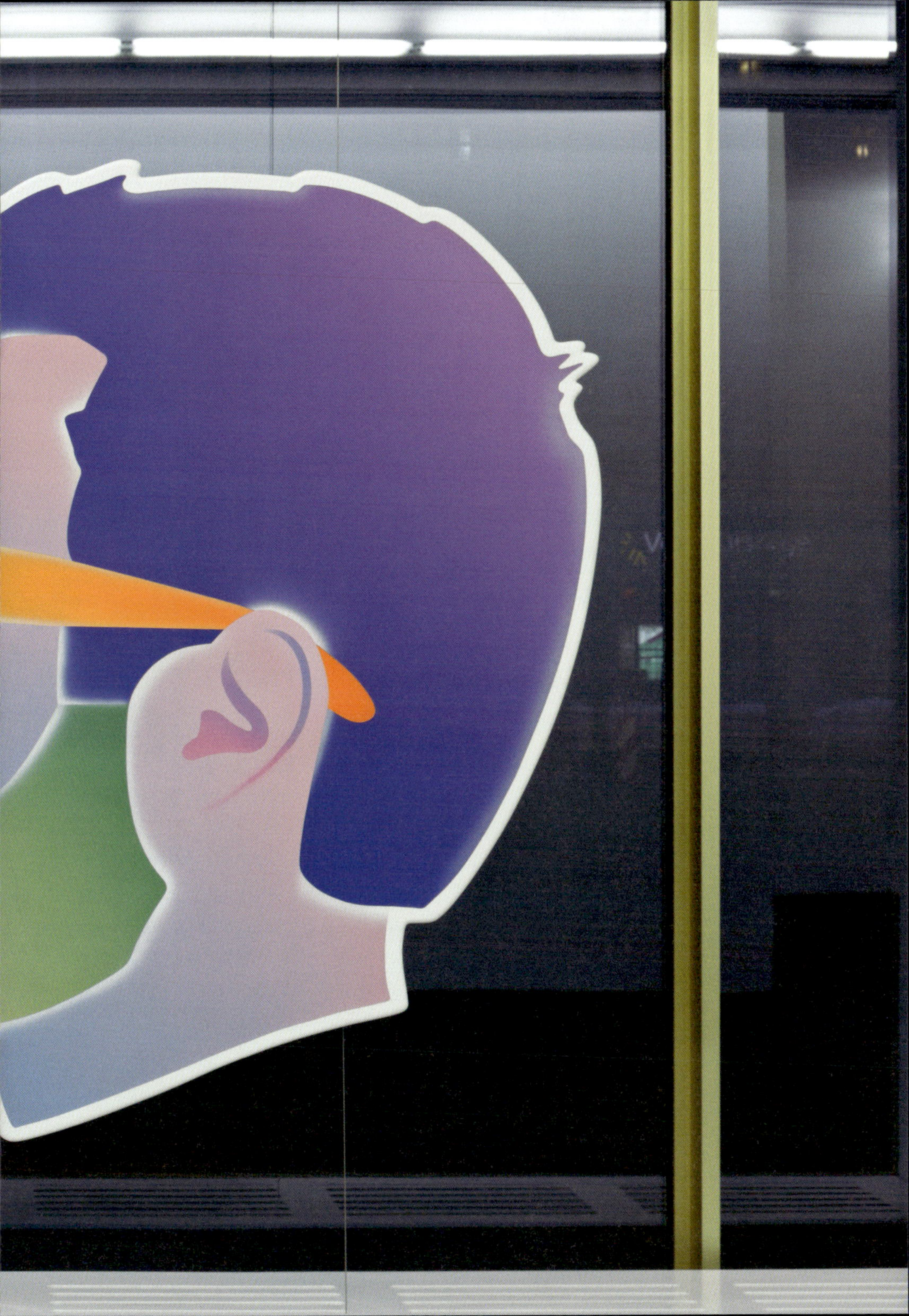

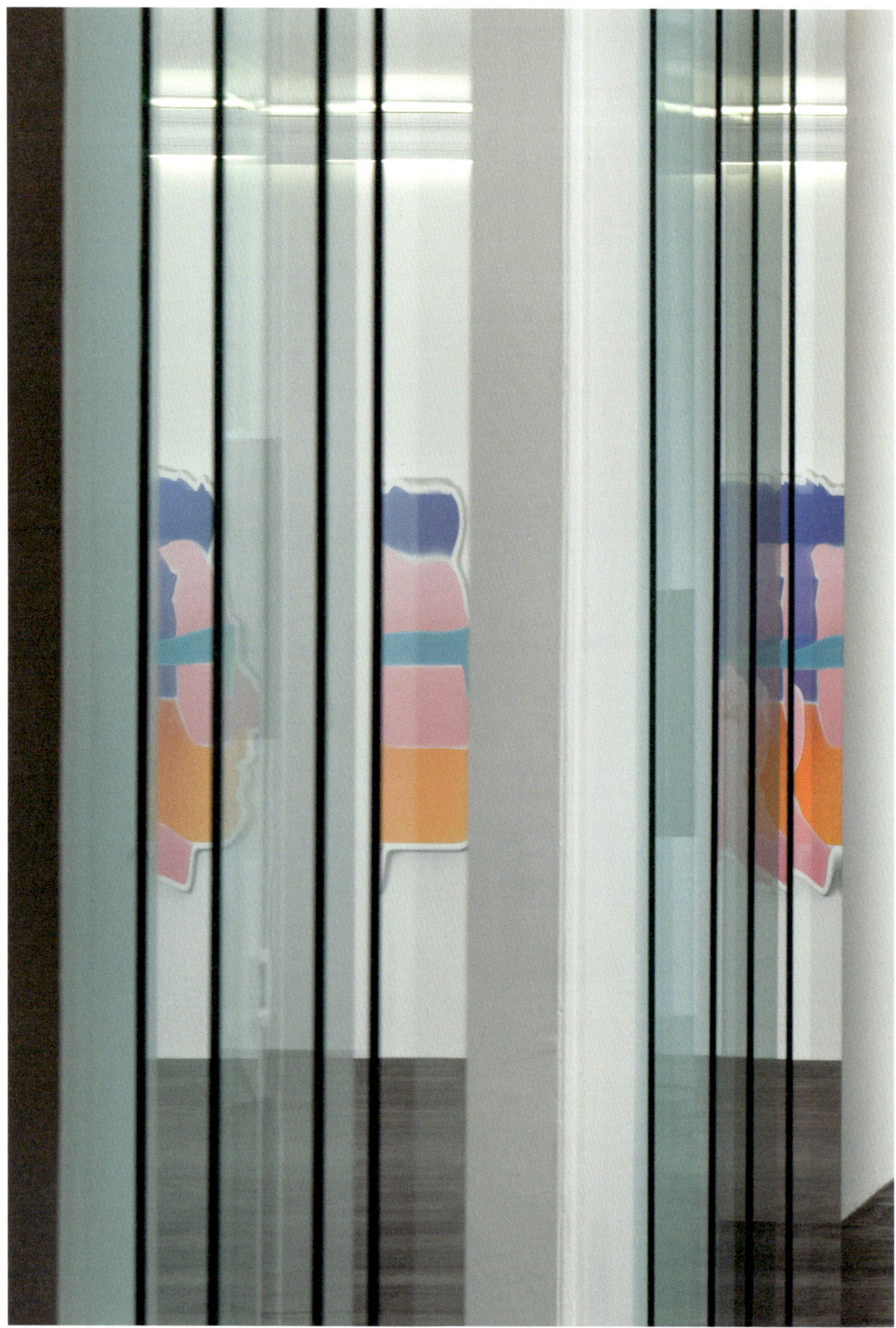

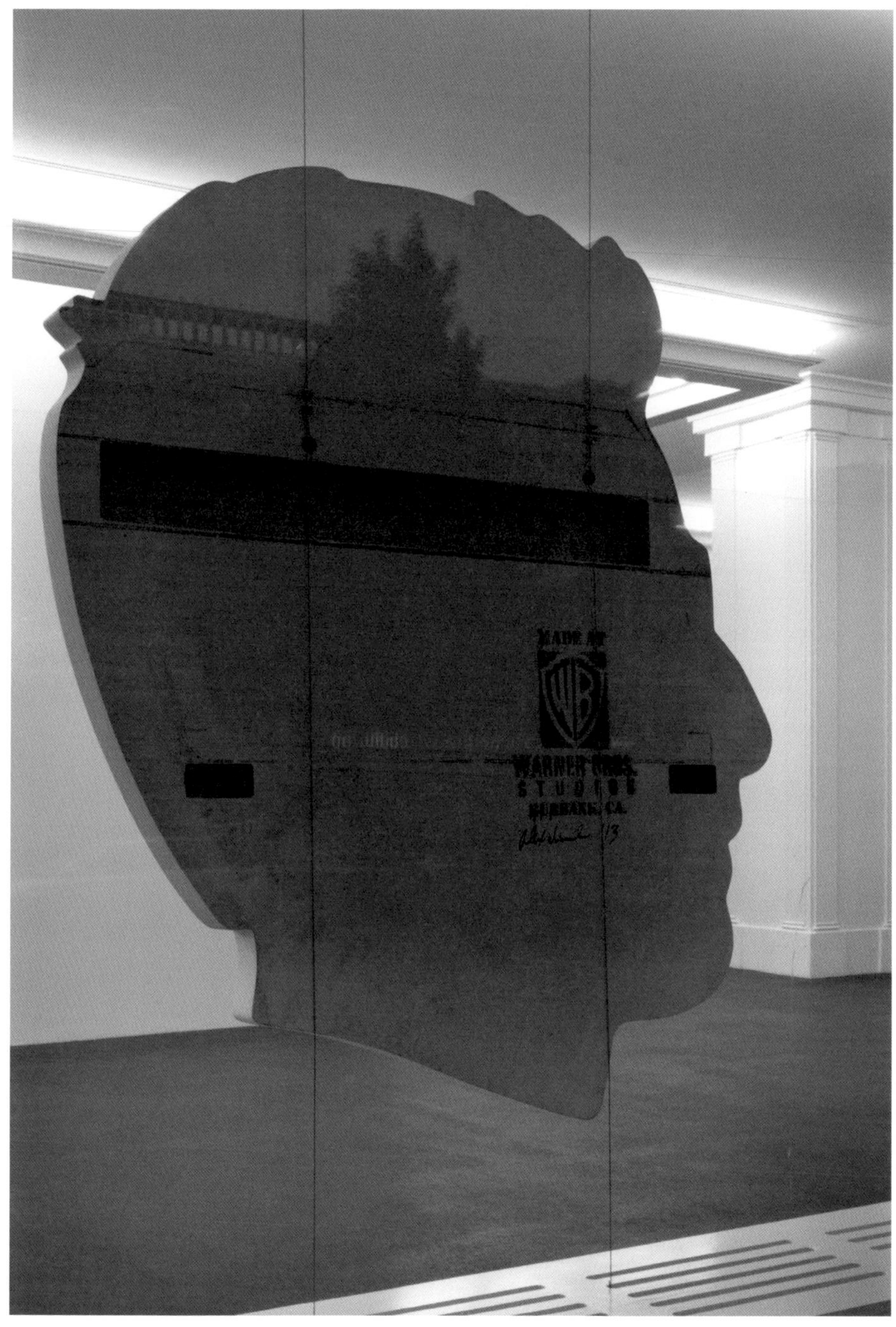

MADE AT
WB
WARNER BROS.
STUDIOS
BURBANK, CA.

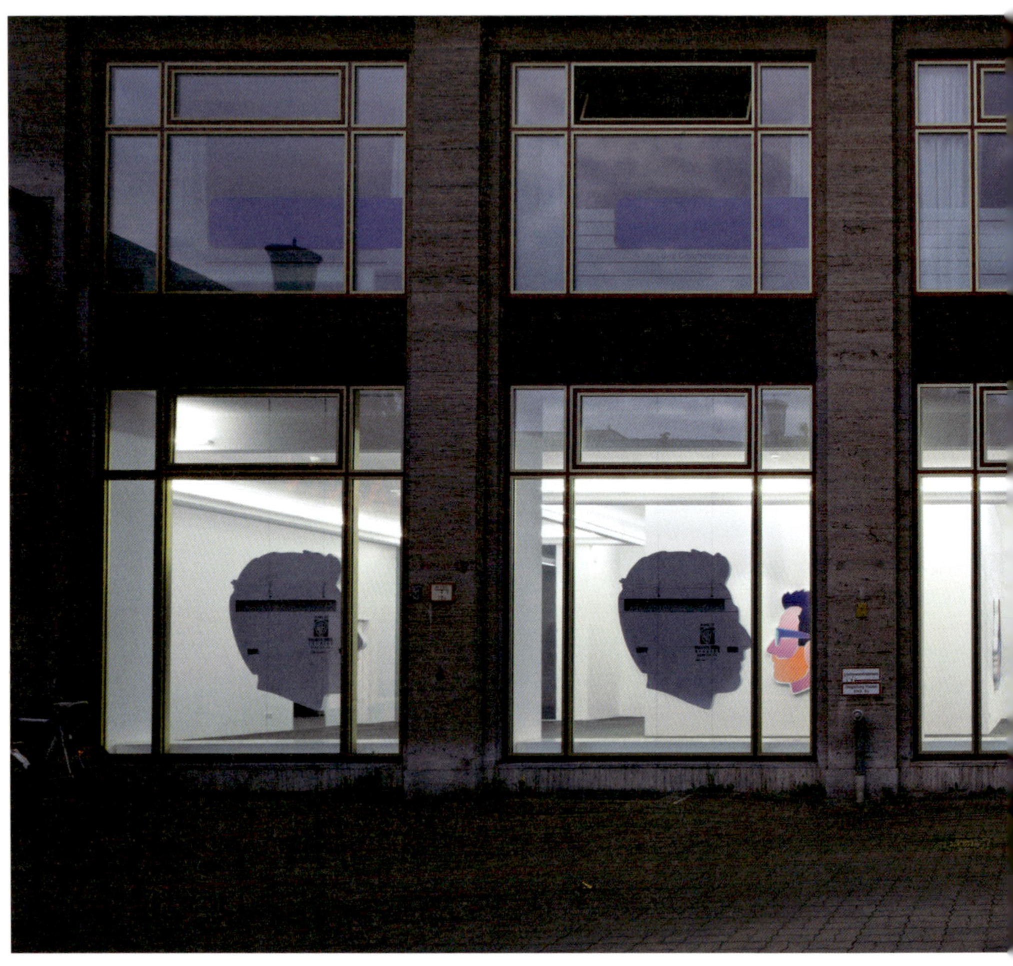

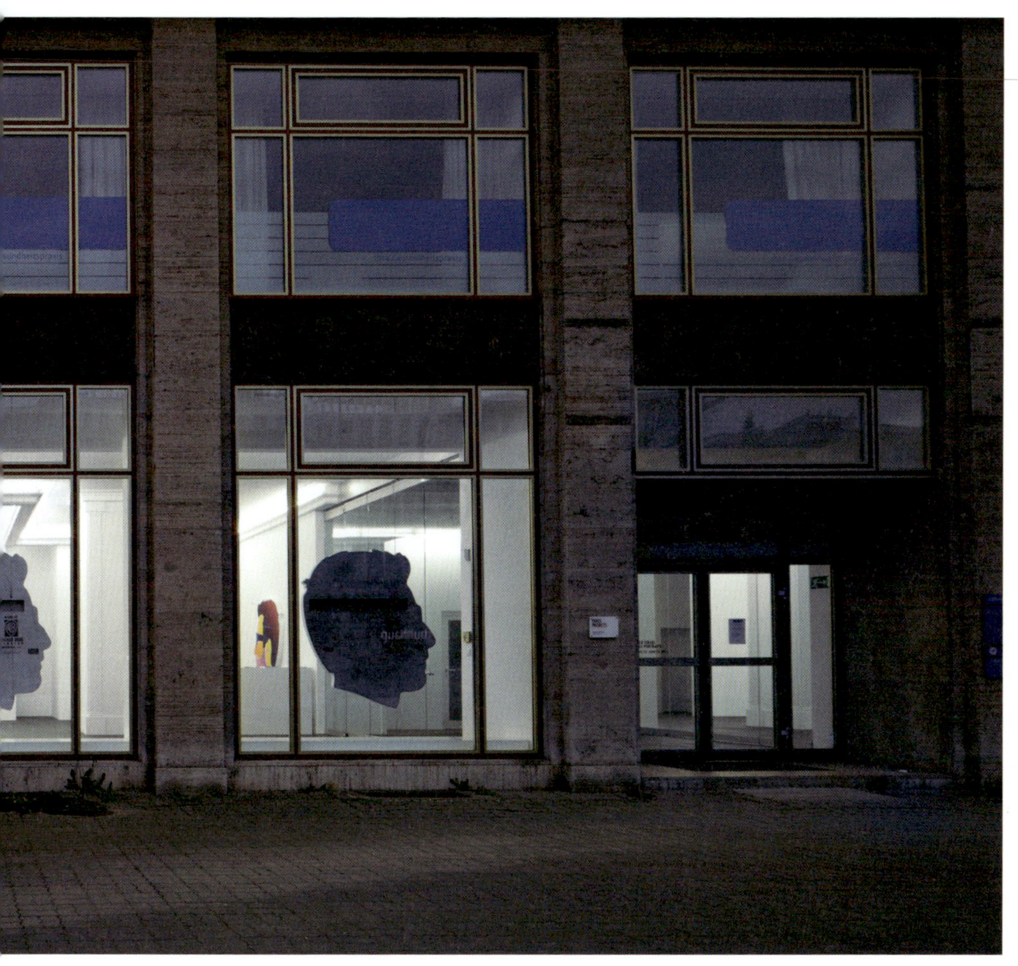

Self-Portrait (Billboard), 2013
Sunset Blvd. at Olive St., West Hollywood
April 2013–April 2016
Produced by LAXART and Art Production Fund

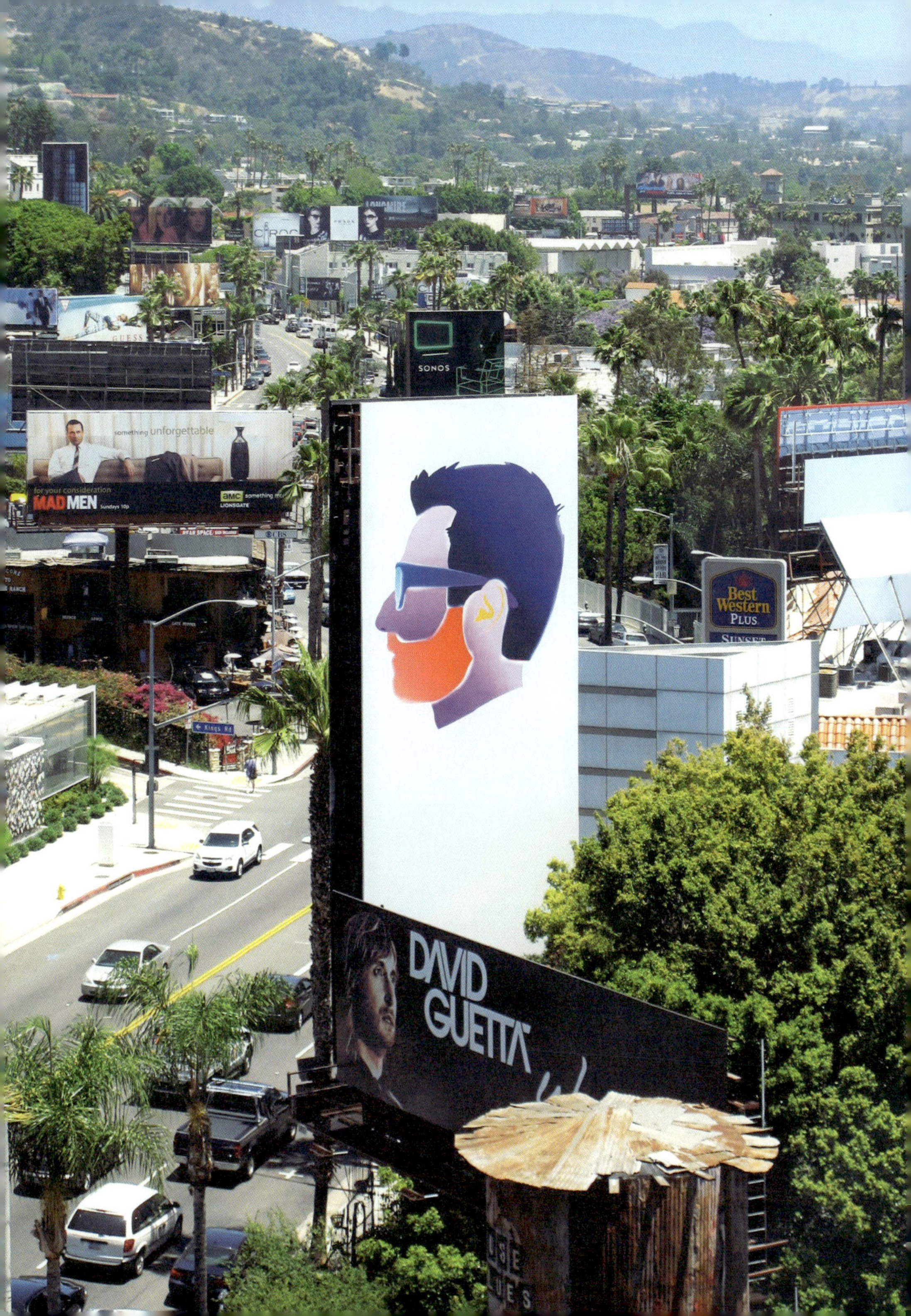

SONOS
something unforgettable
for your consideration
MAD MEN
Sundays 10p
amc something more
LIONSGATE
GUESS
CBS
Kings Rd
Best Western
PLUS
SUNSET
DAVID
GUETTA

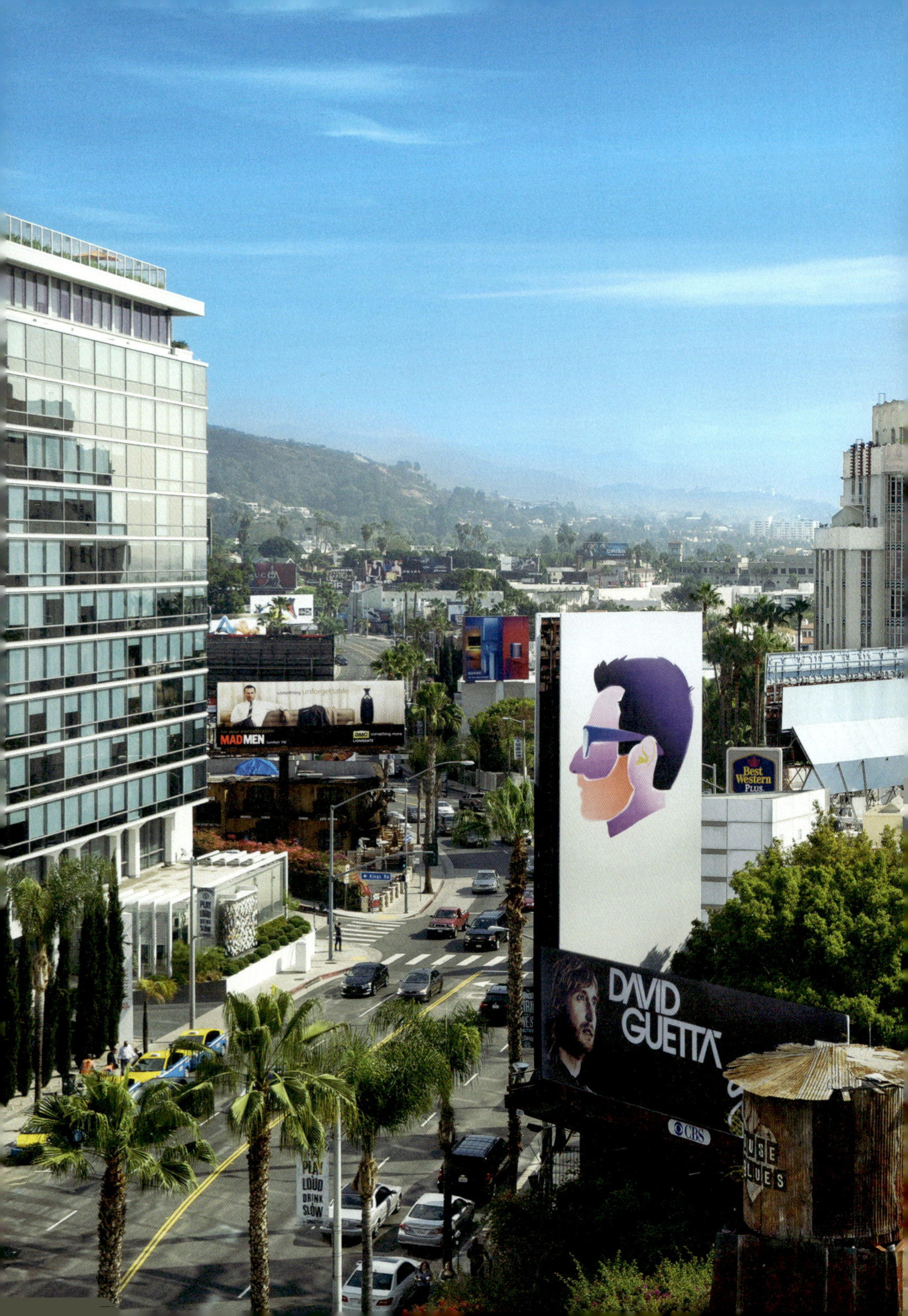

everything unforgettable
MADMEN
AMC something more
LIONSGATE
DAVID
GUETTA
Best Western
PLUS
CBS
PLAY
LOUD
DRINK
SLOW
Kings Rd

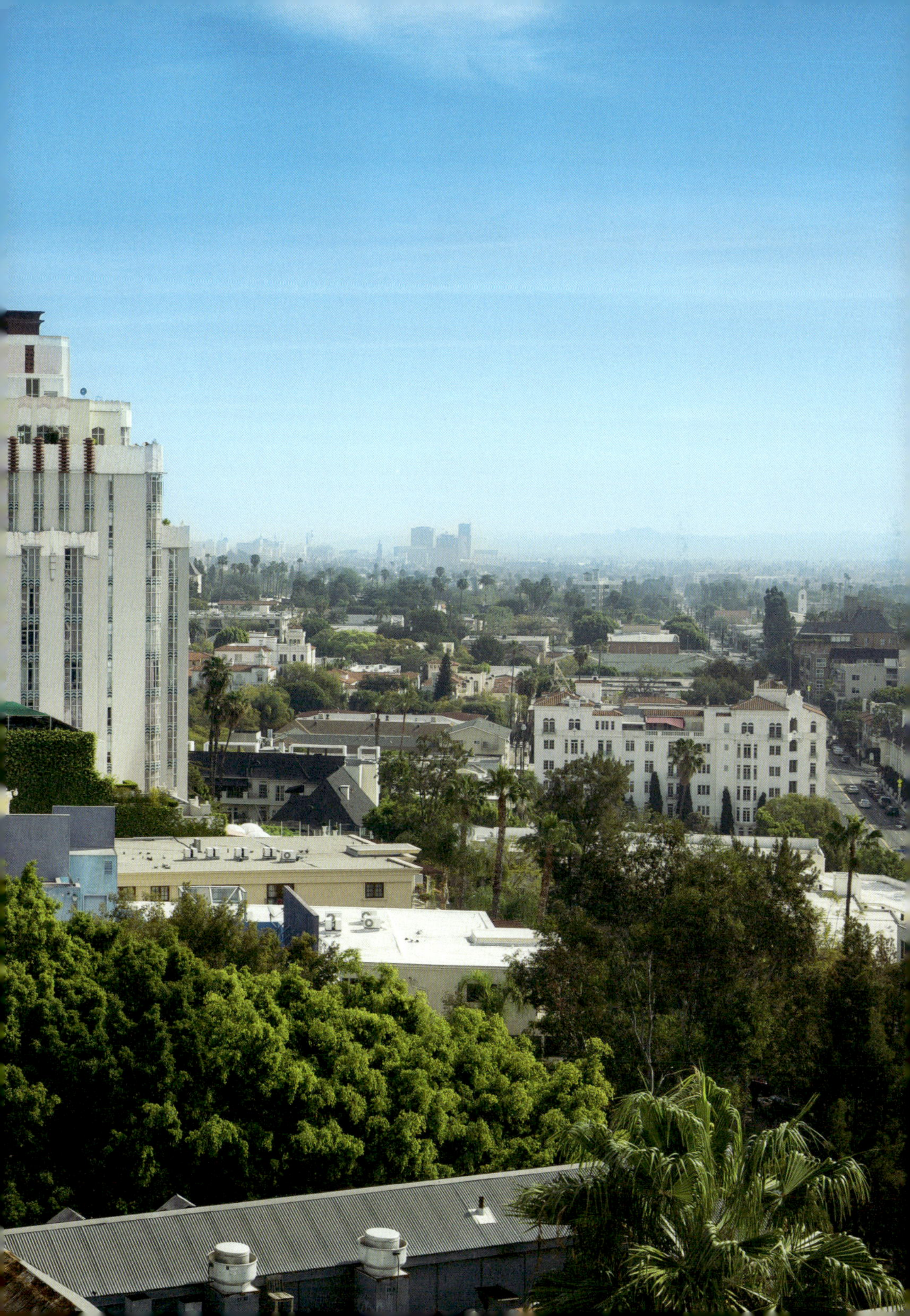

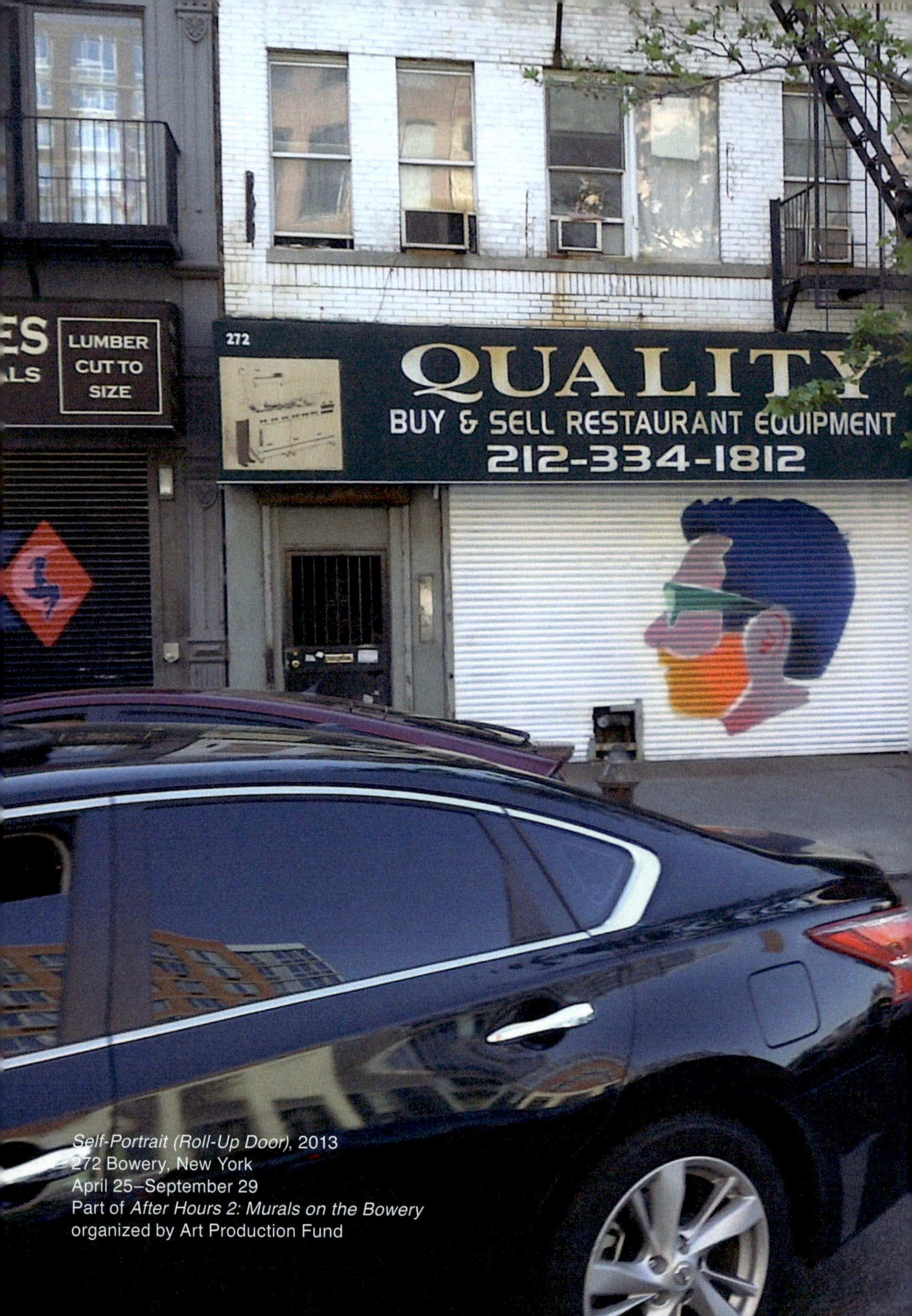

Self-Portrait (Roll-Up Door), 2013
272 Bowery, New York
April 25–September 29
Part of *After Hours 2: Murals on the Bowery*
organized by Art Production Fund

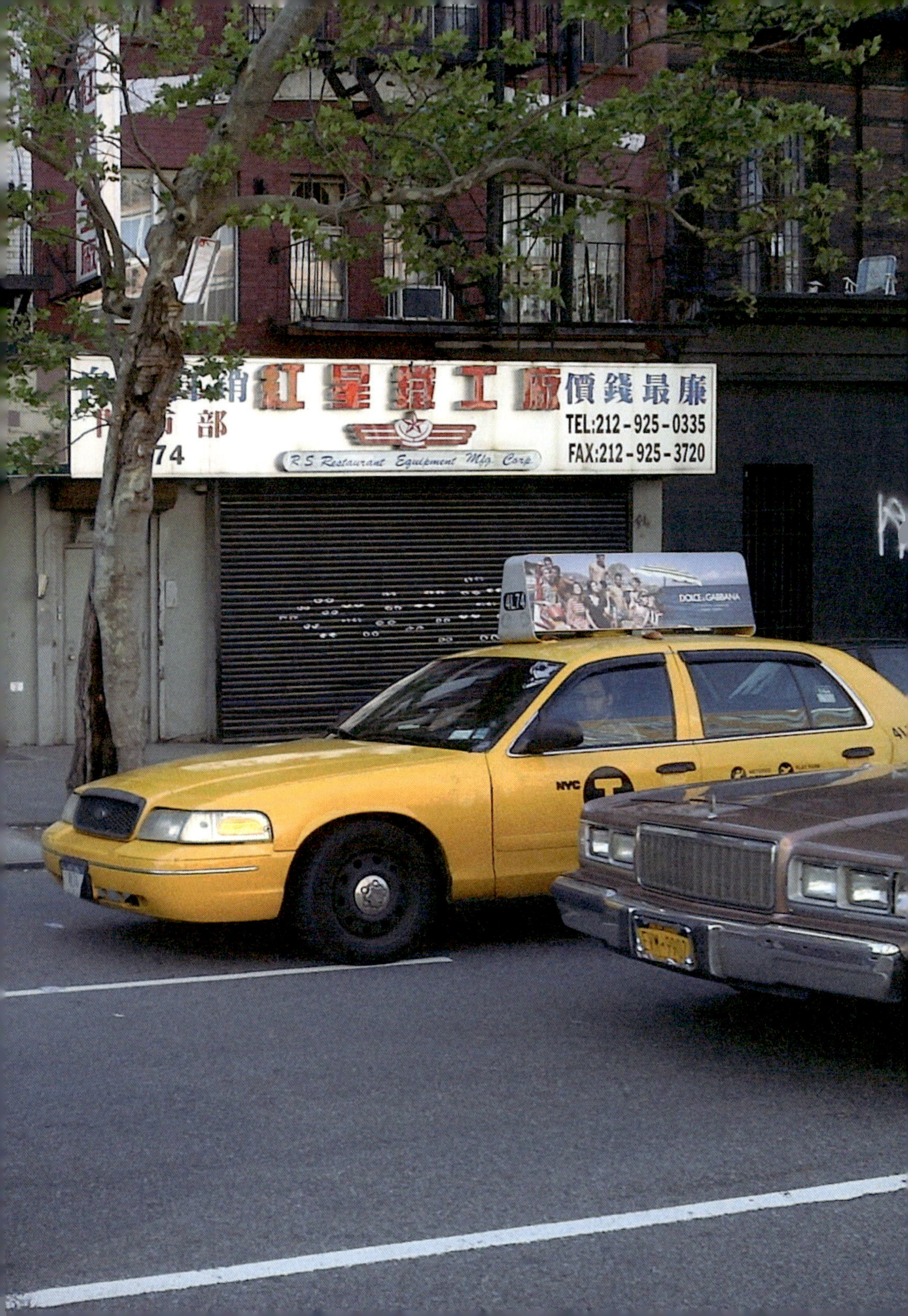
紅星鑧工廠 價錢最廉
TEL:212-925-0335
FAX:212-925-3720
R.S. Restaurant Equipment Mfg. Corp.
部
74
NYC
DOLCE&GABBANA

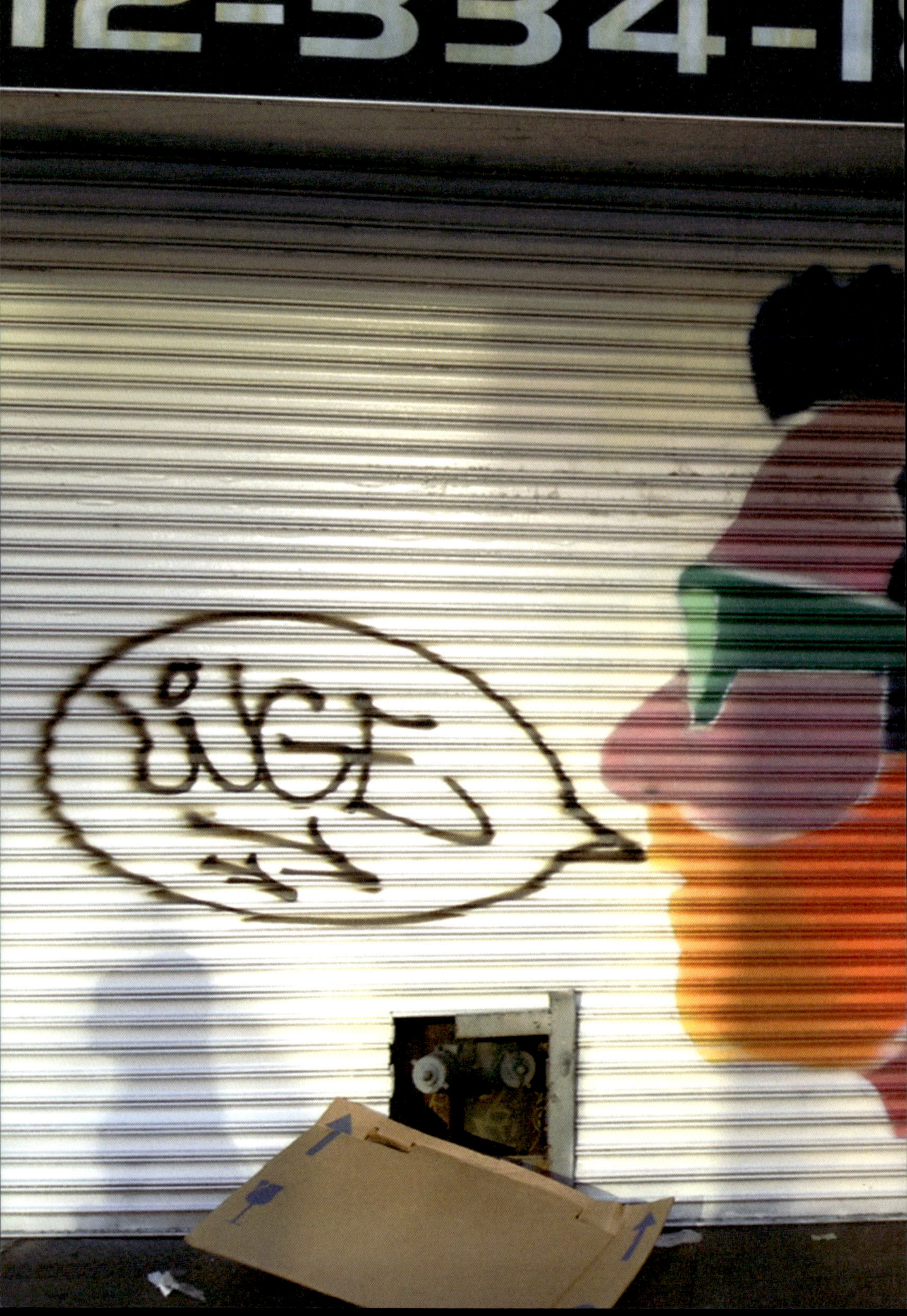
12-334-1

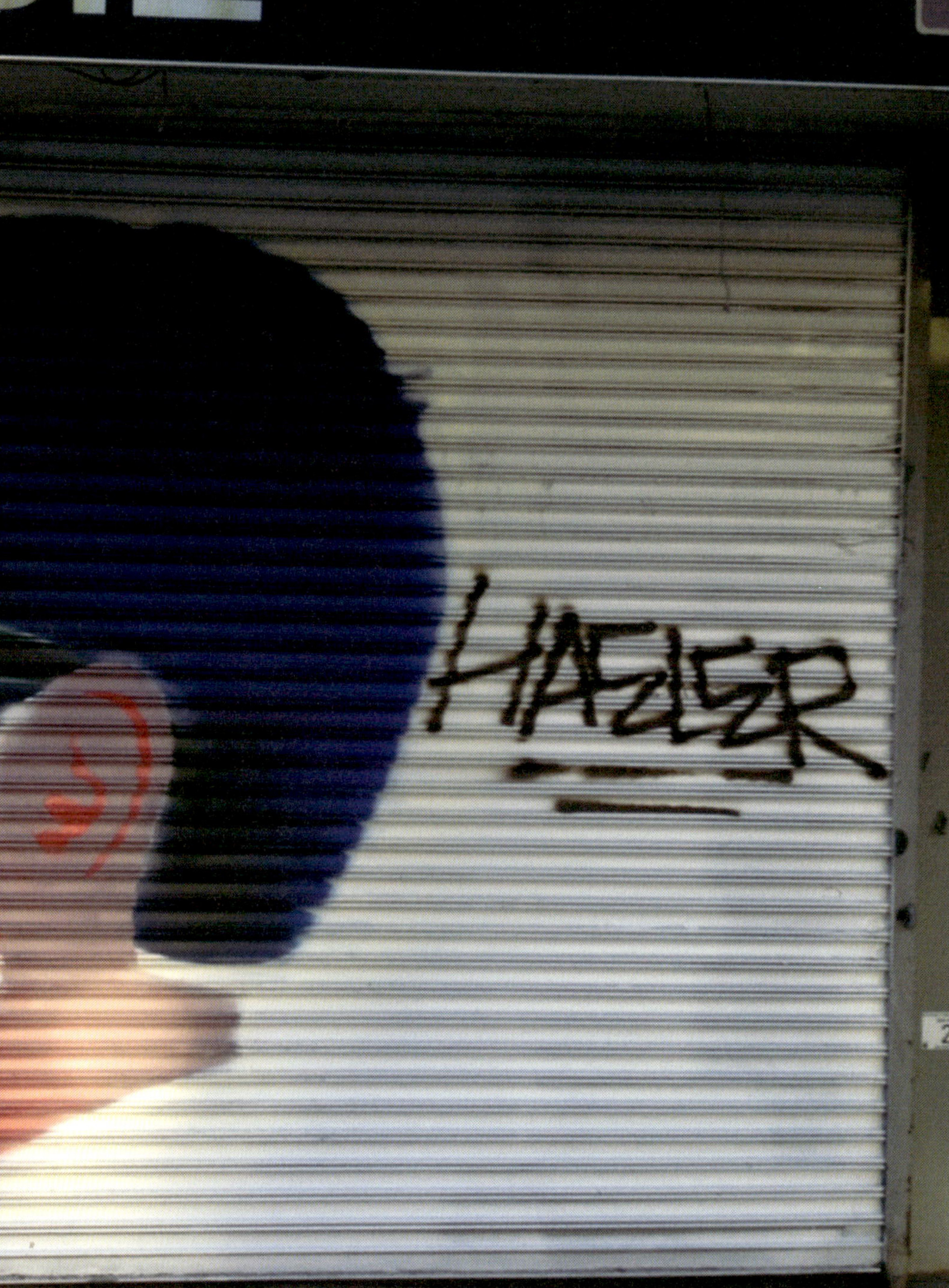
312

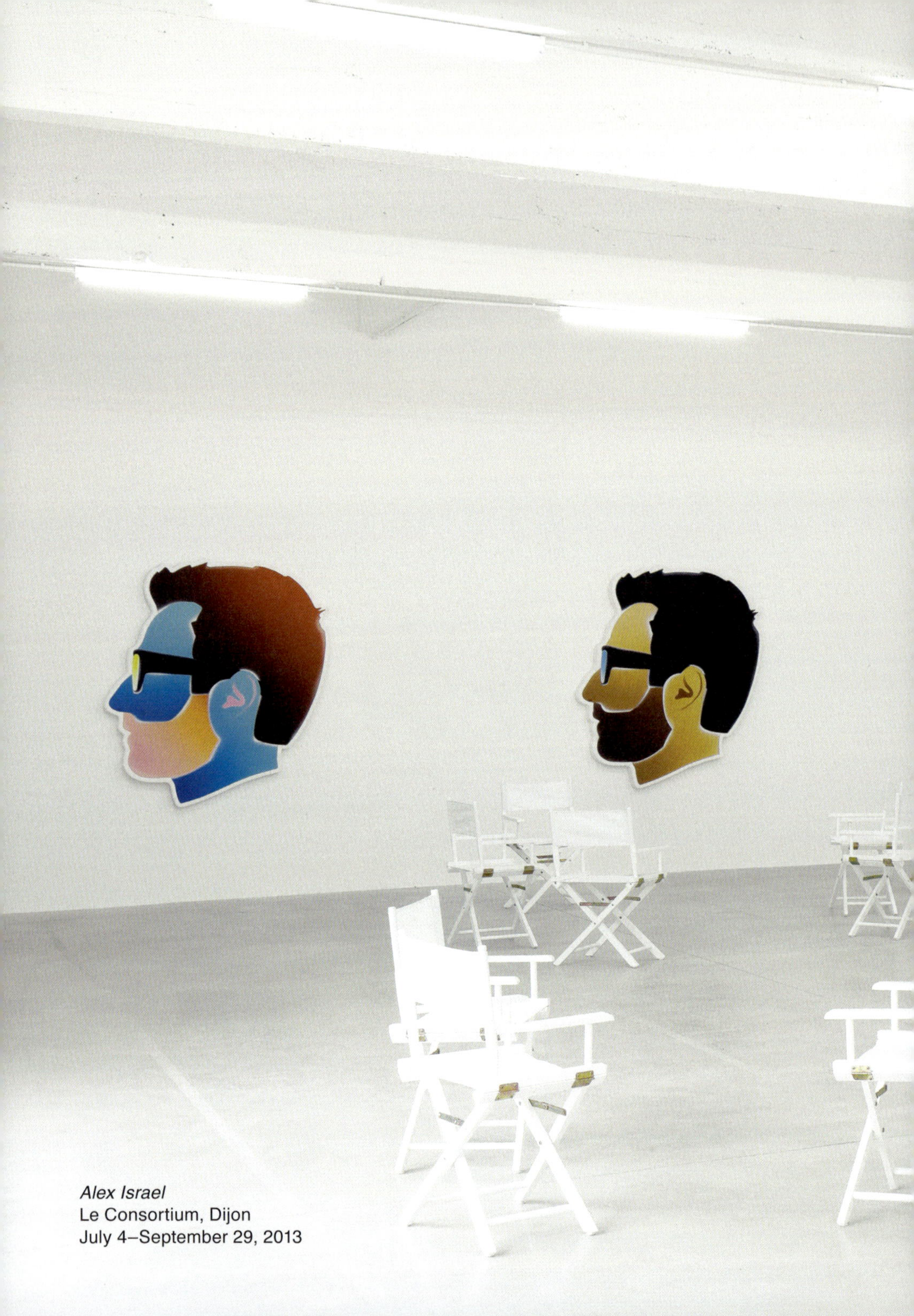

Alex Israel
Le Consortium, Dijon
July 4–September 29, 2013

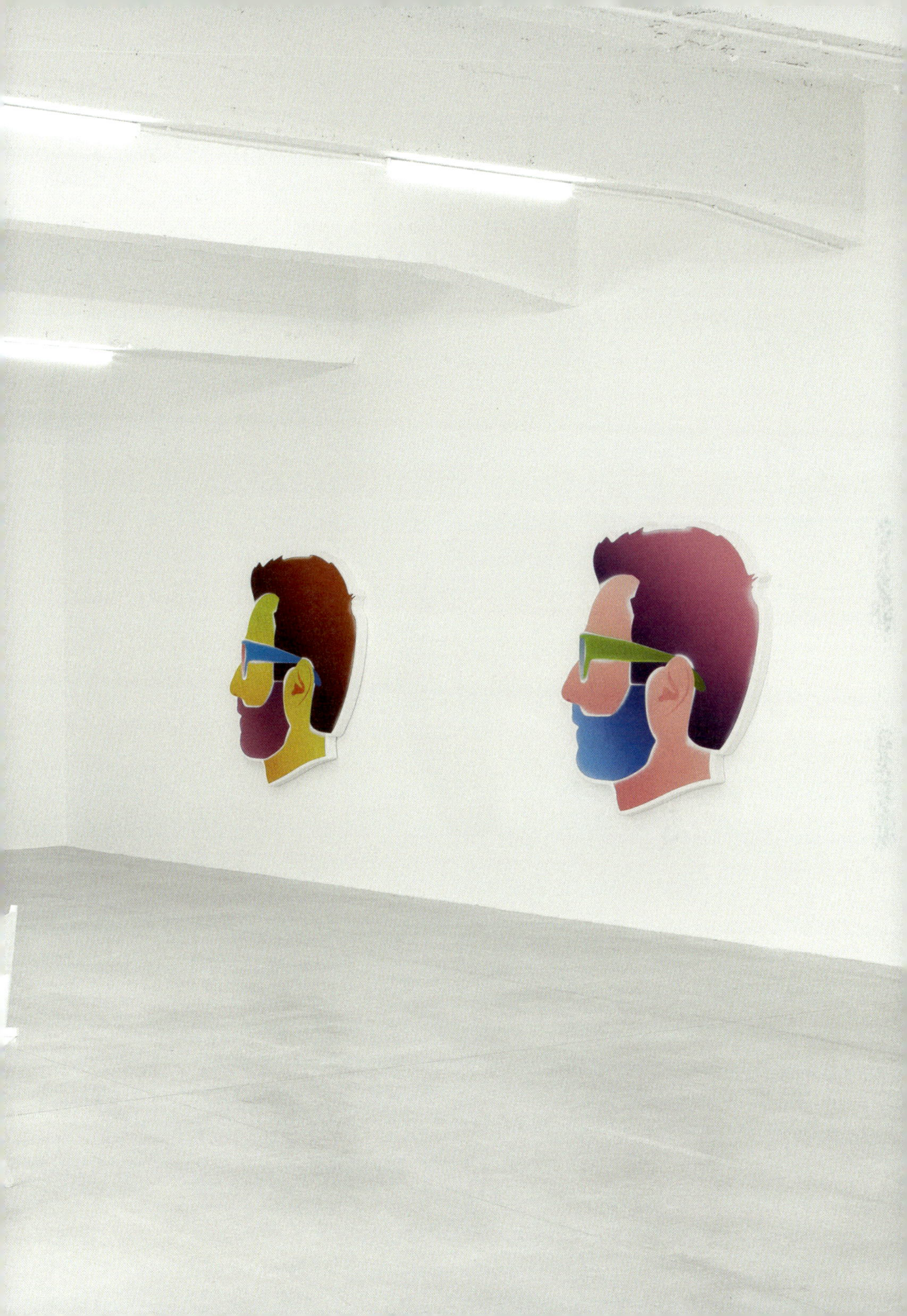

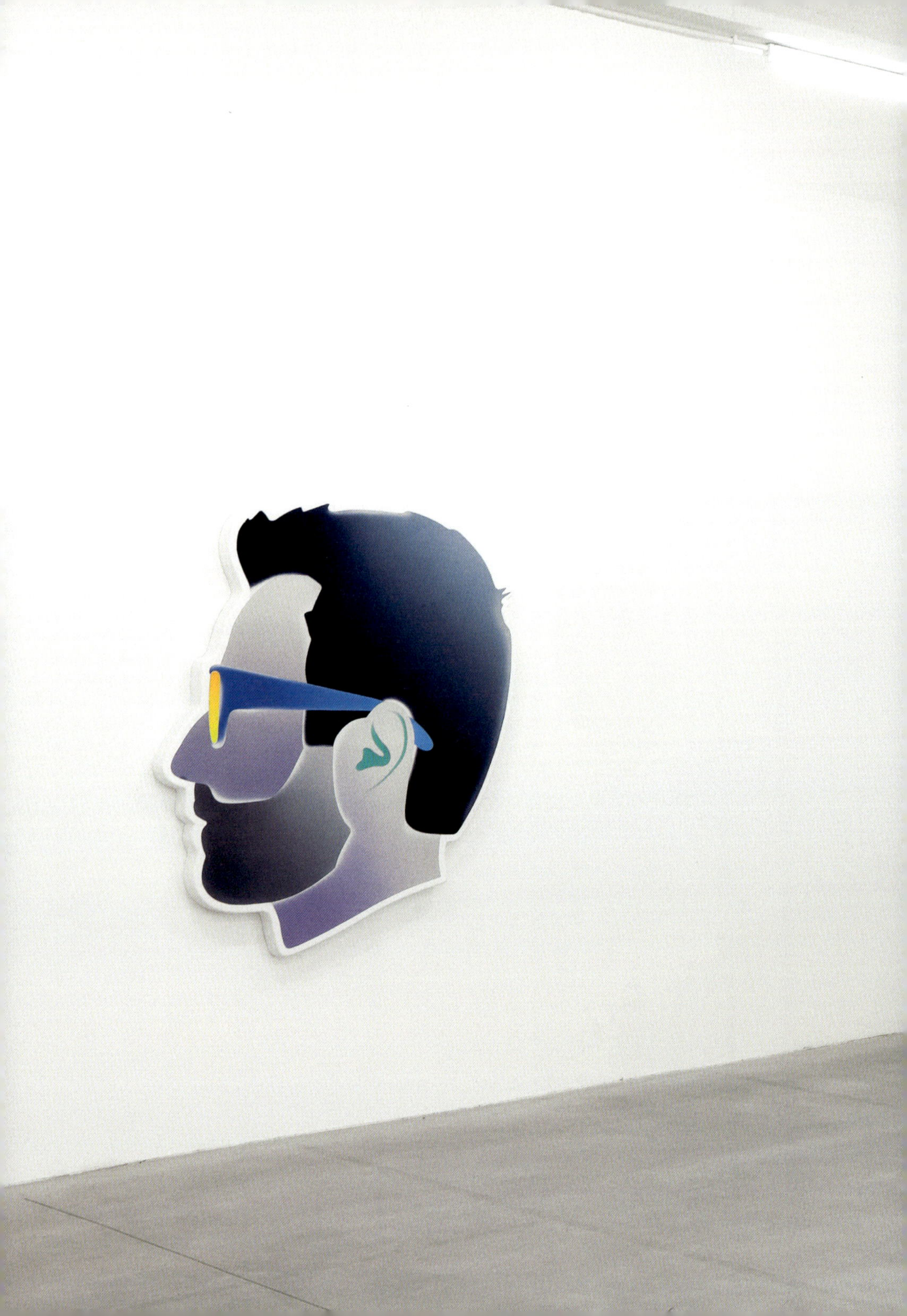

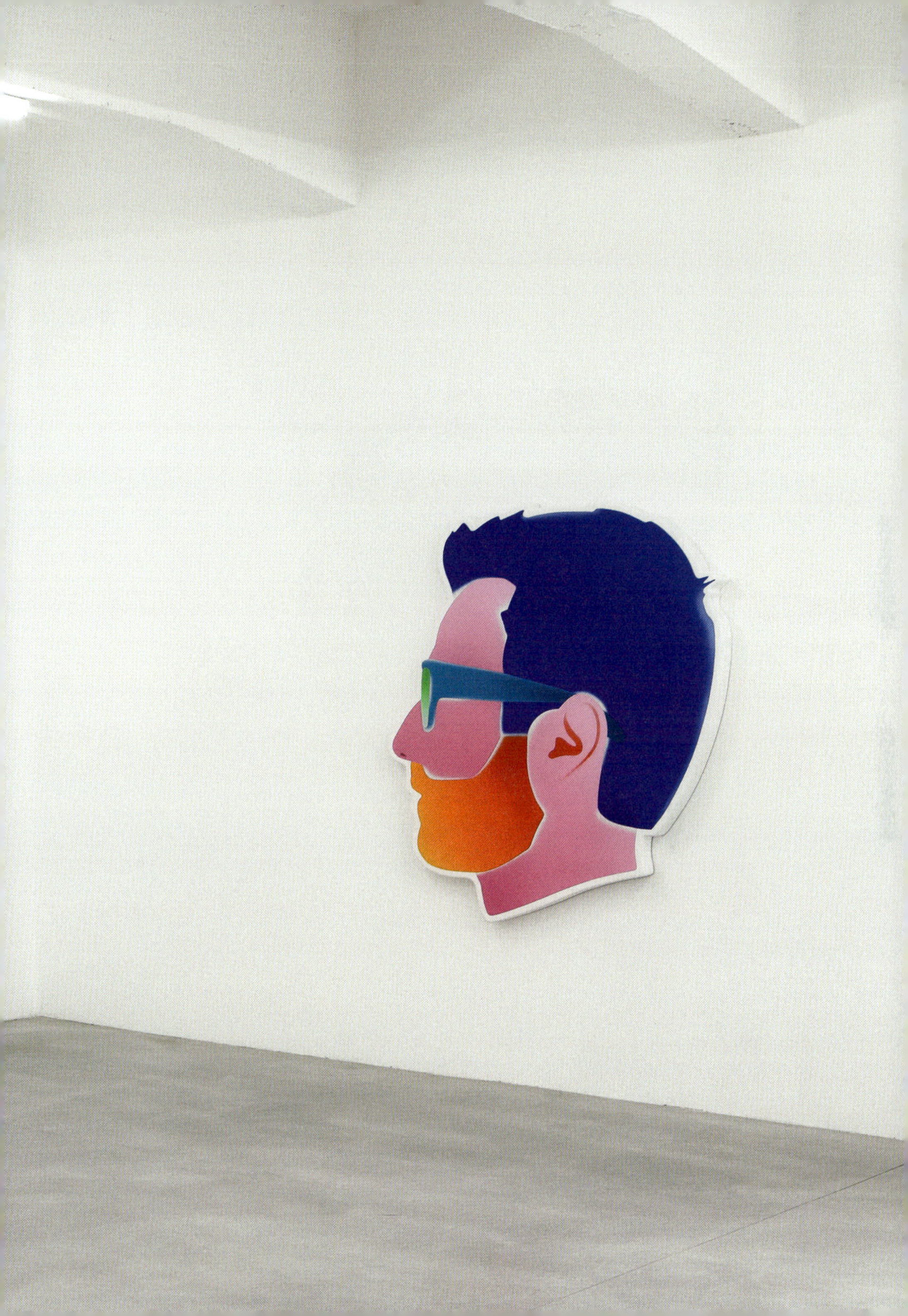

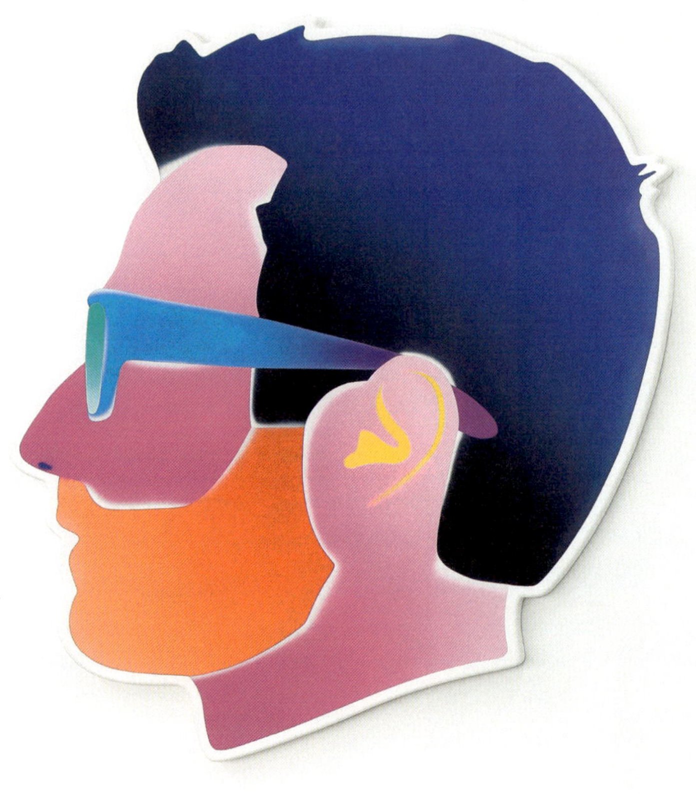

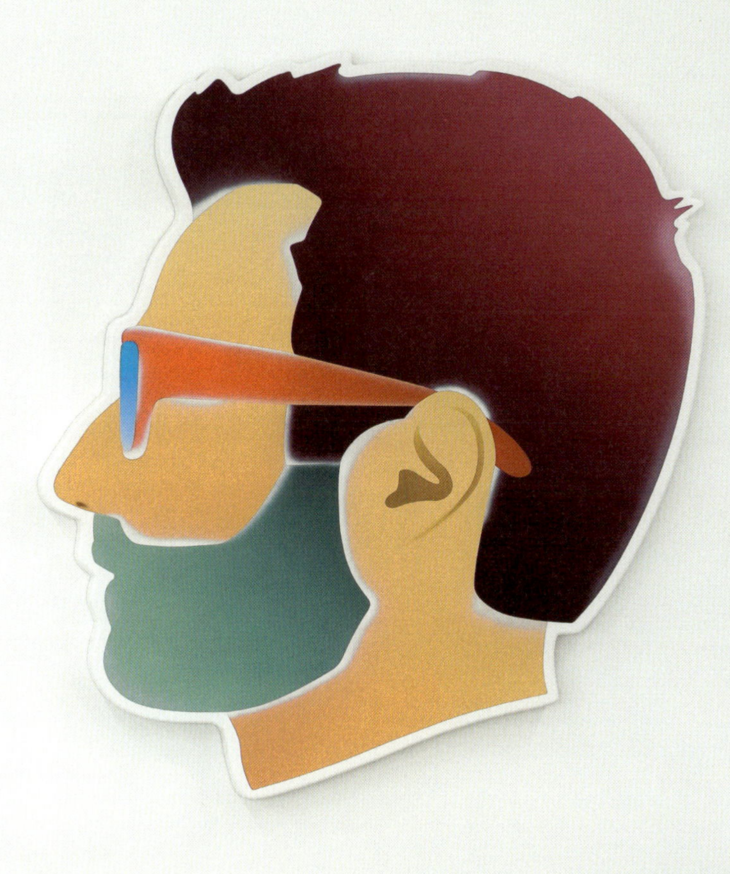

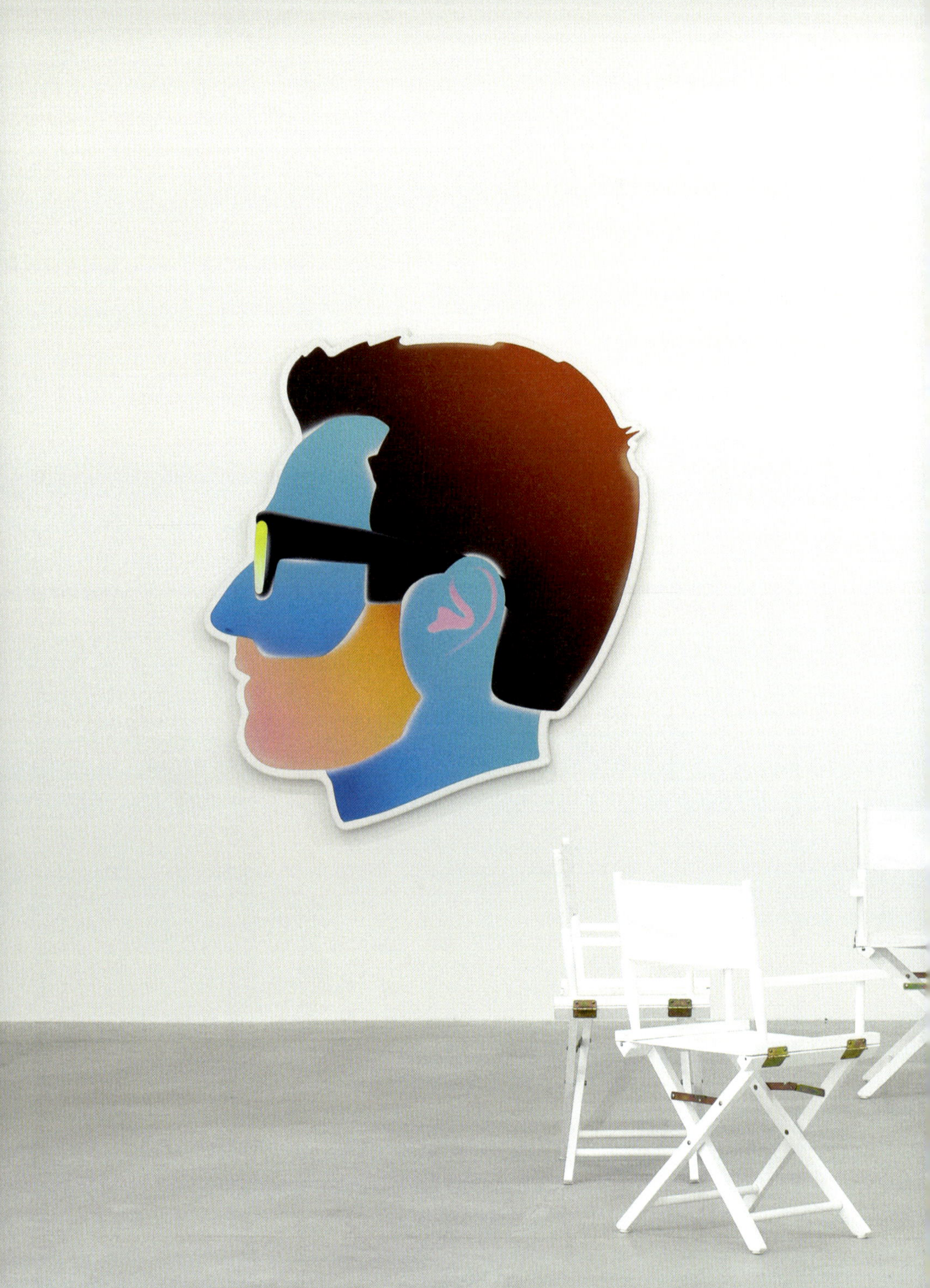

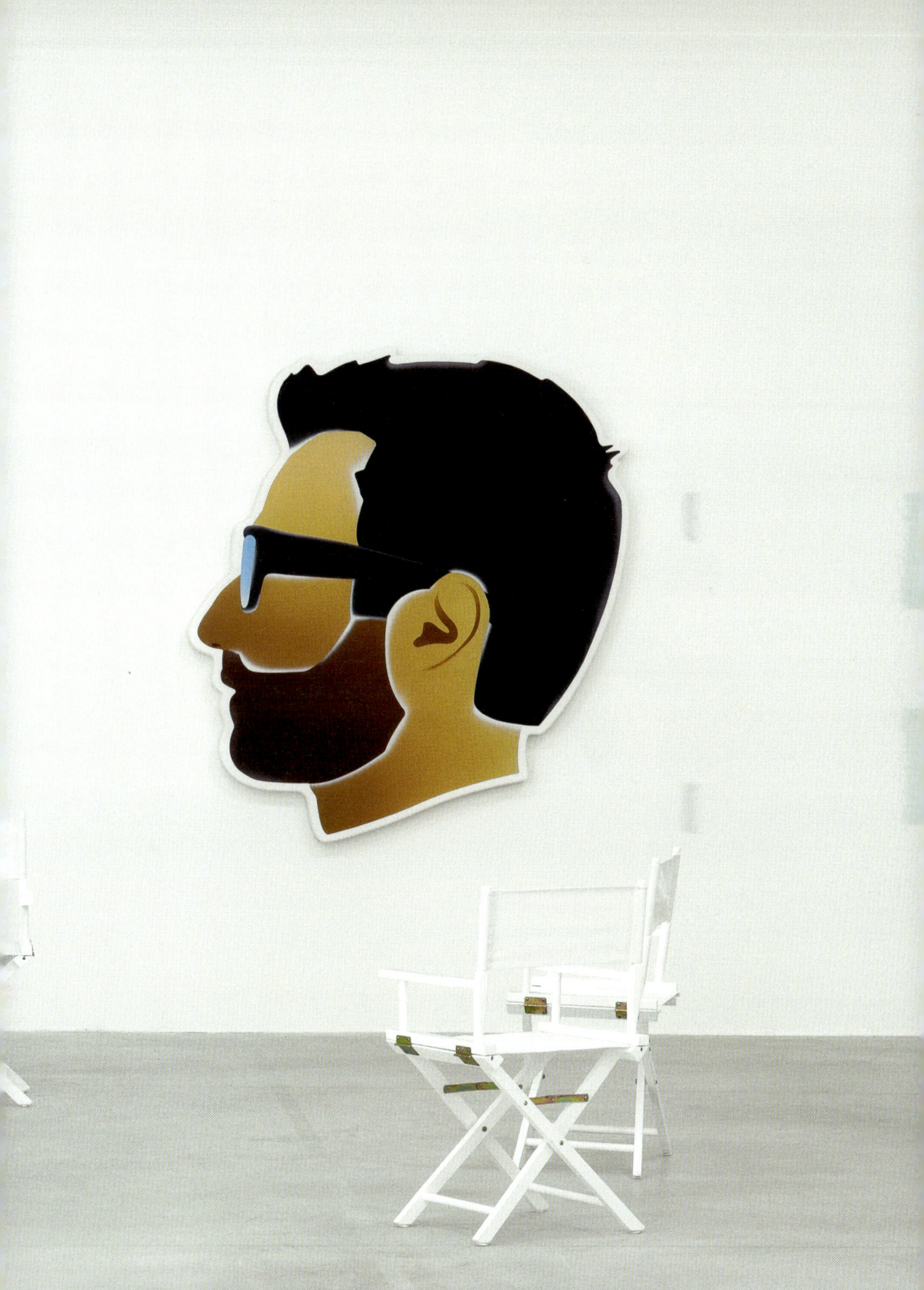

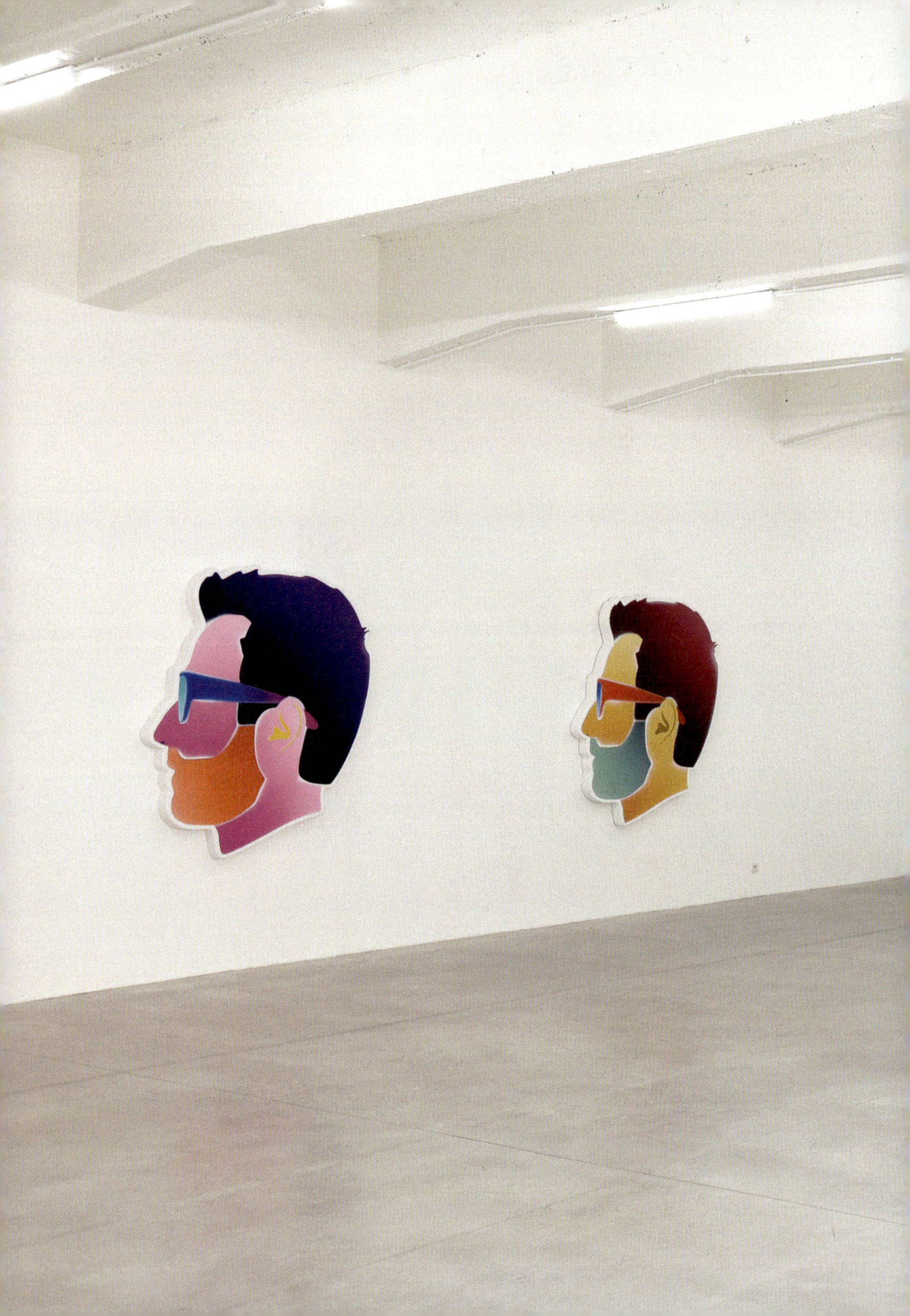

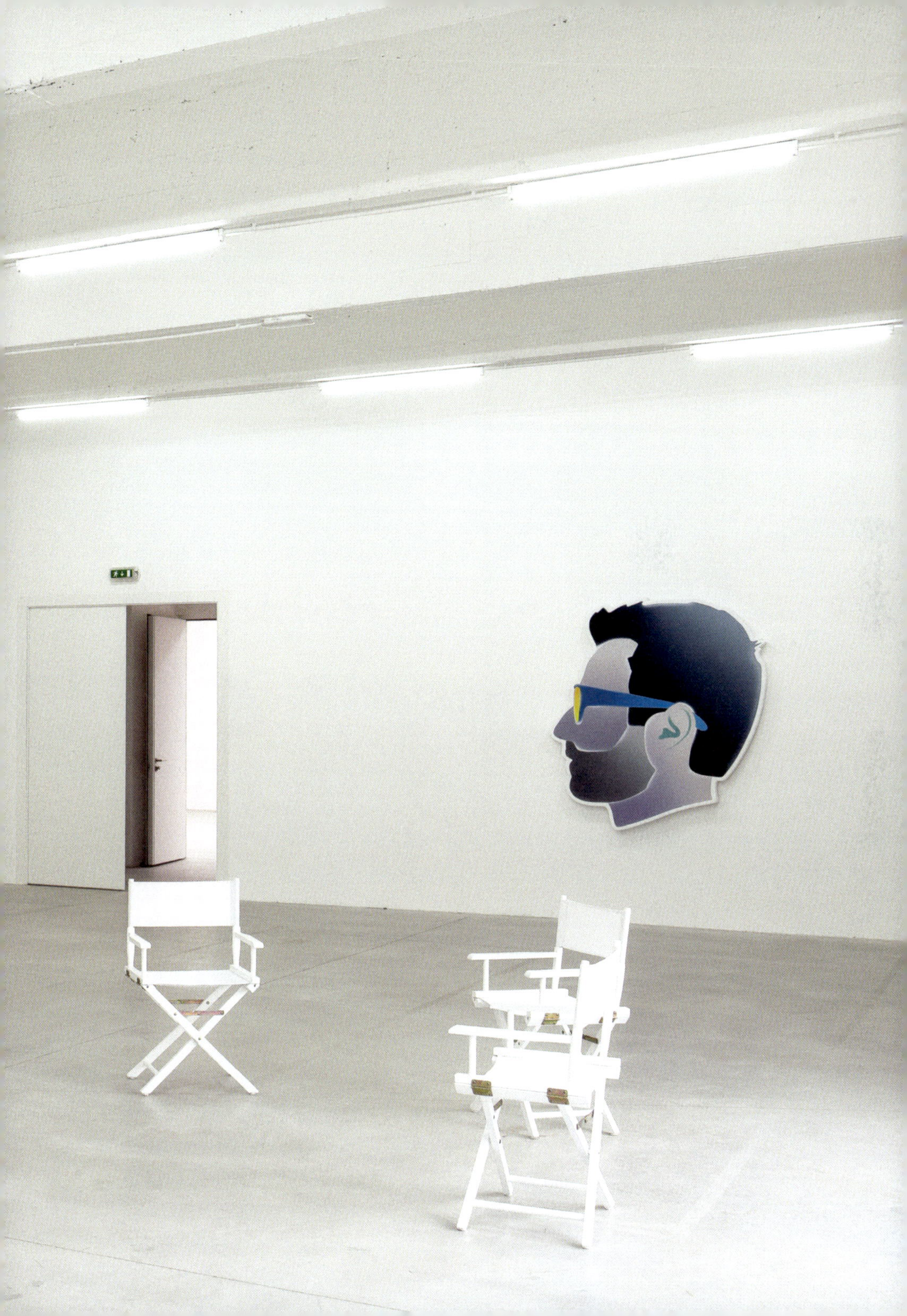

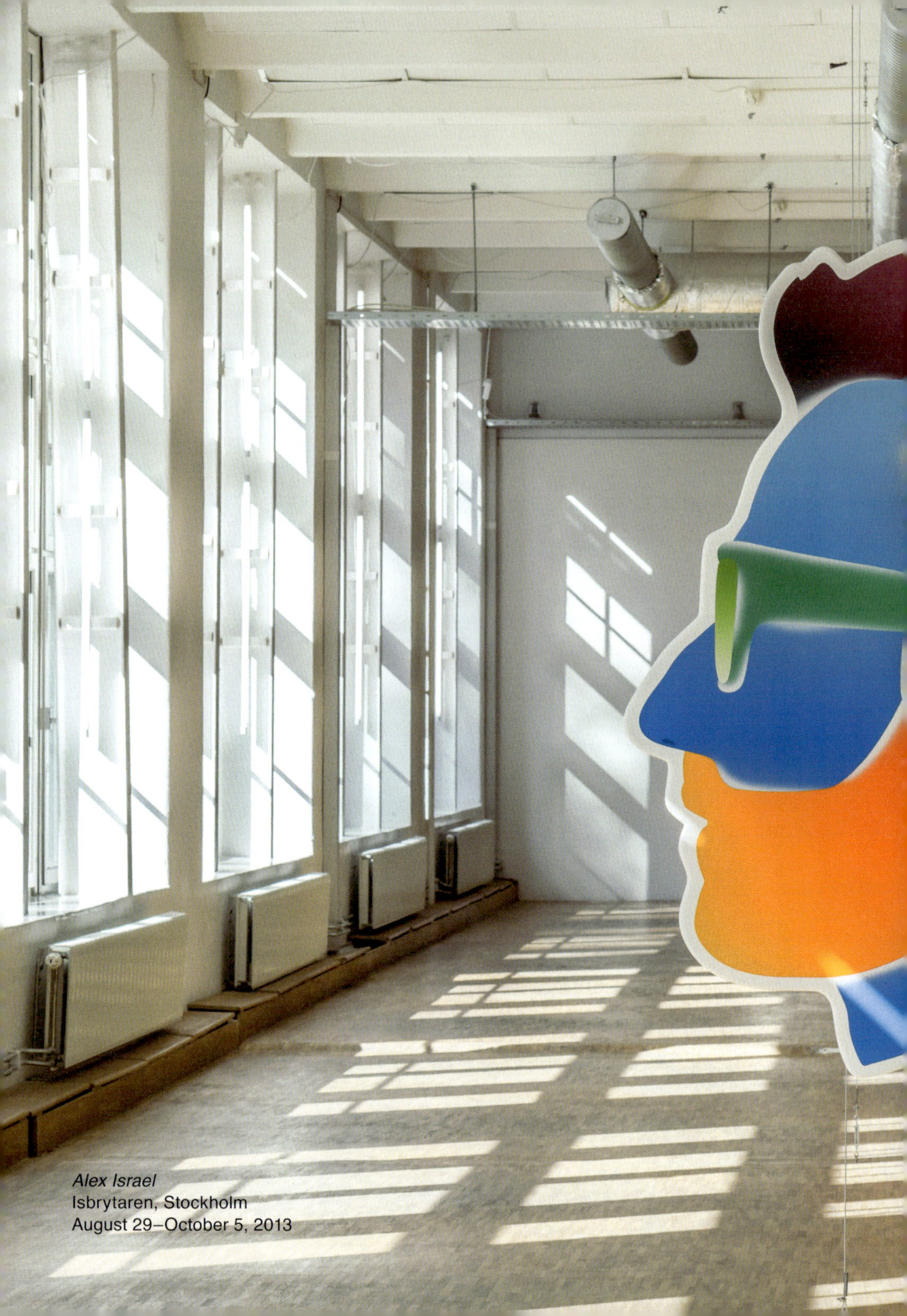

Alex Israel
Isbrytaren, Stockholm
August 29–October 5, 2013

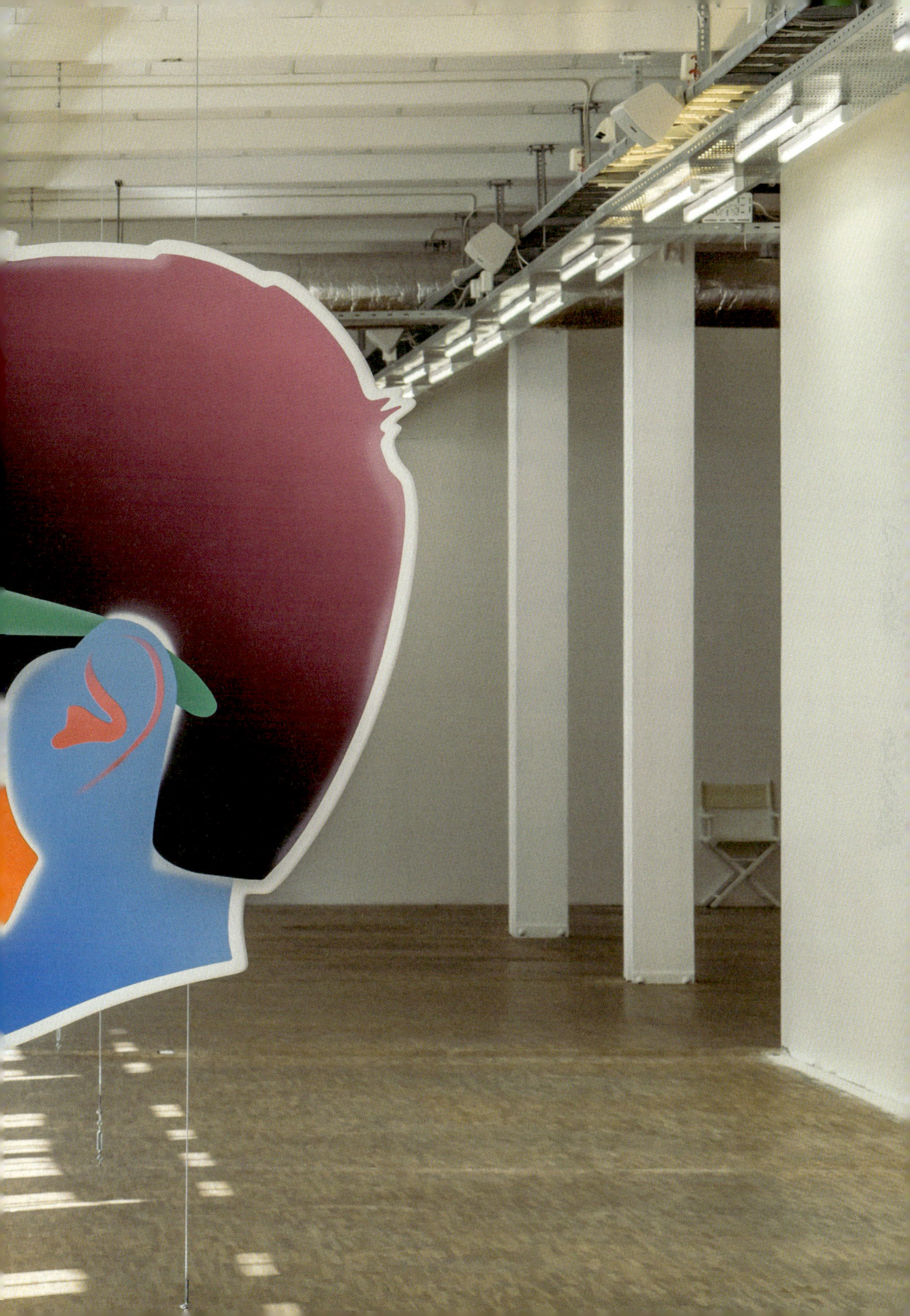

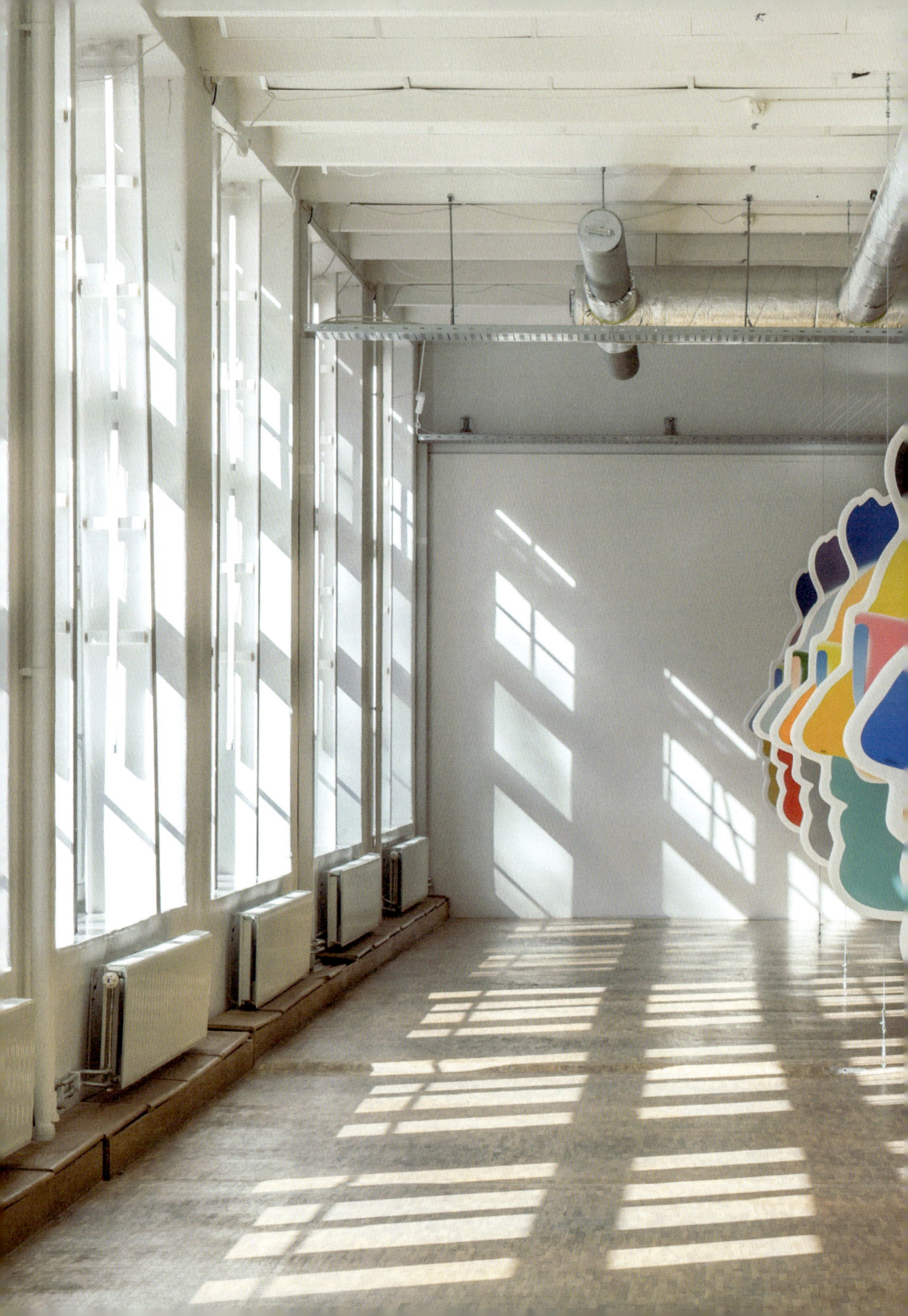

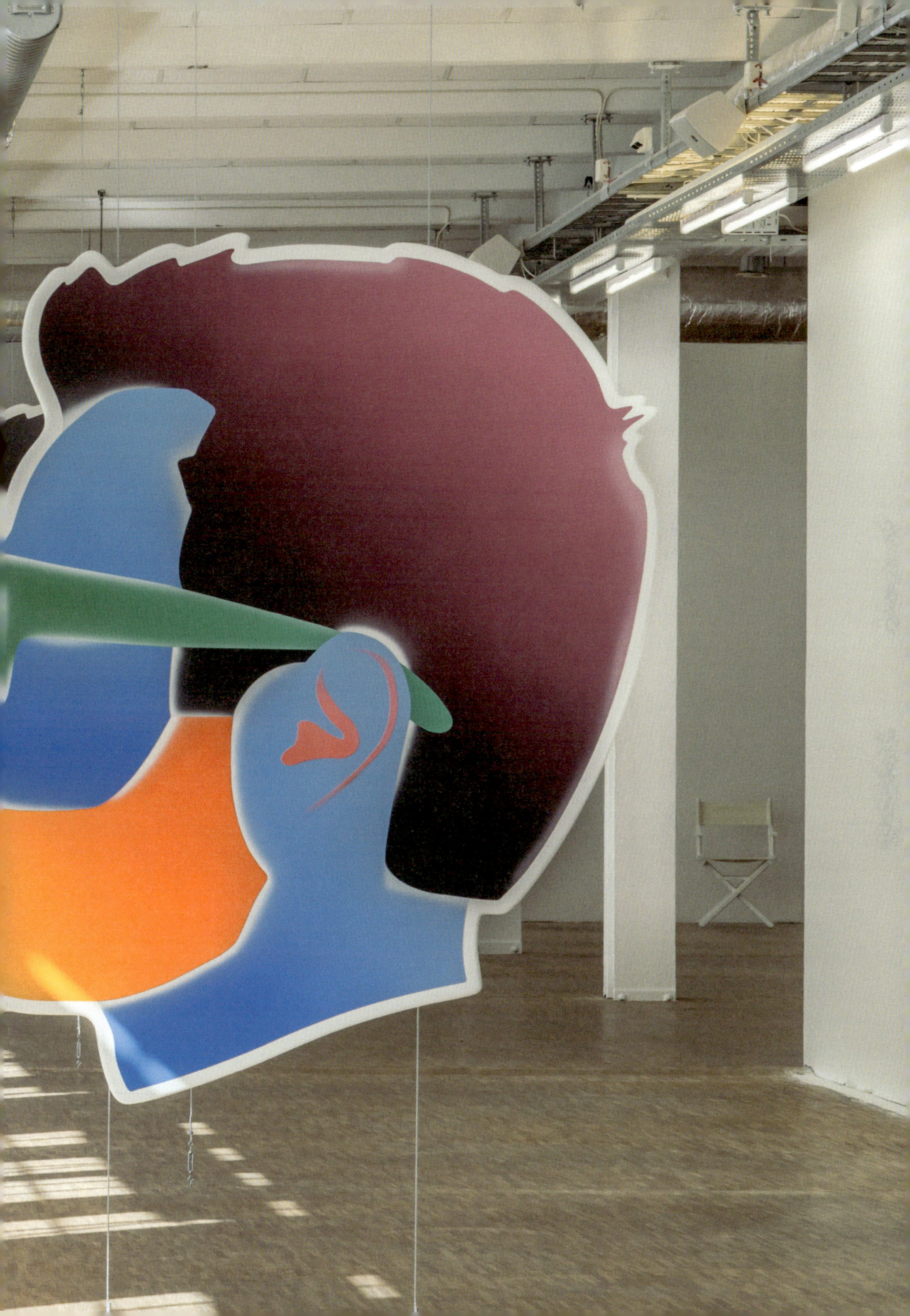

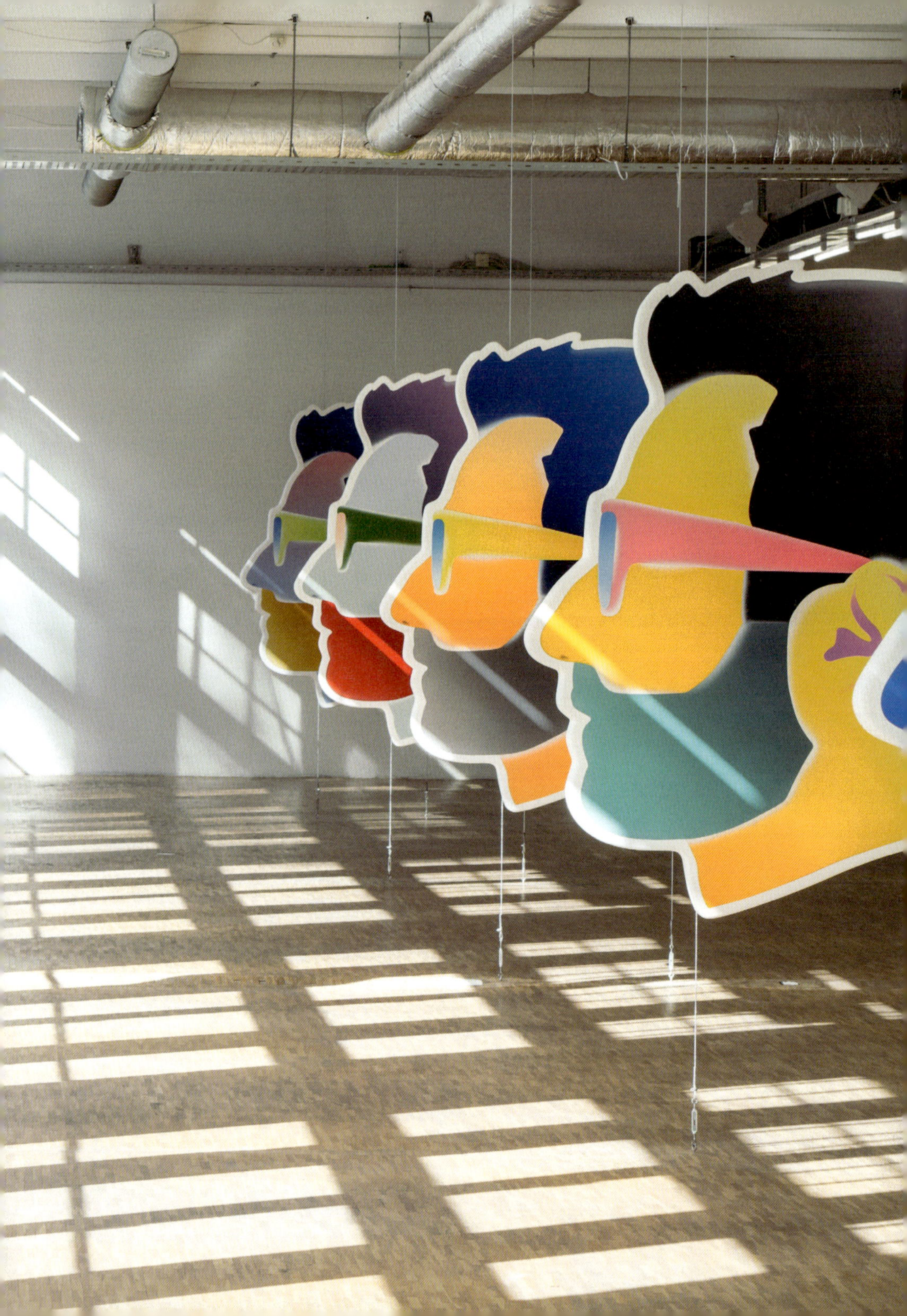

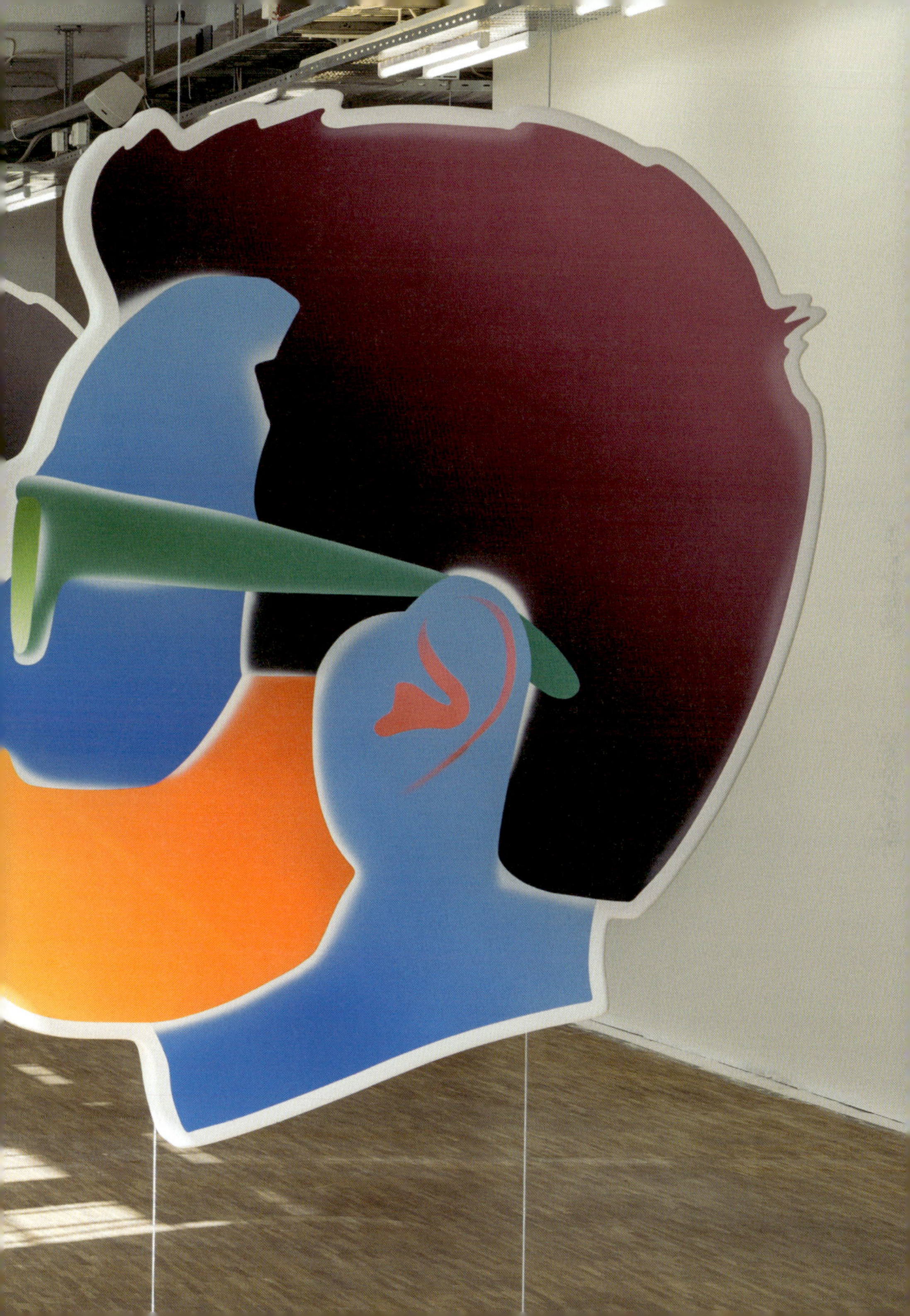

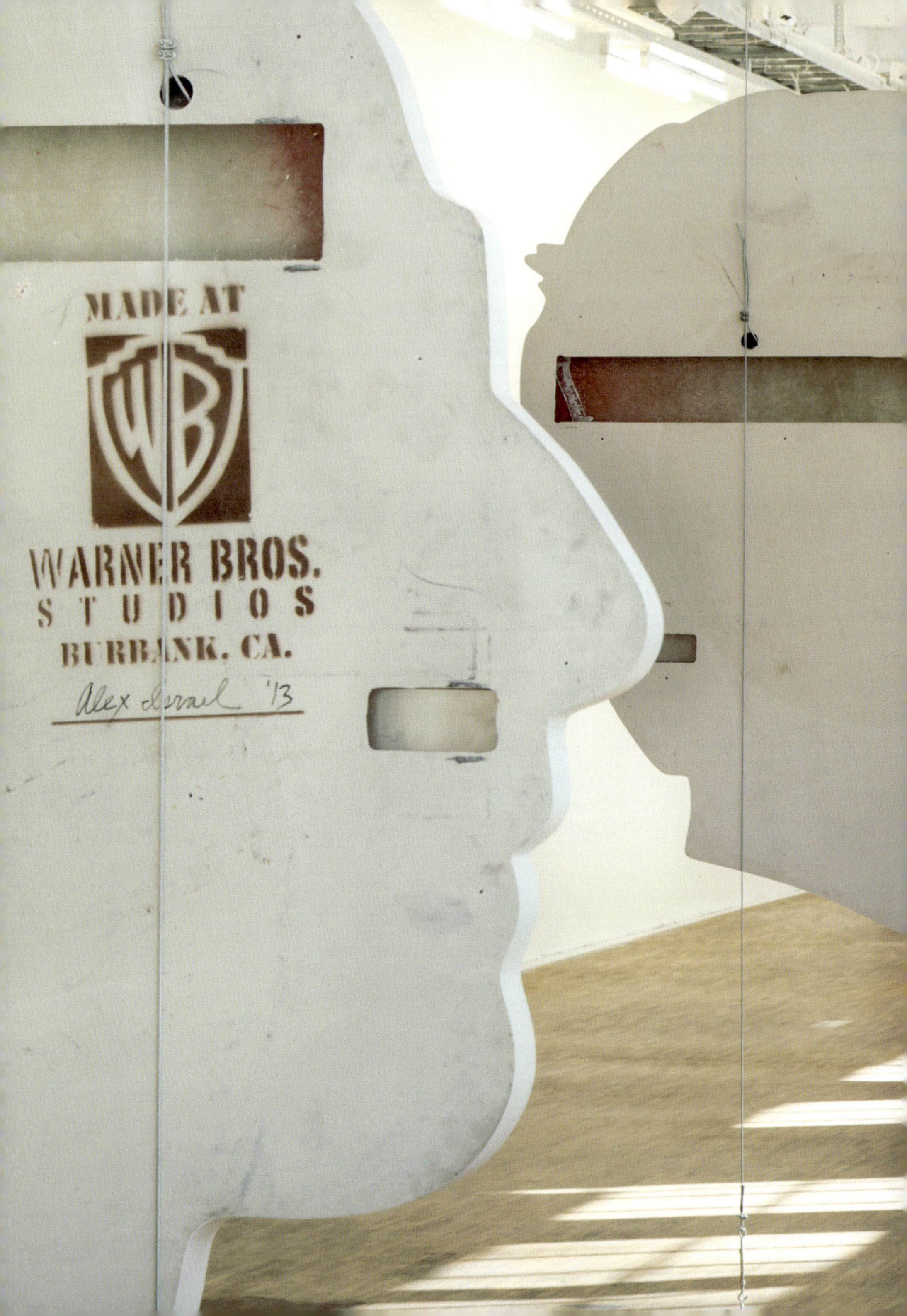
MADE AT
WB
WARNER BROS.
STUDIOS
BURBANK, CA.
Alex Israel '13

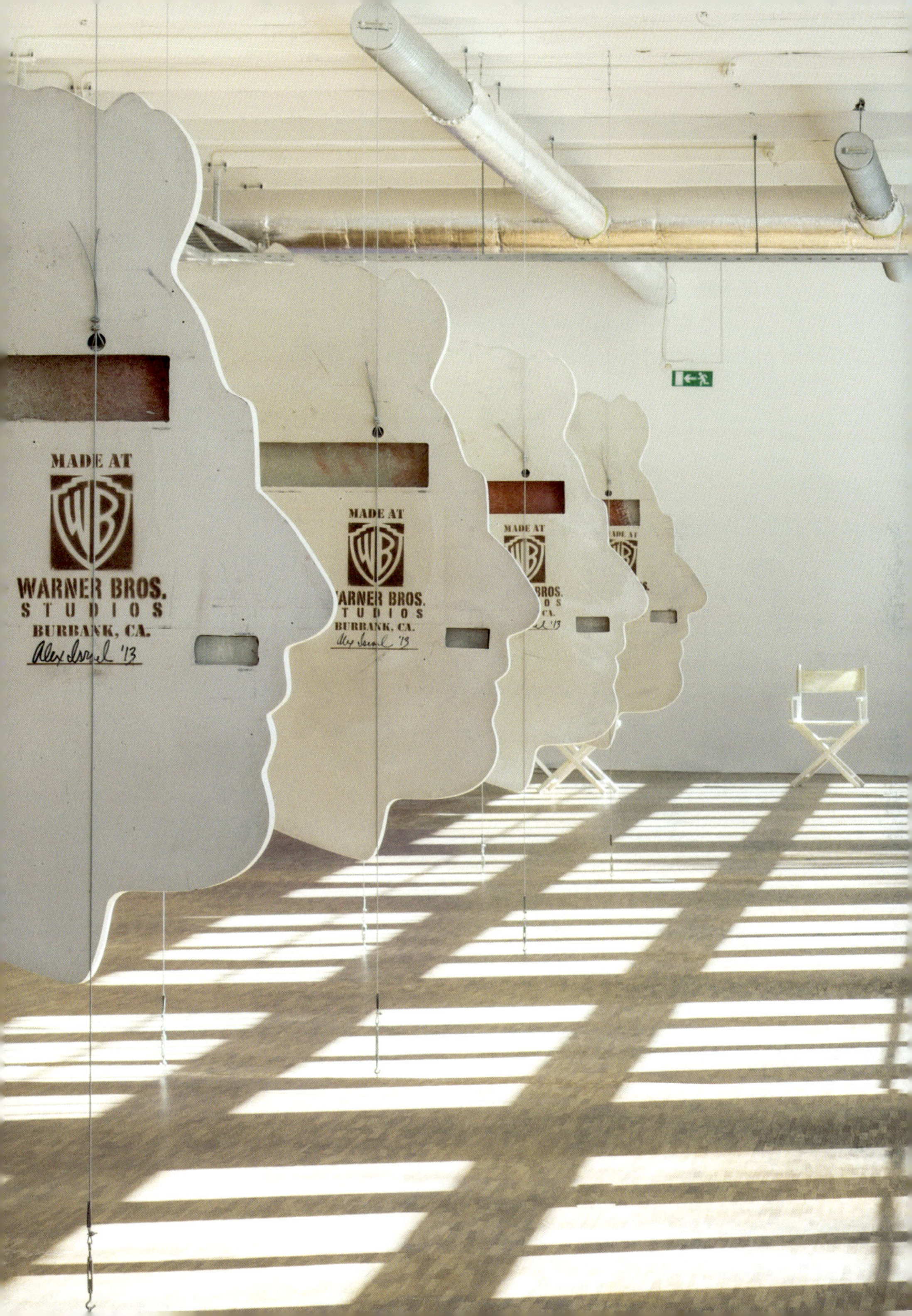

MADE AT
WB
WARNER BROS.
STUDIOS
BURBANK, CA.
Alex Israel '13
MADE AT
WB
WARNER BROS.
STUDIOS
BURBANK, CA.
Alex Israel '13

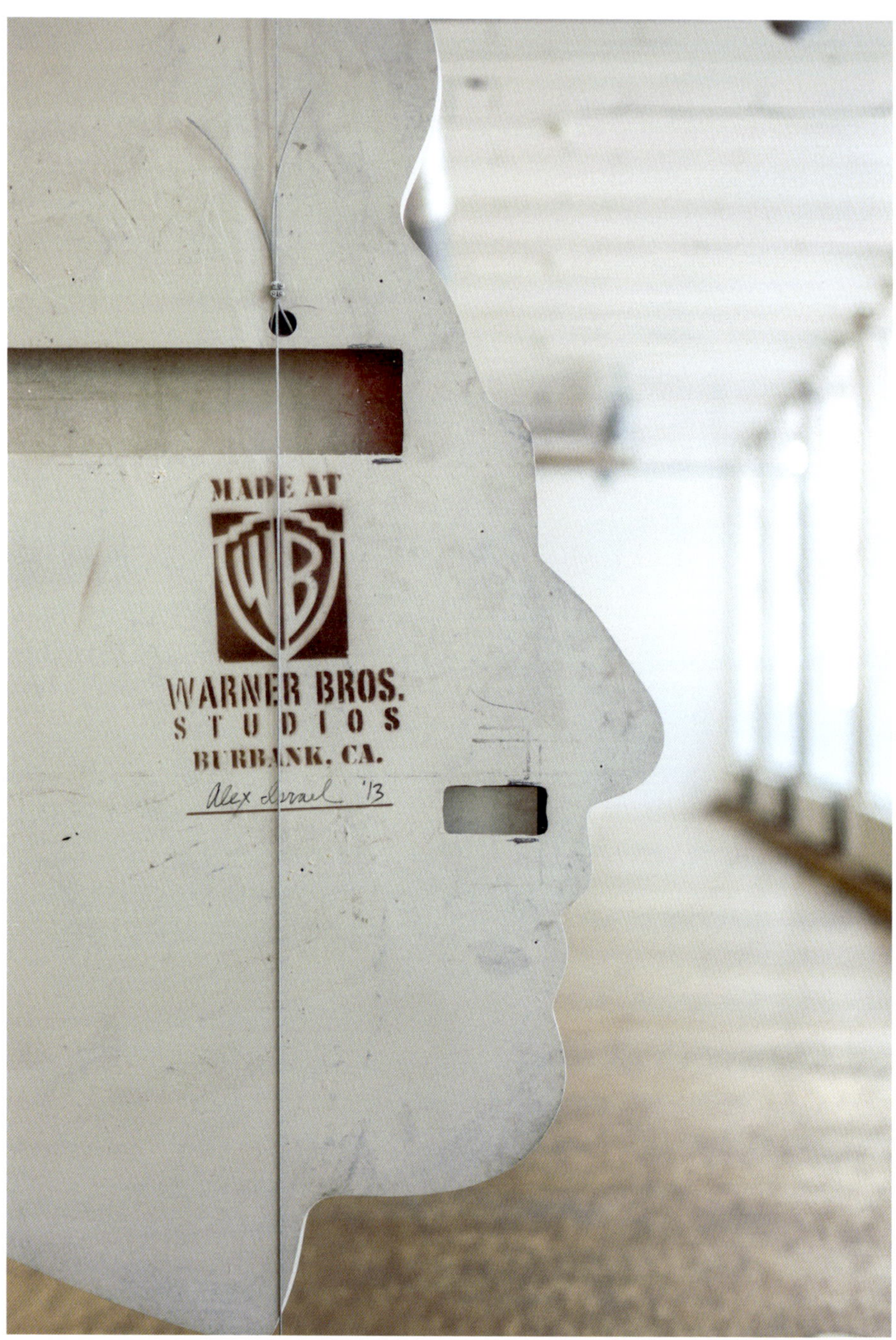
MADE AT
WARNER BROS.
STUDIOS
BURBANK, CA.
Alex Israel '13

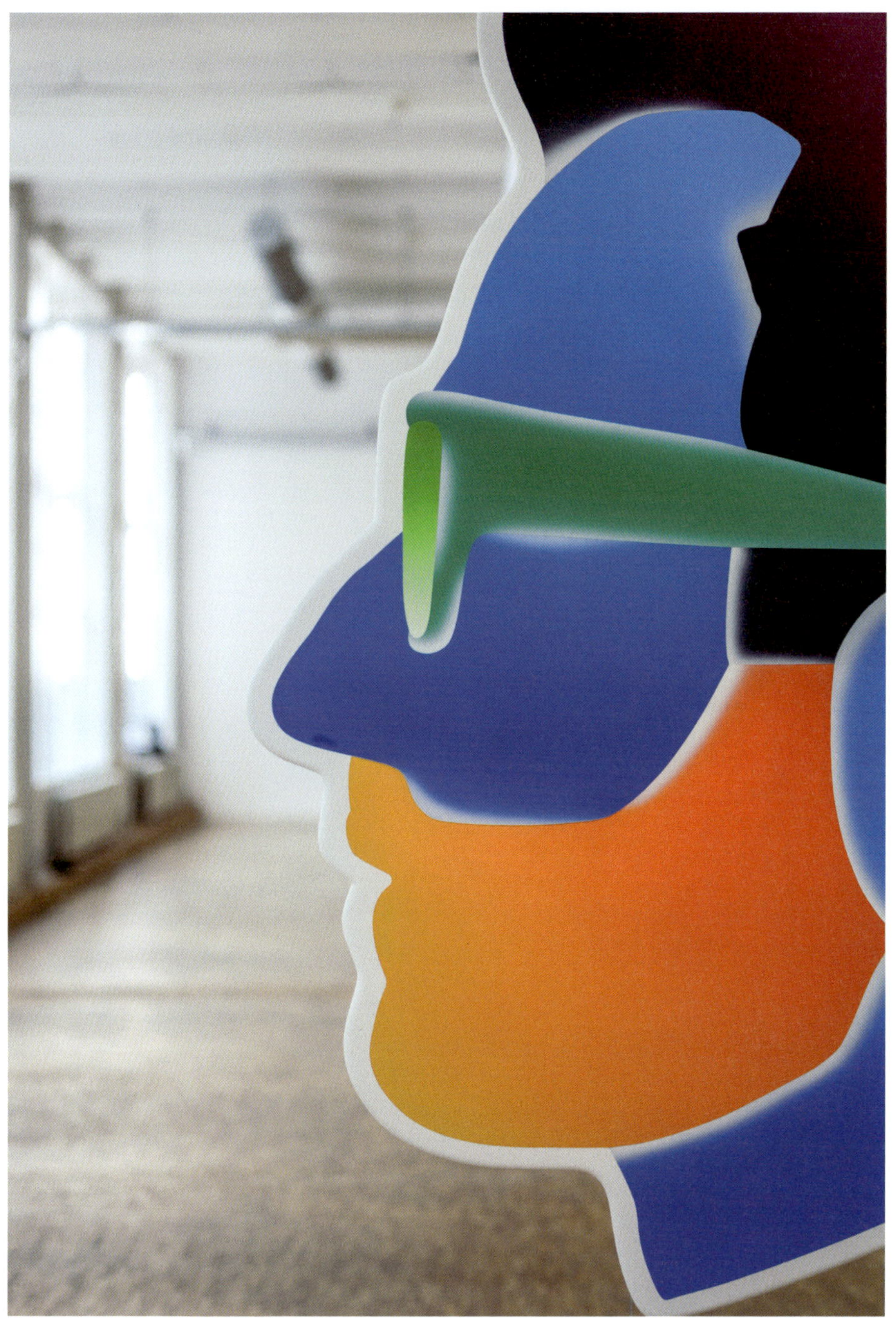

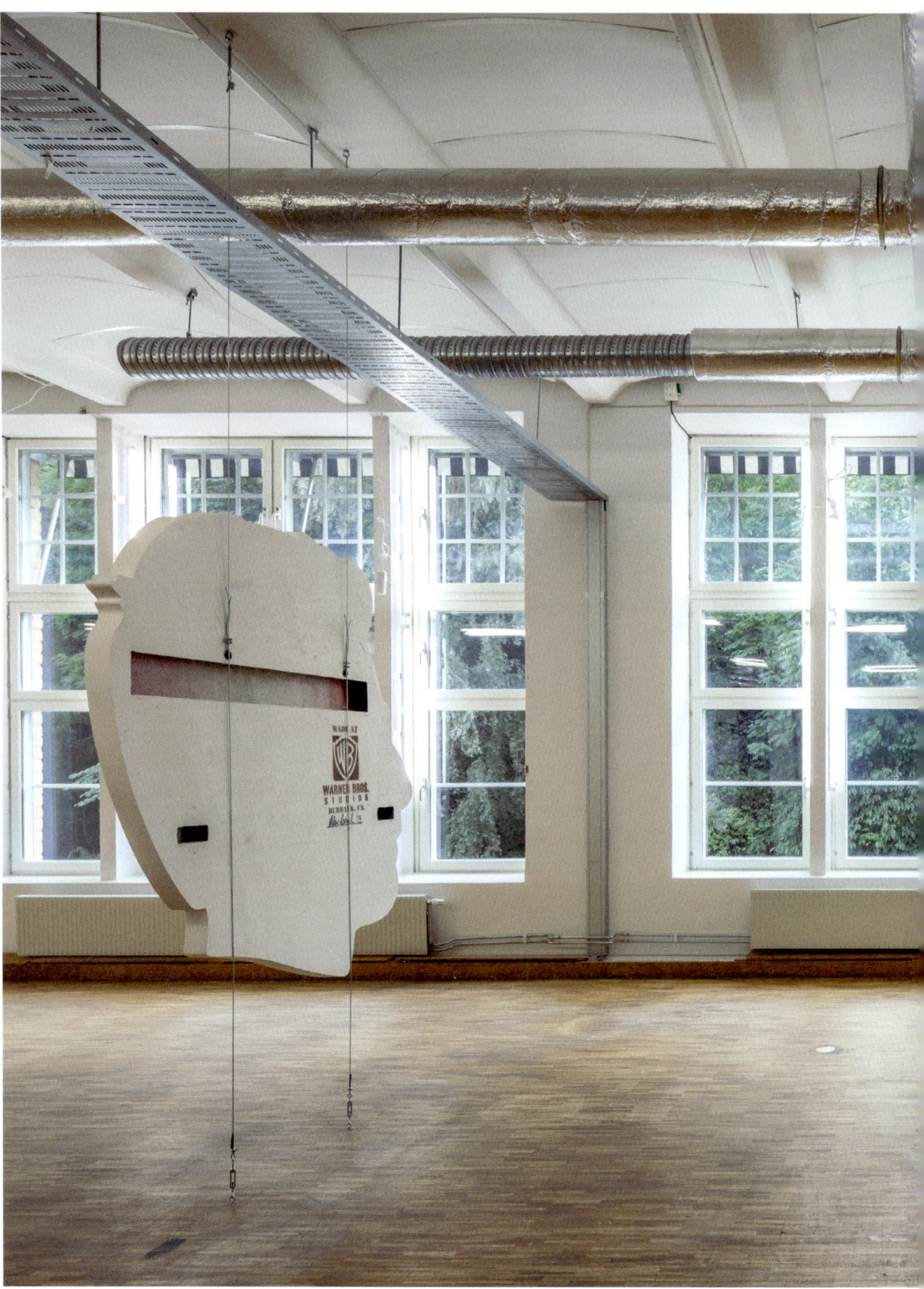
MADE AT
WARNER BROS.
STUDIOS
BURBANK, CA.

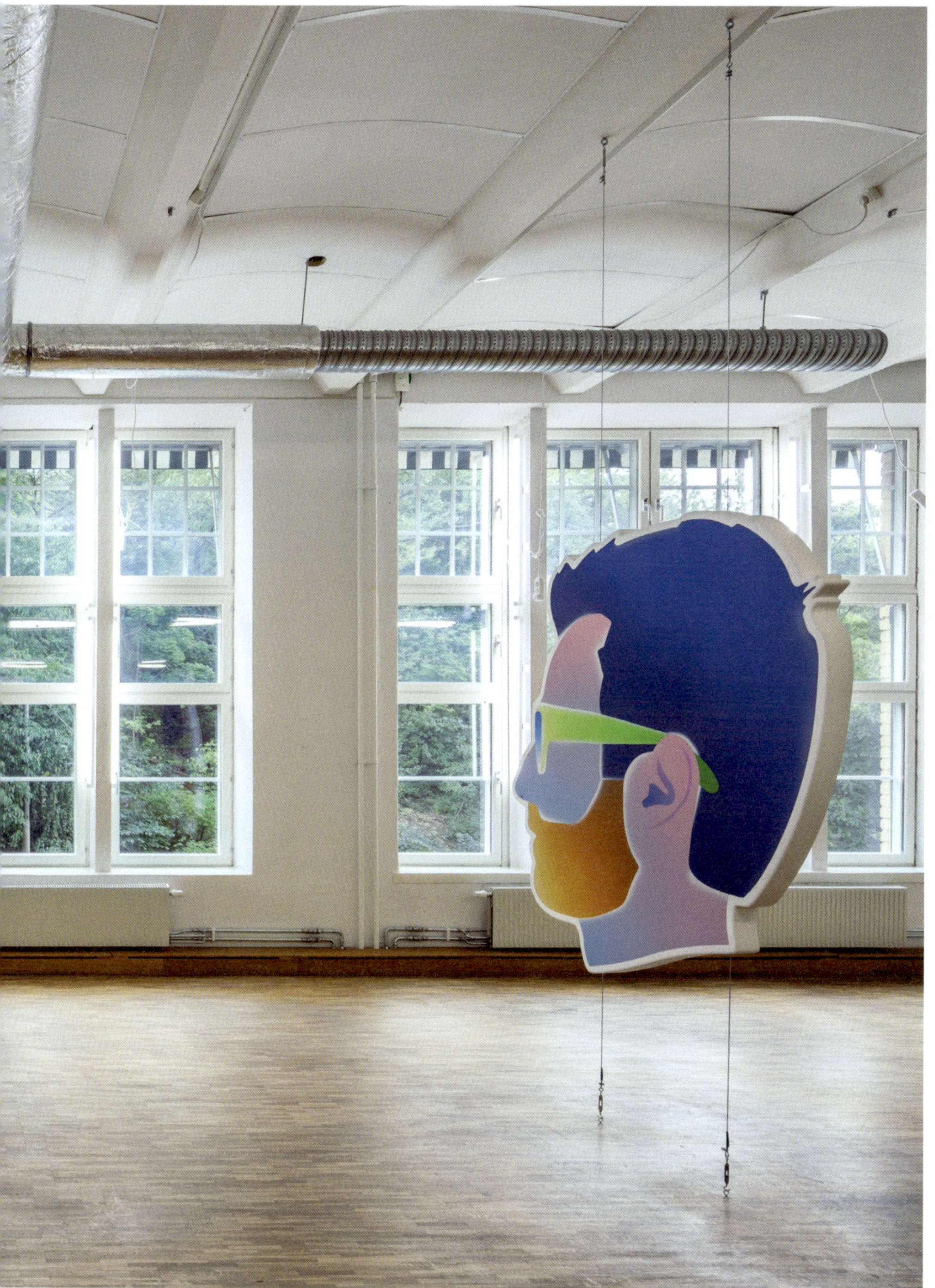

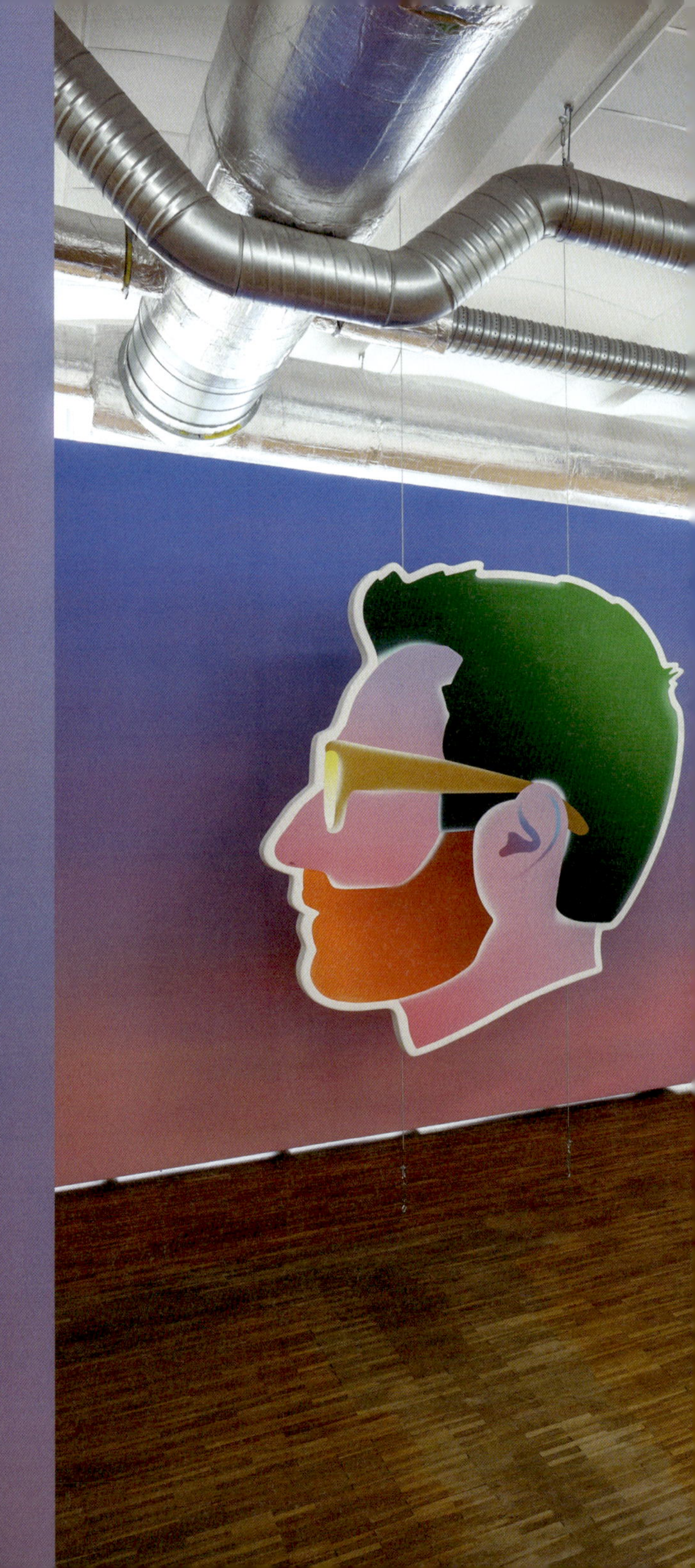

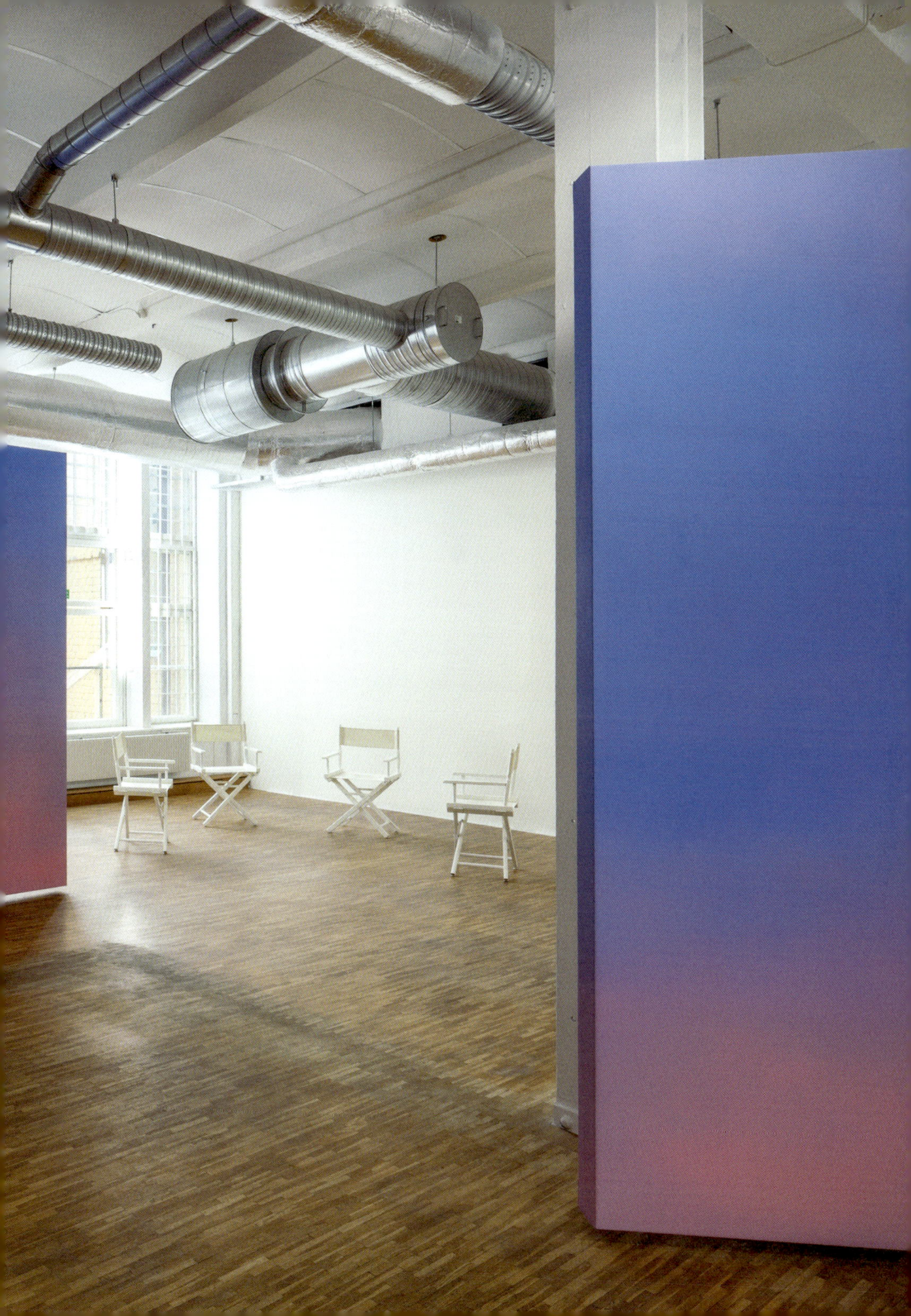

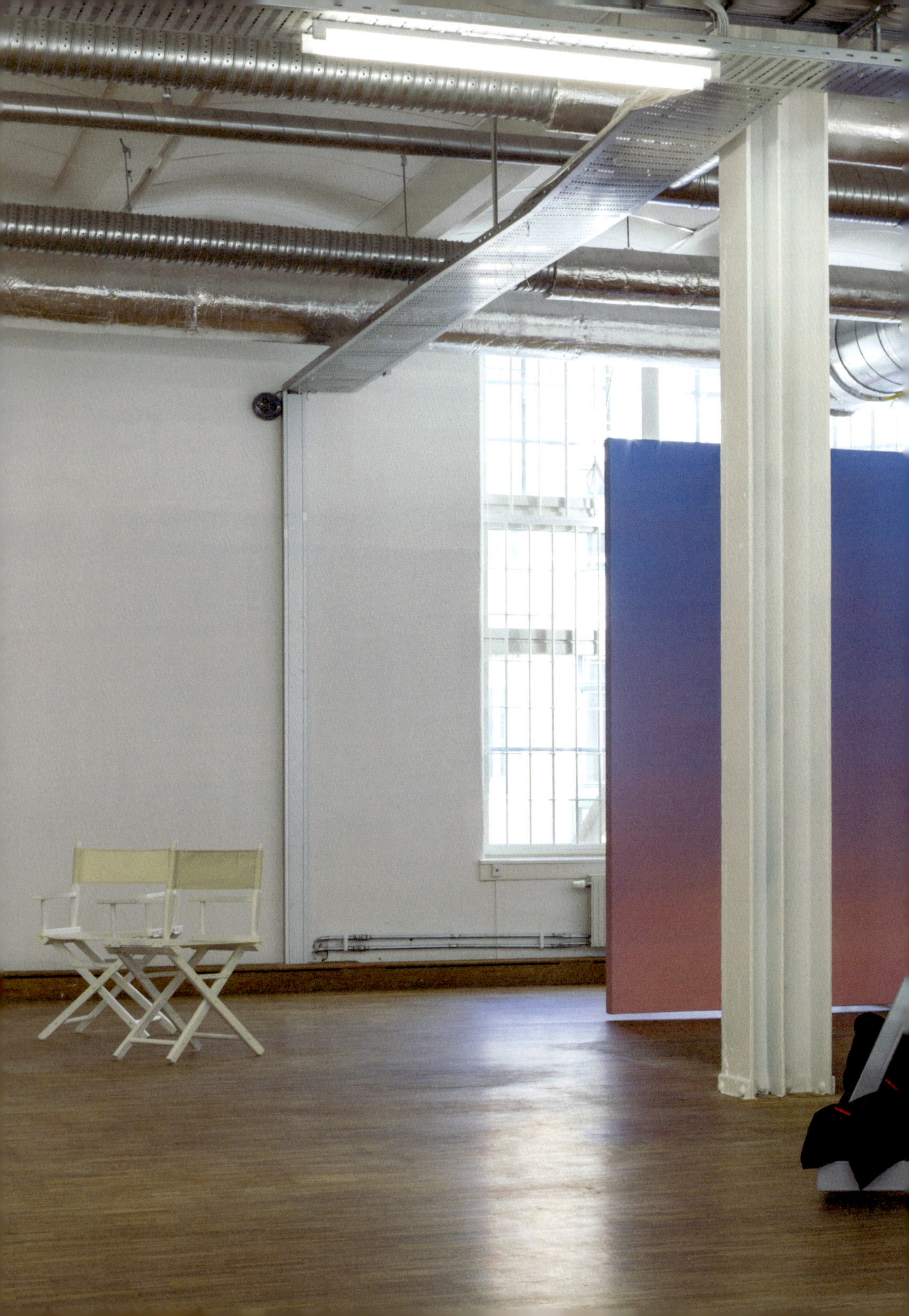

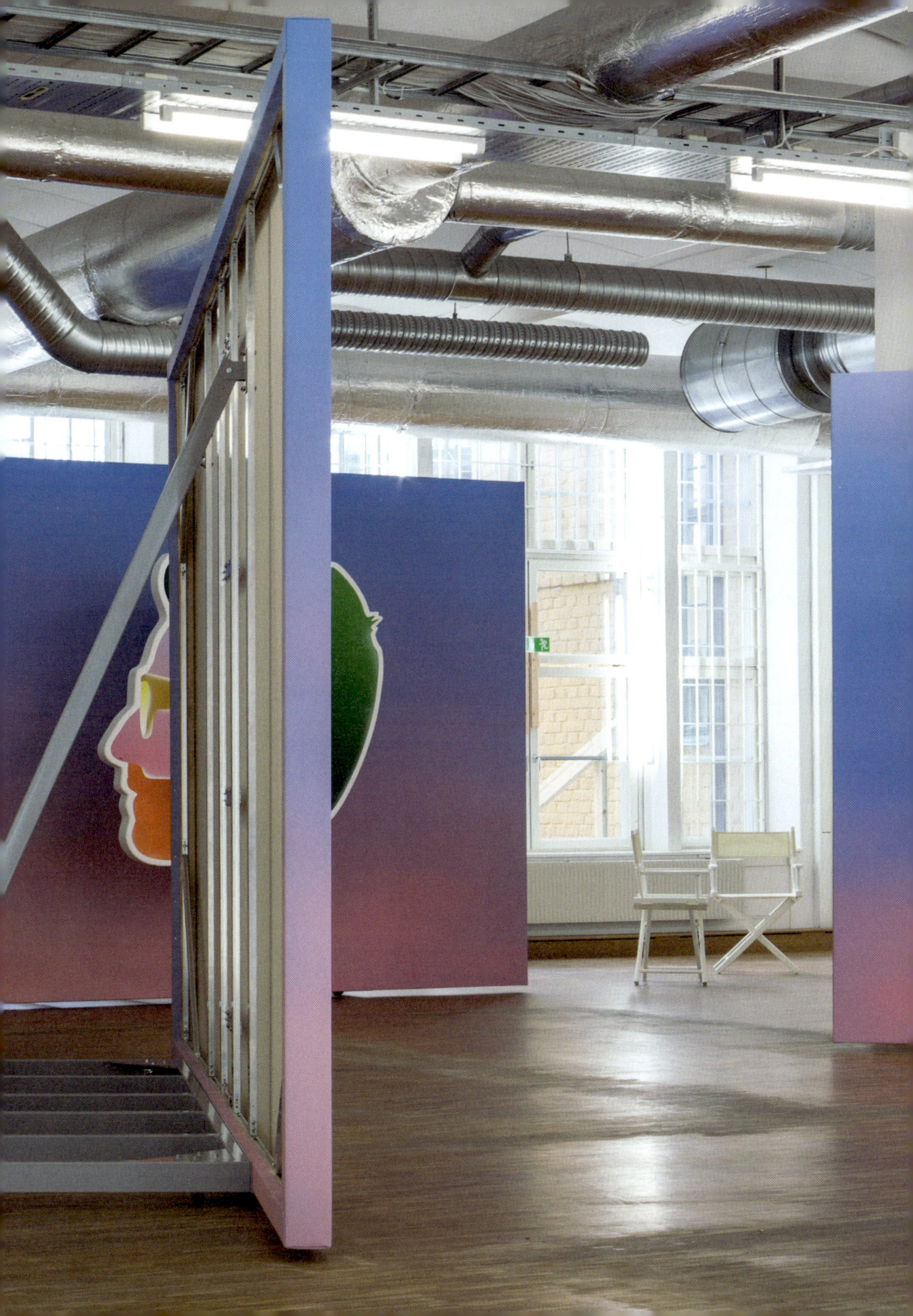

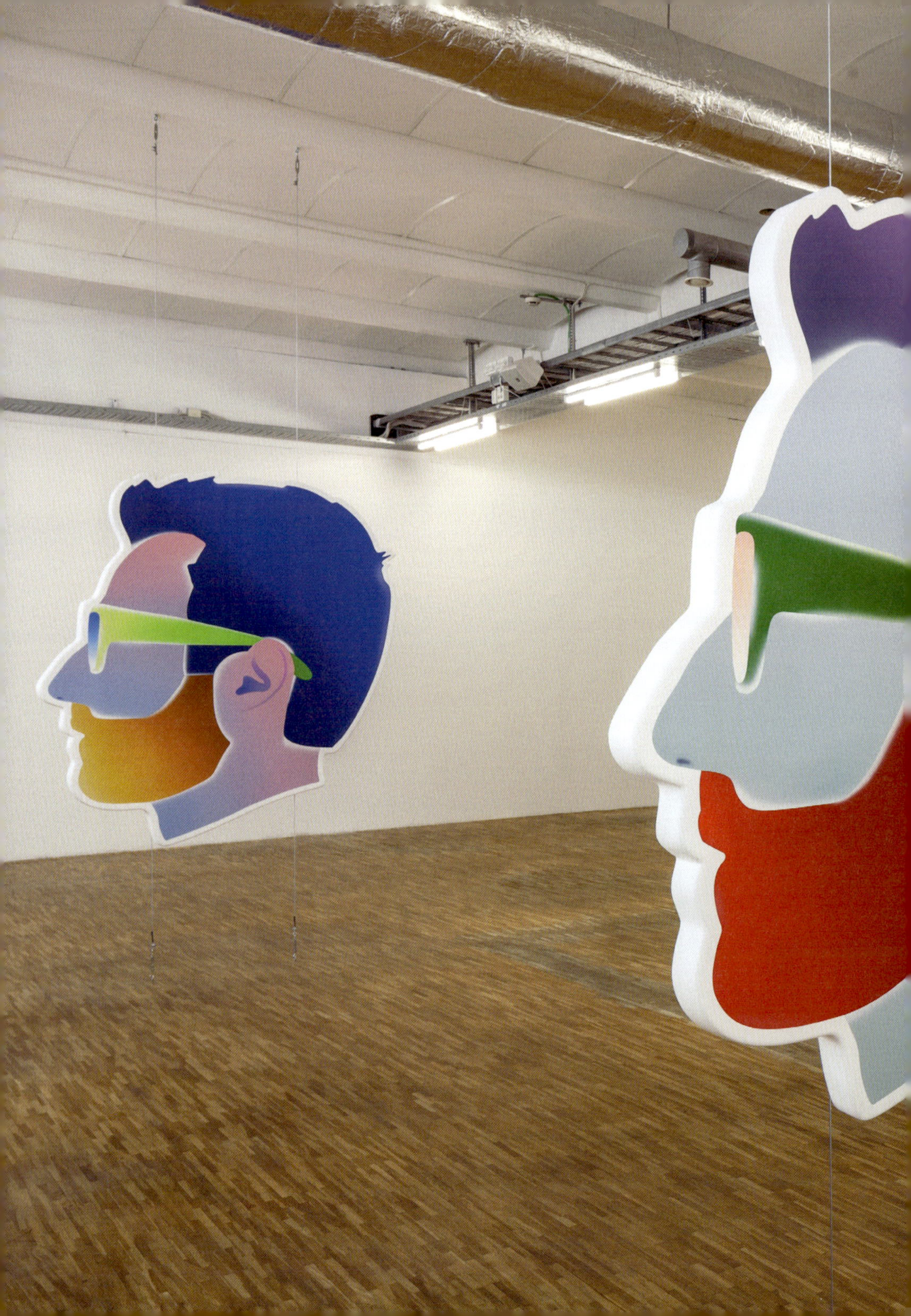

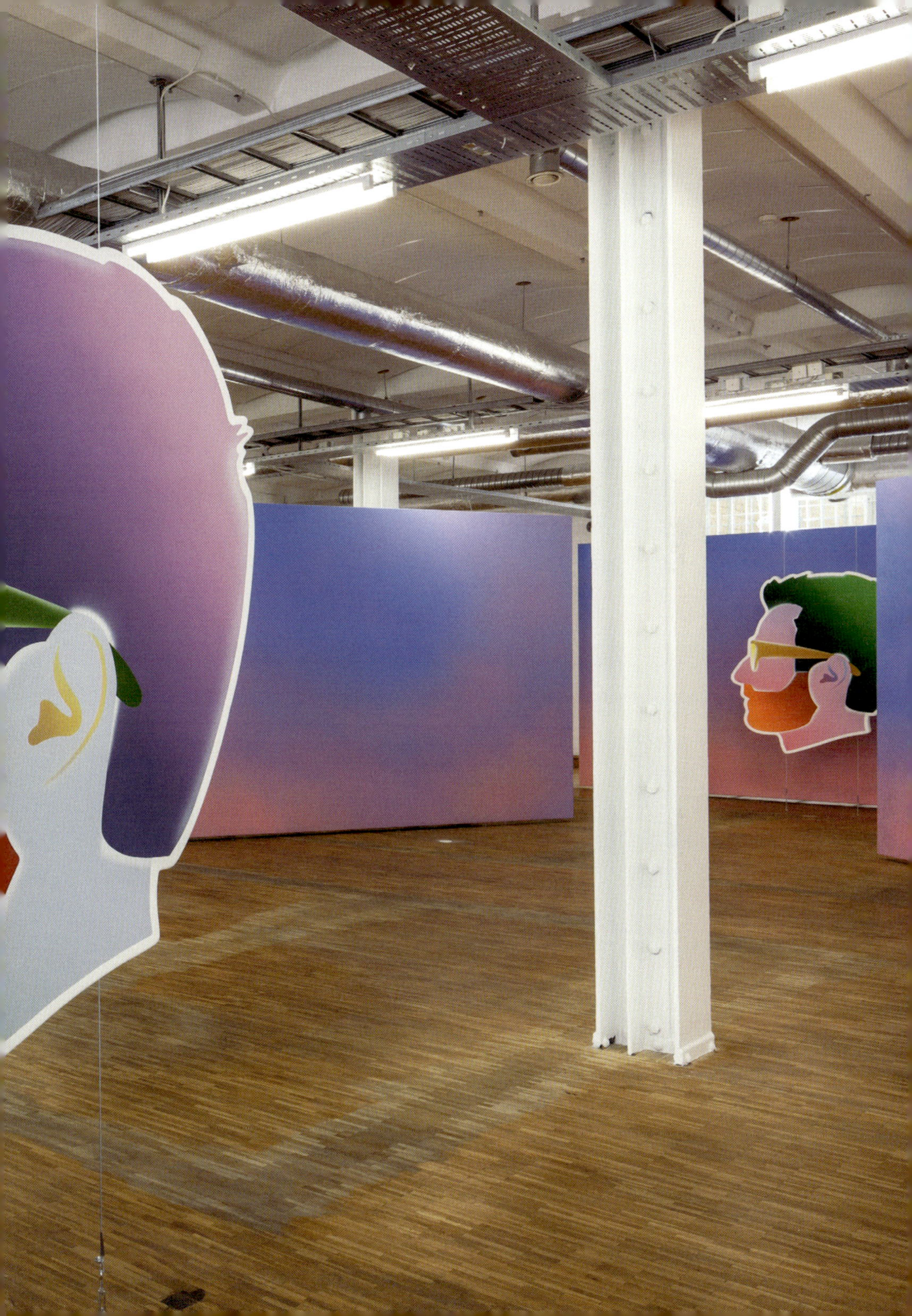

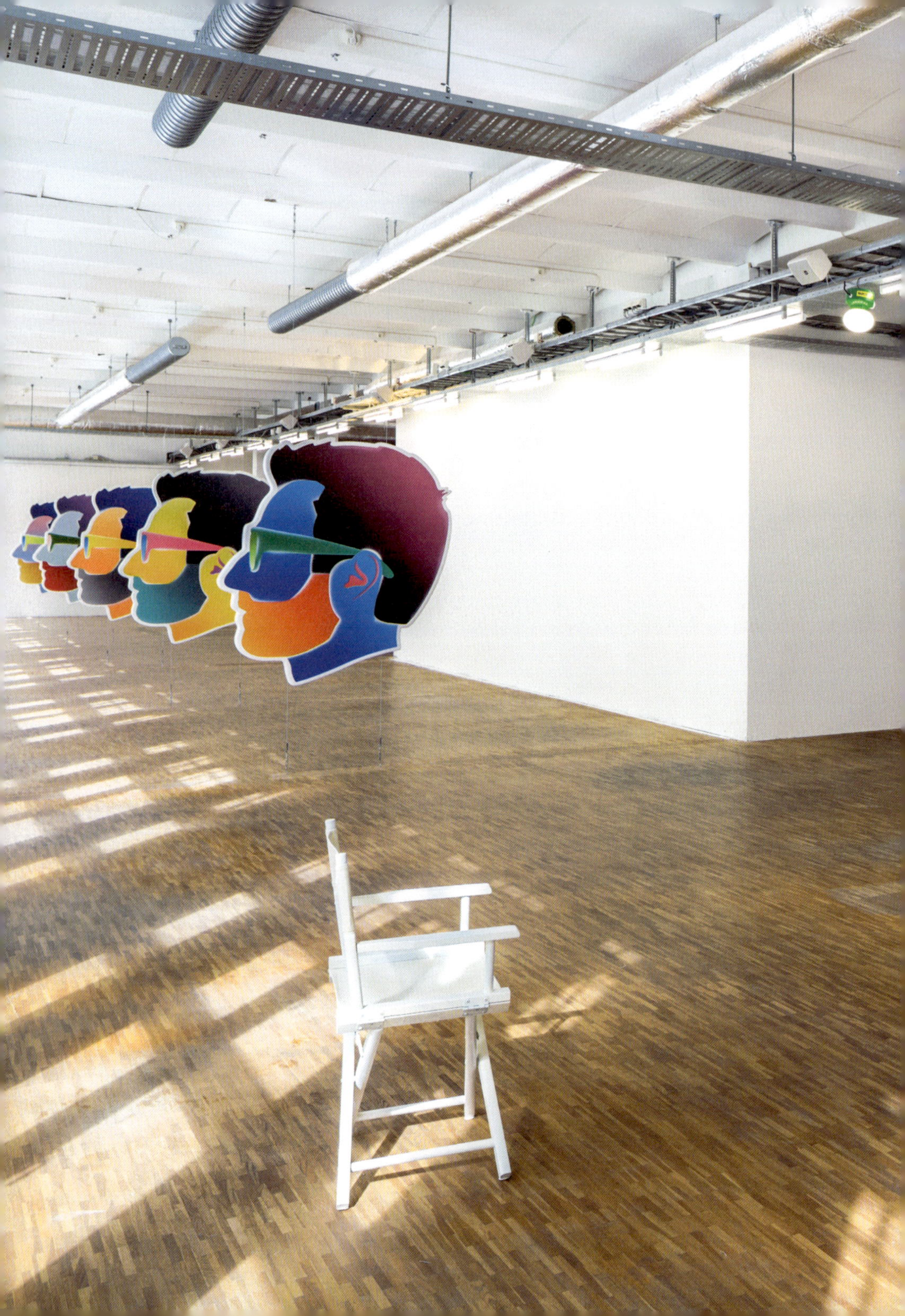

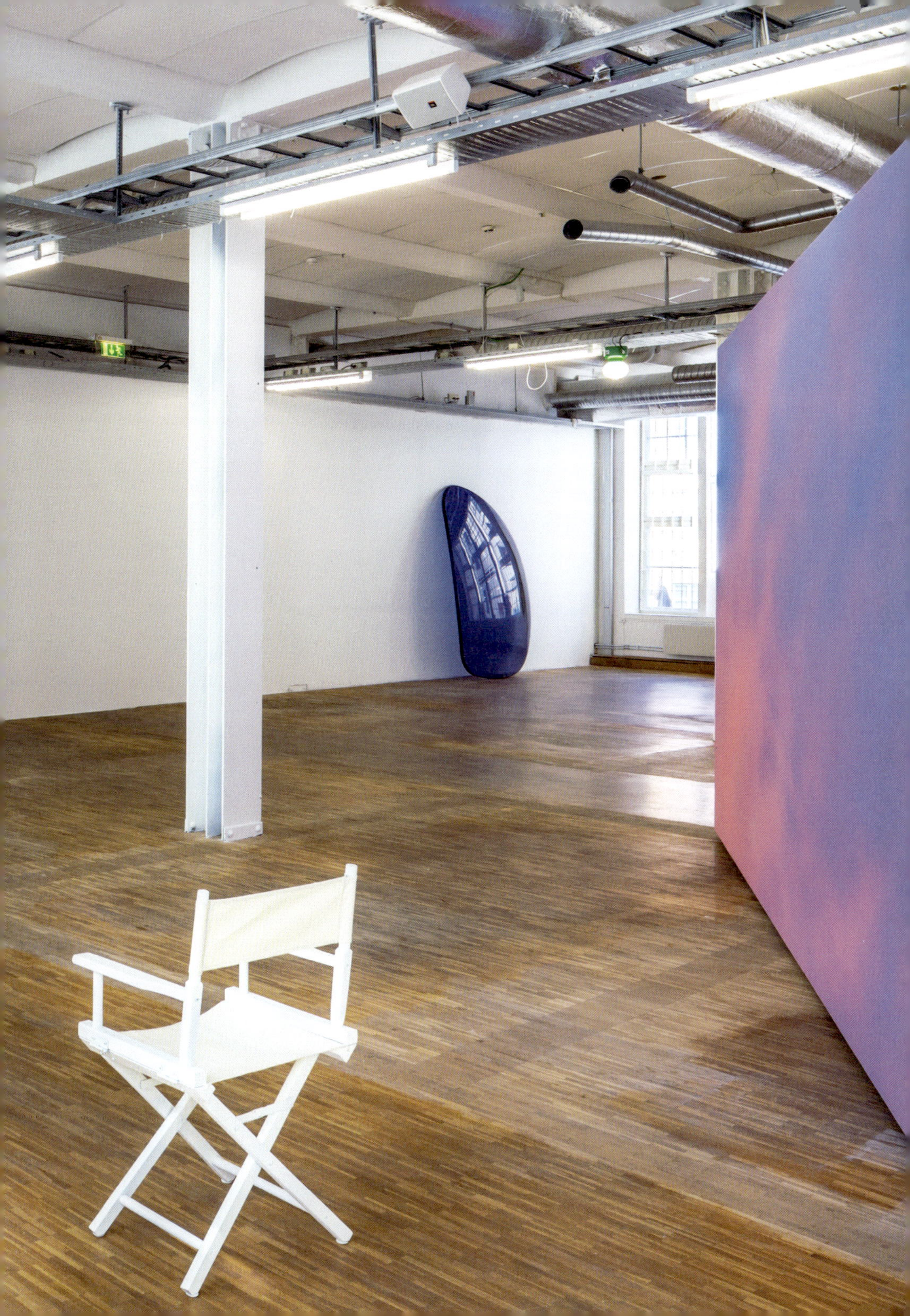

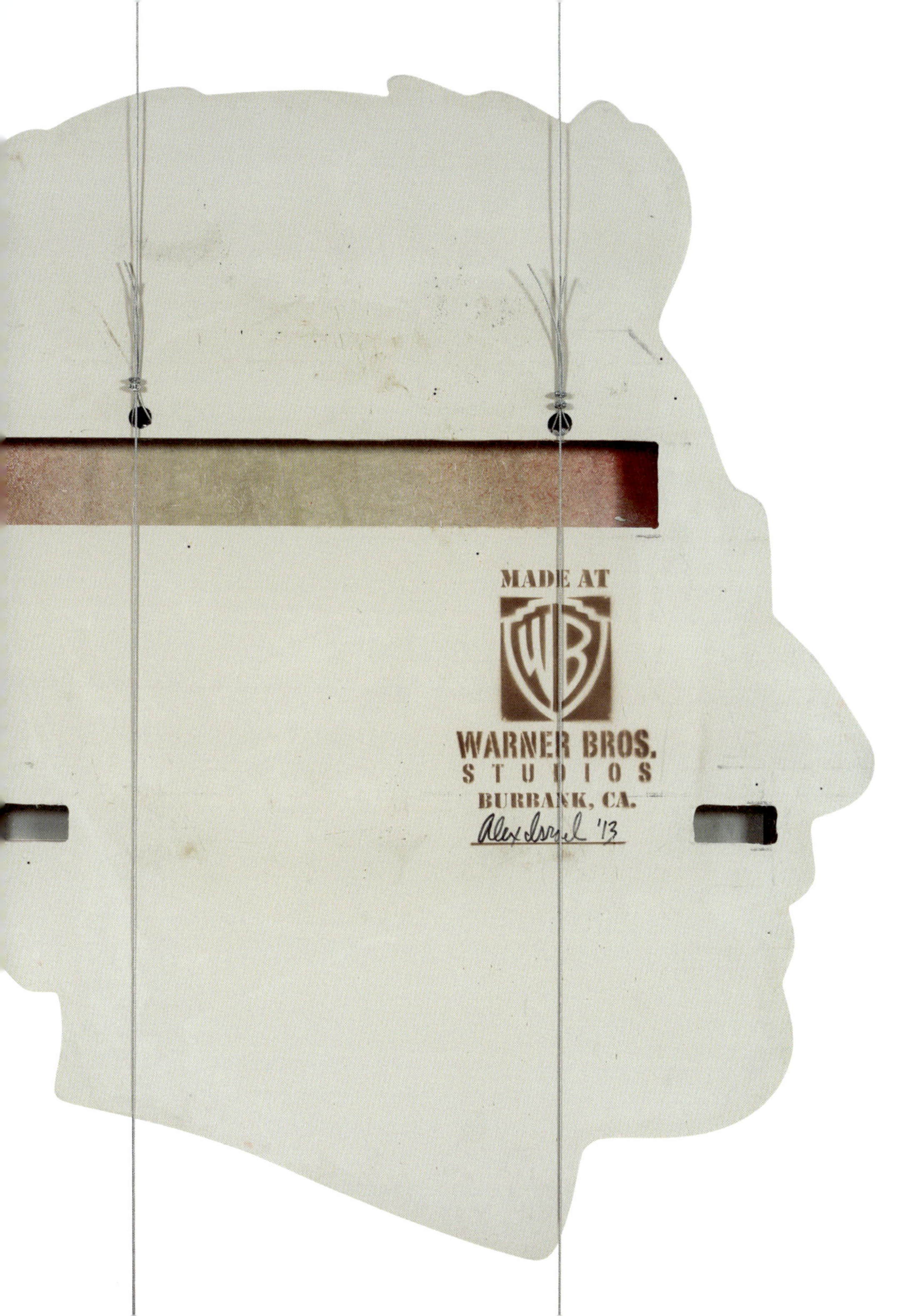

MADE AT
WARNER BROS.
STUDIOS
BURBANK, CA.
Alex Israel '13

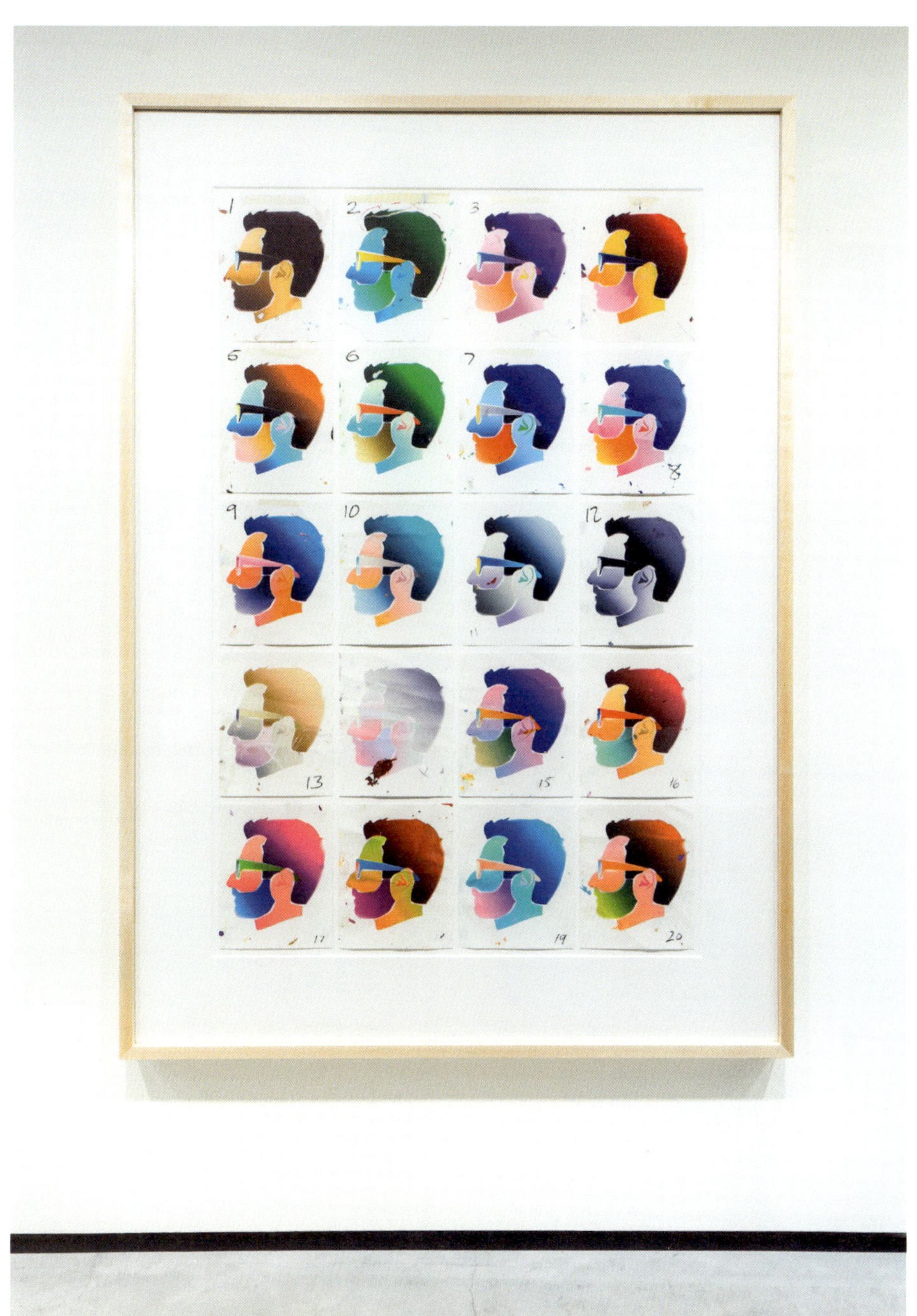

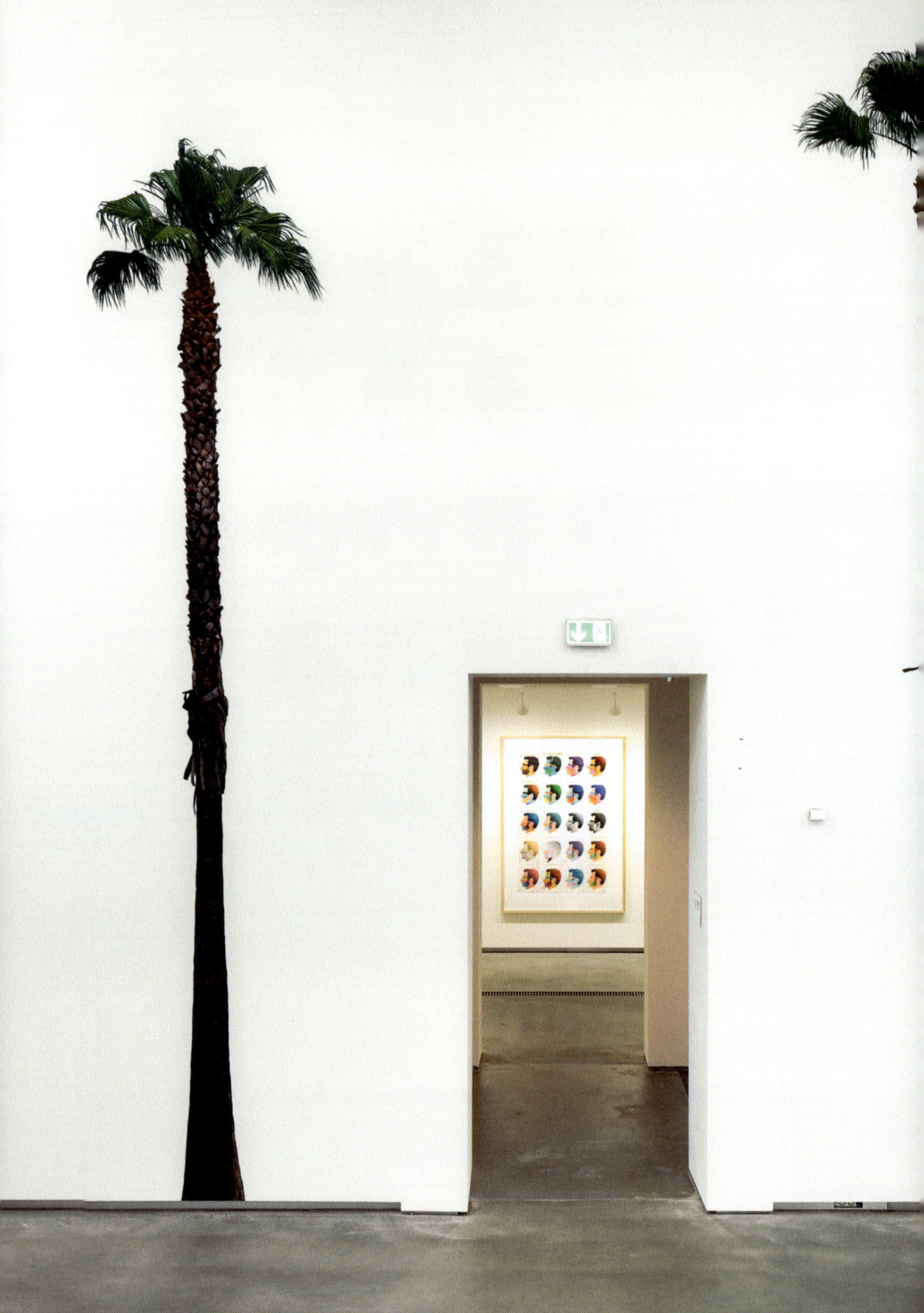

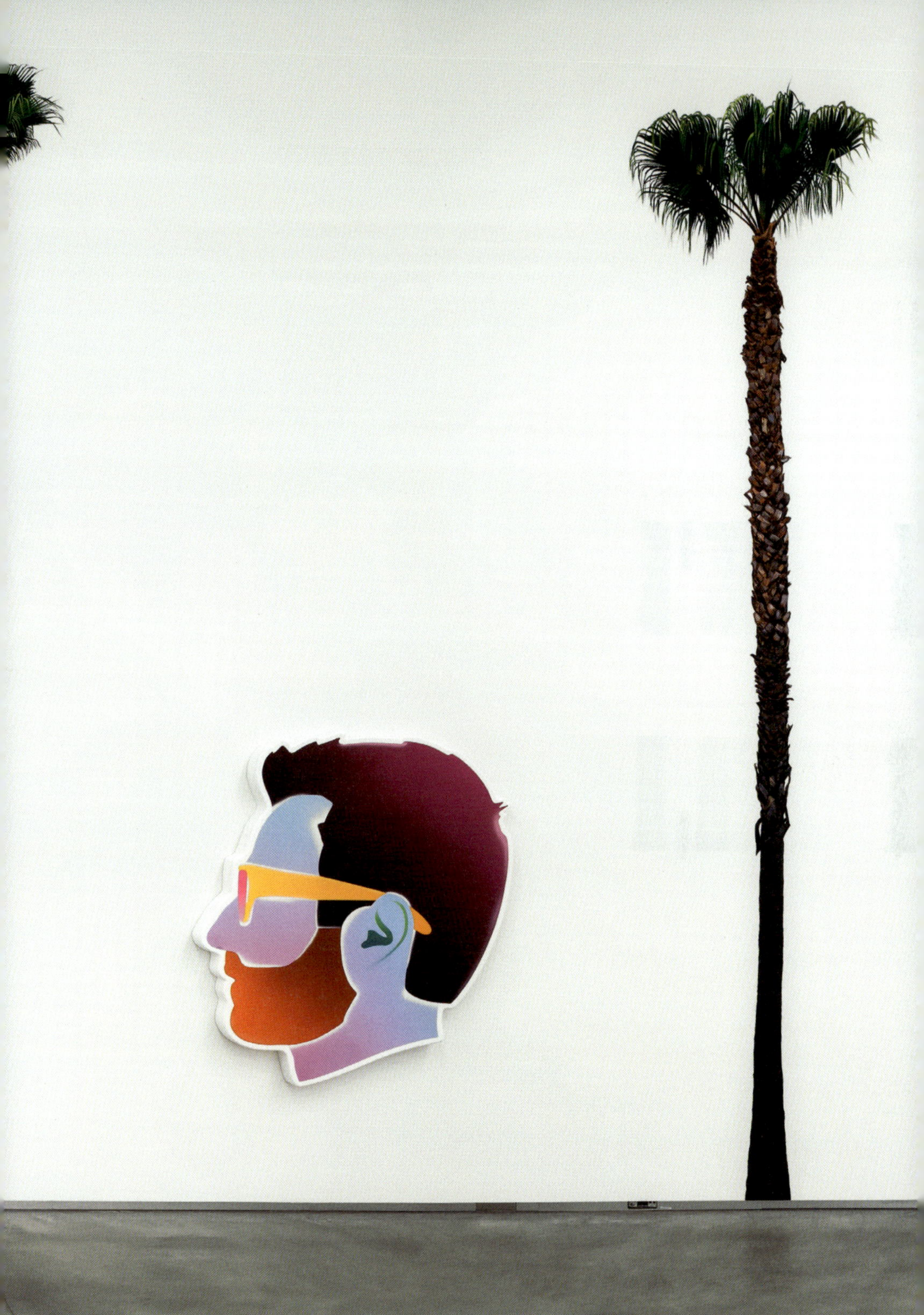

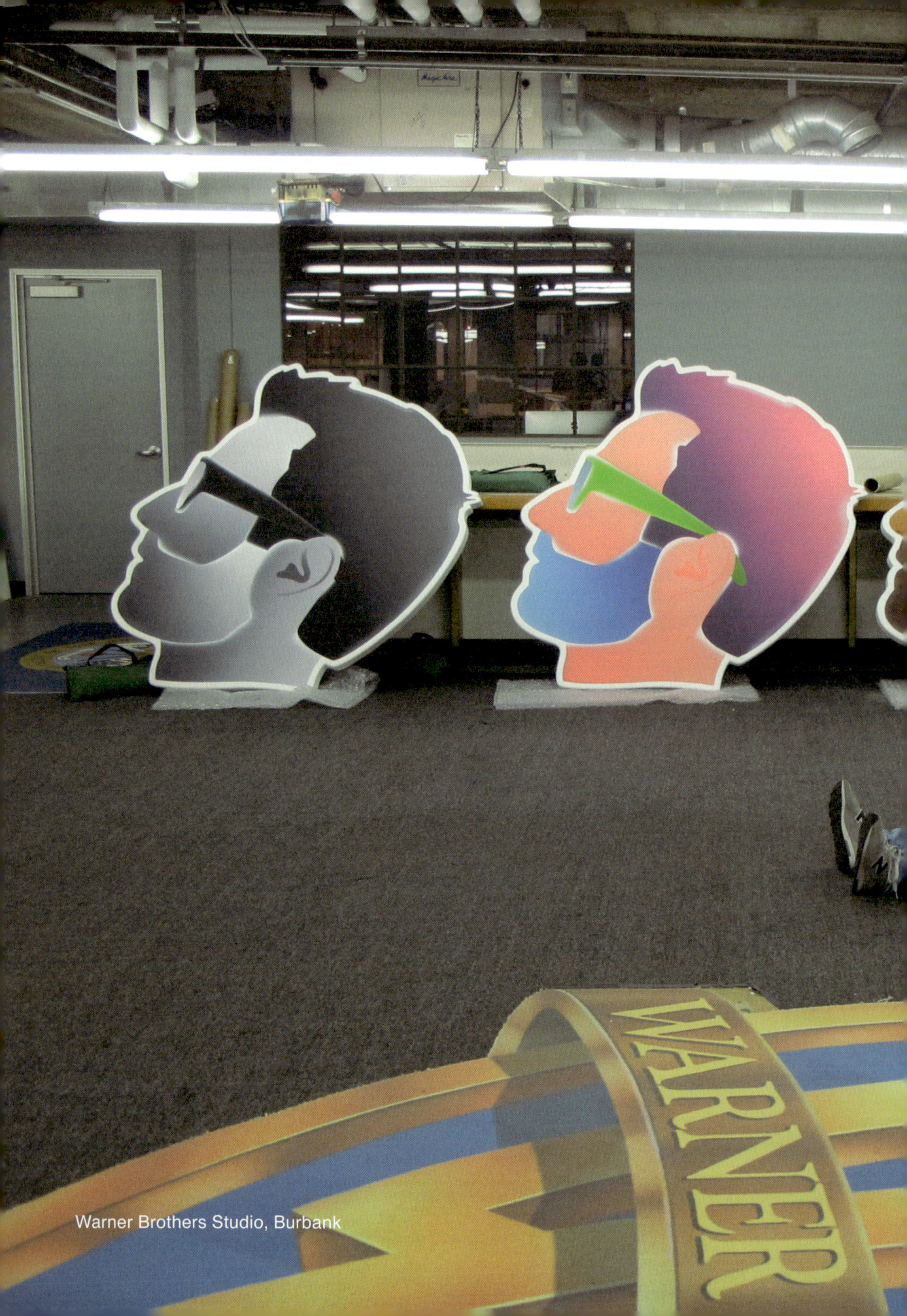

Warner Brothers Studio, Burbank

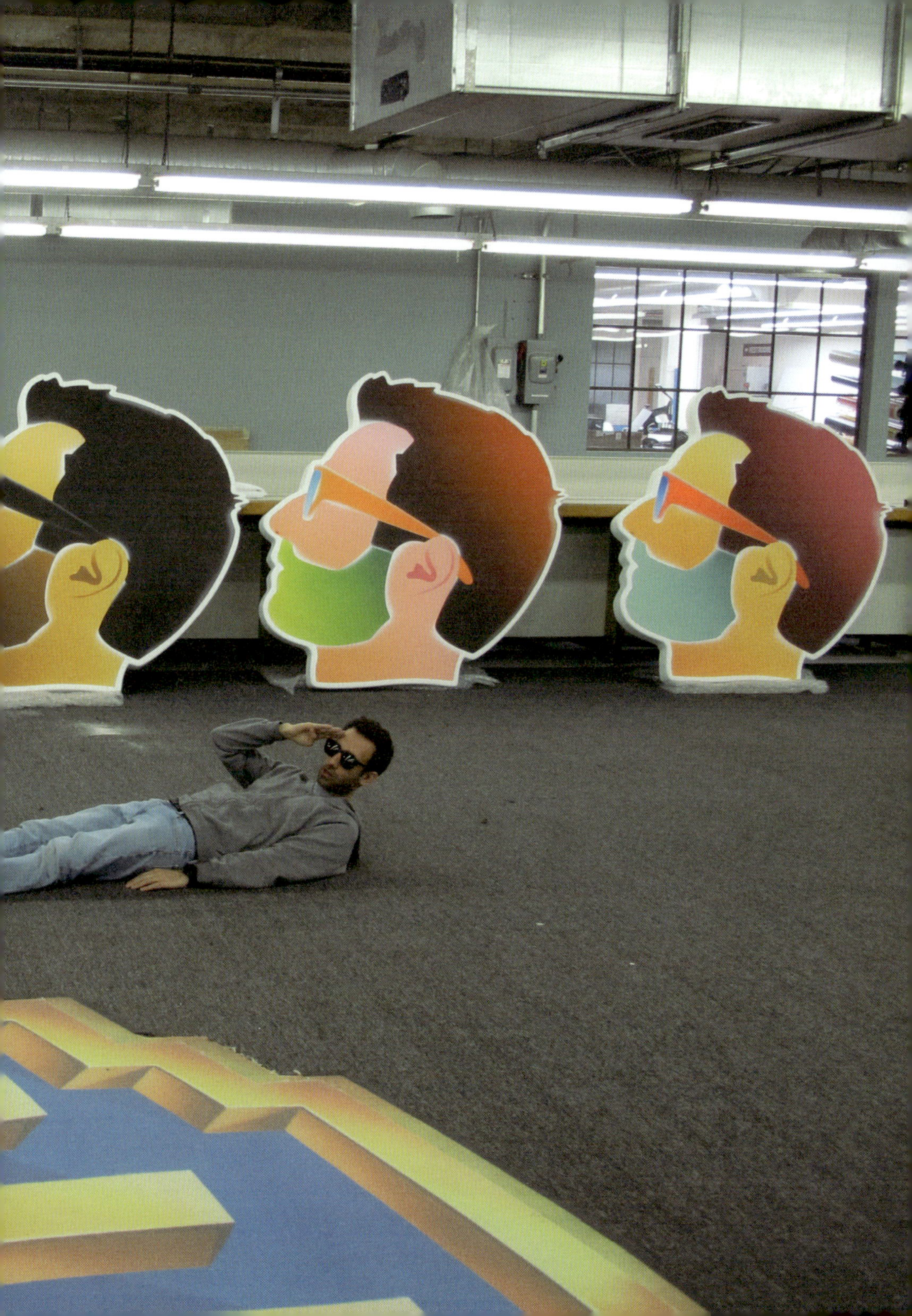

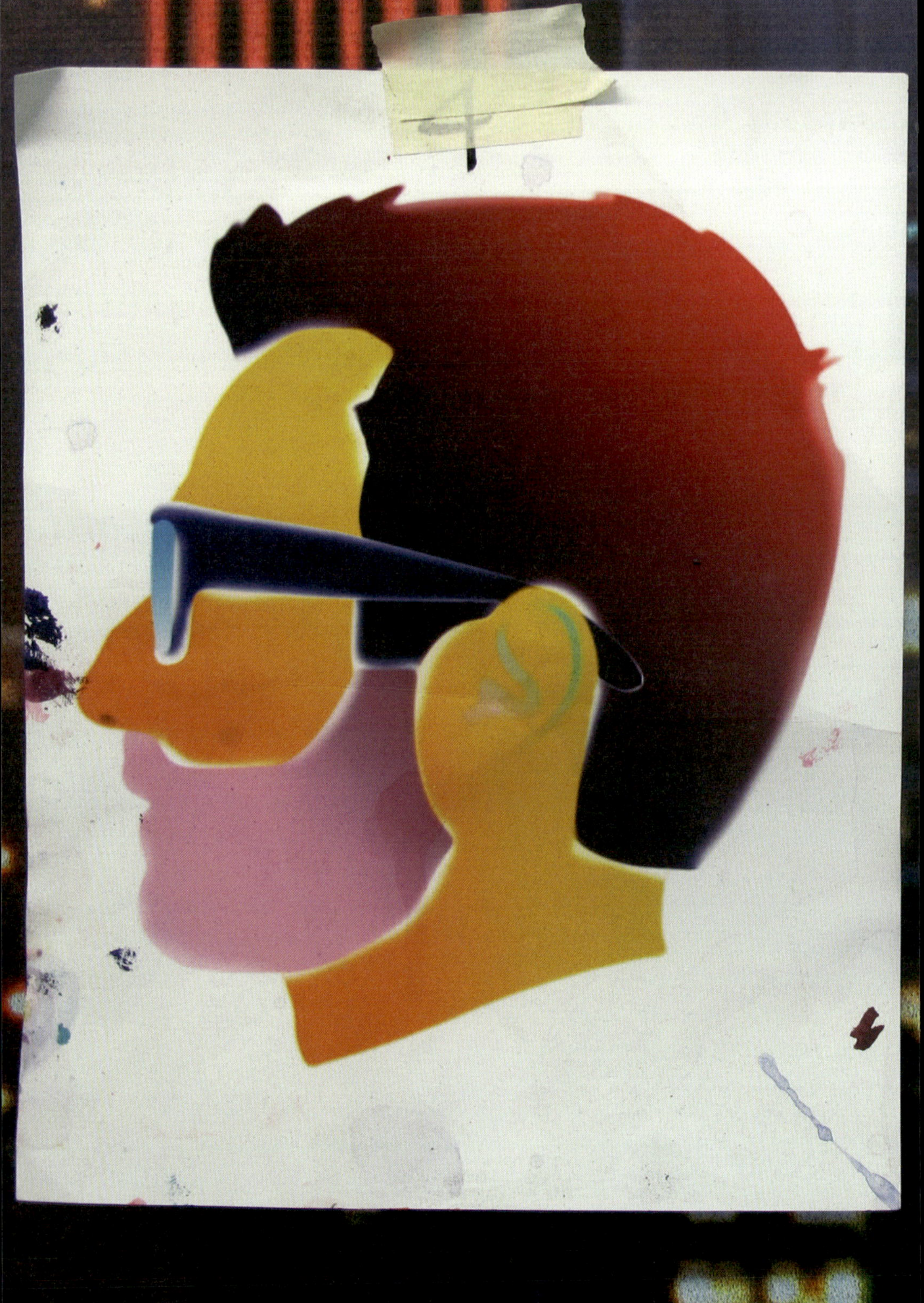

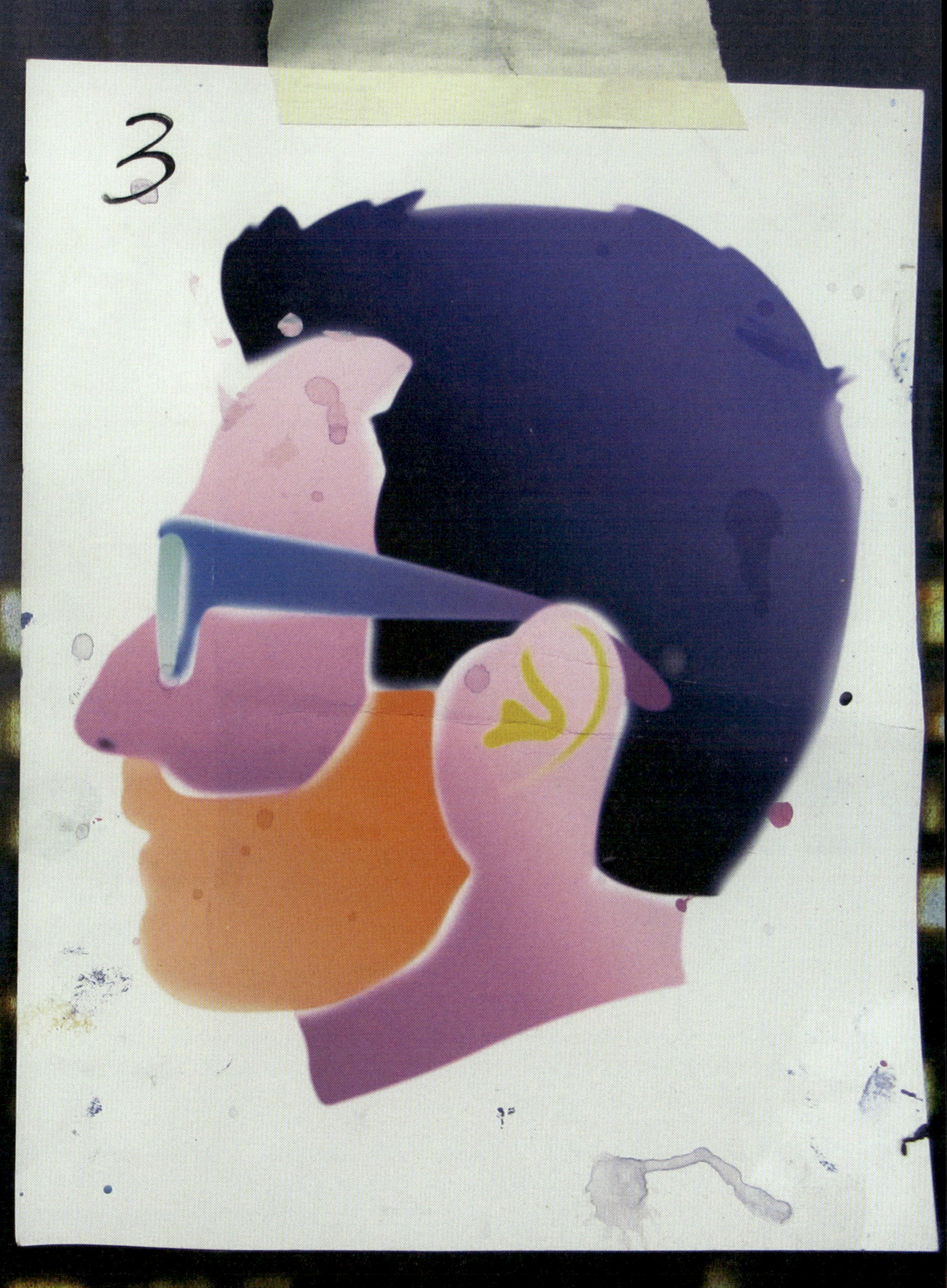
3

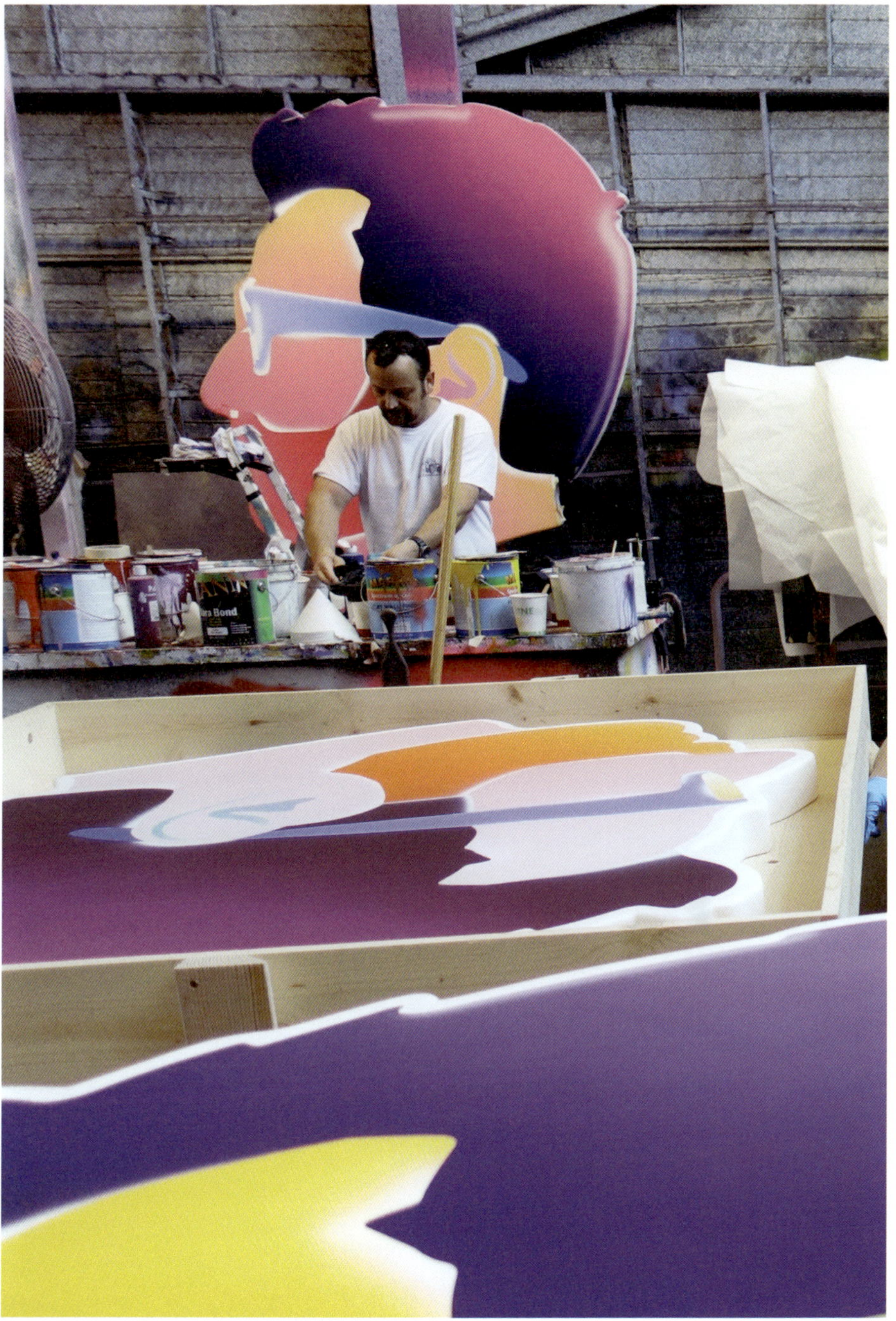

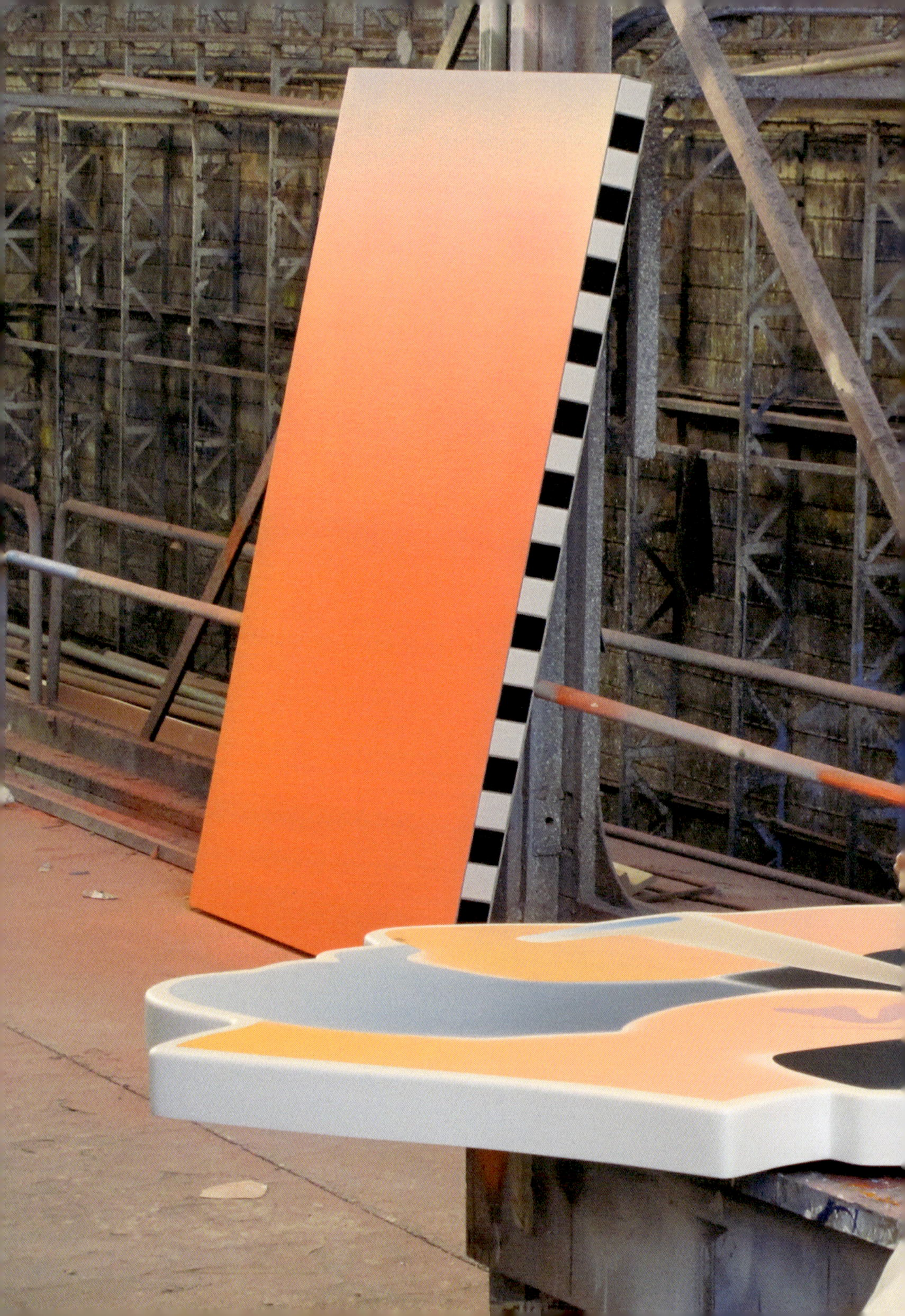

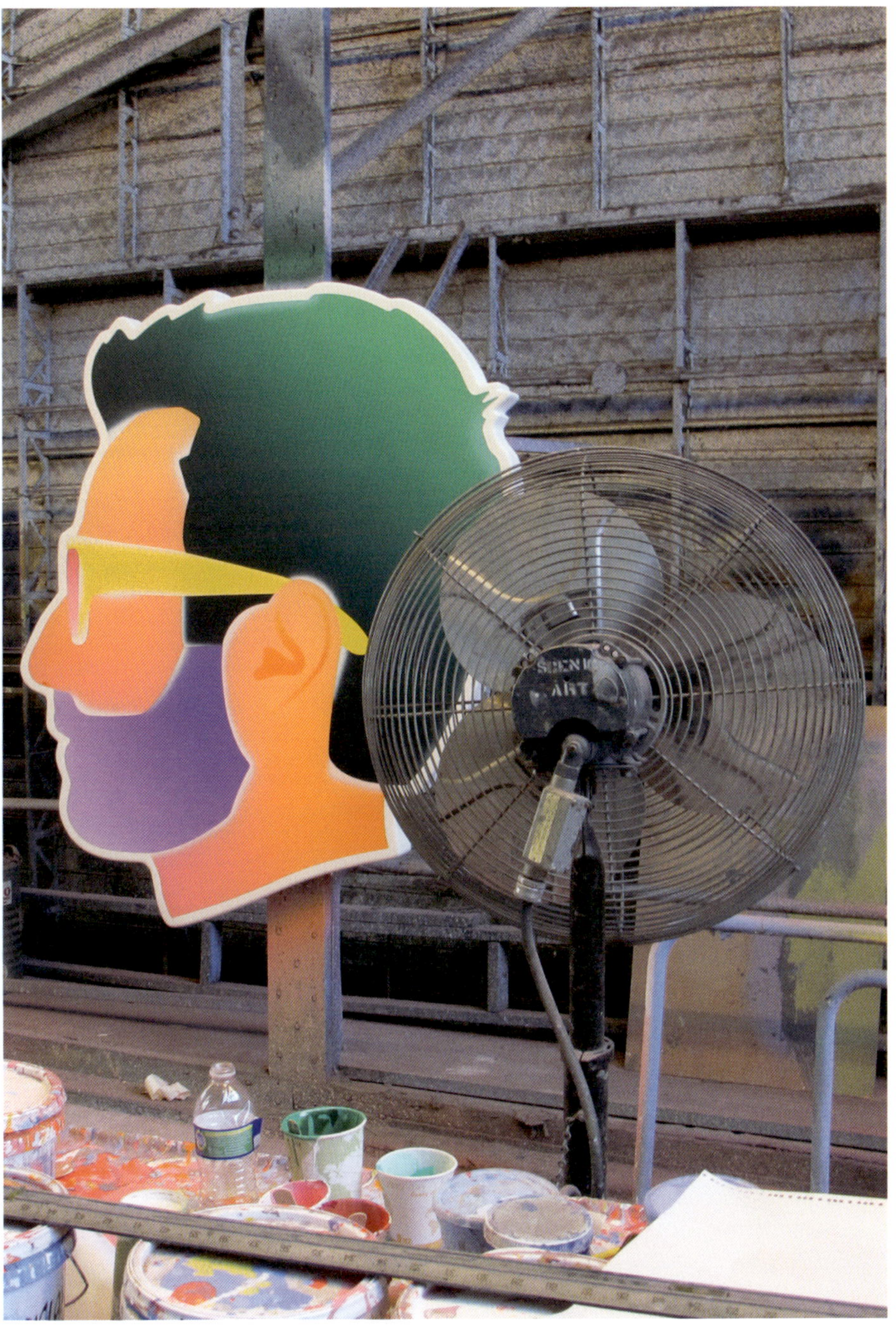

SIEN
ART

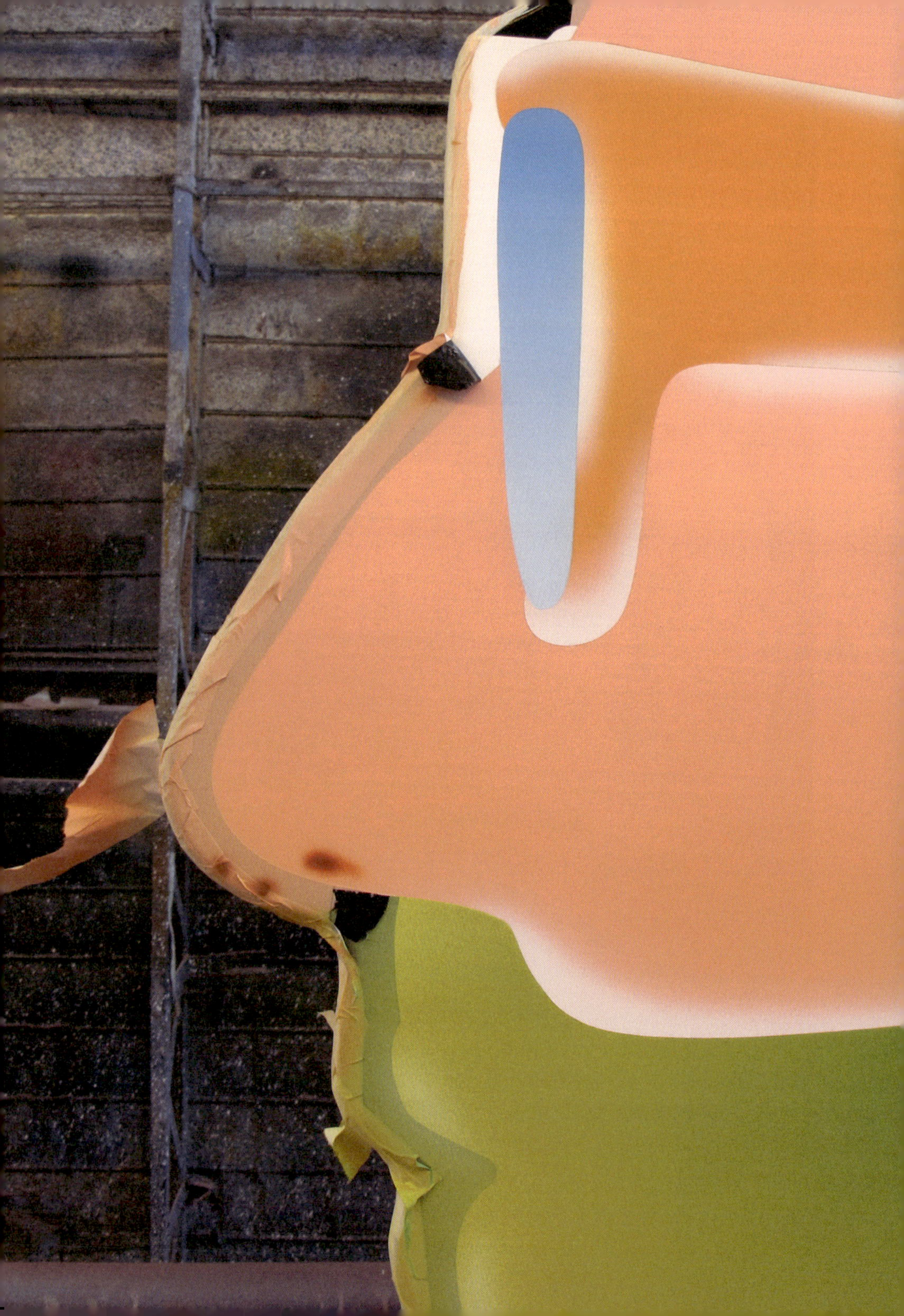

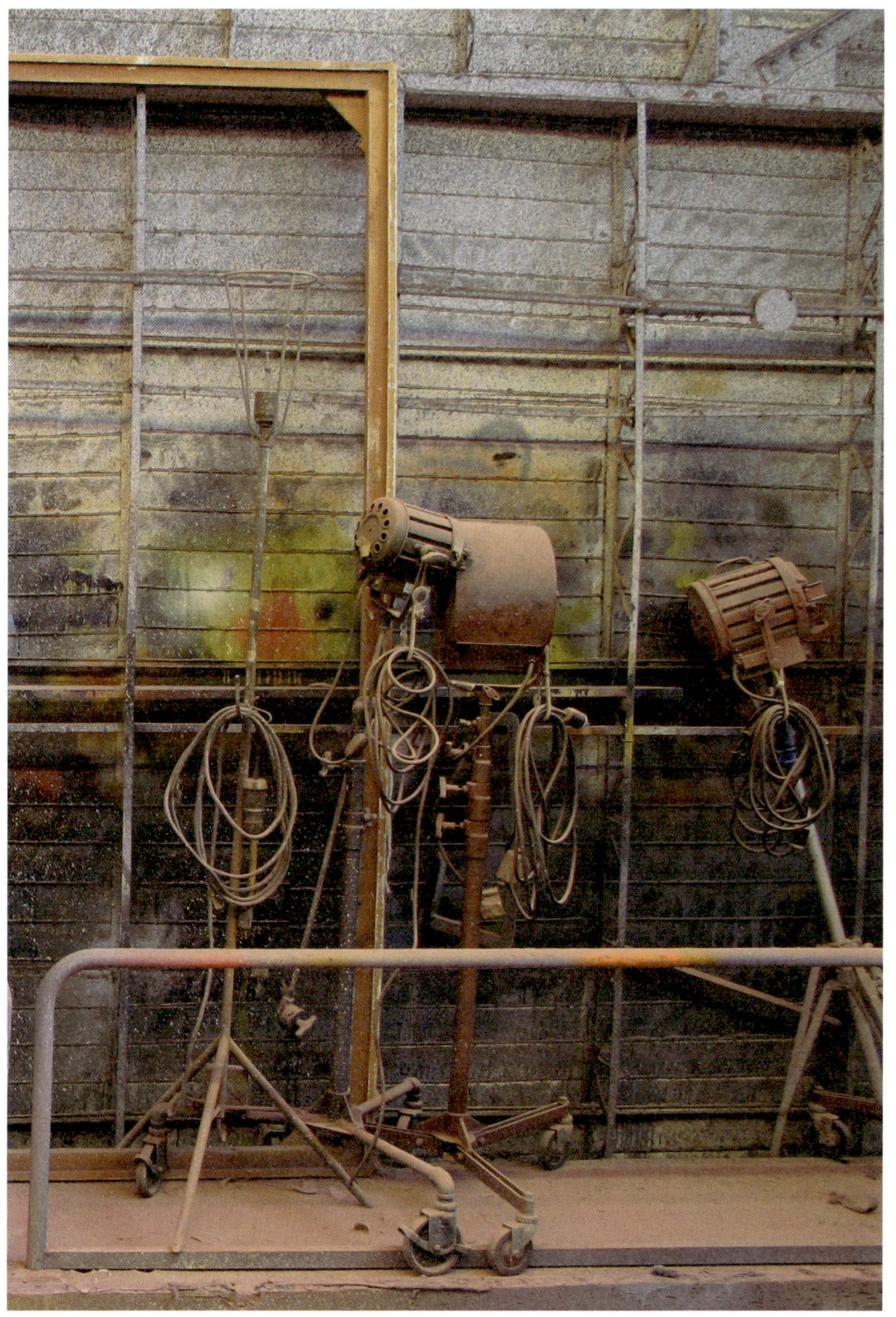

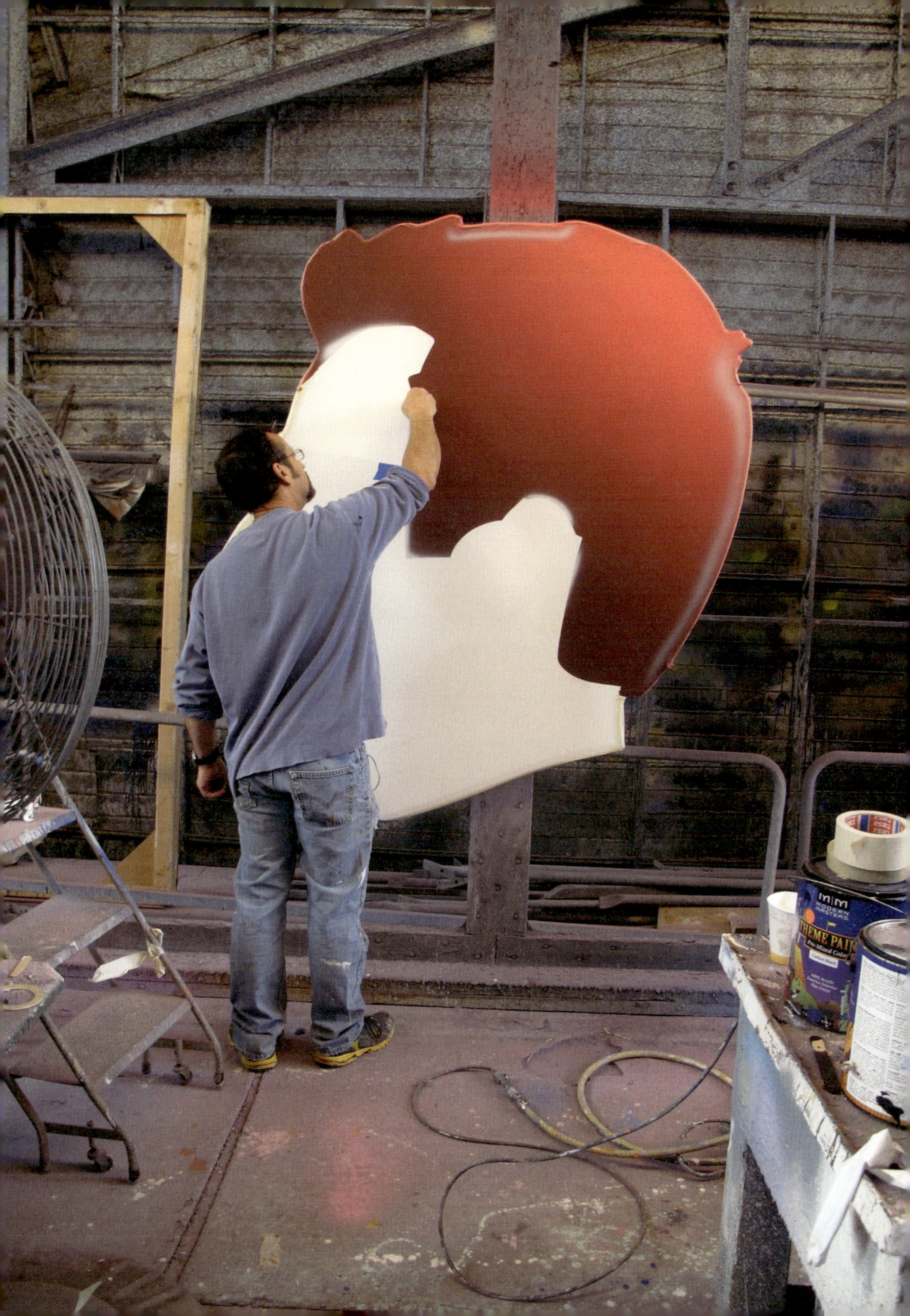

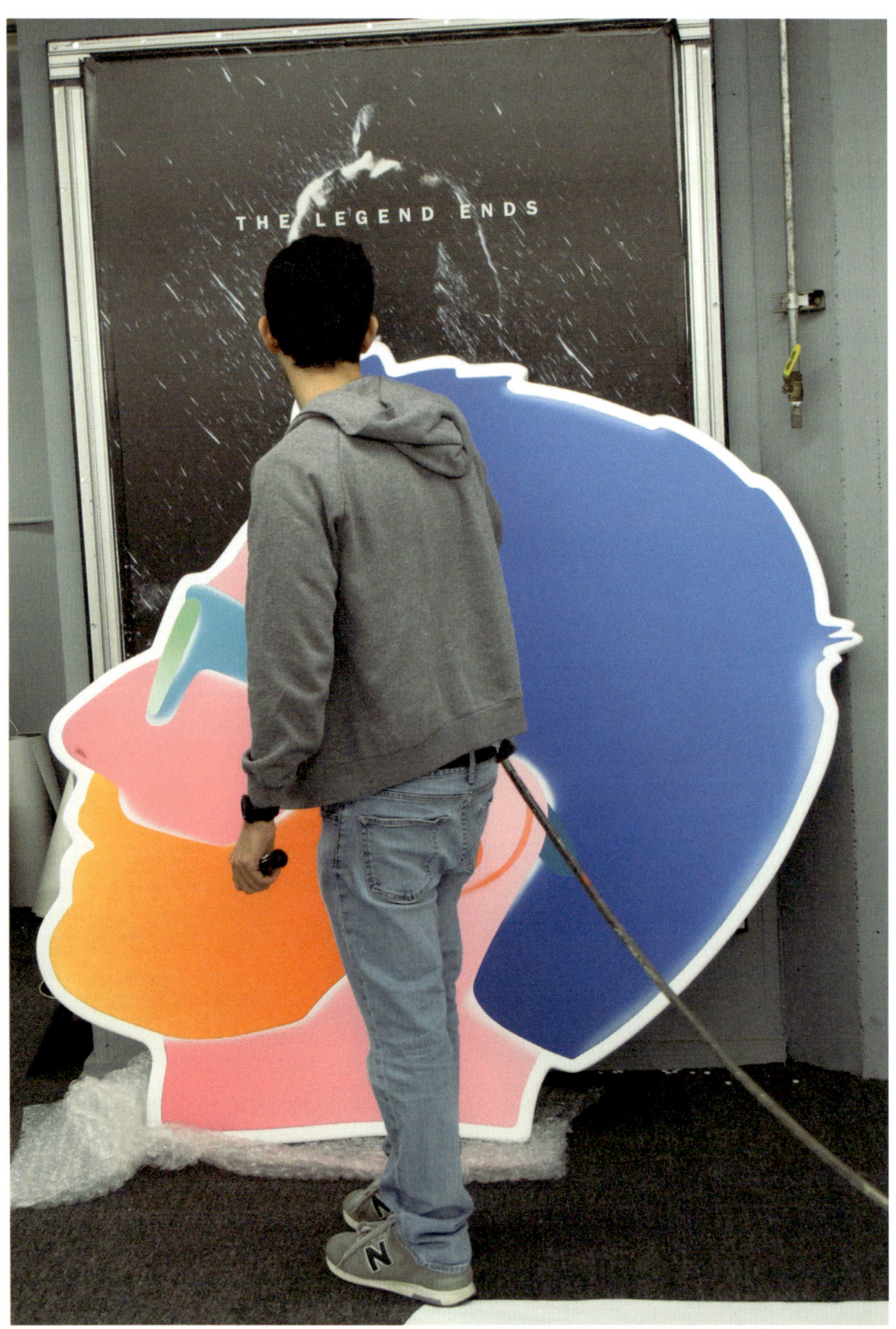

THE LEGEND ENDS

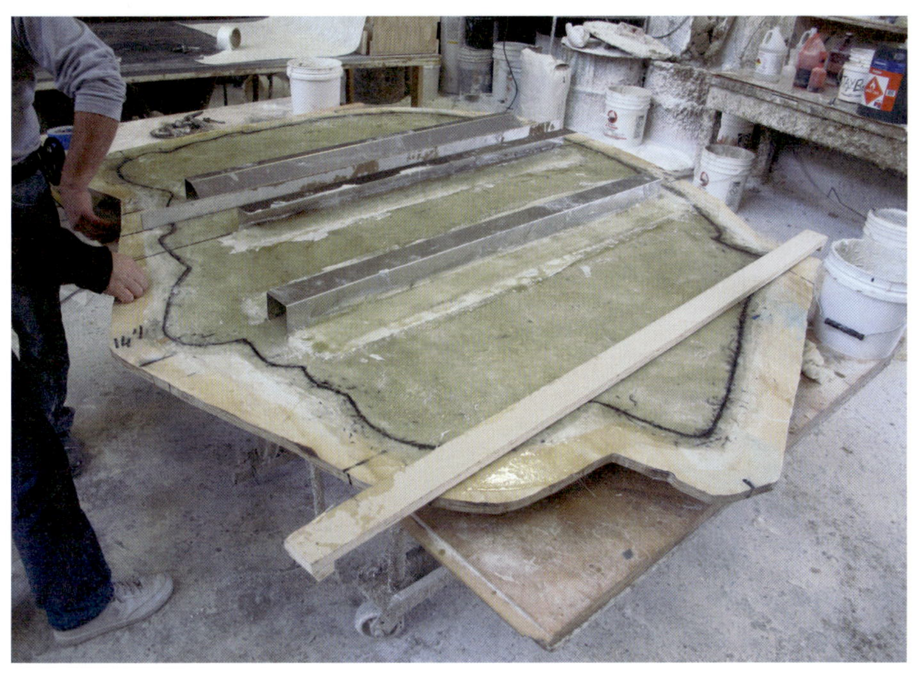

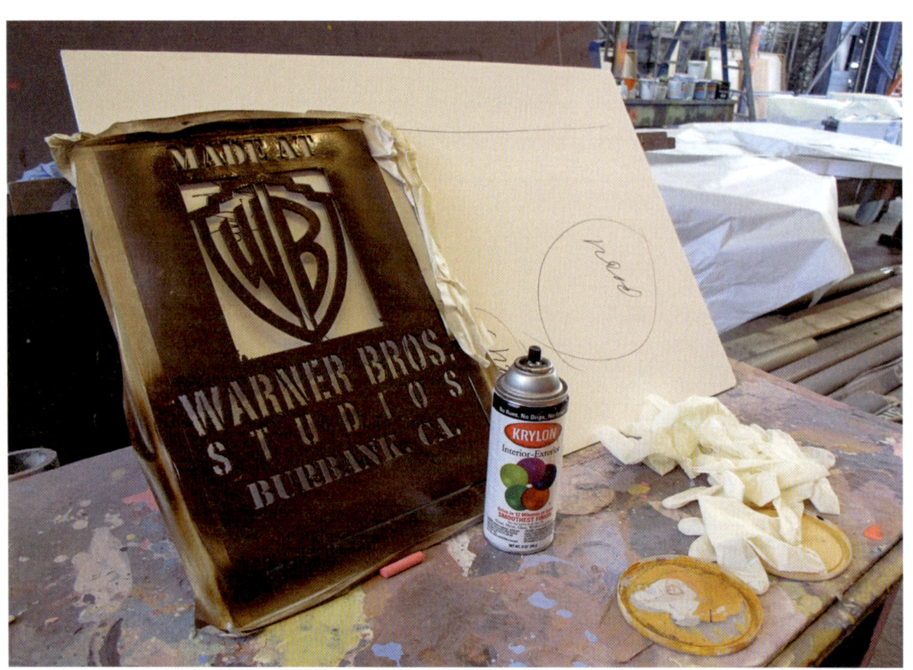

MADE AT
WB
WARNER BROS.
STUDIOS
BURBANK, CA.
KRYLON
Interior-Exterior

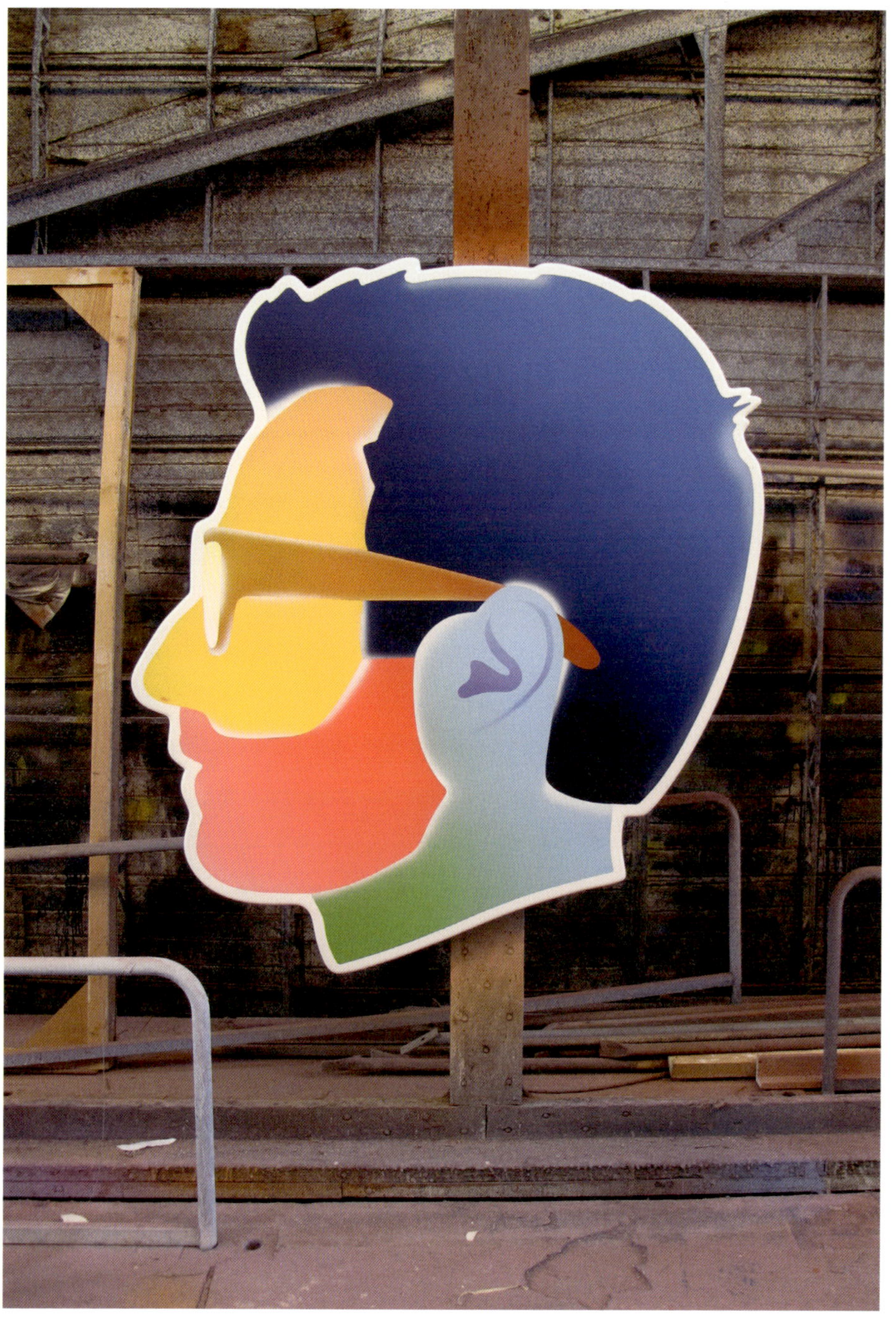

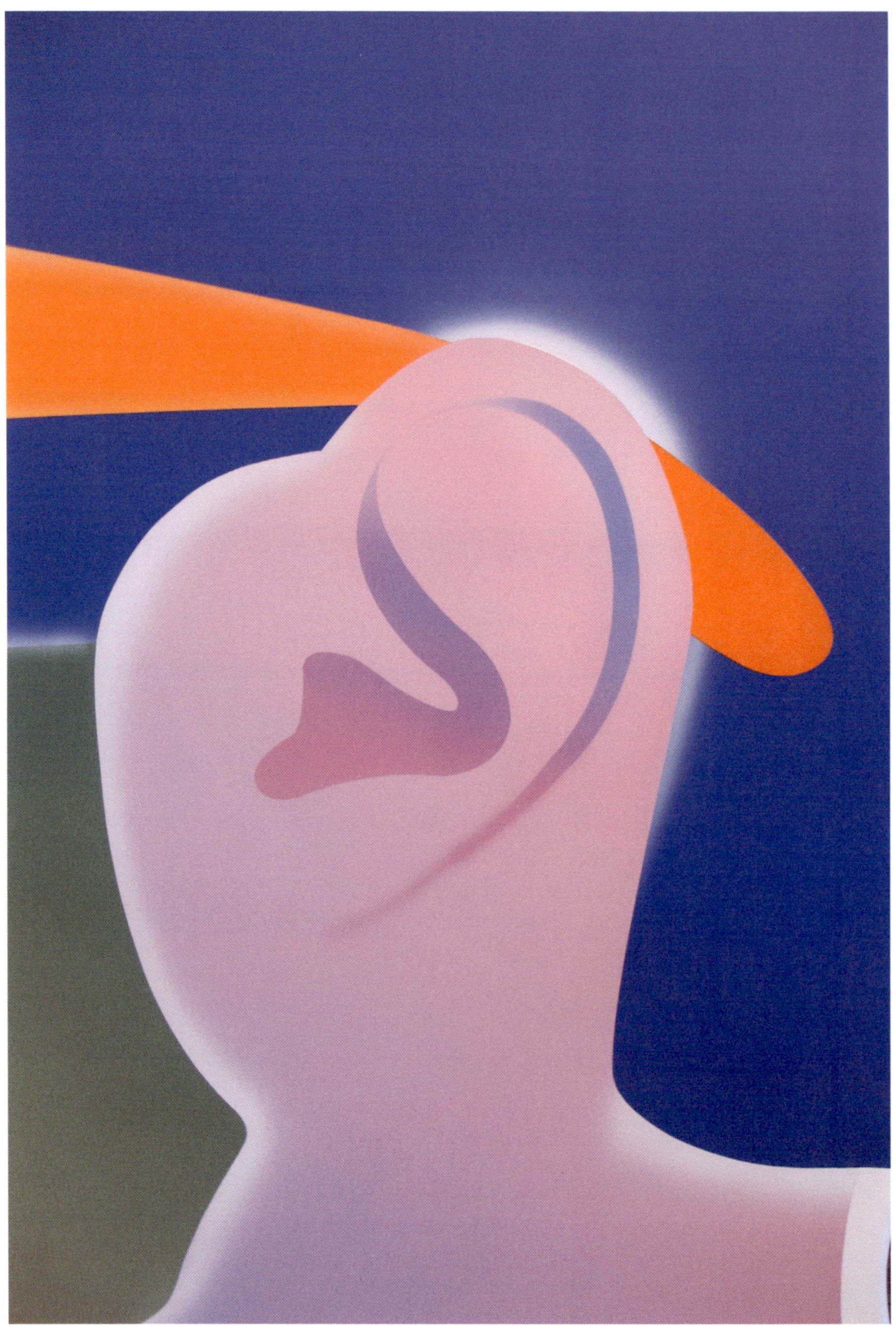

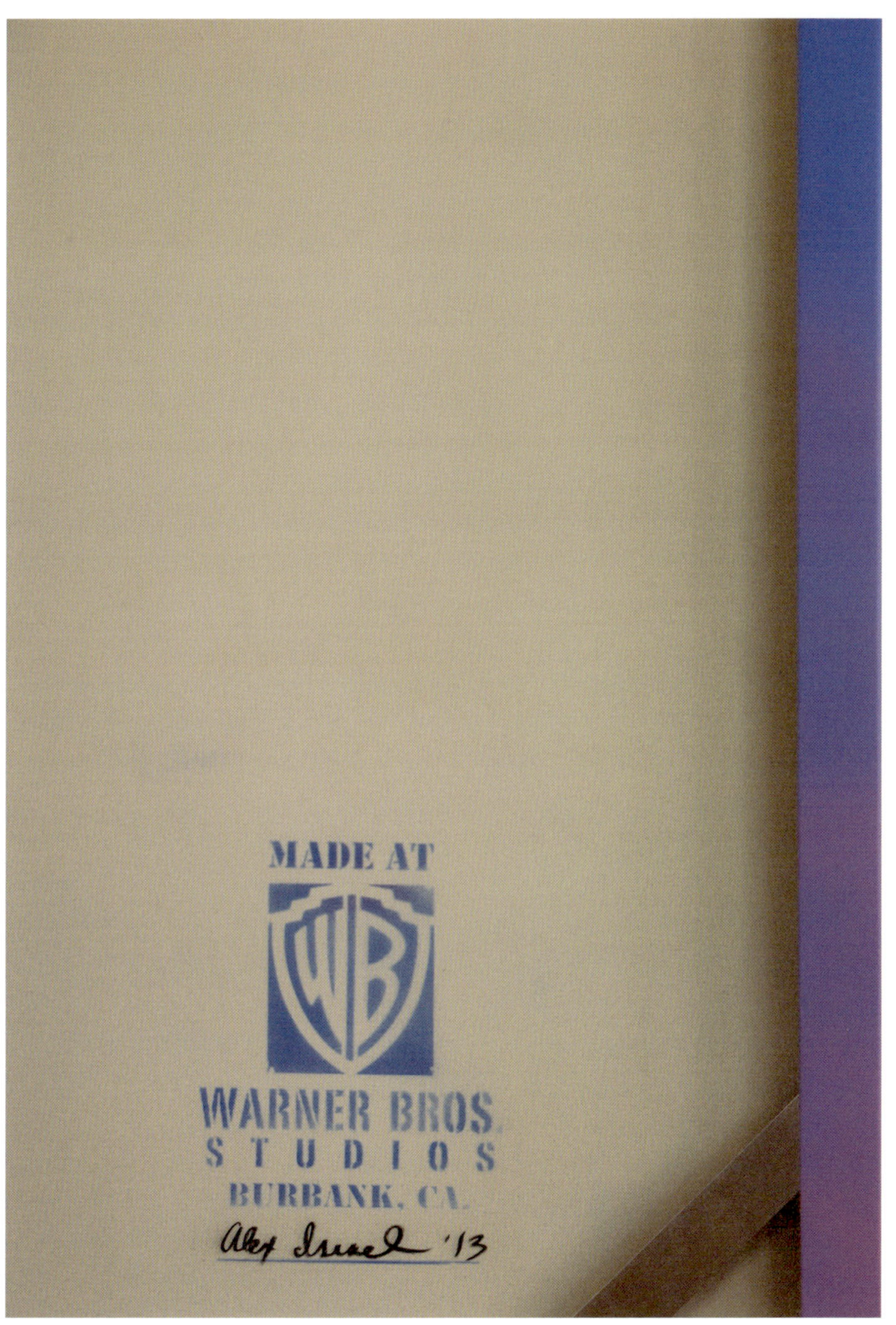

MADE AT
WARNER BROS.
STUDIOS
BURBANK, CA.

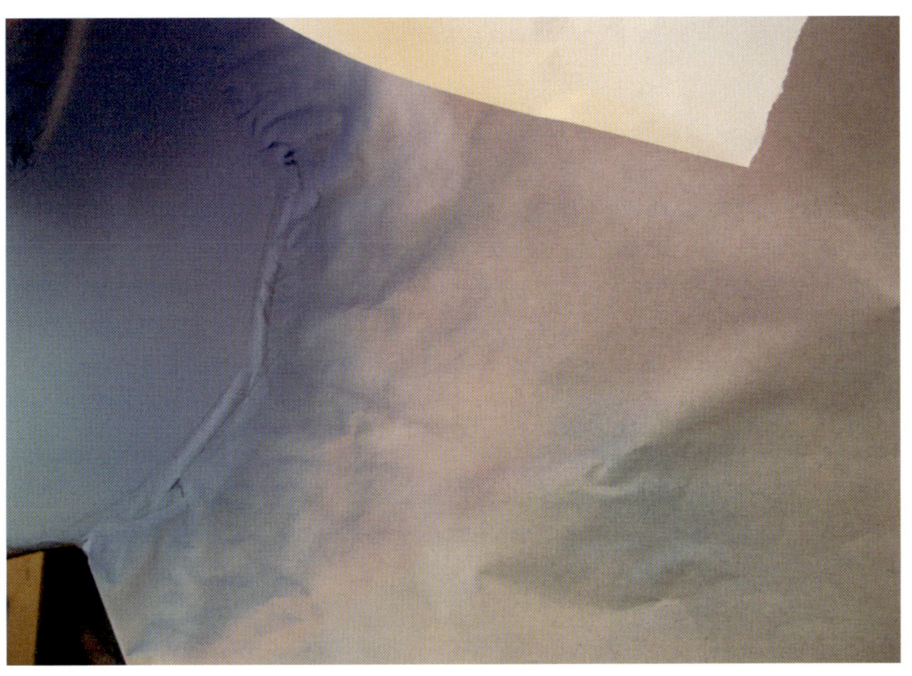

TimeWa

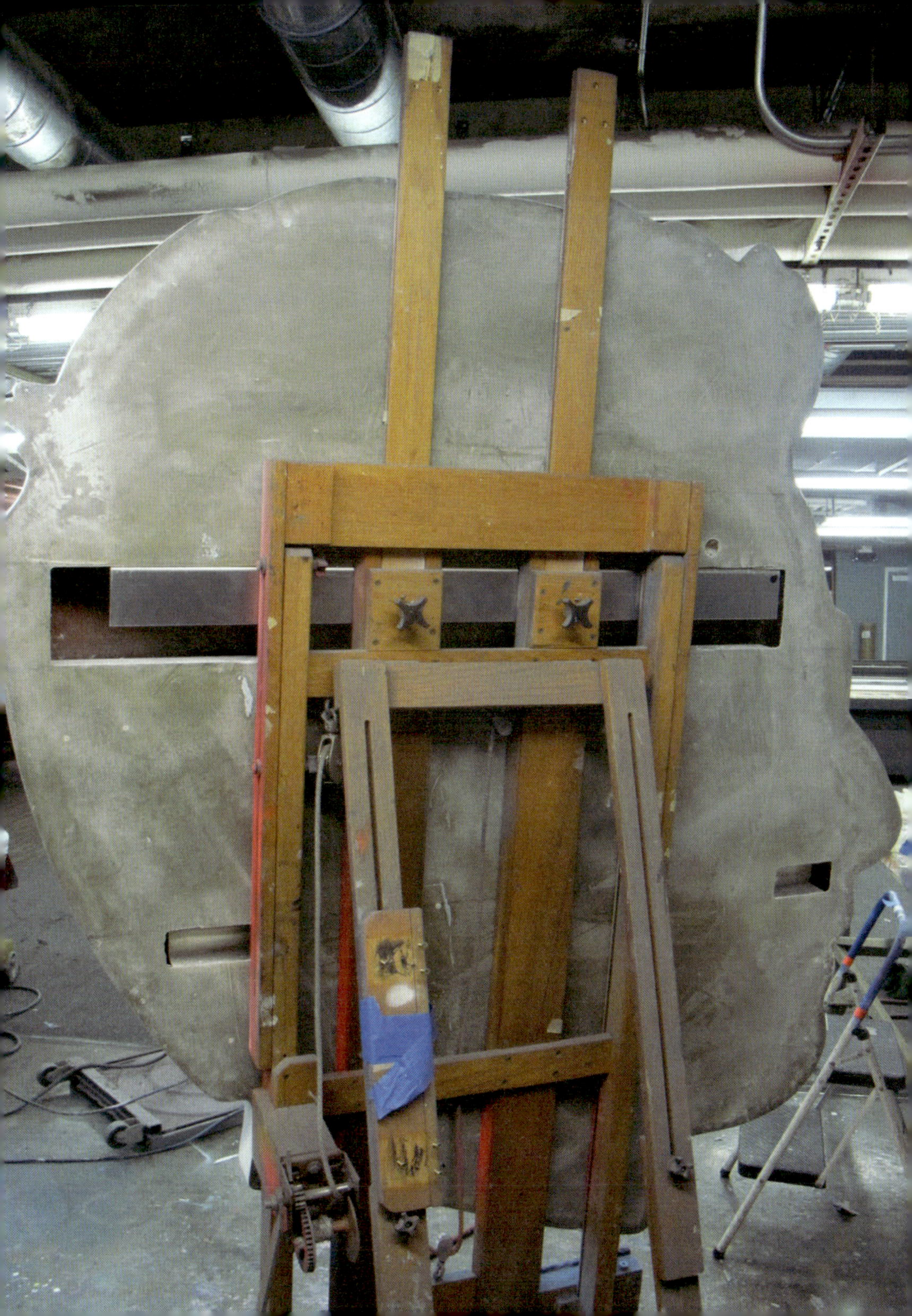

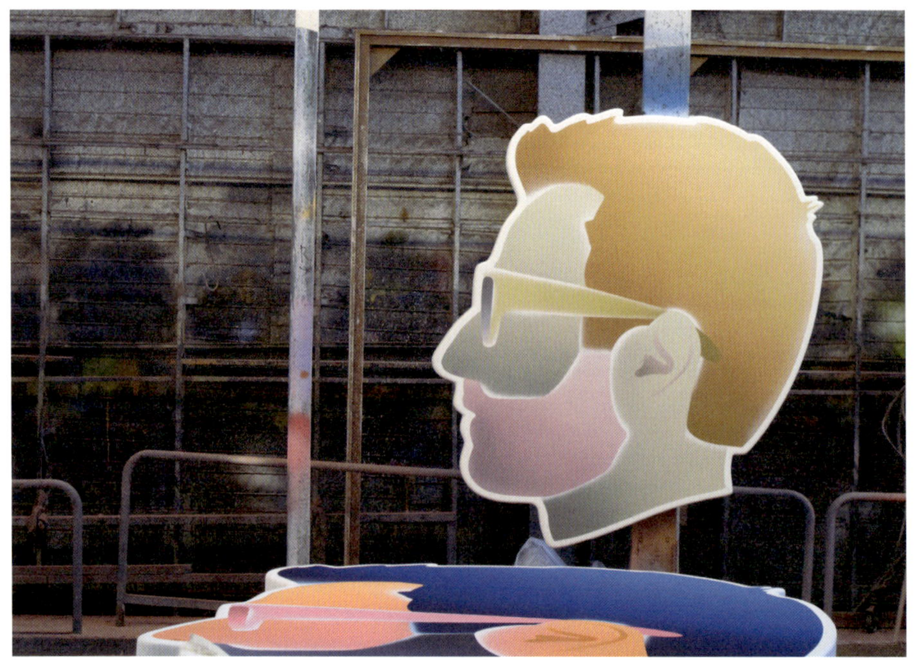

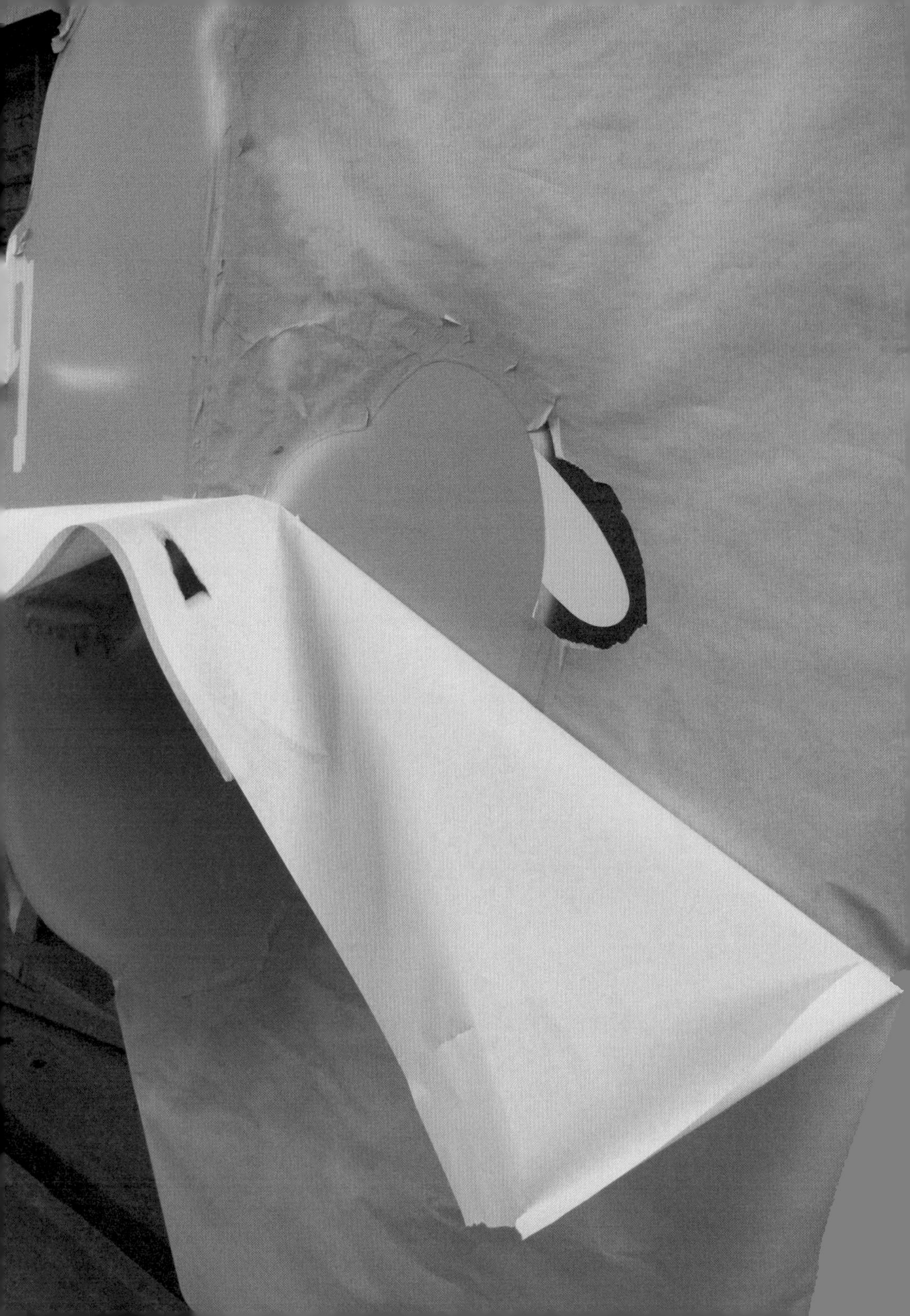

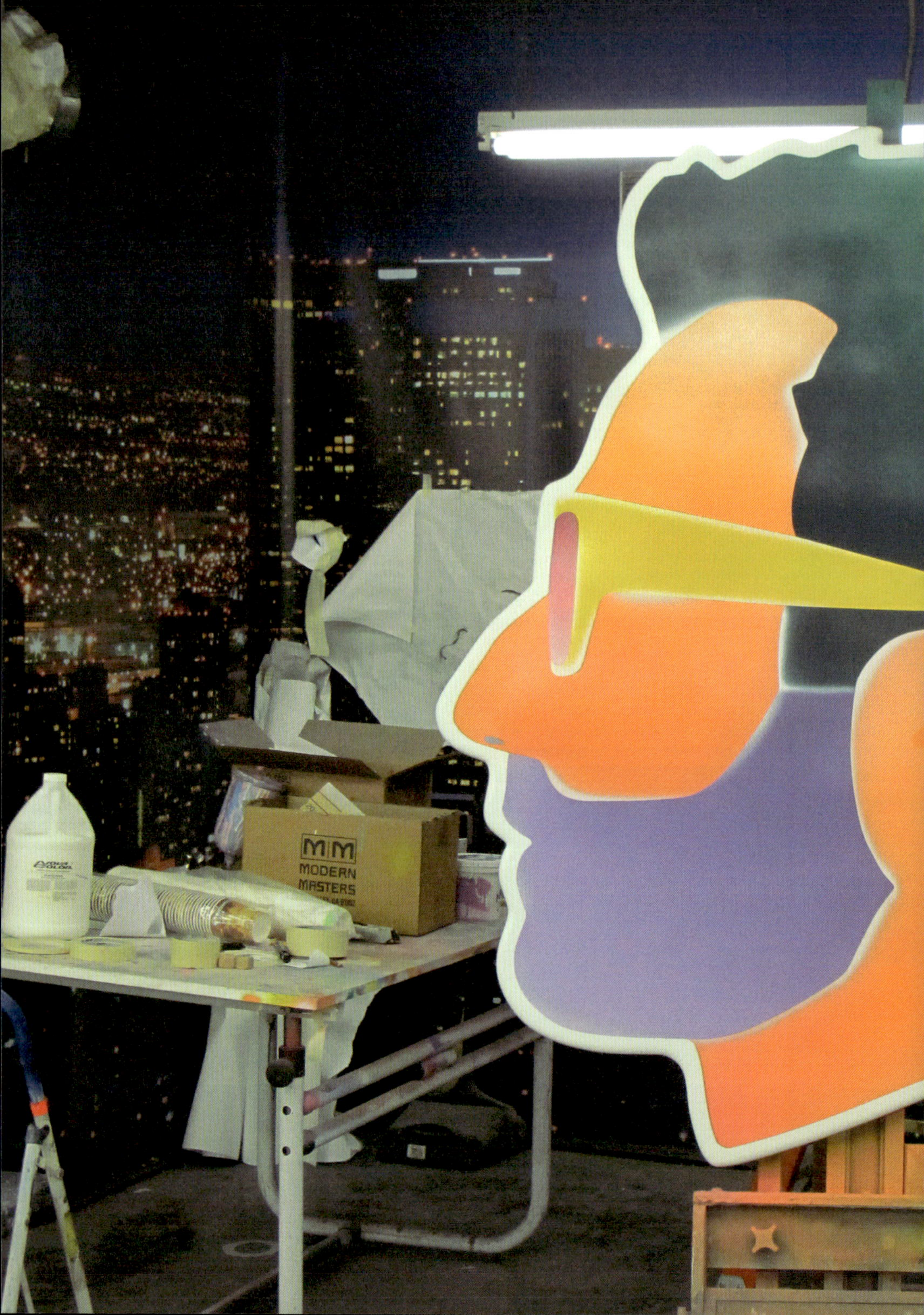
MM
MODERN
MASTERS

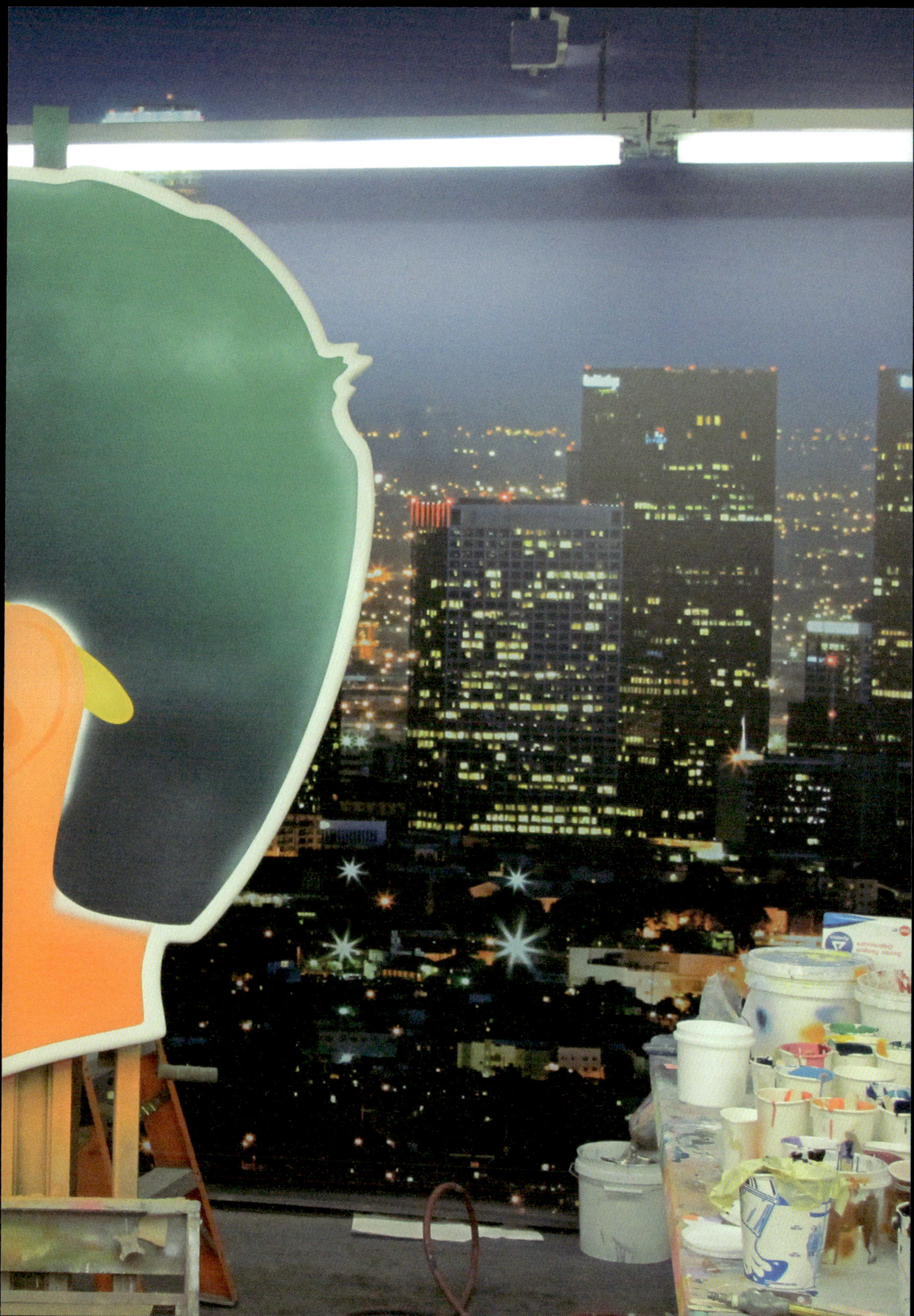

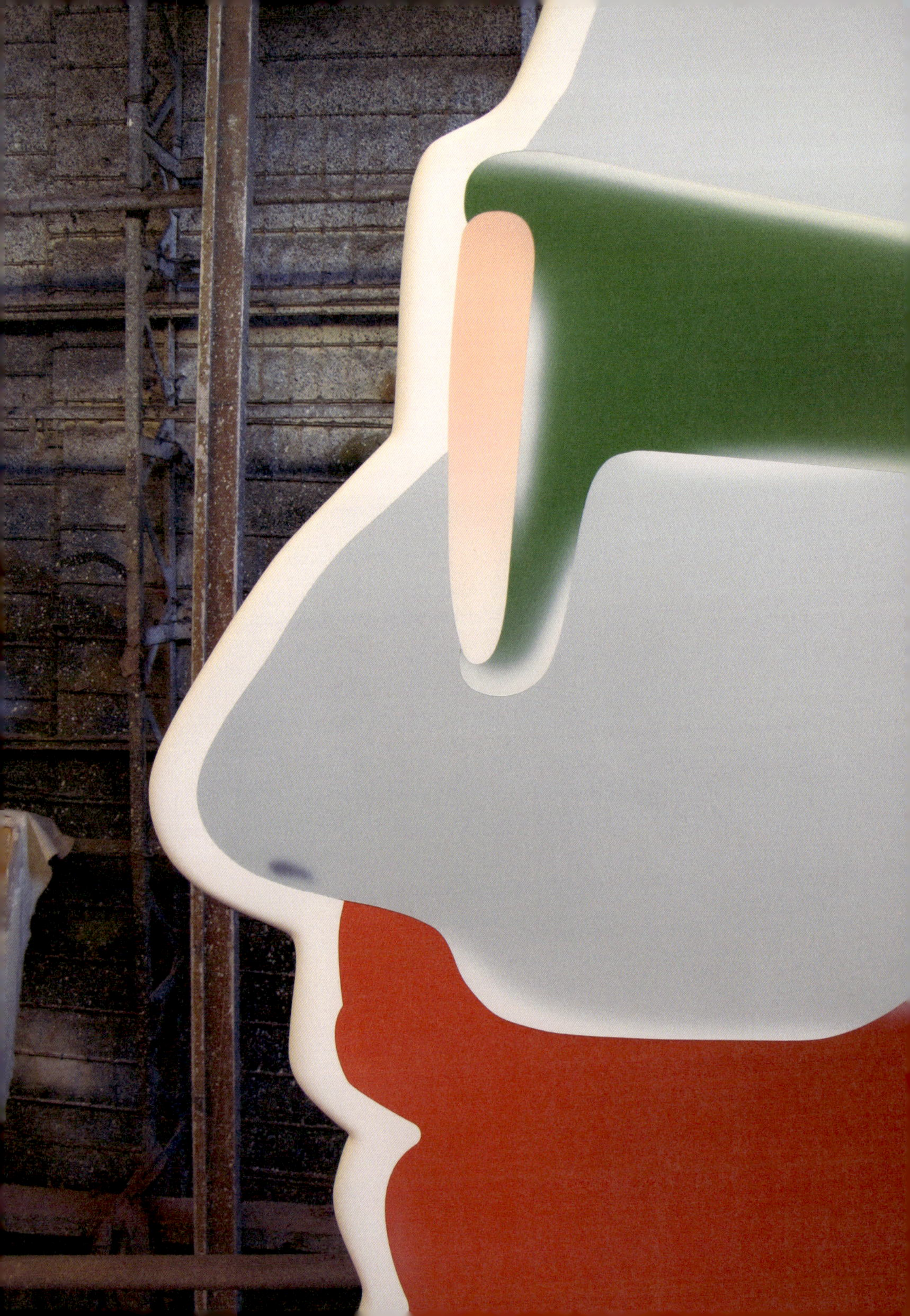

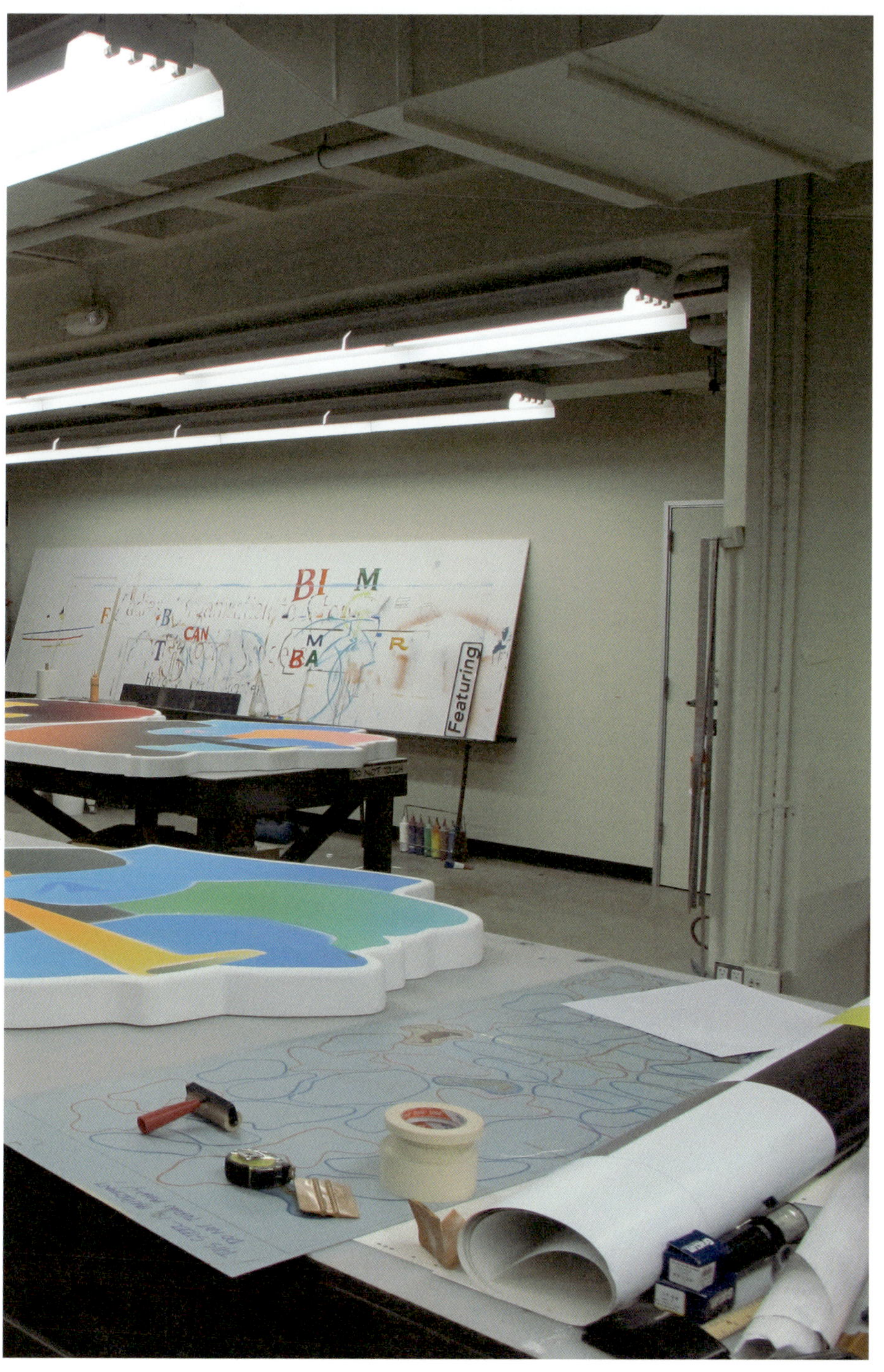
BI M
B
CAN
T
M
BA R
Featuring

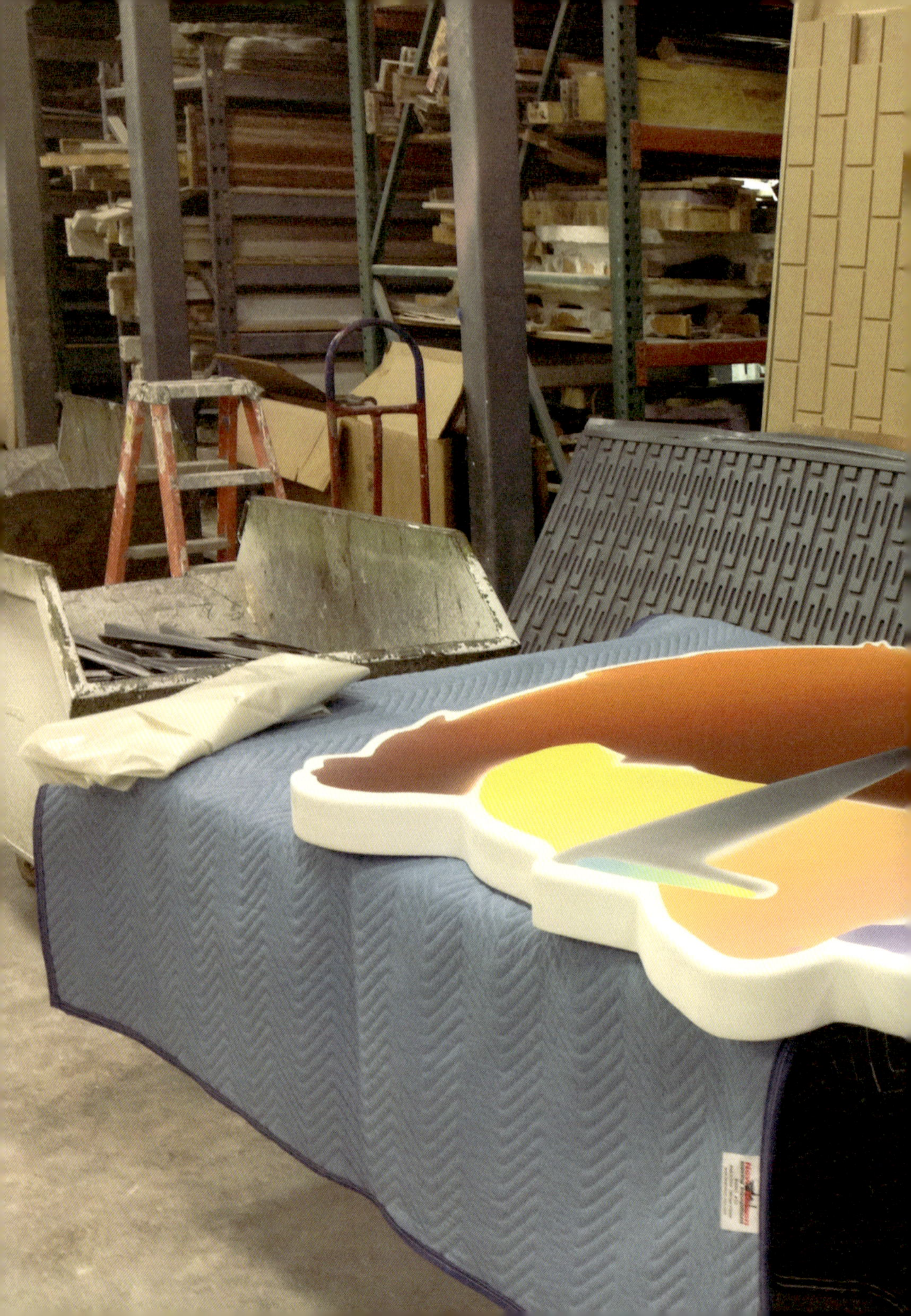

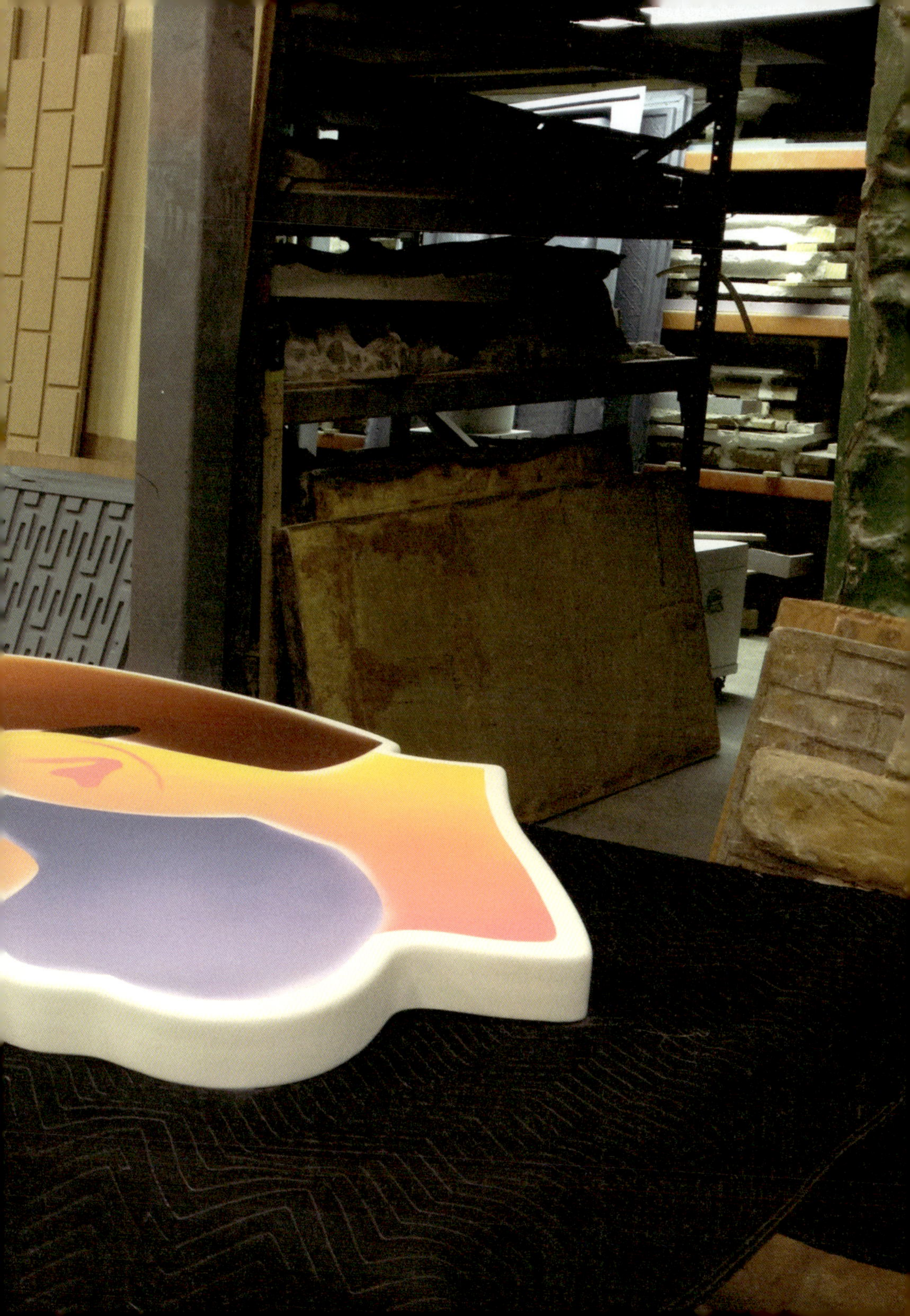

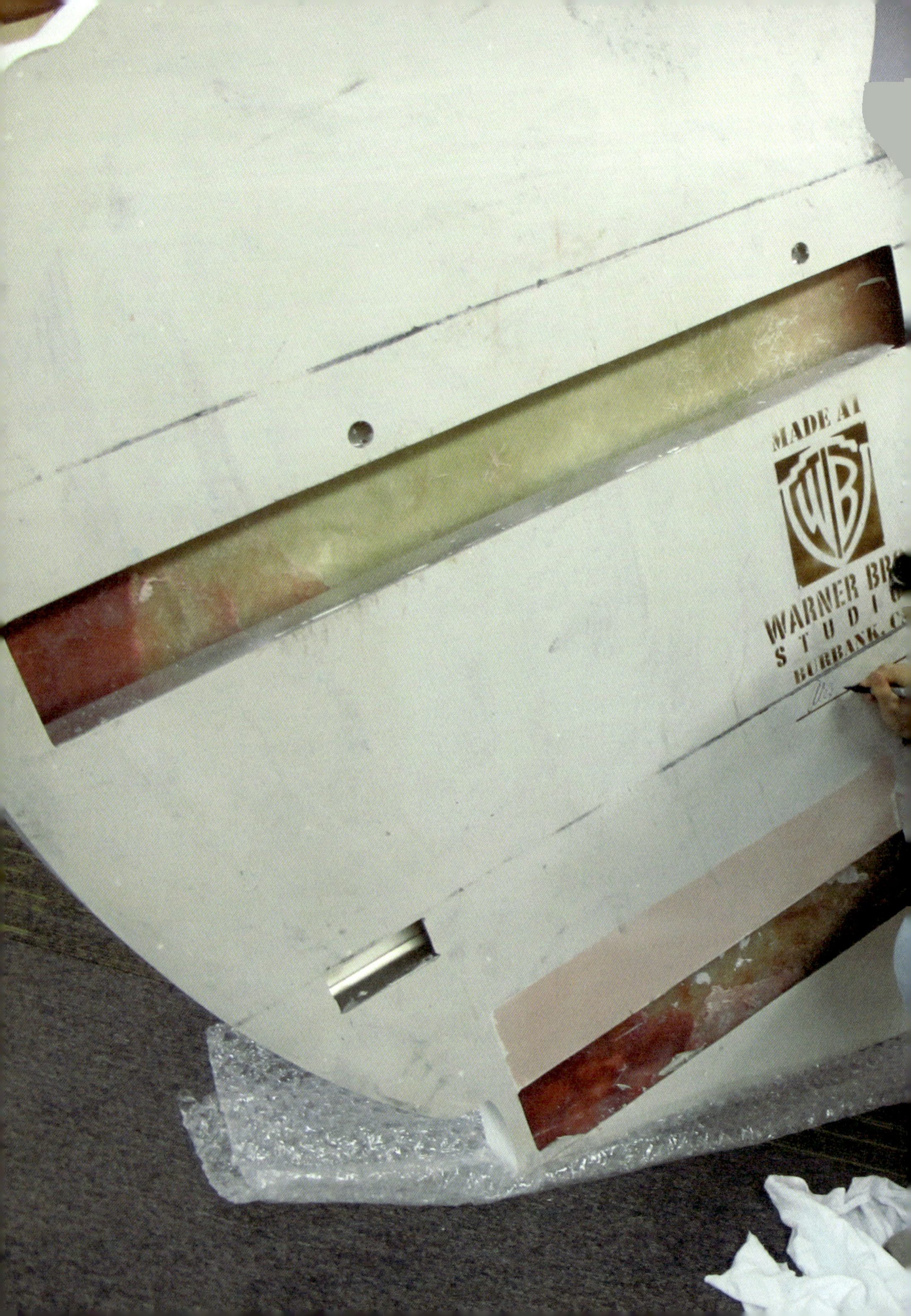
MADE AT
WARNER BR
STUDIO
BURBANK, C

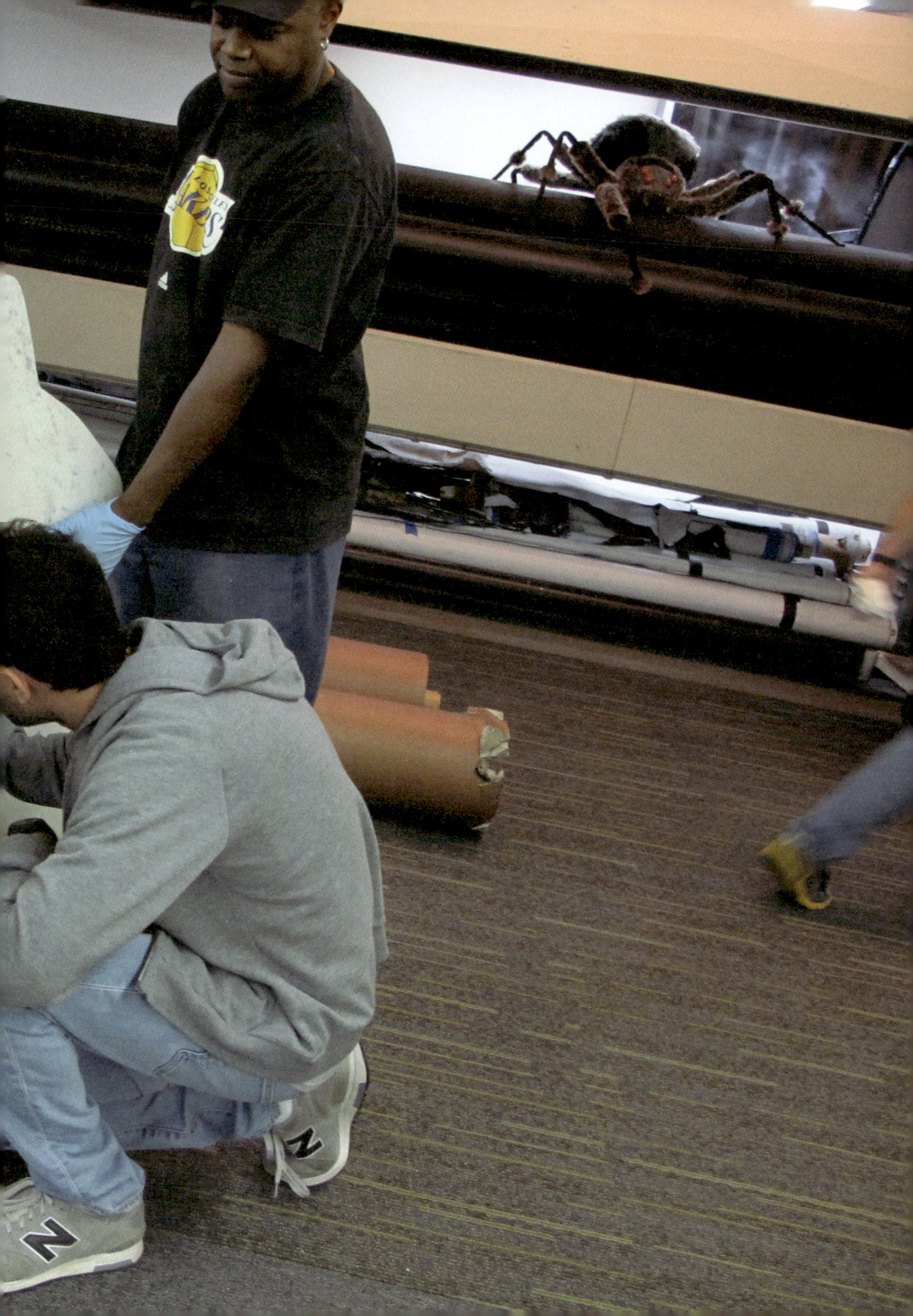

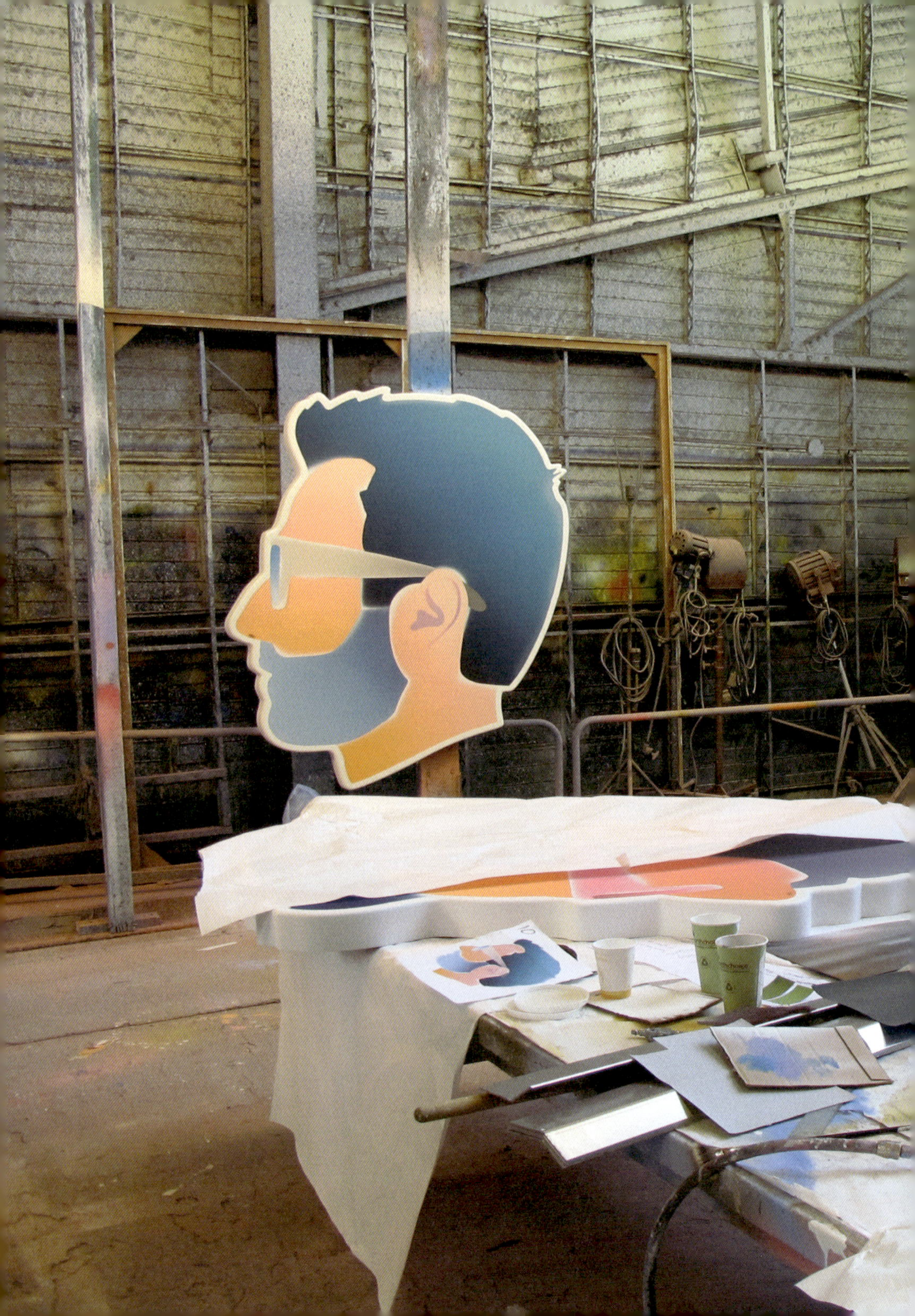

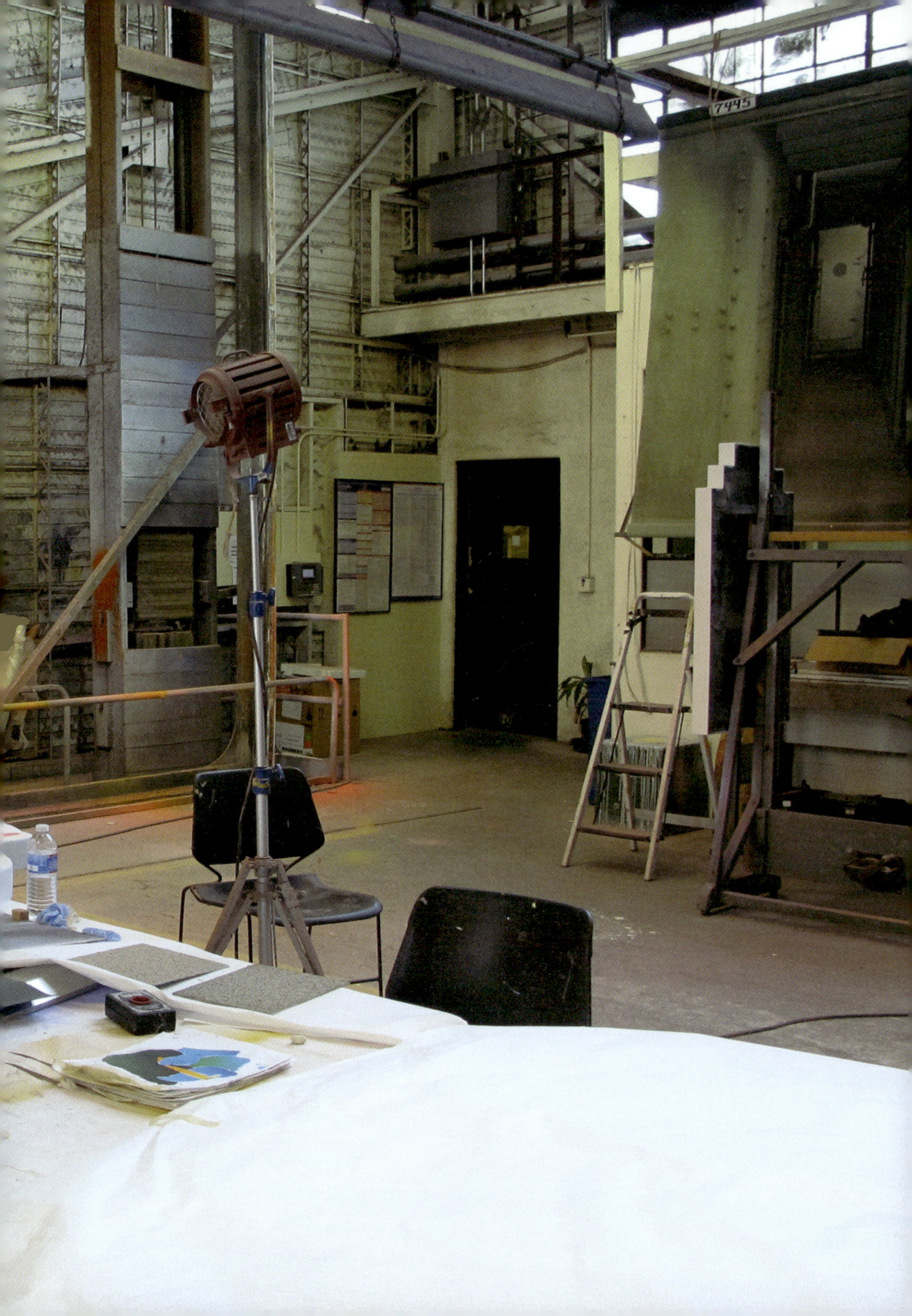

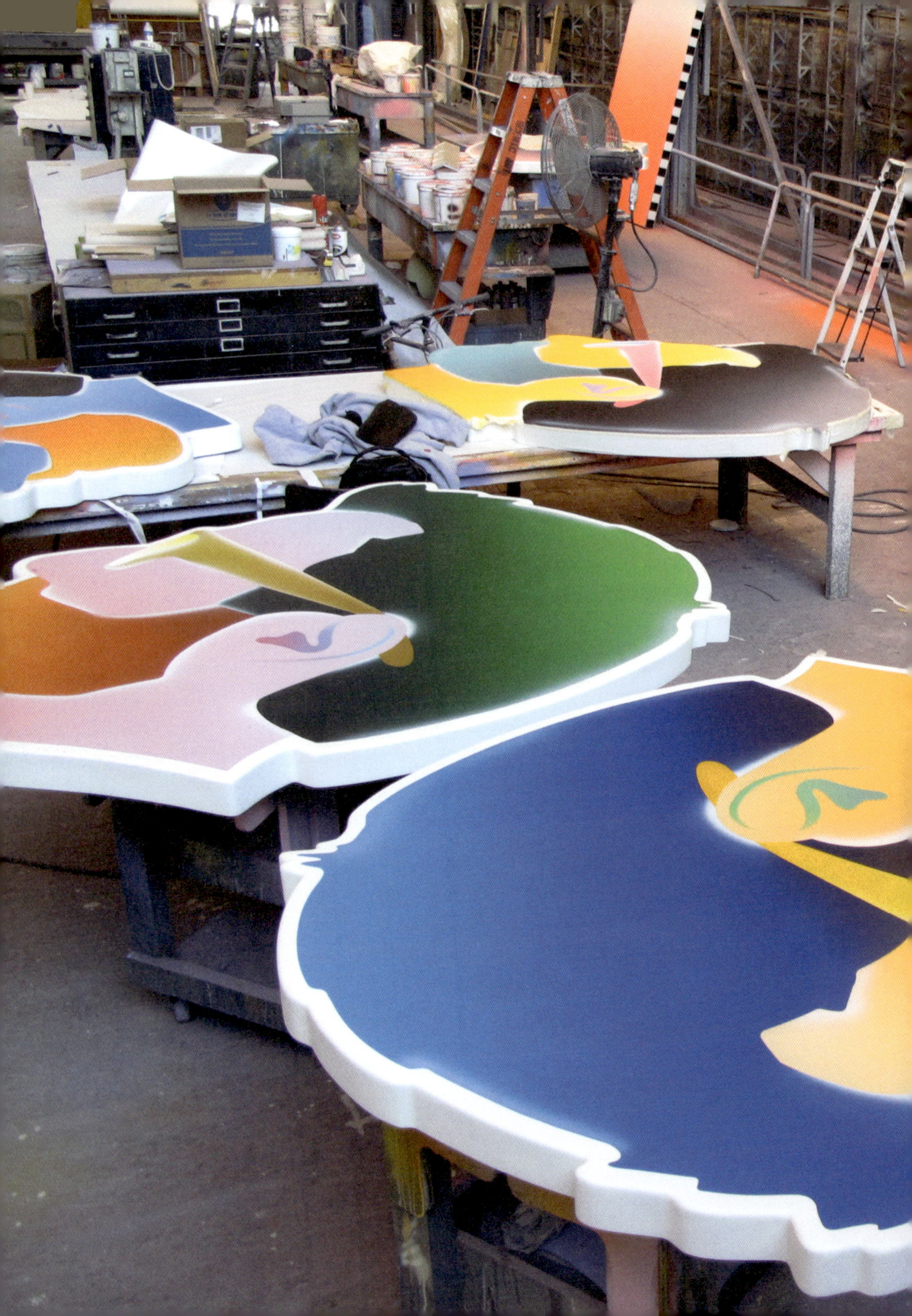

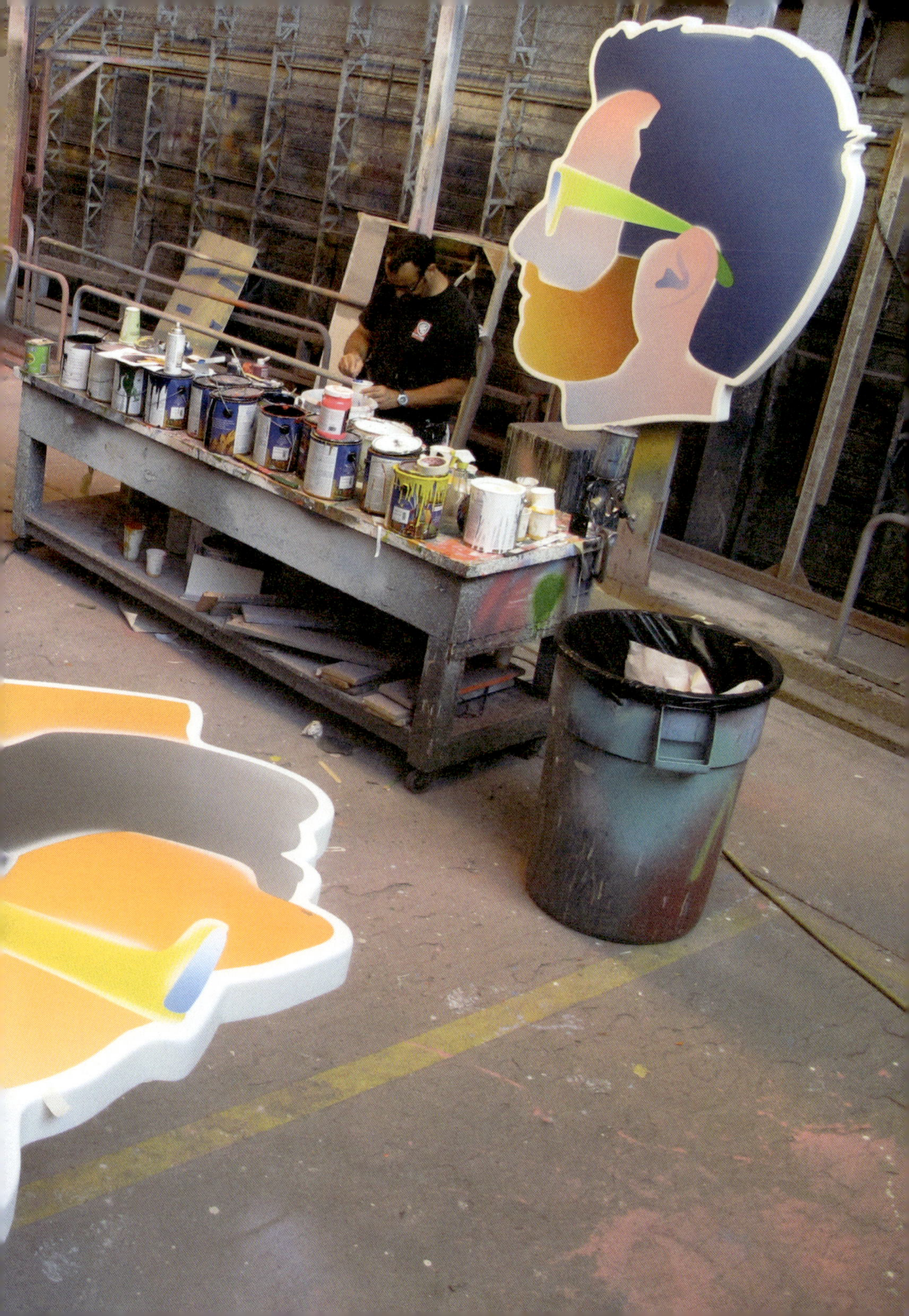

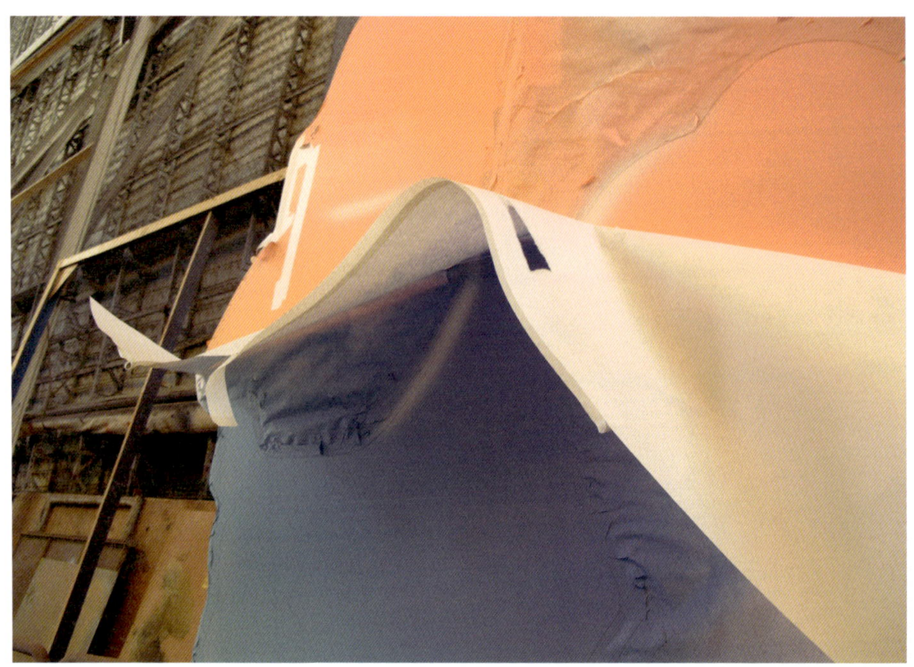

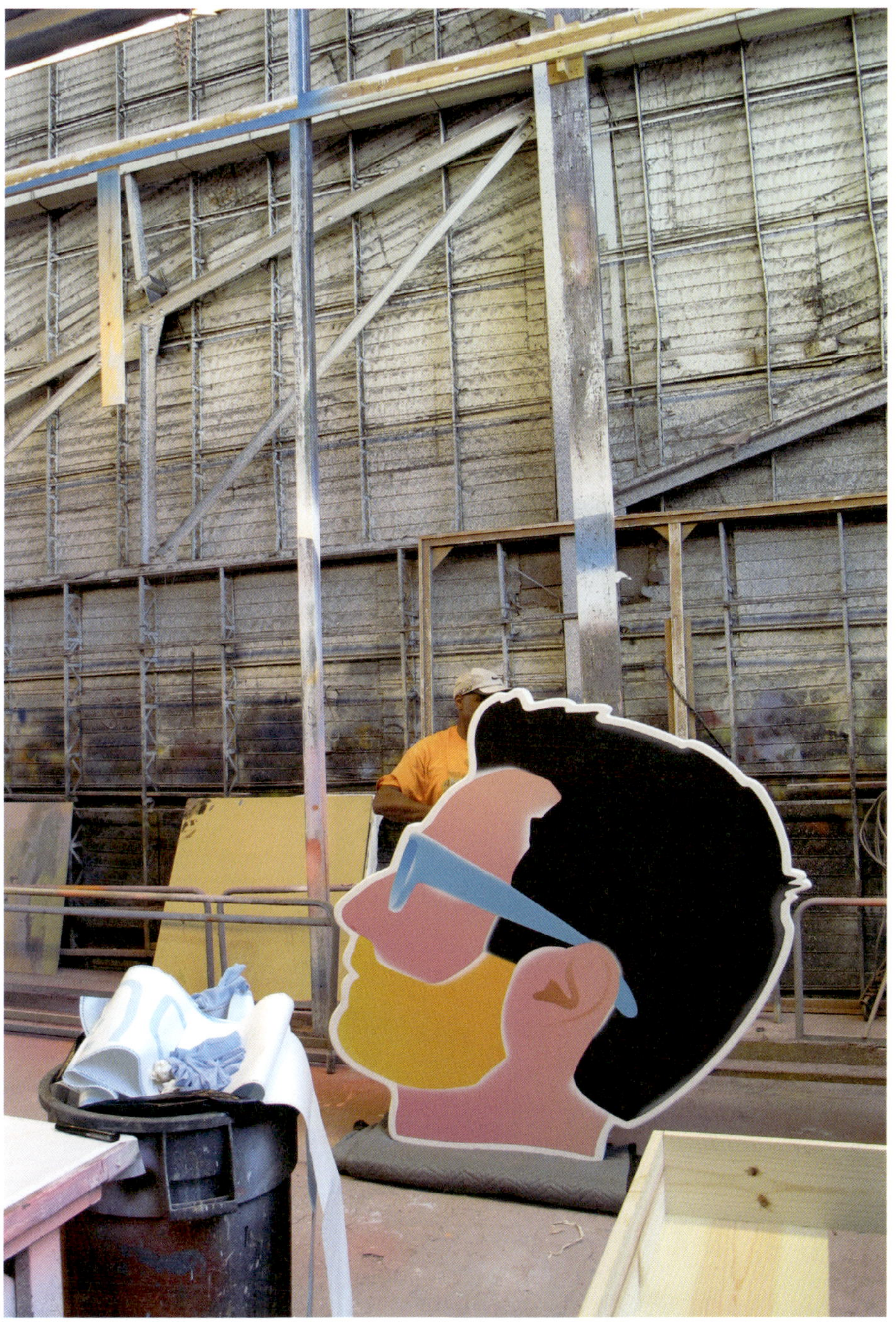

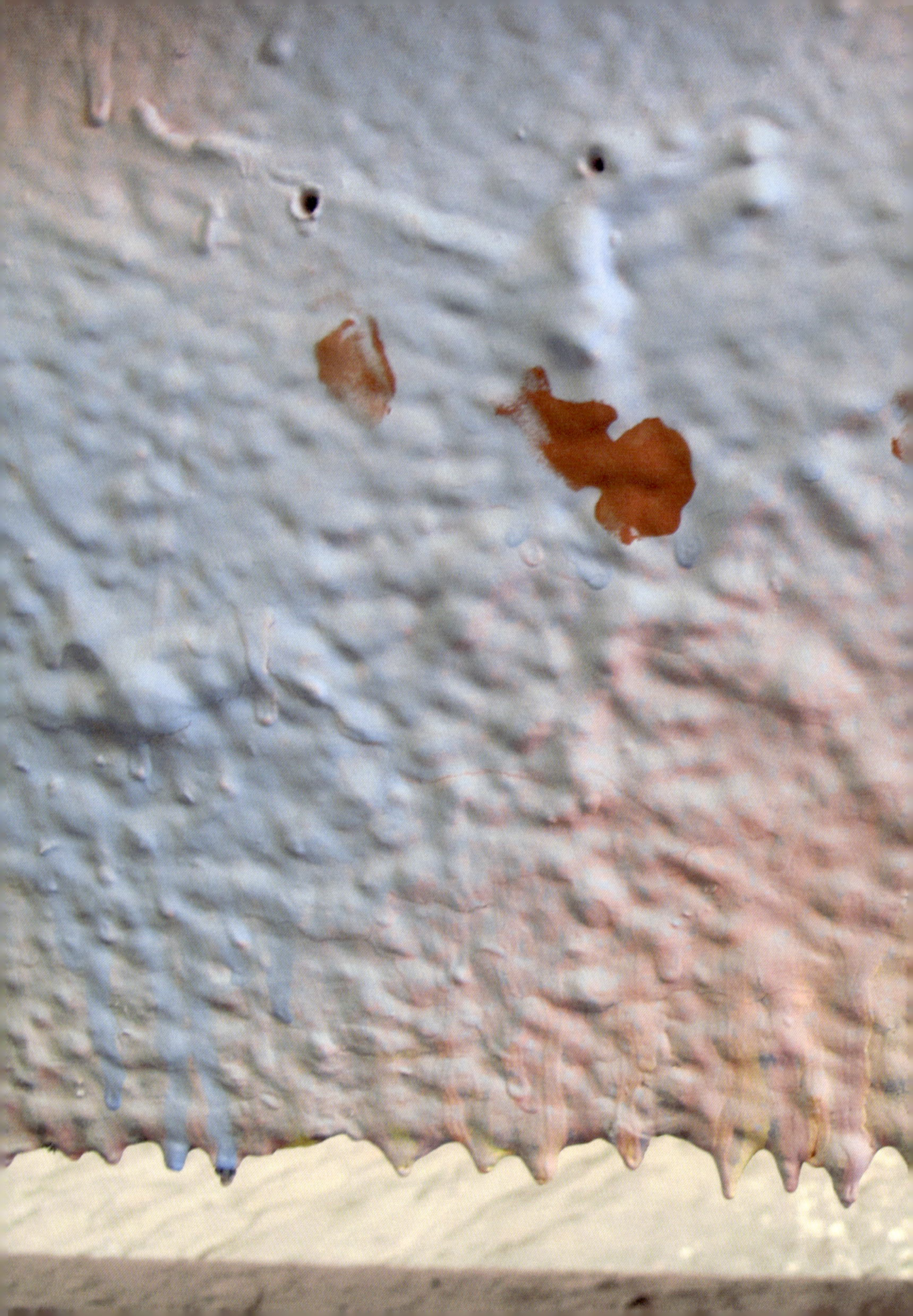

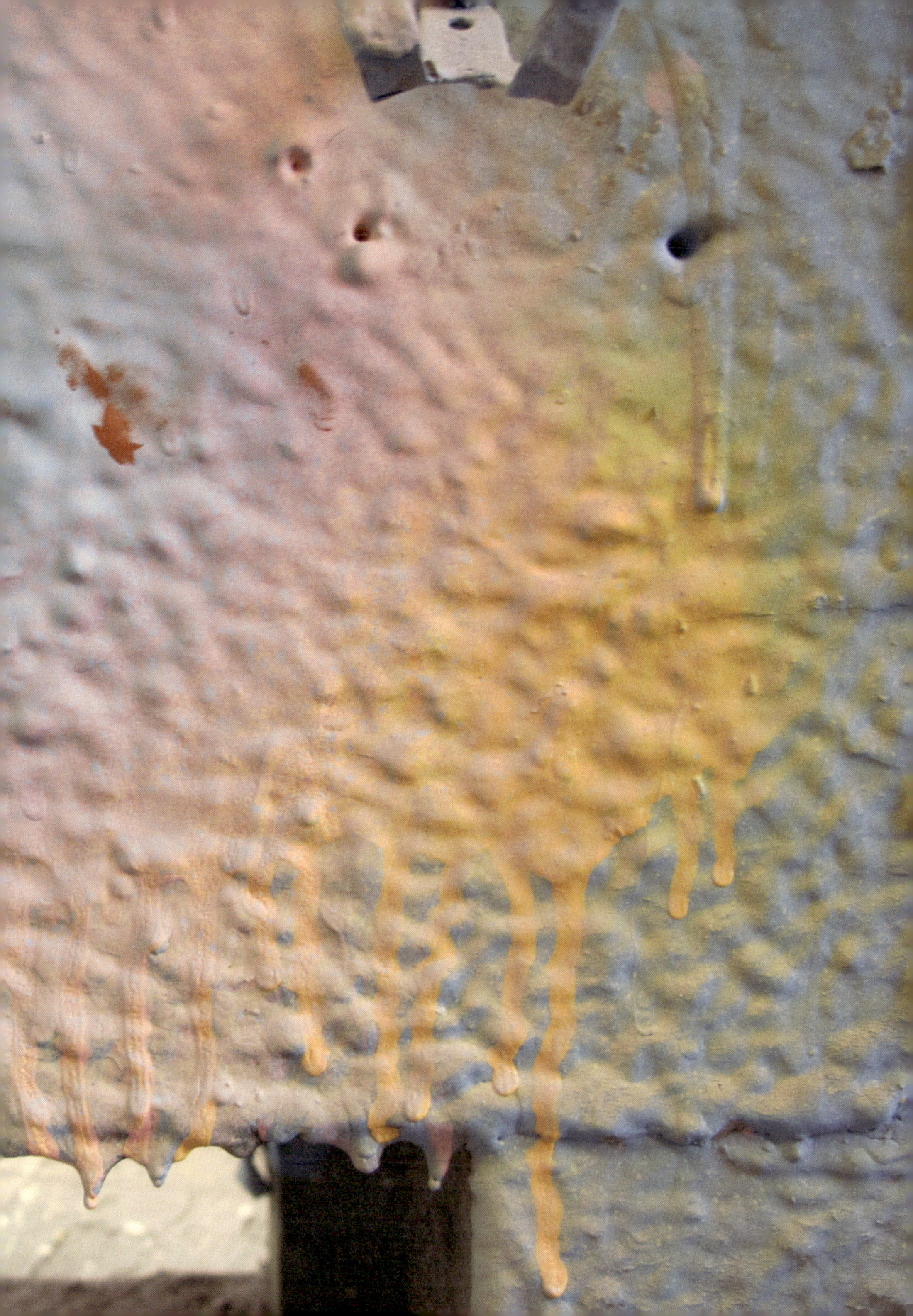

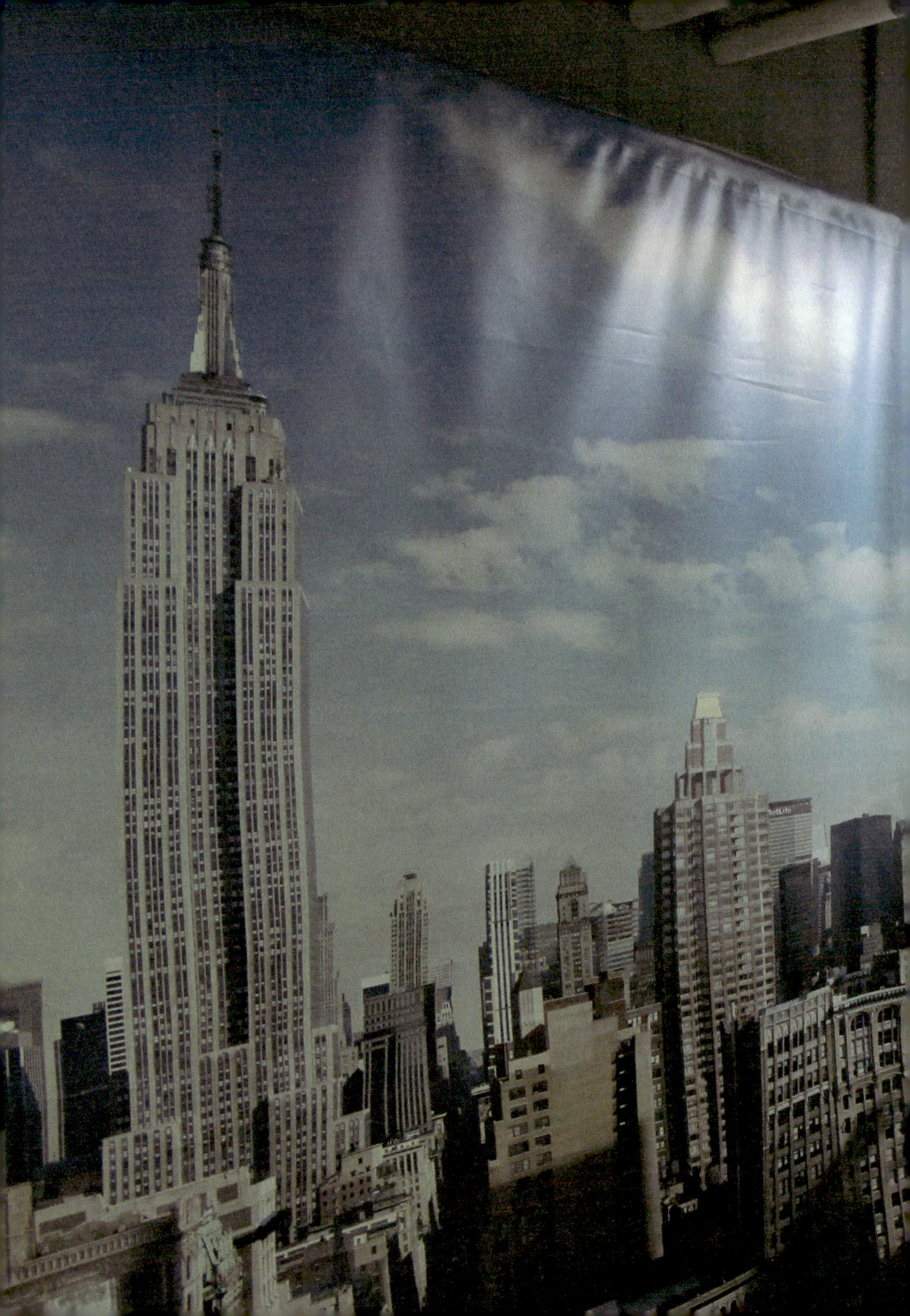

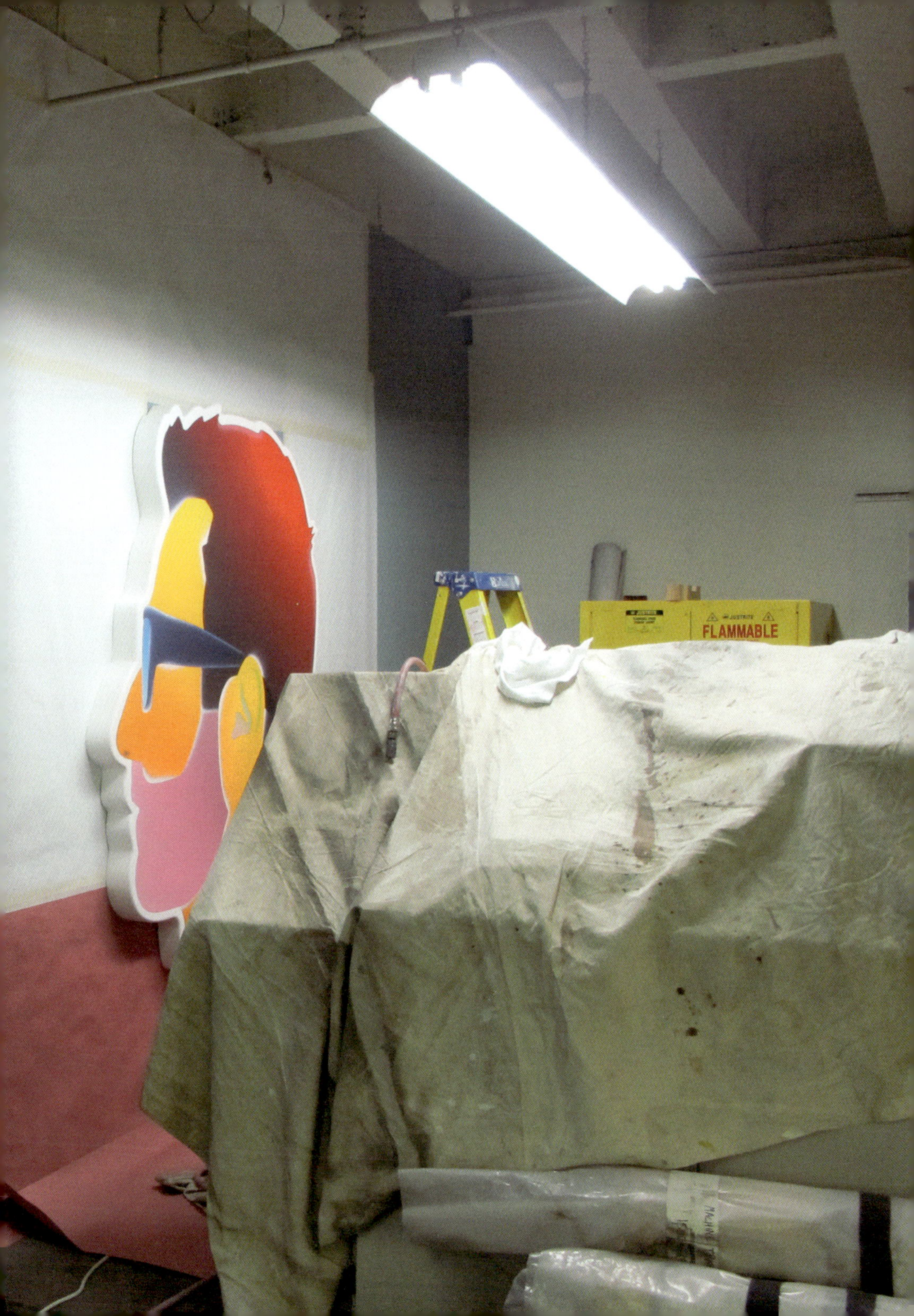

FLAMMABLE

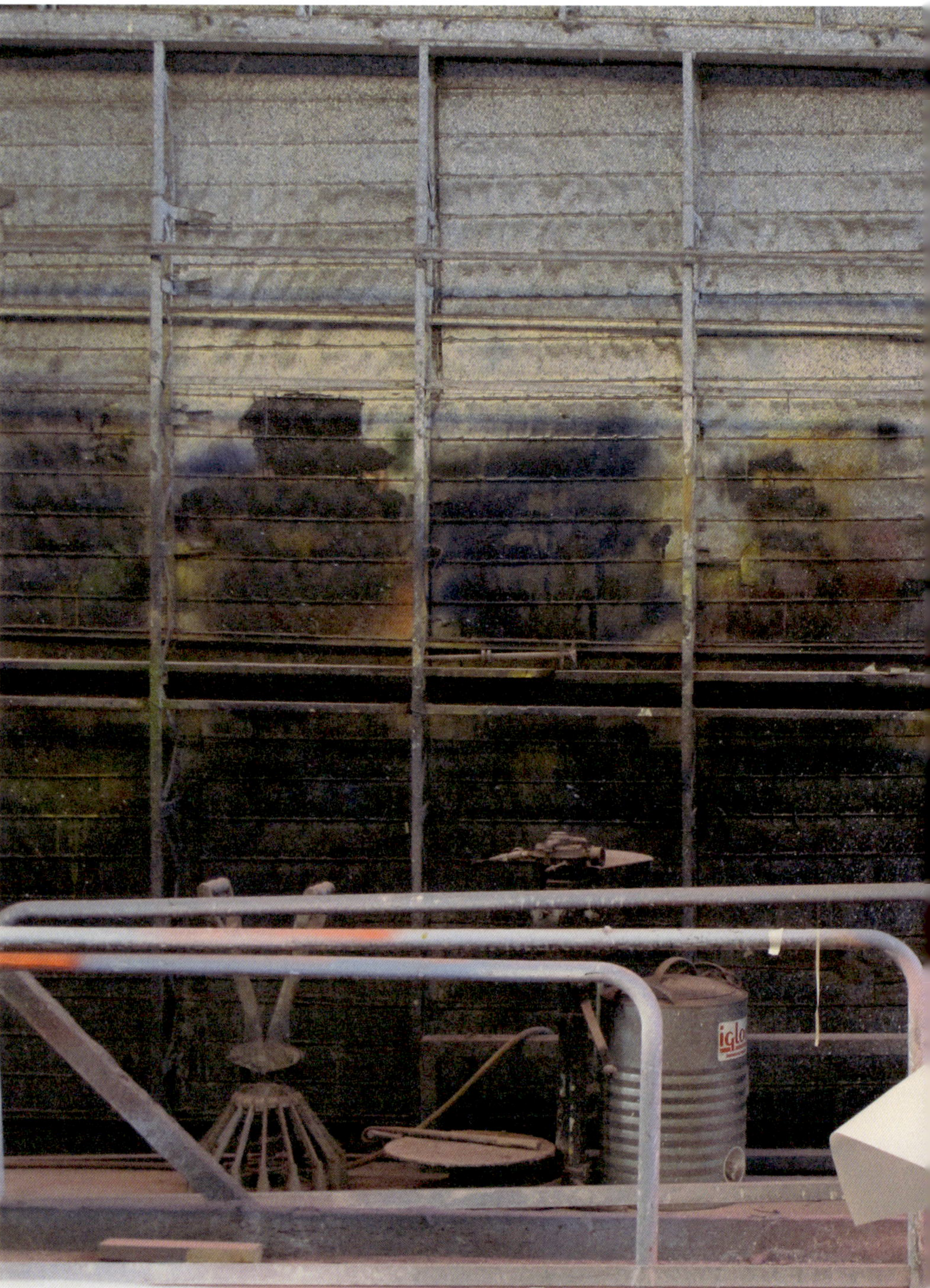

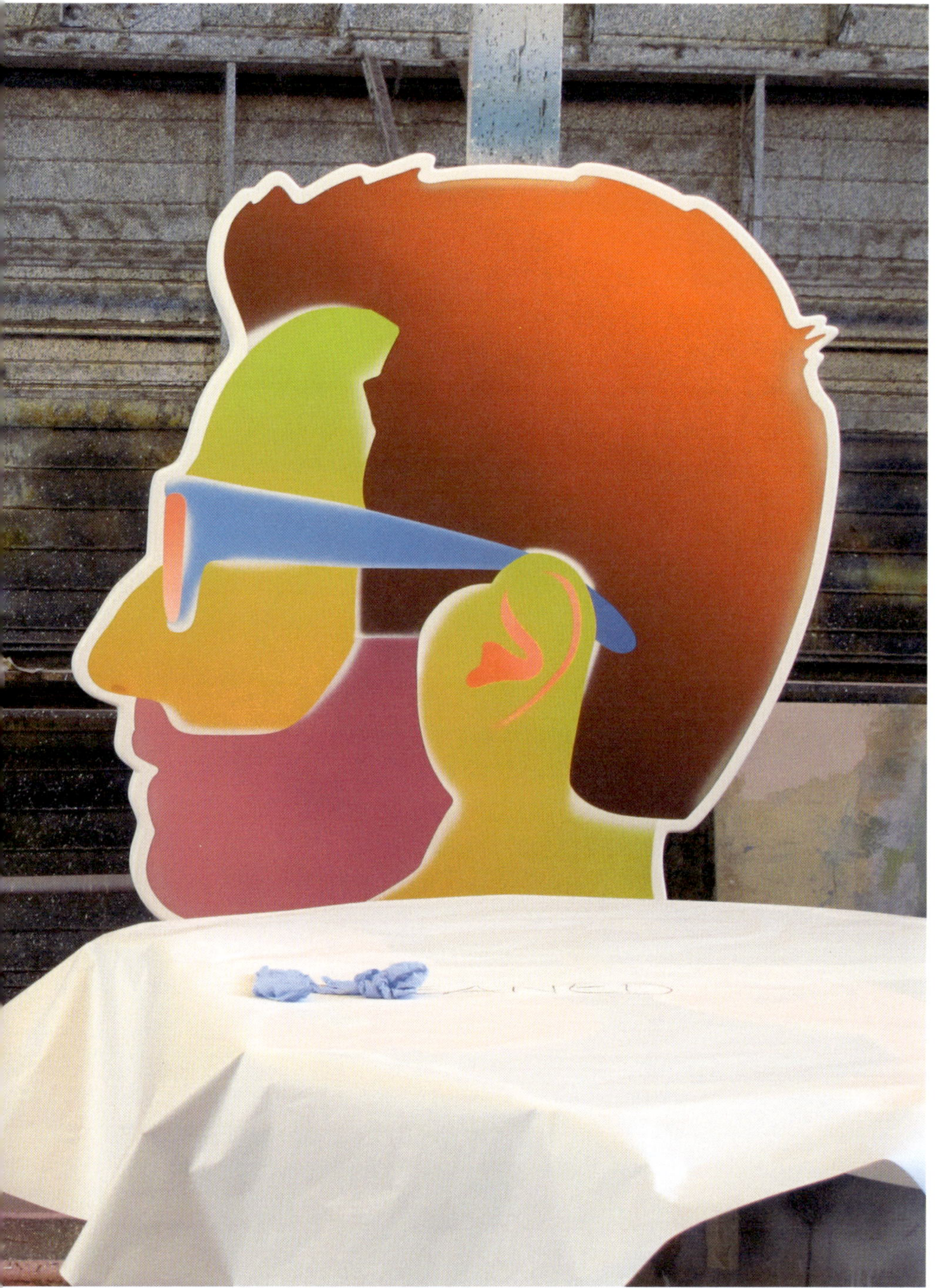

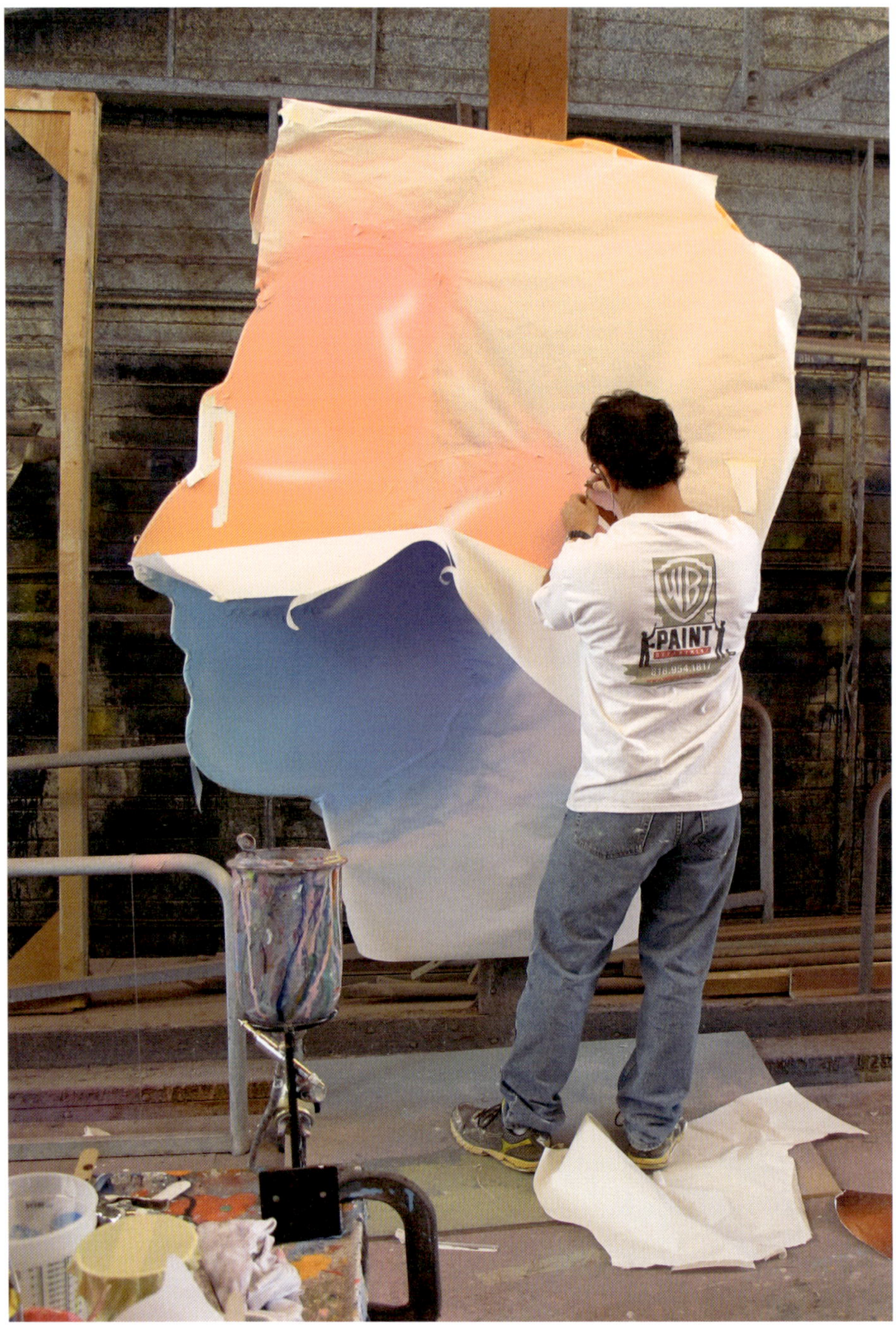

WB
PAINT

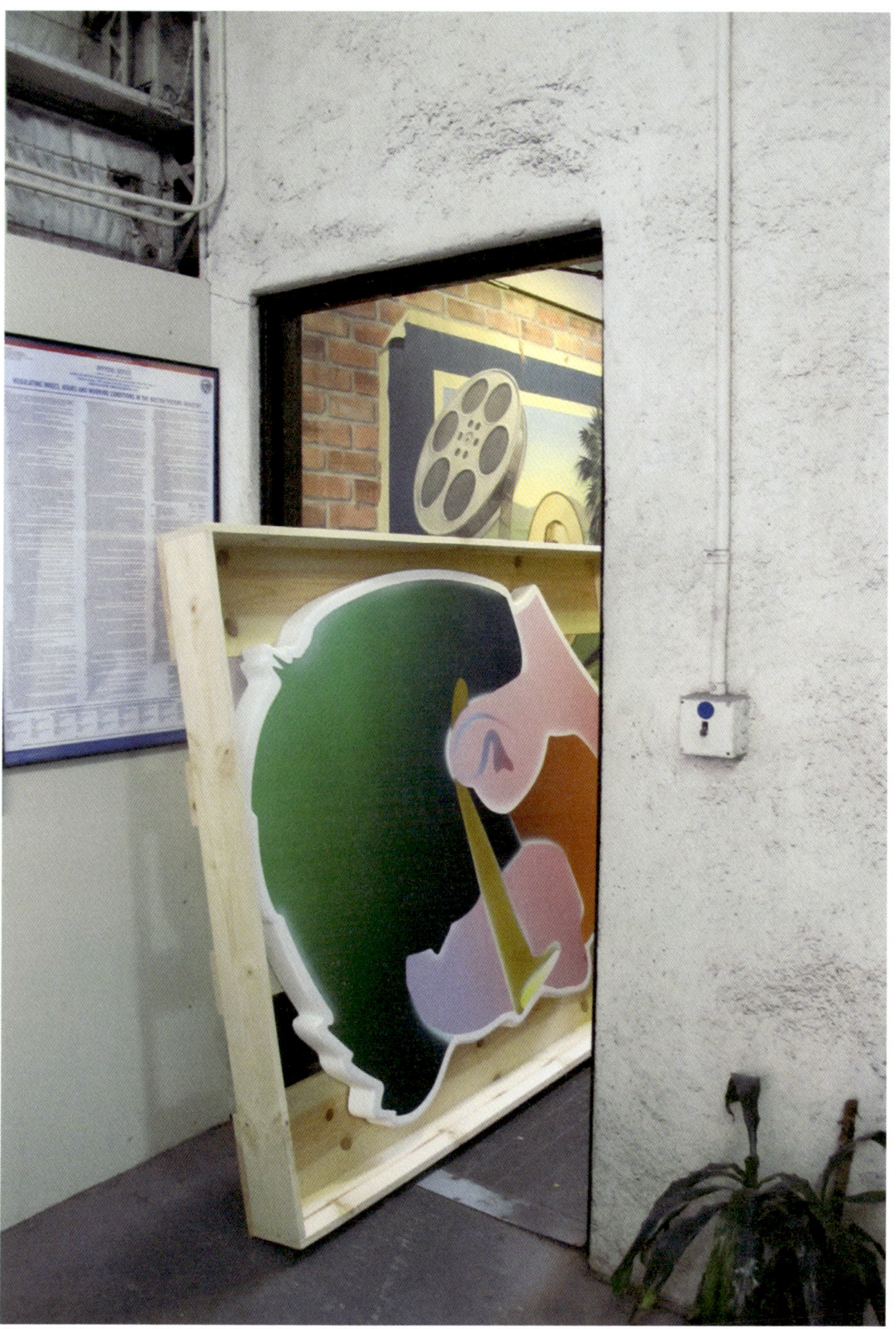

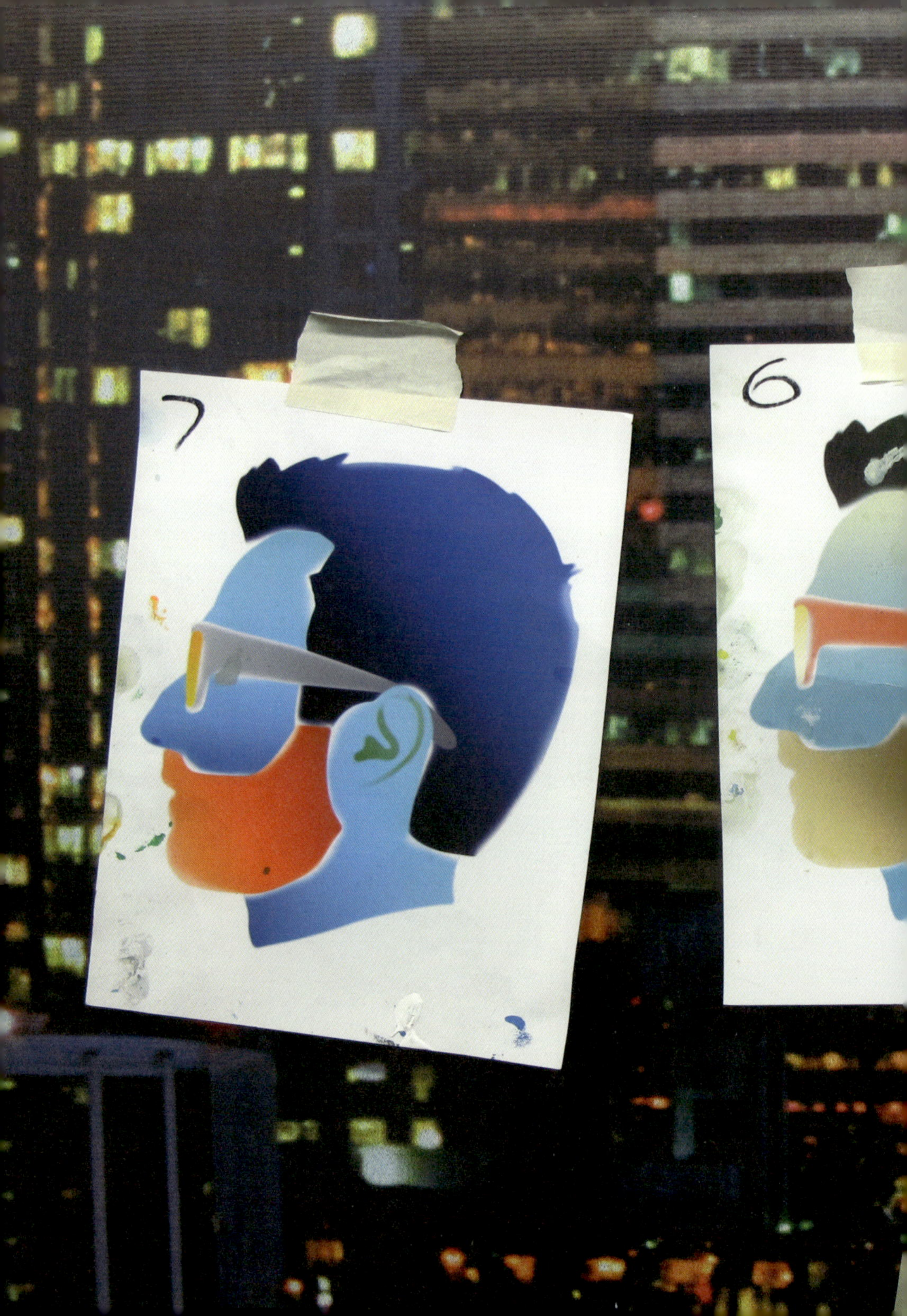
7
6

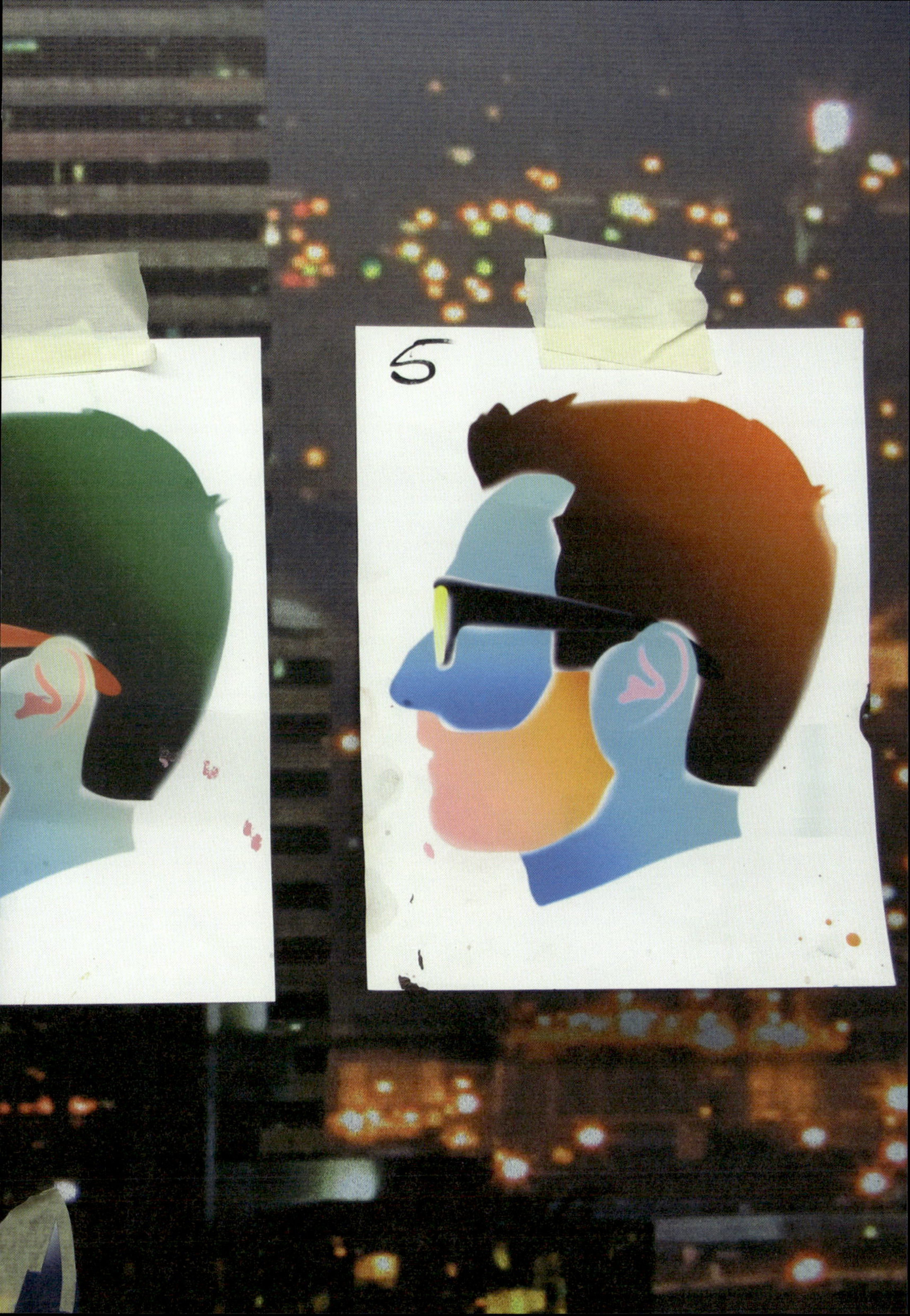
5

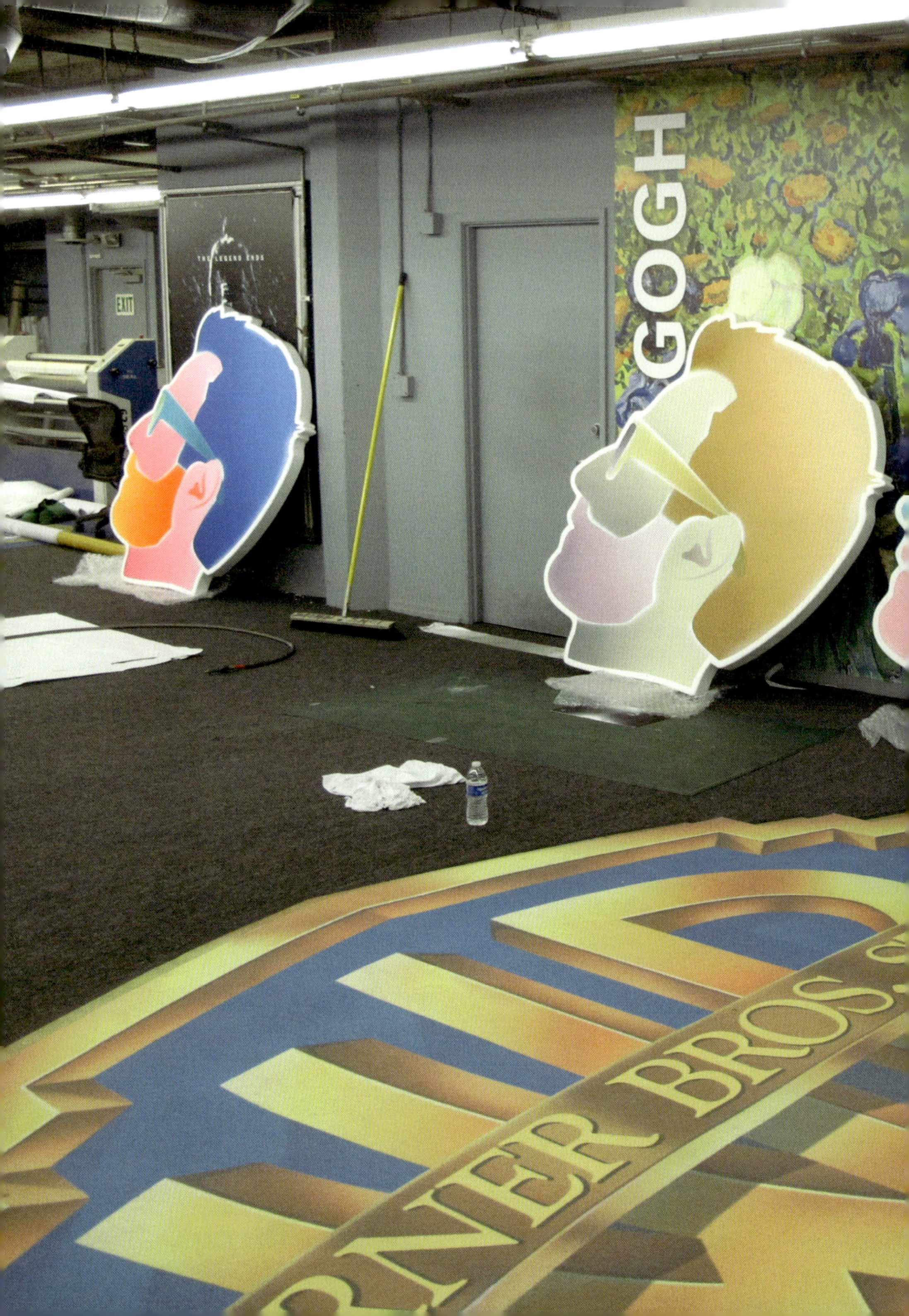
EXIT
GOGH
RNER BROS

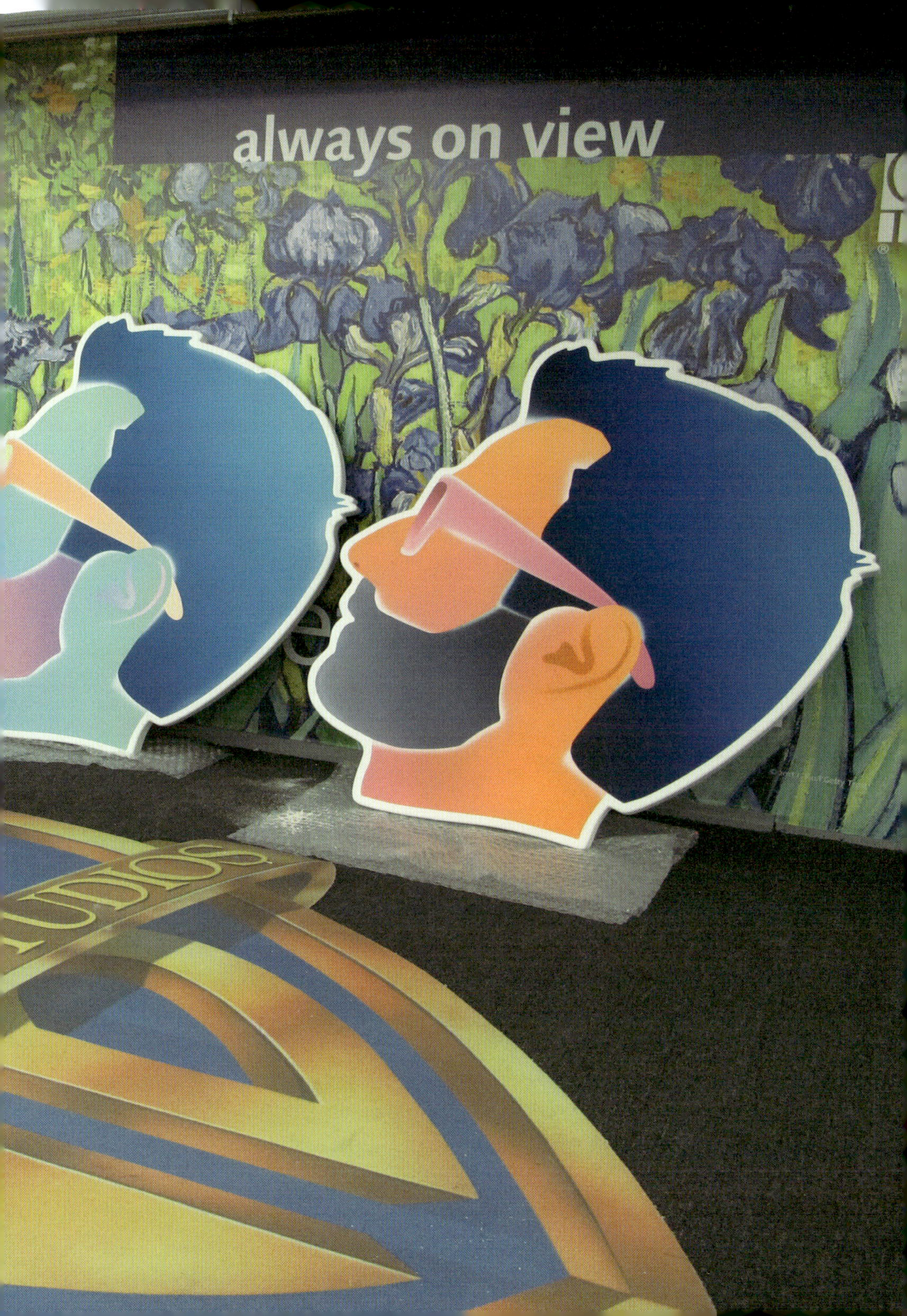

always on view

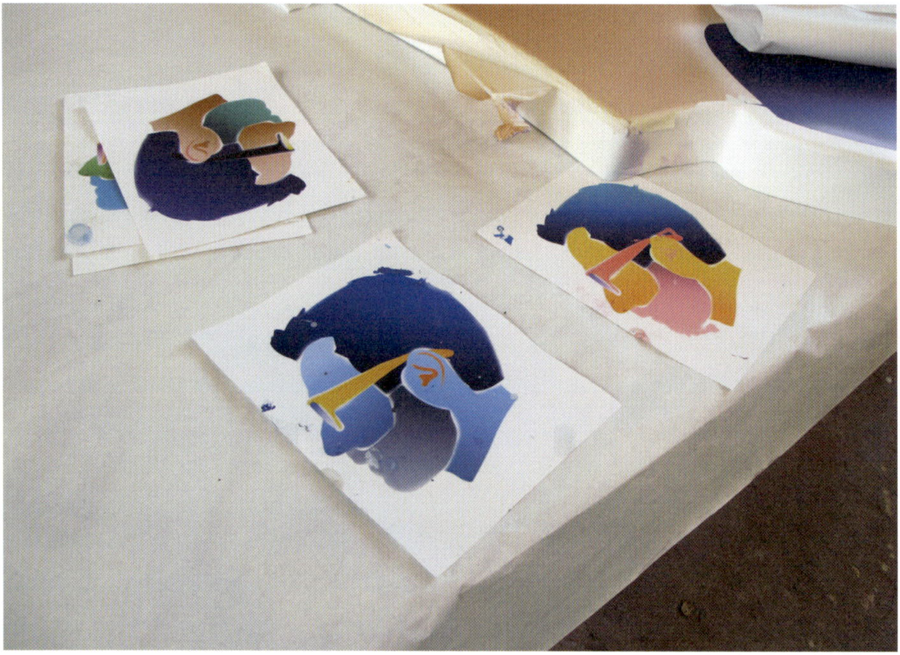

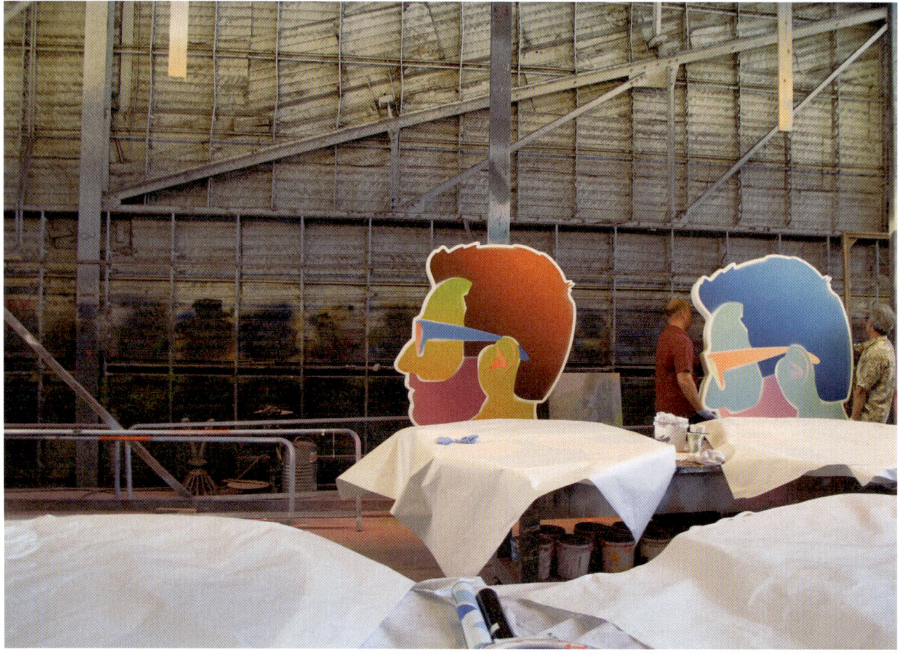

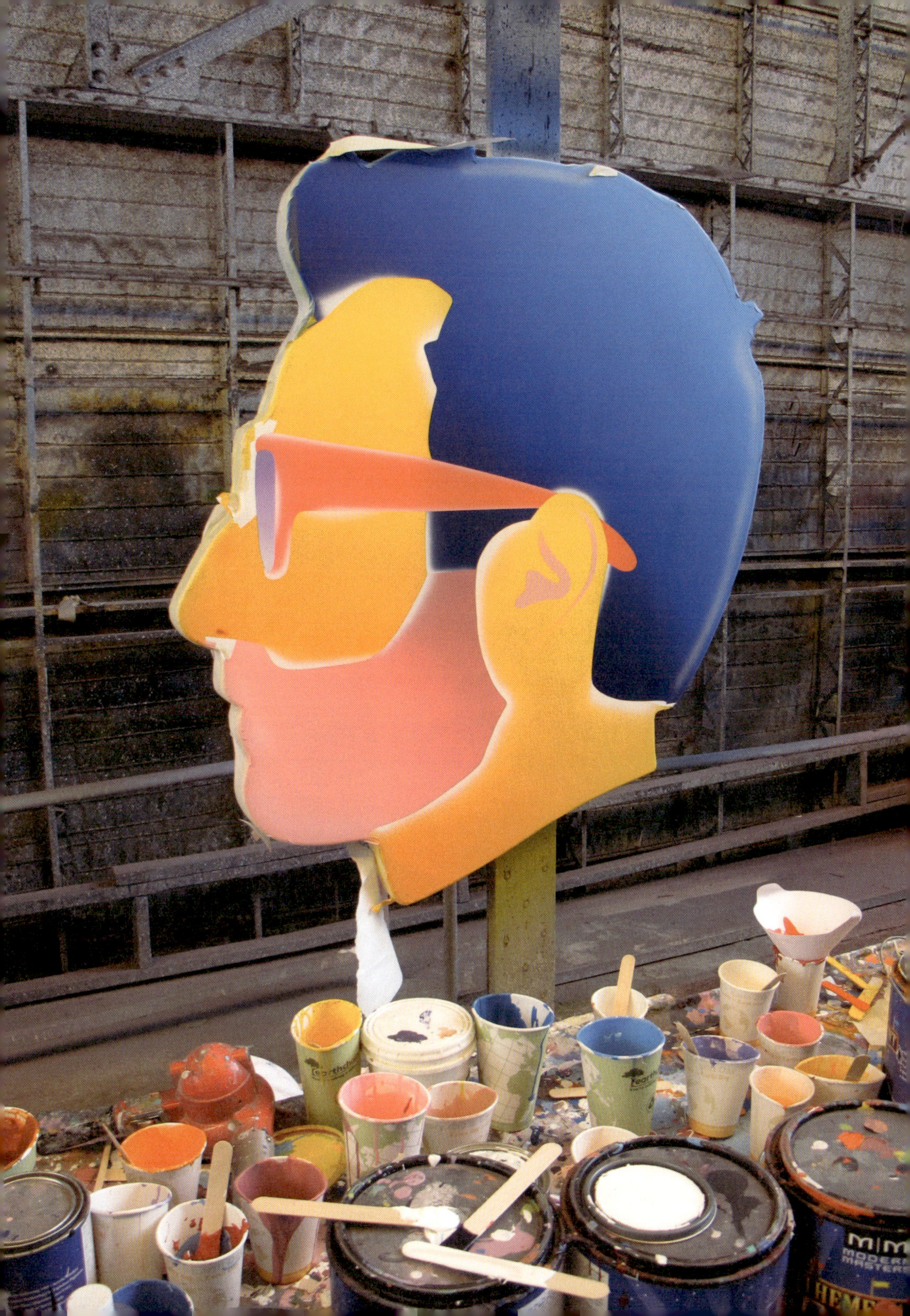

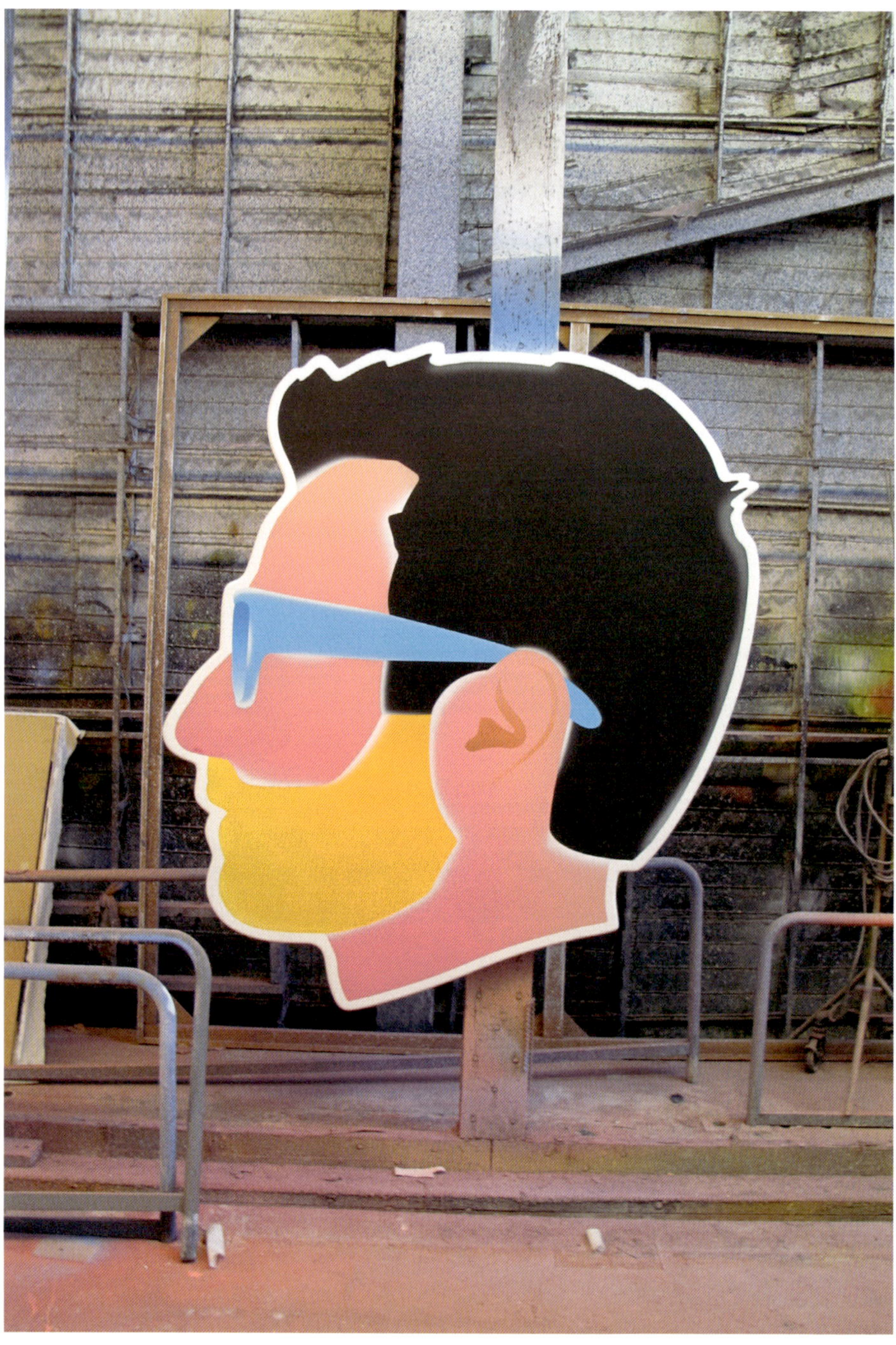

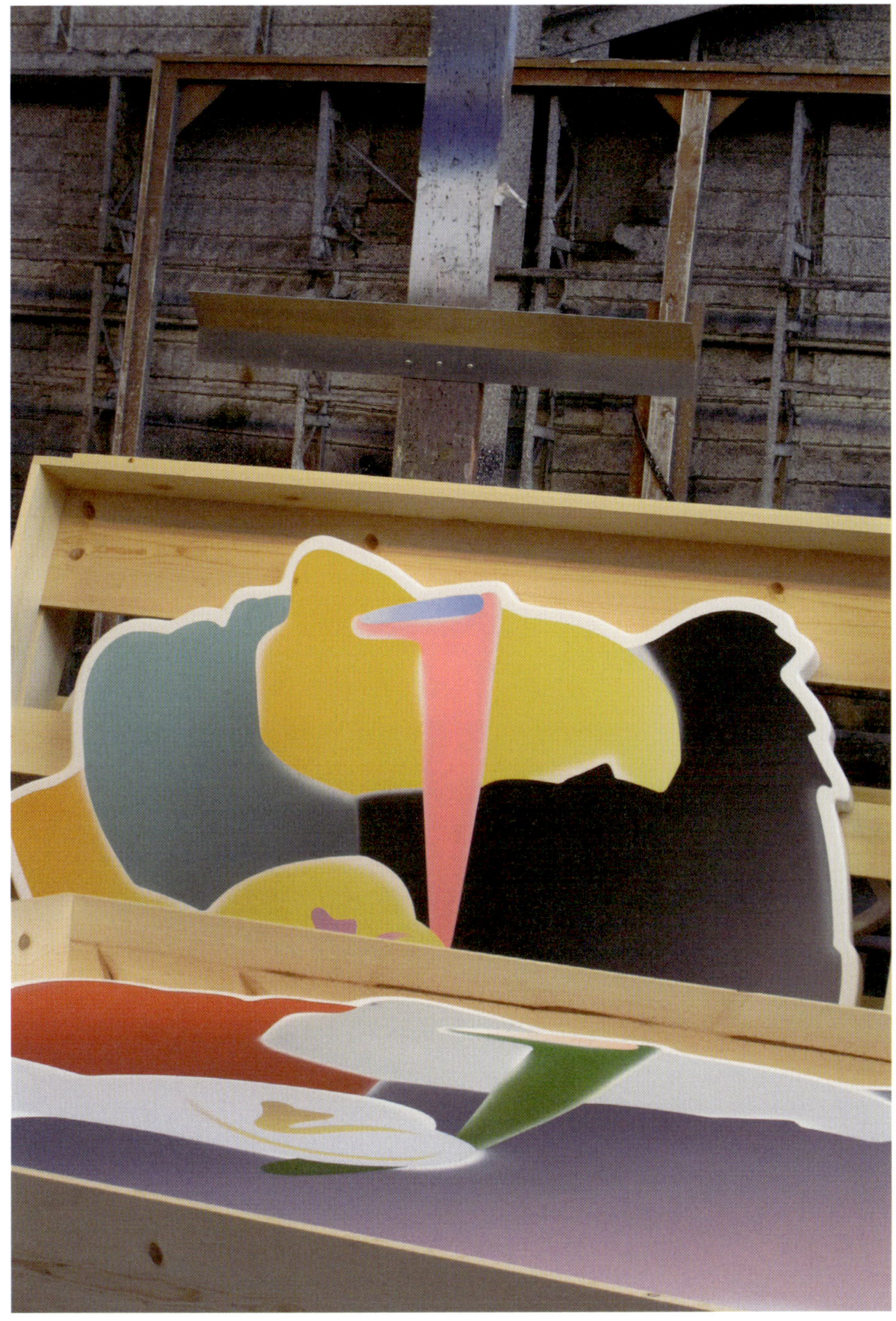

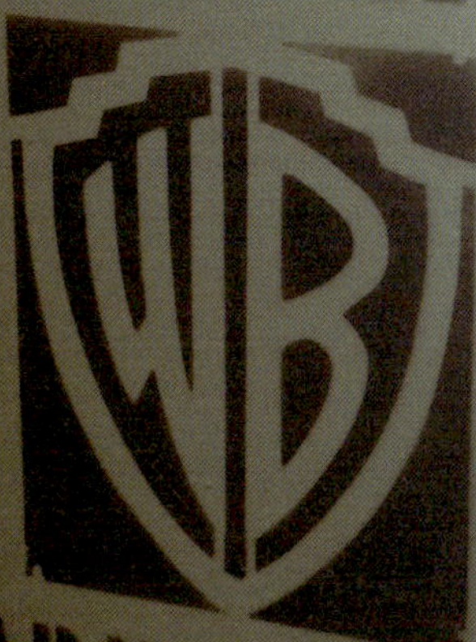
MADE AT
WARNER BROS.
STUDIOS
BURBANK, CA.

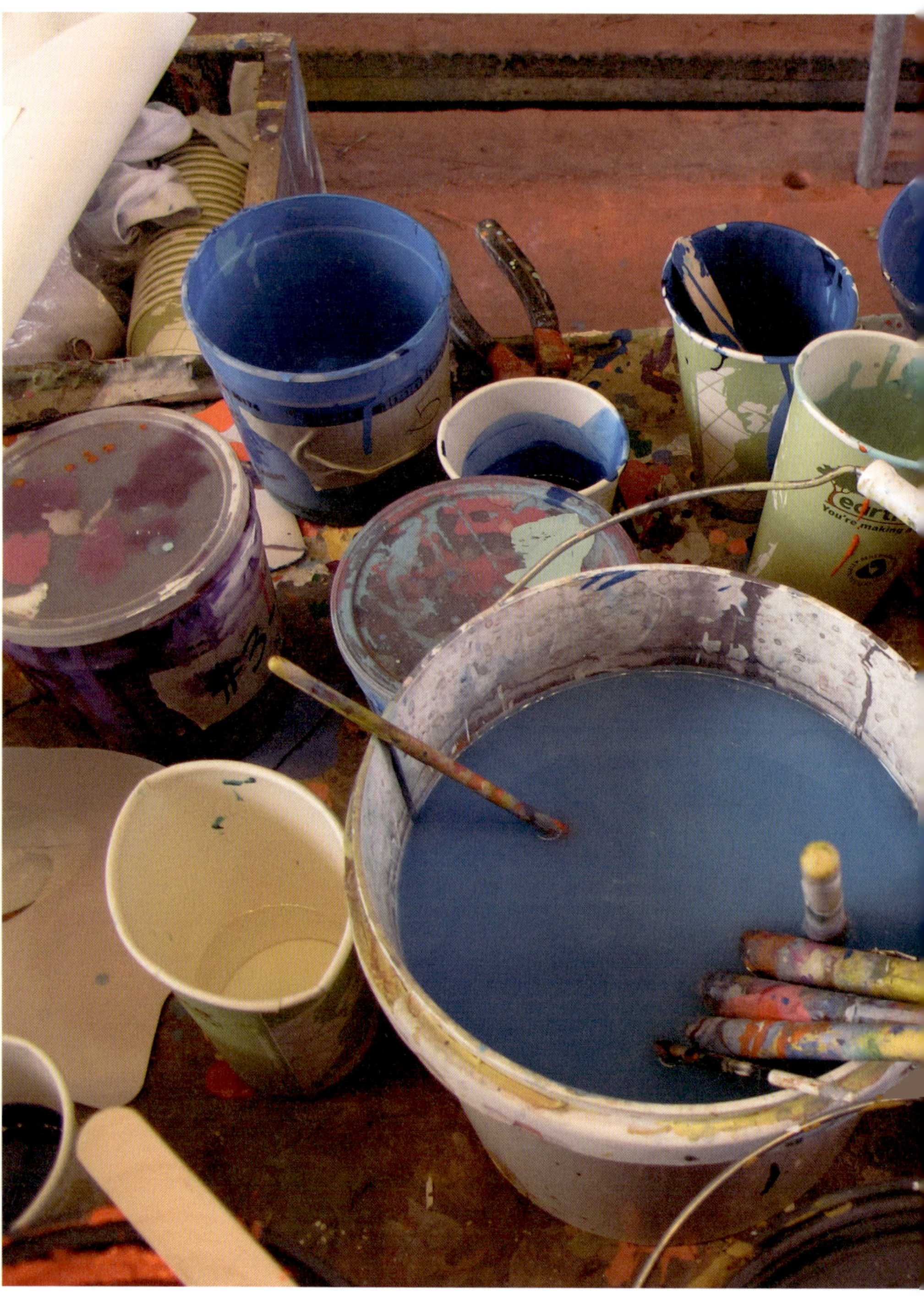

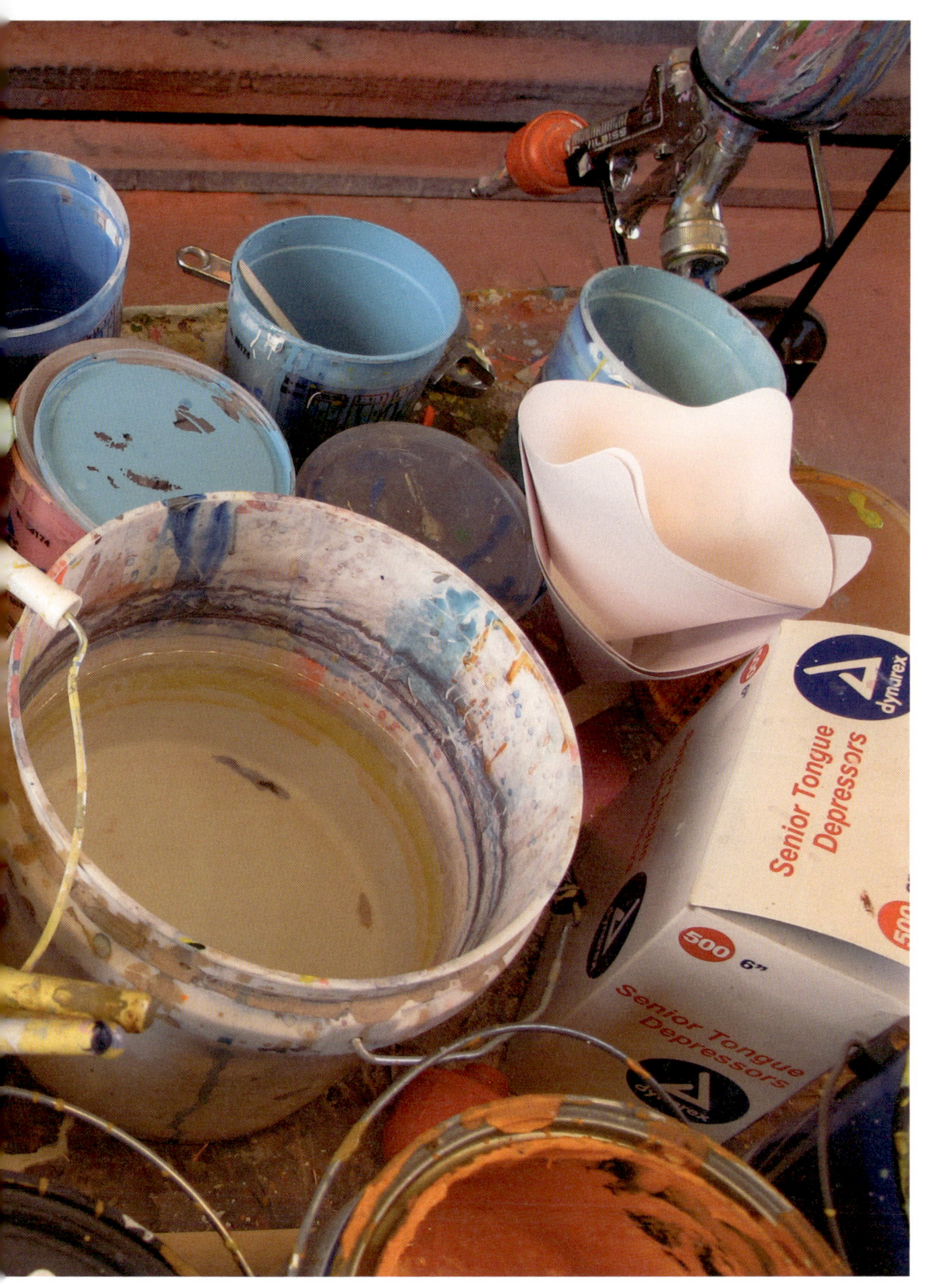

dynarex
Senior Tongue Depressors
500
6"
Senior Tongue Depressors
dynarex

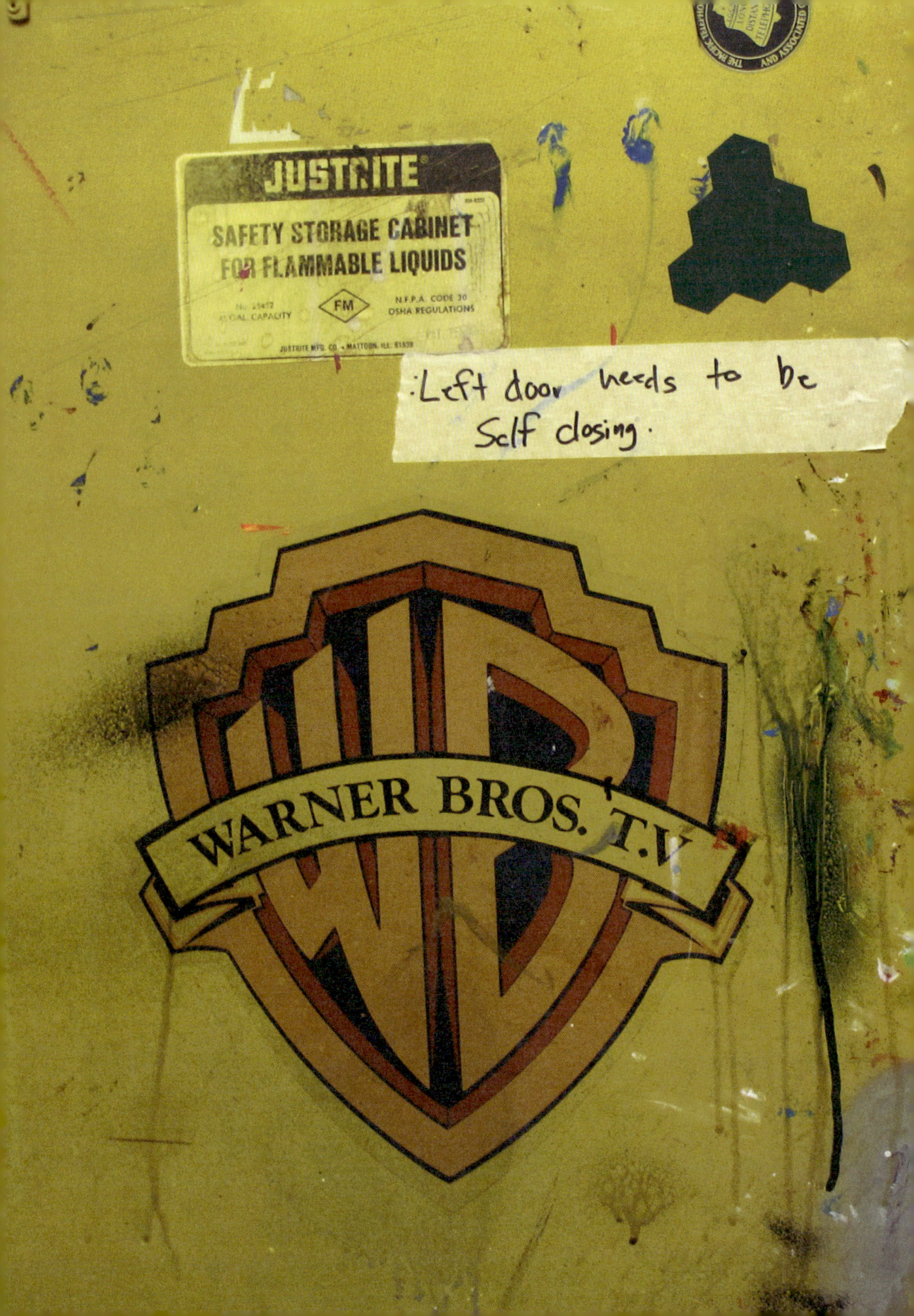

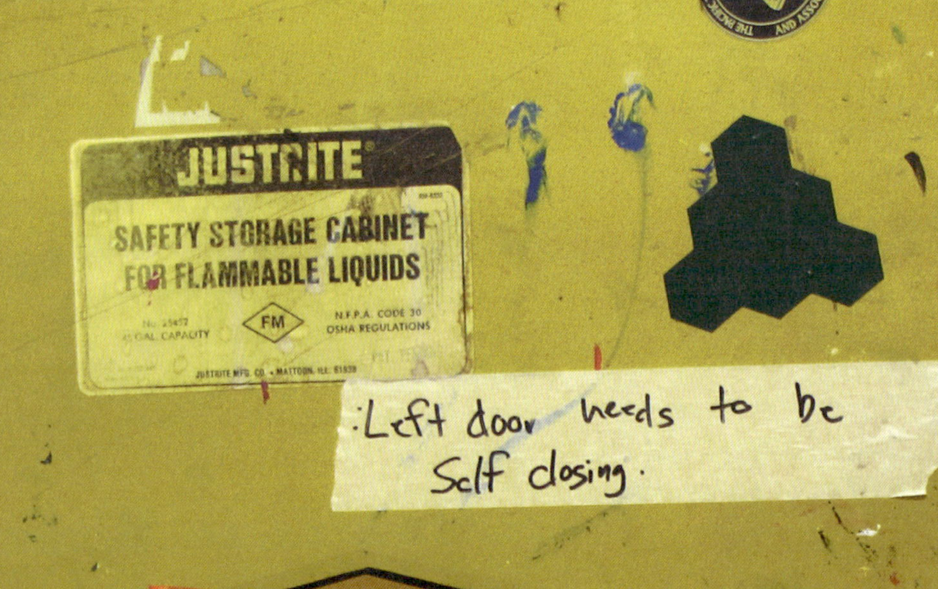

JUSTRITE
SAFETY STORAGE CABINET
FOR FLAMMABLE LIQUIDS
FM
N.F.P.A. CODE 30
OSHA REGULATIONS
Left door needs to be self closing.
WARNER BROS. T.V

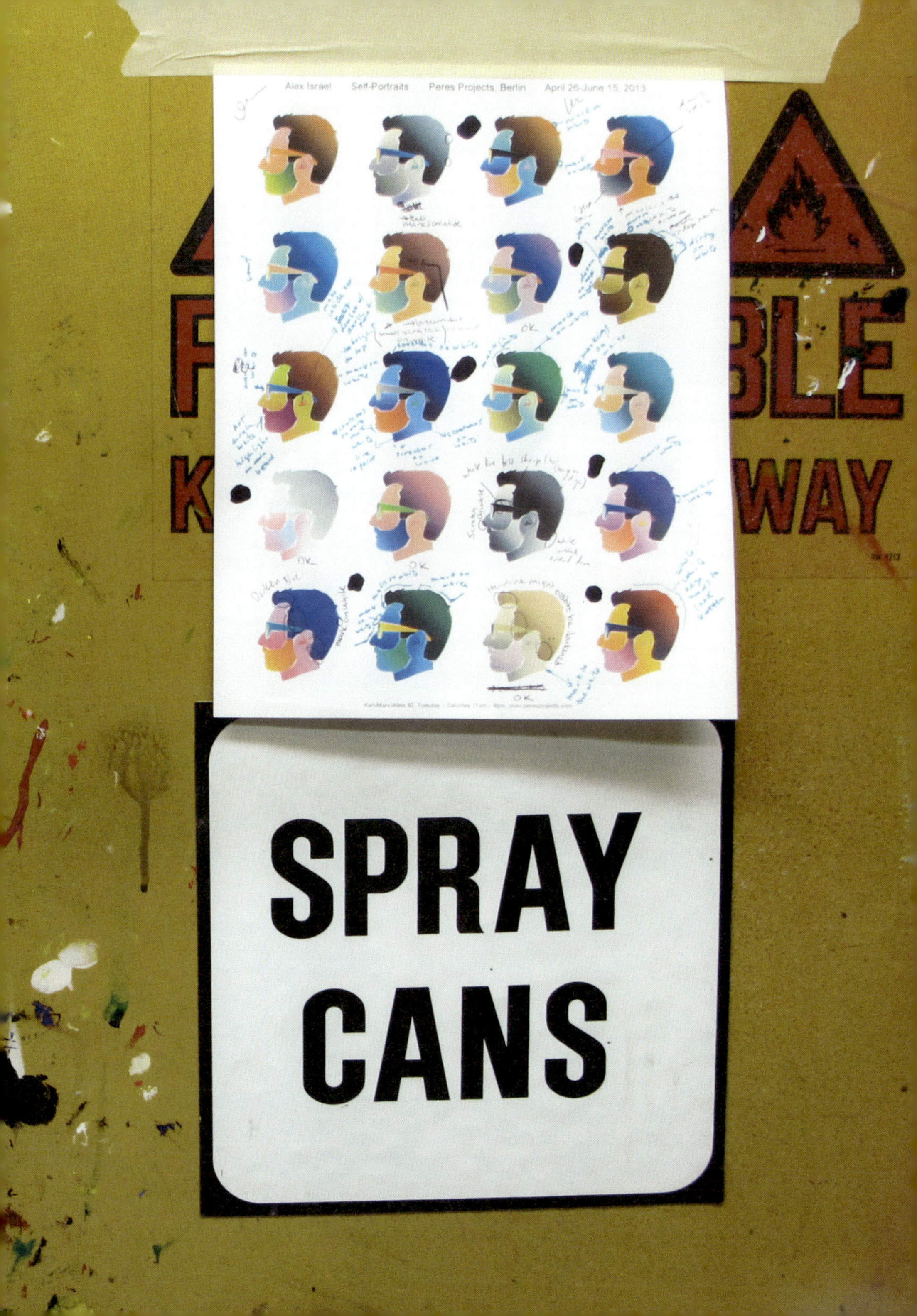

Alex Israel   Self-Portraits   Peres Projects, Berlin   April 26-June 15, 2013
SPRAY
CANS
FLAMMABLE
KEEP AWAY

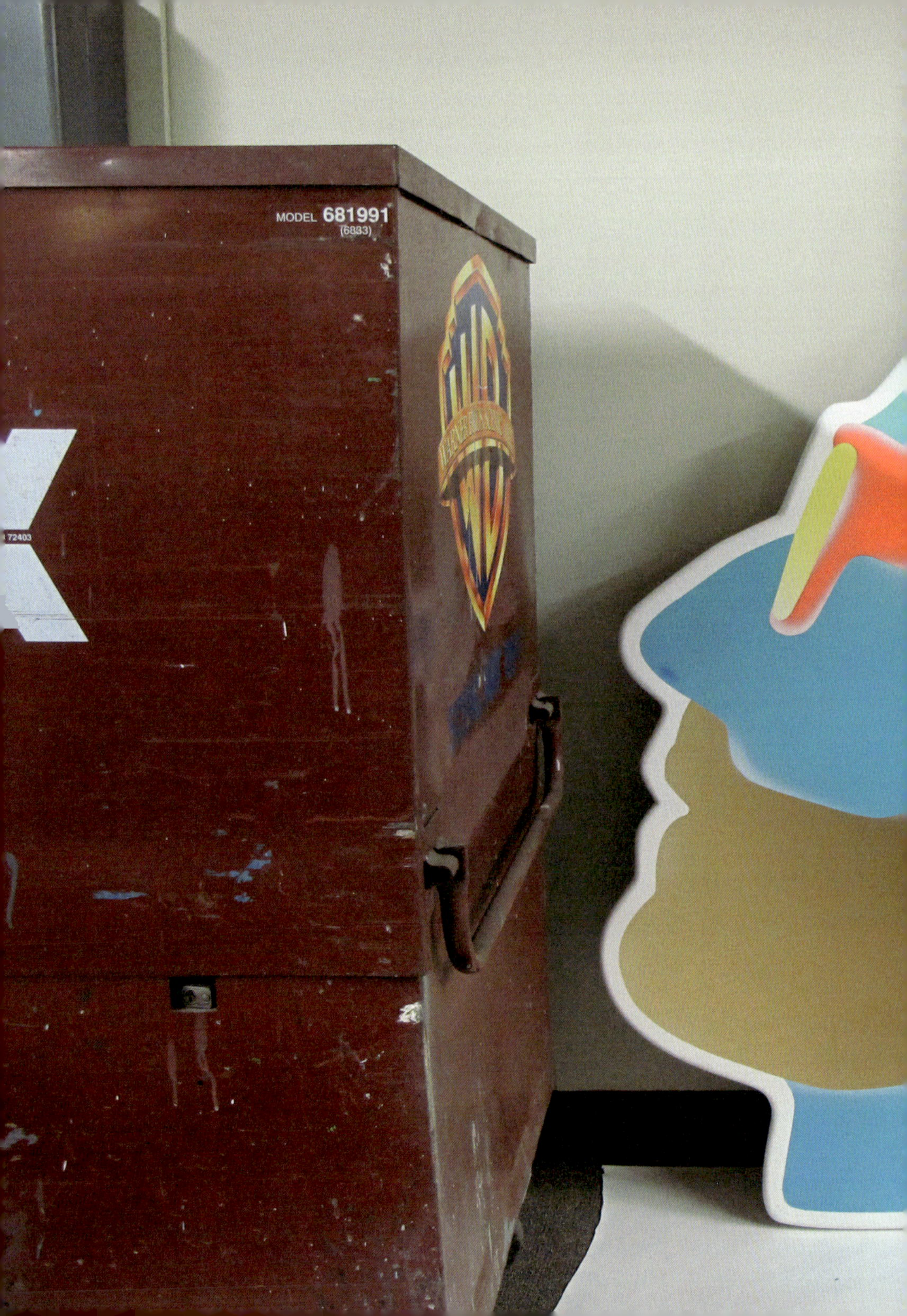

MODEL 681991
(6833)
72403

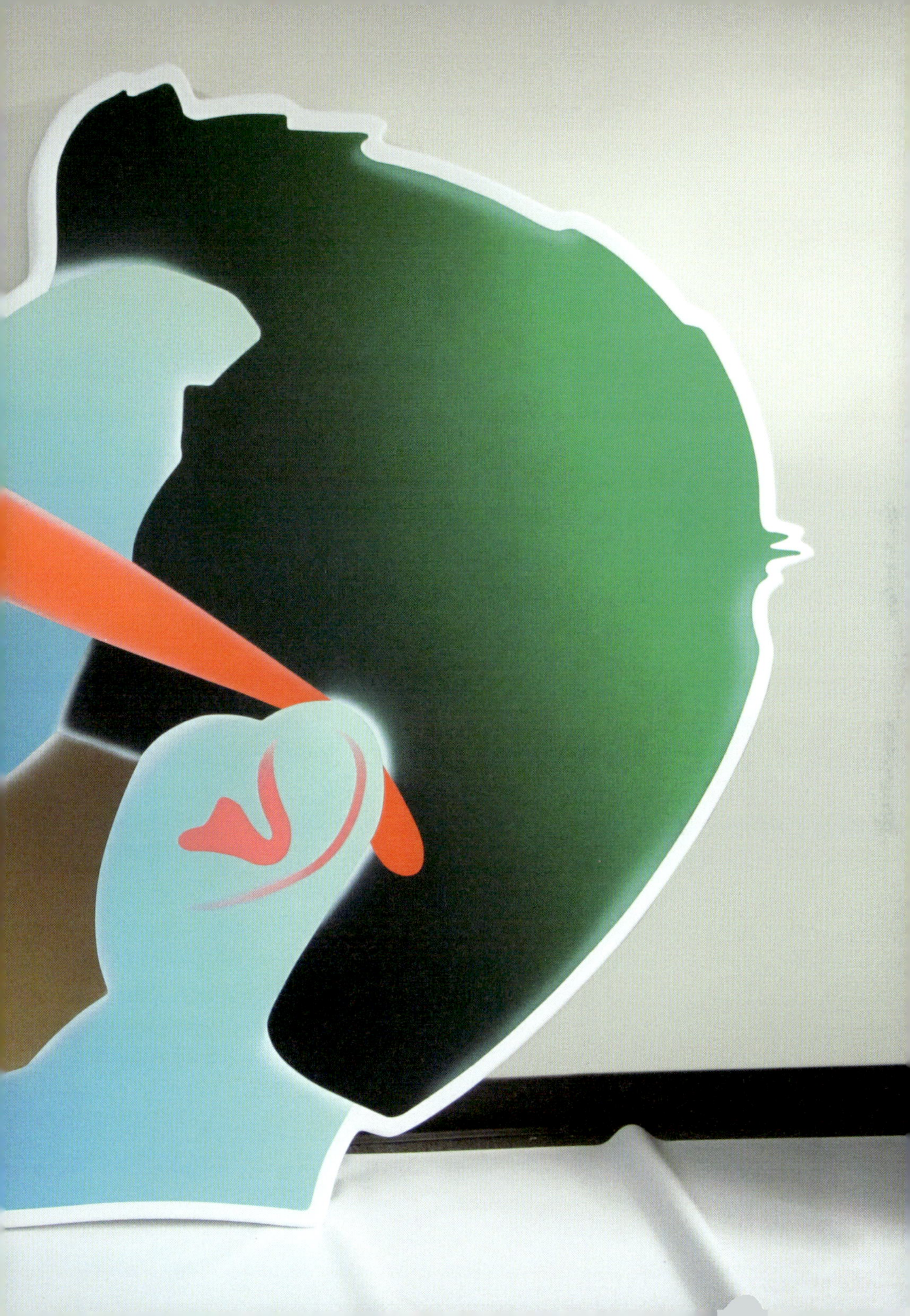

Products, Media, and Interiors

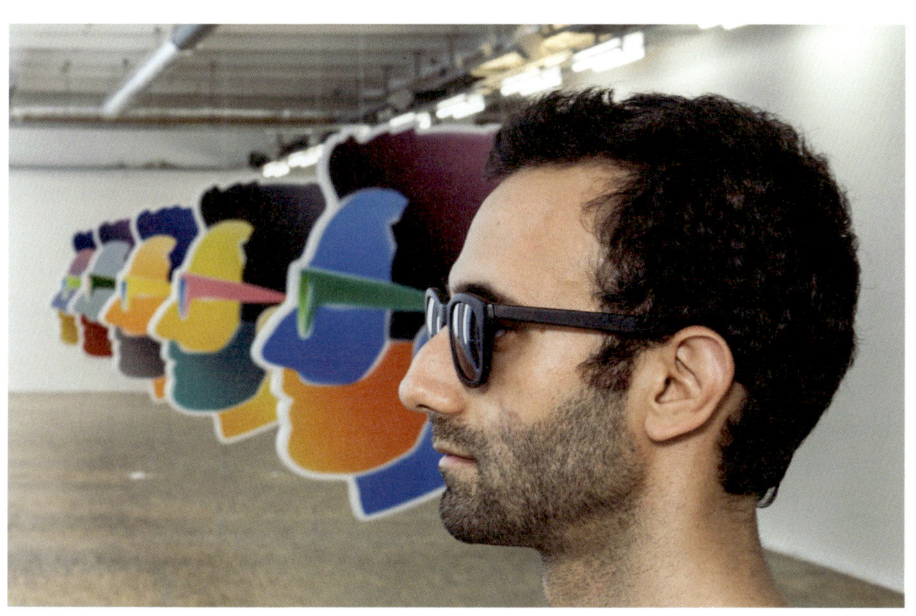

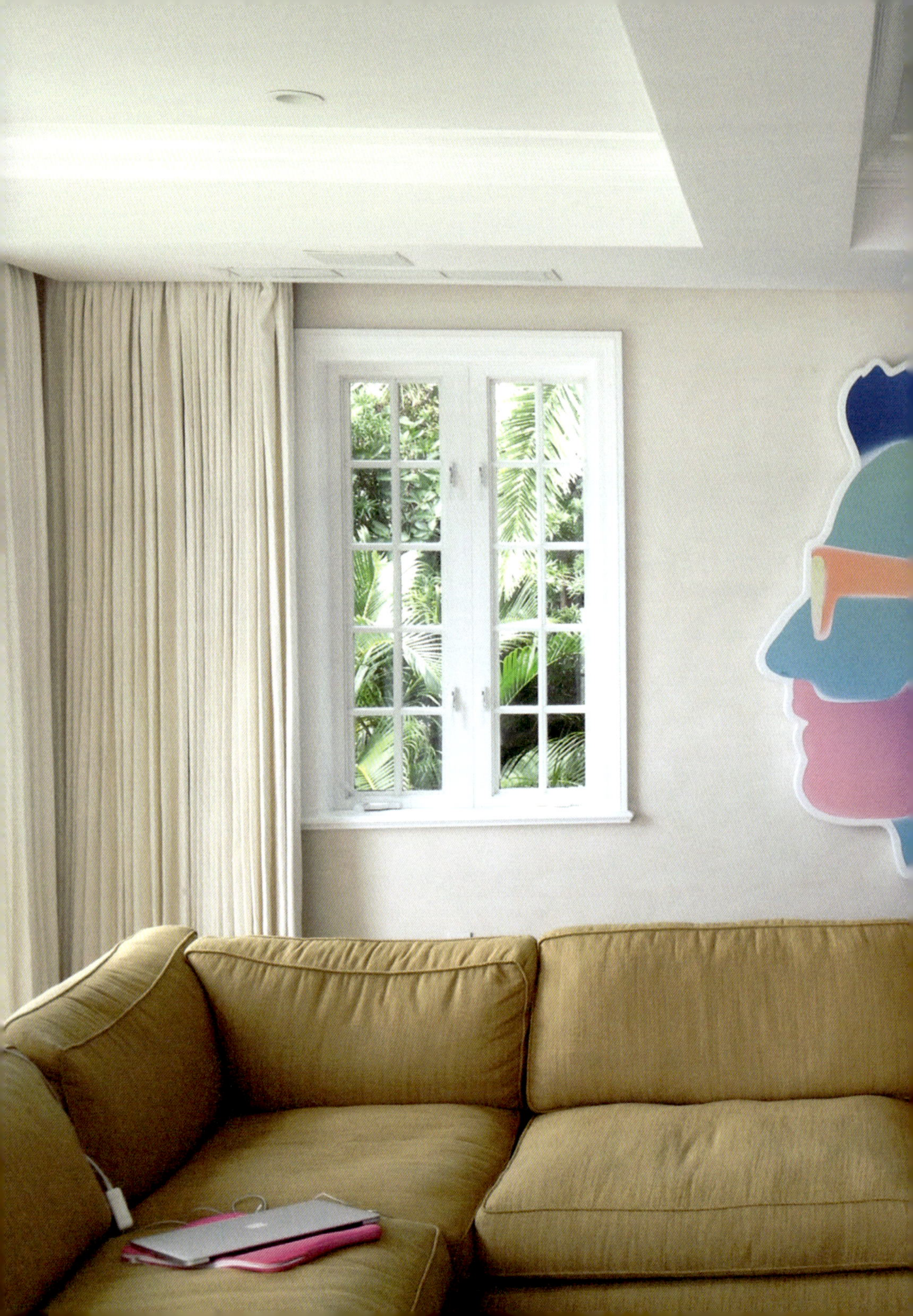

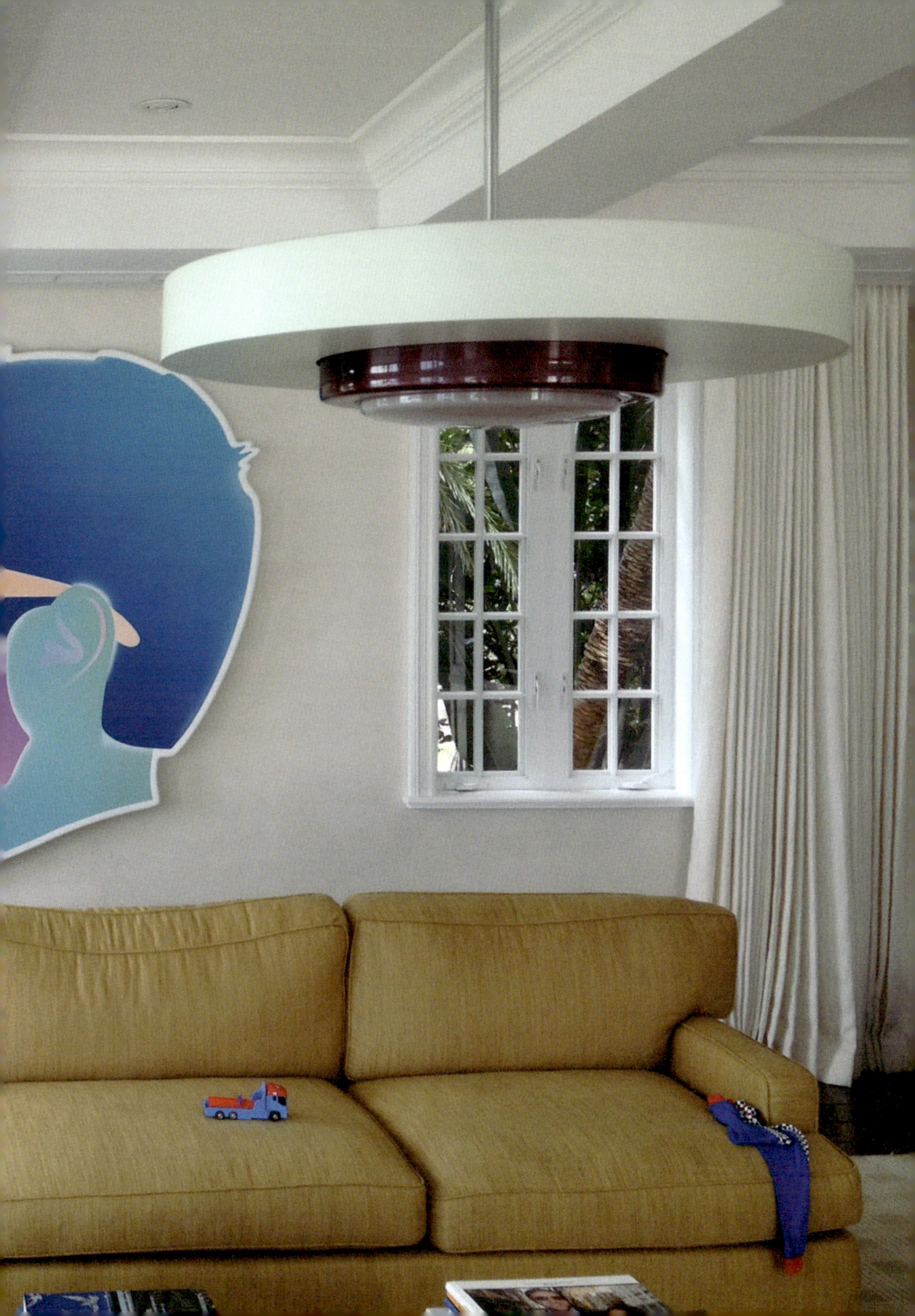

alex israel self portrait

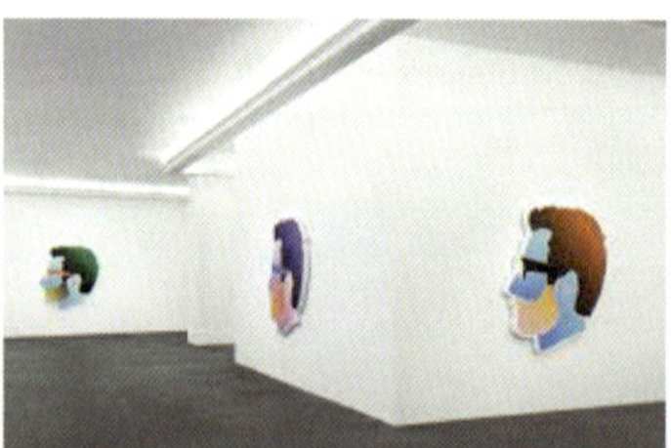
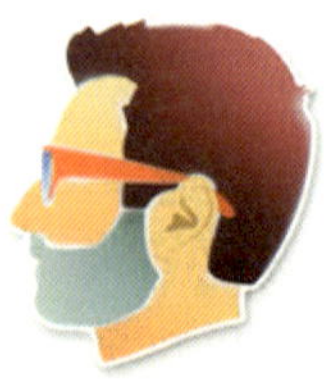
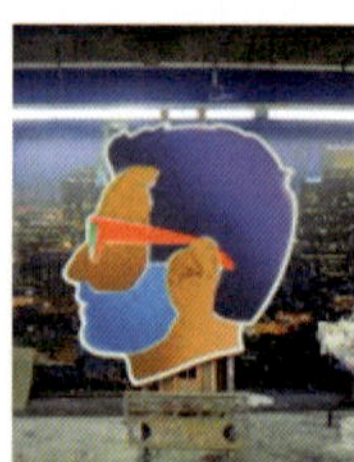
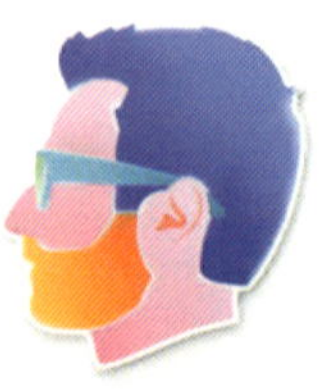

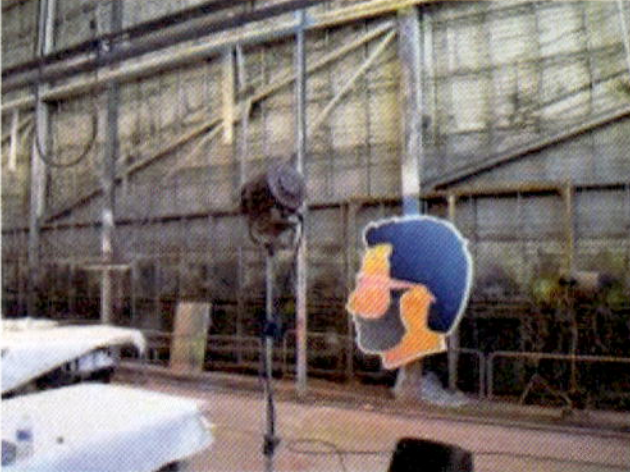
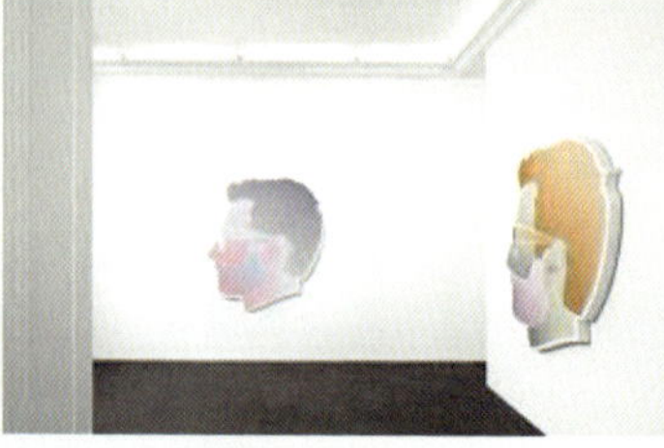
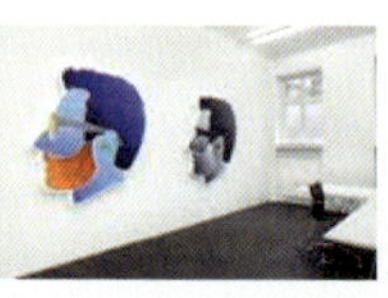
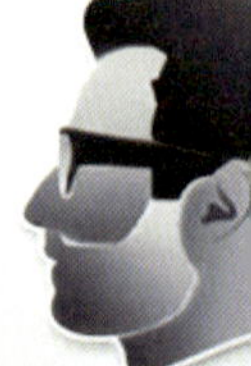

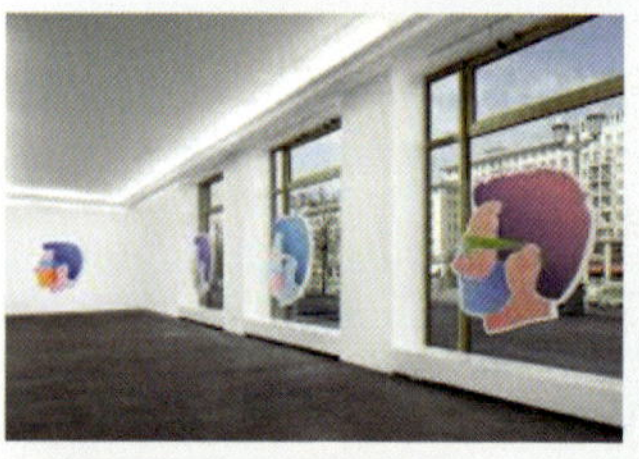
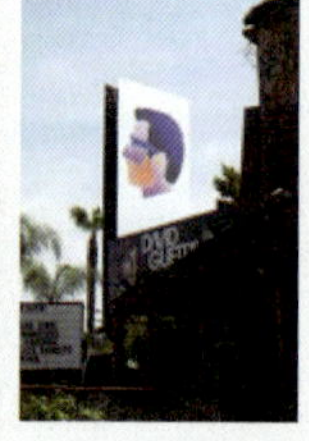
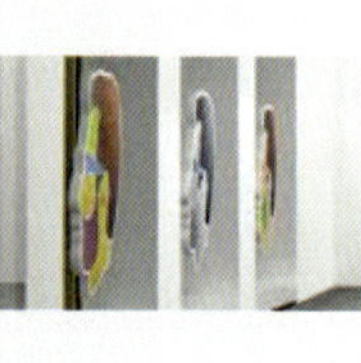
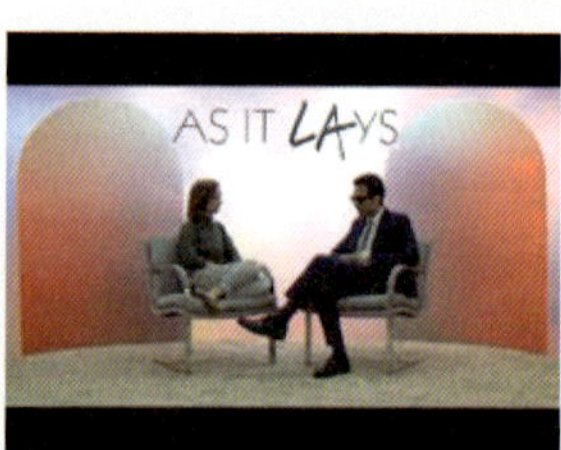

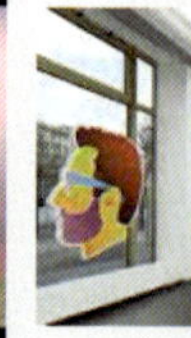

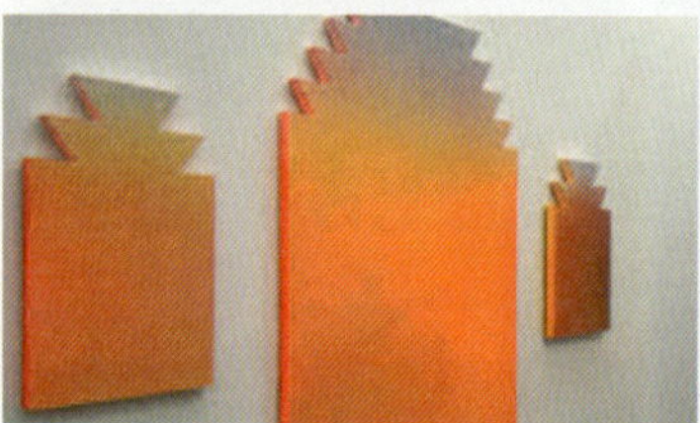
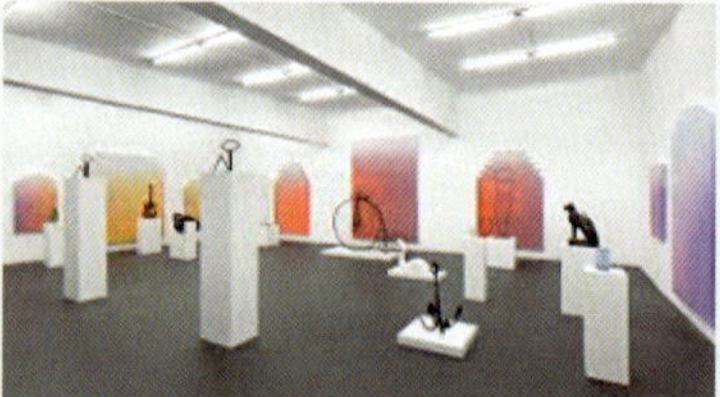
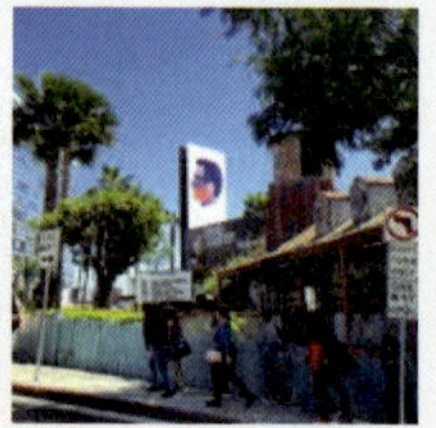
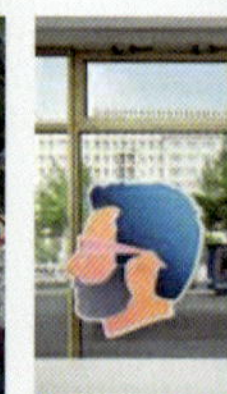

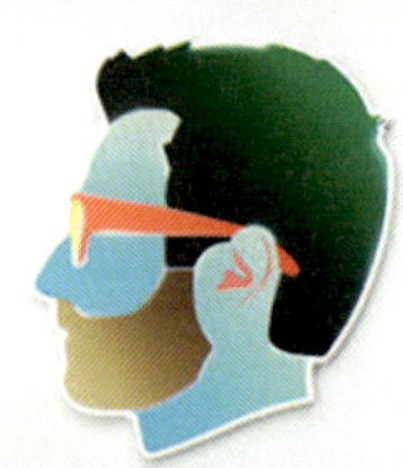
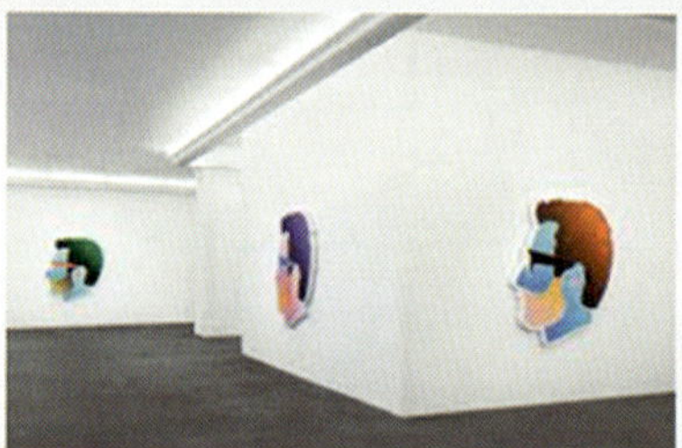
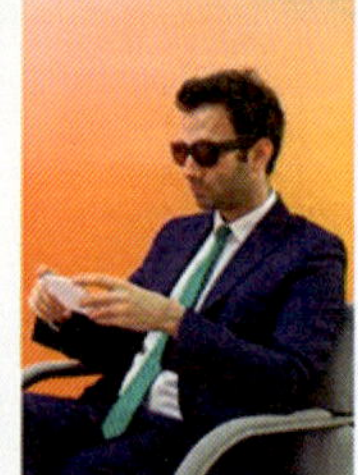
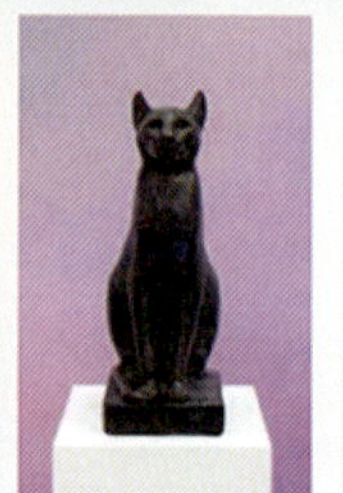

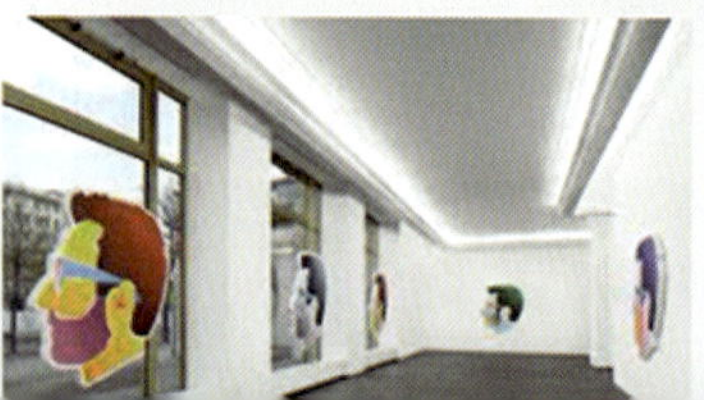
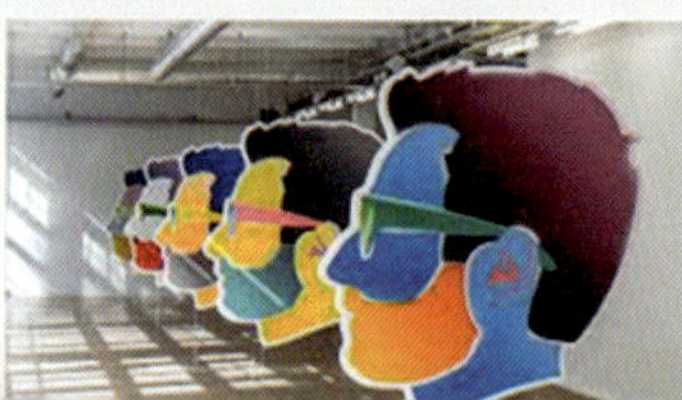
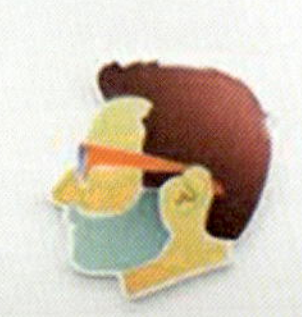

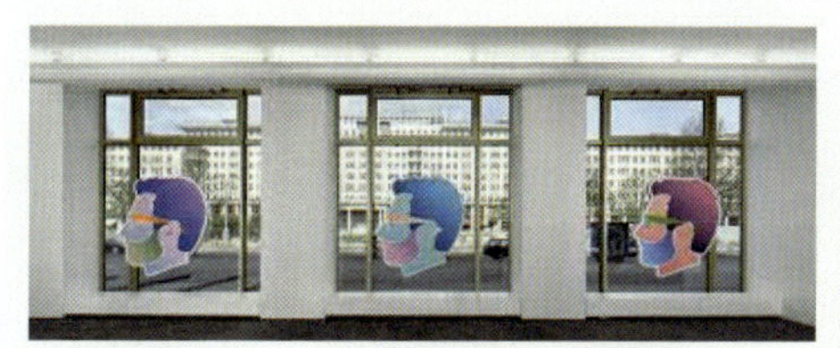
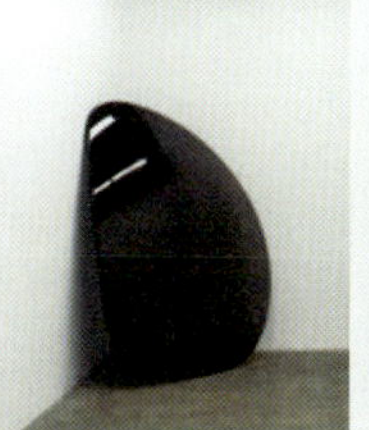
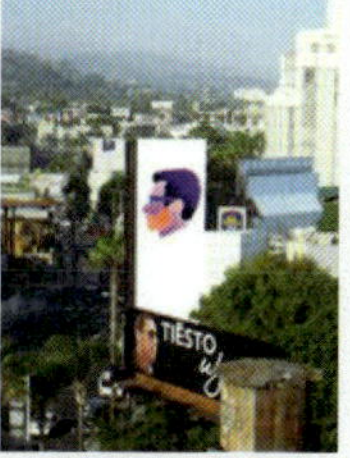
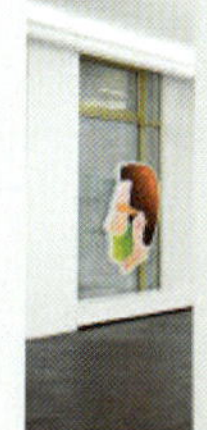
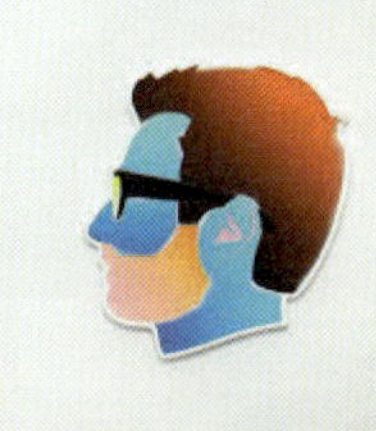
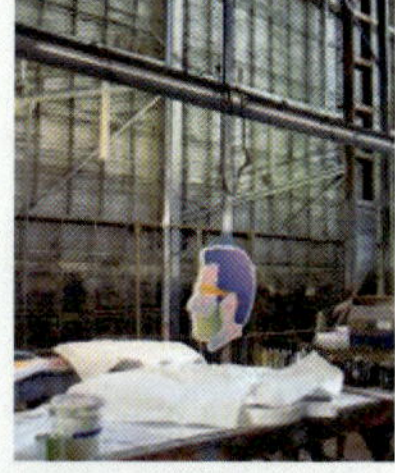
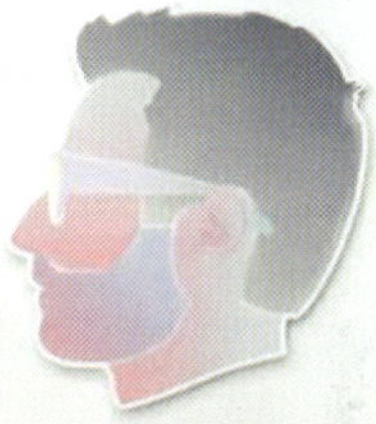
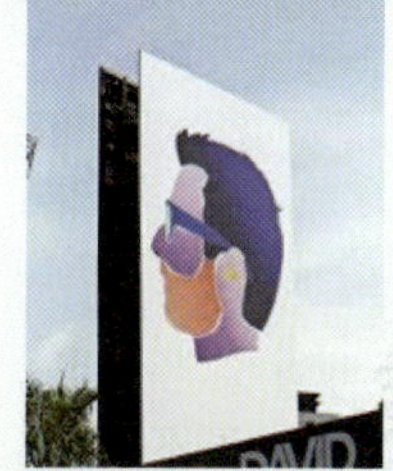
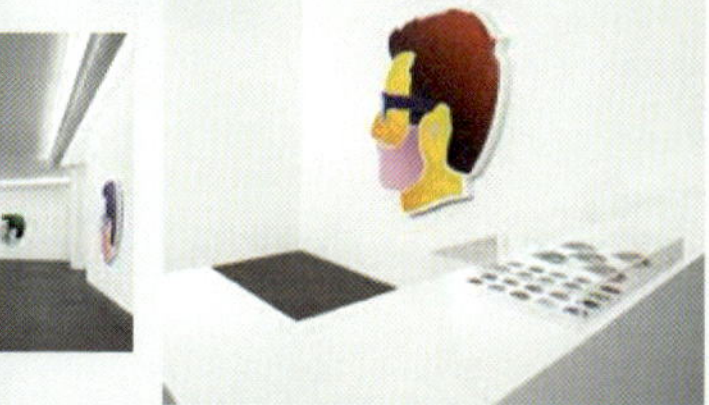
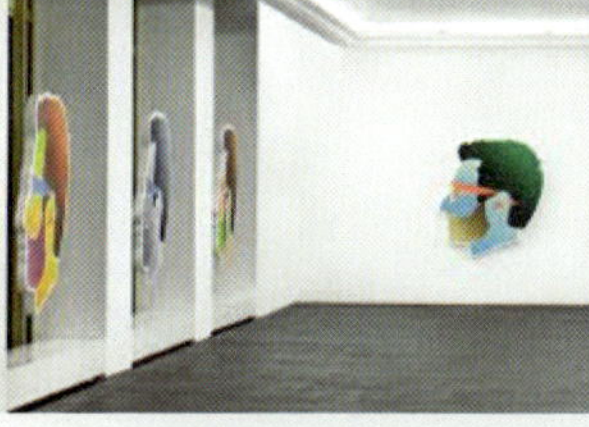
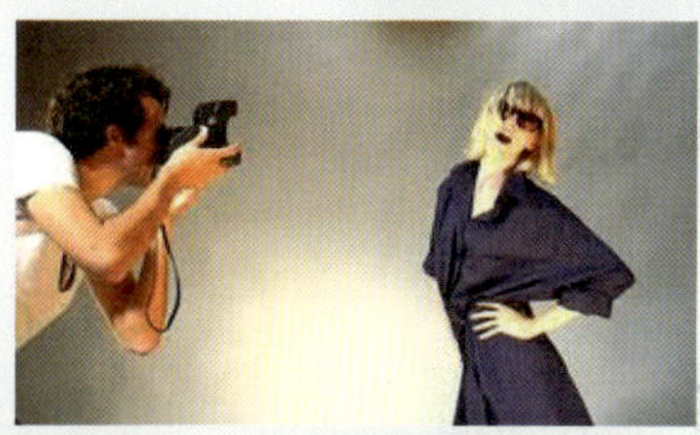
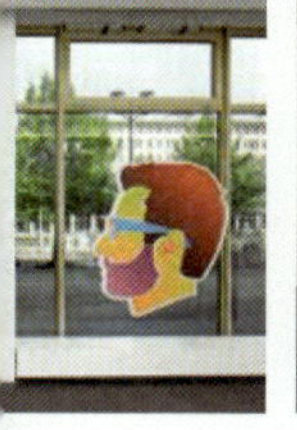
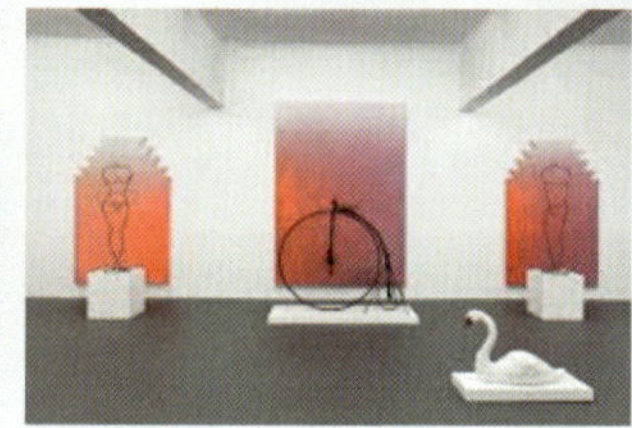
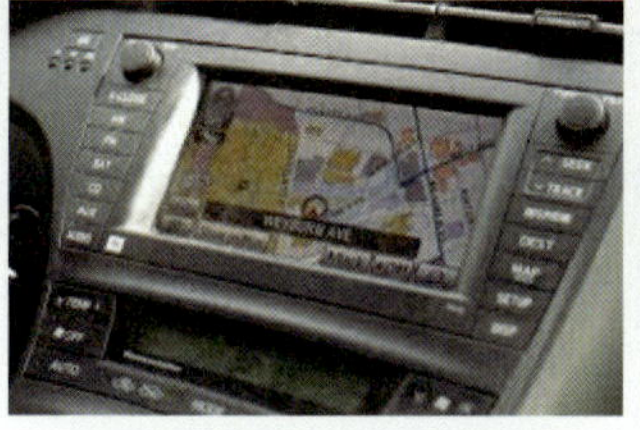
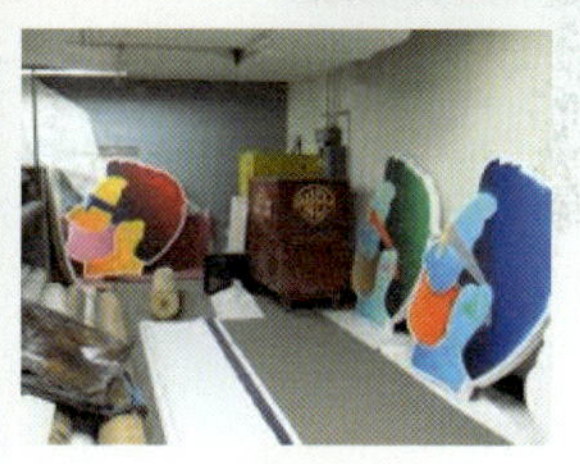
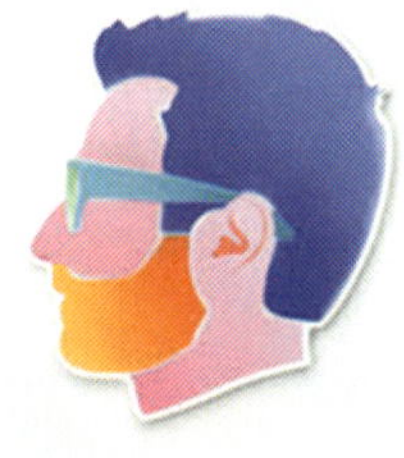
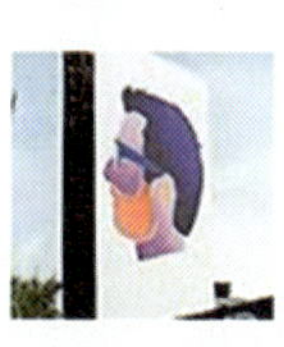
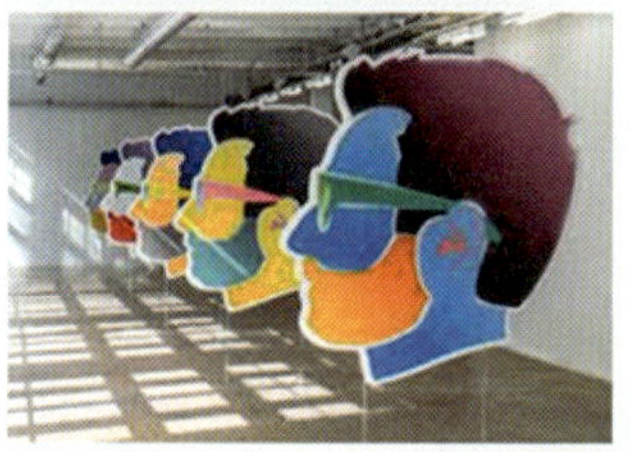
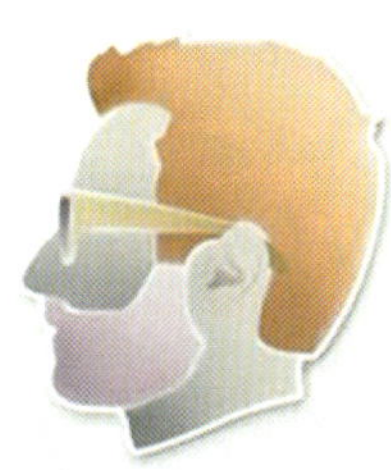
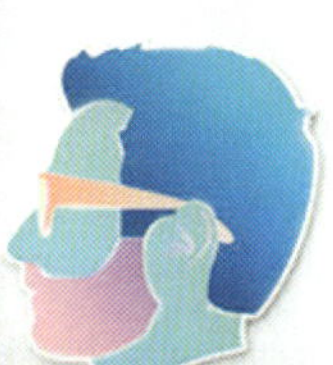
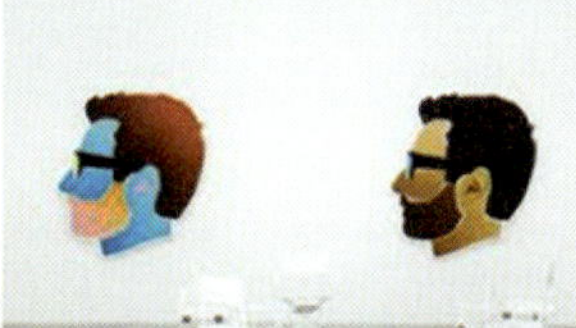
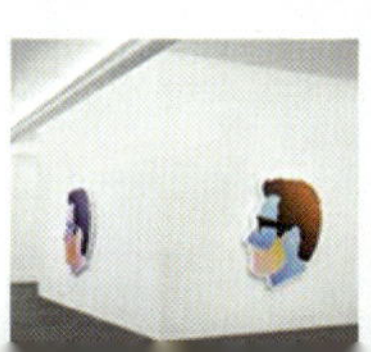
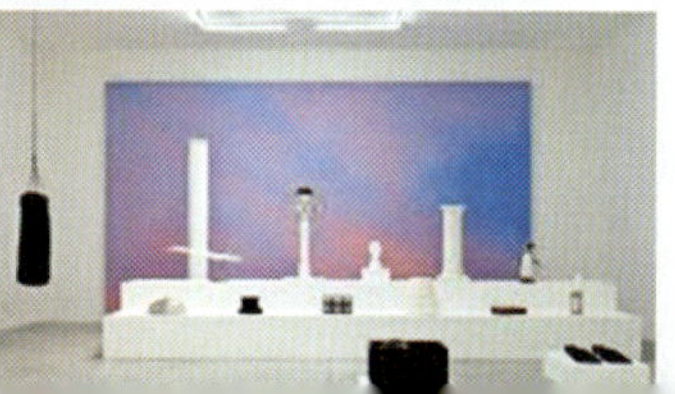

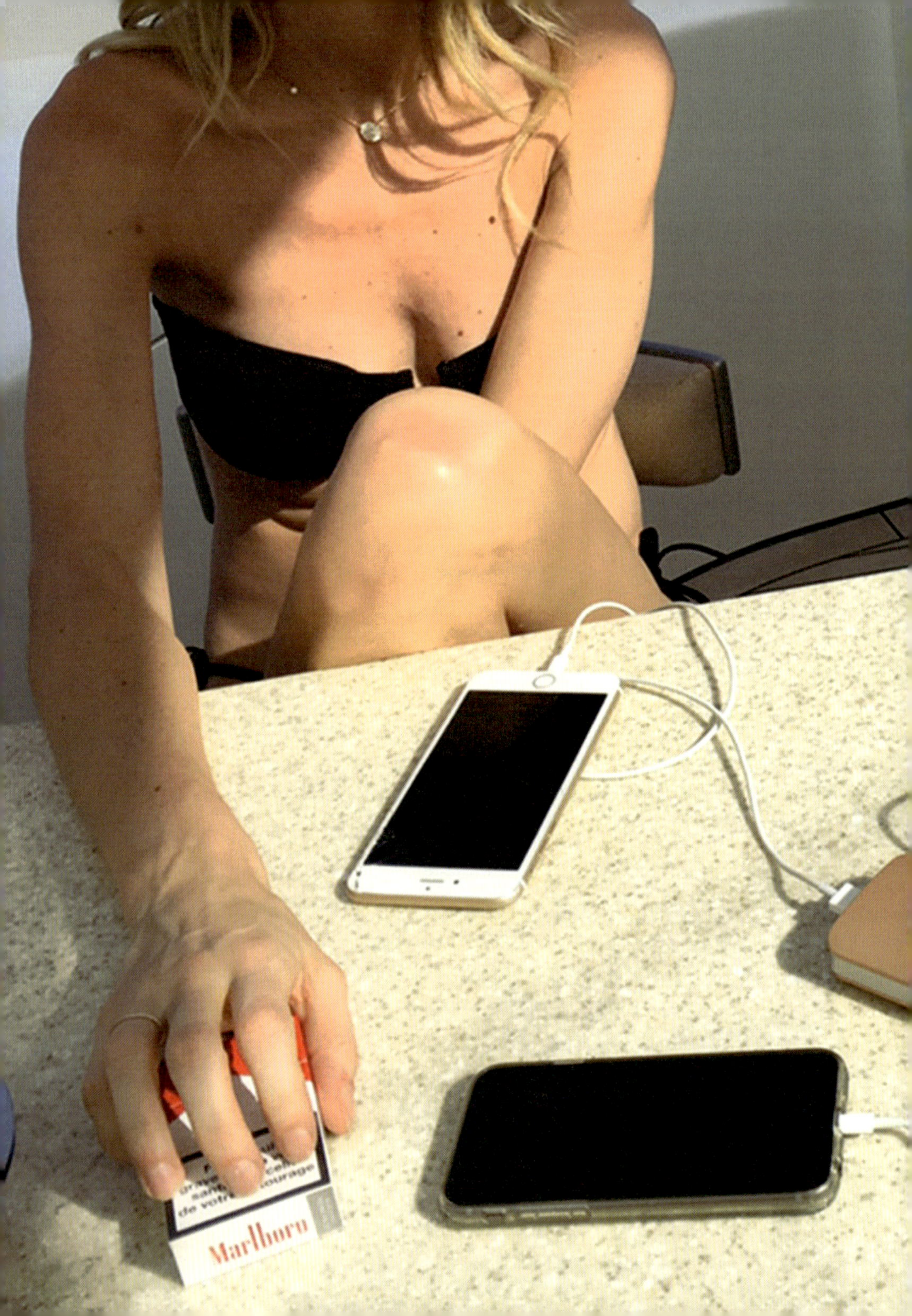

Marlboro

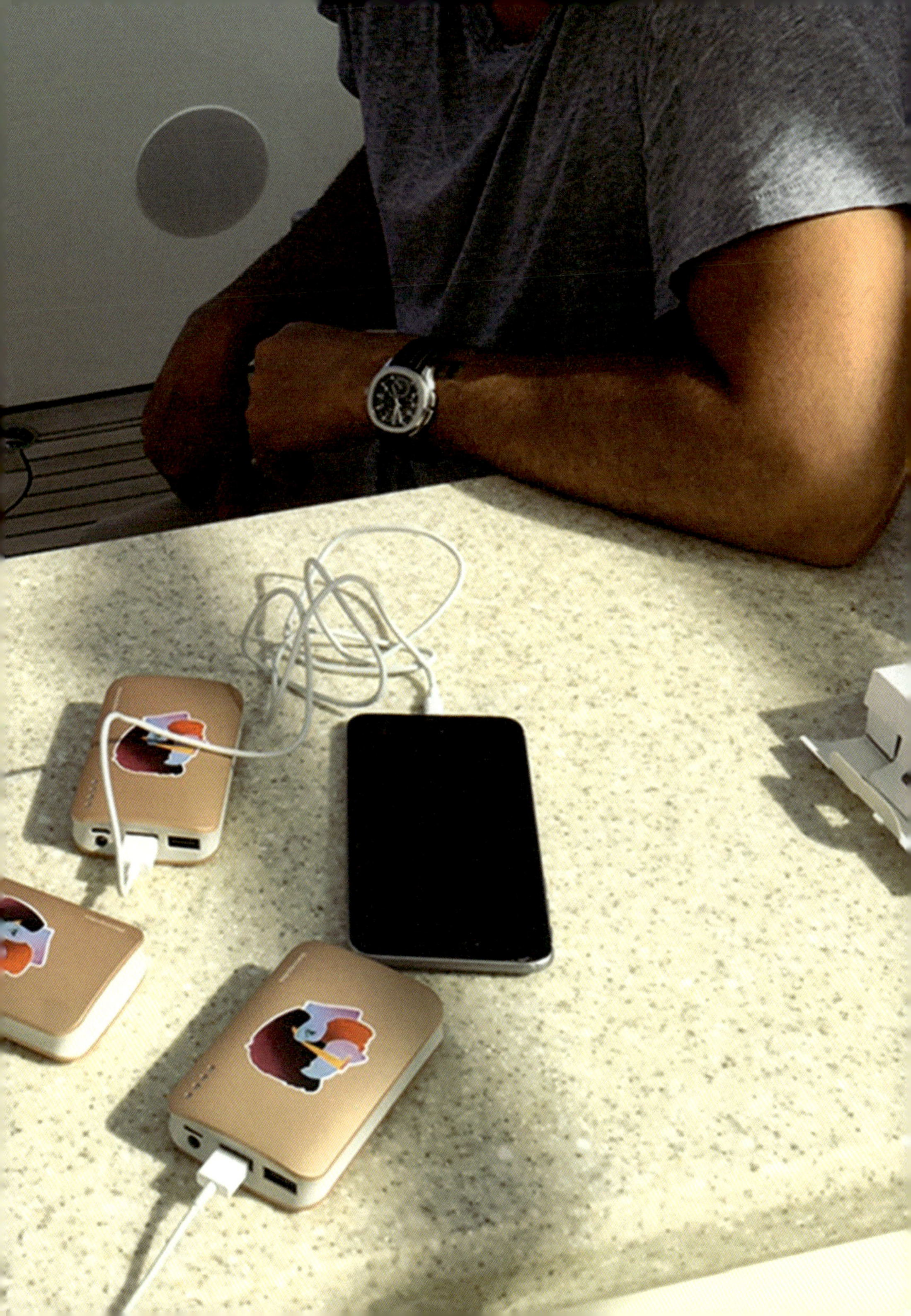

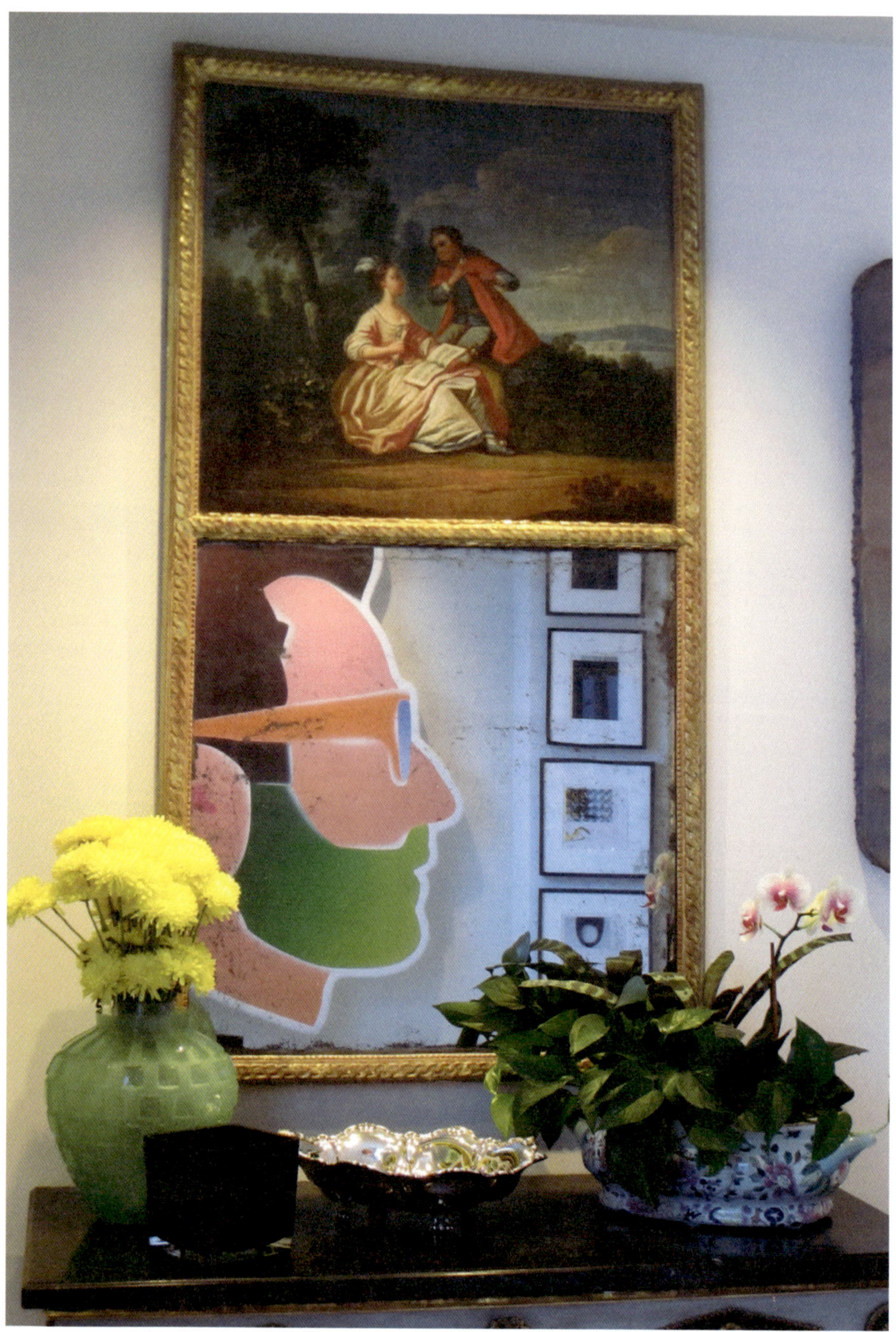

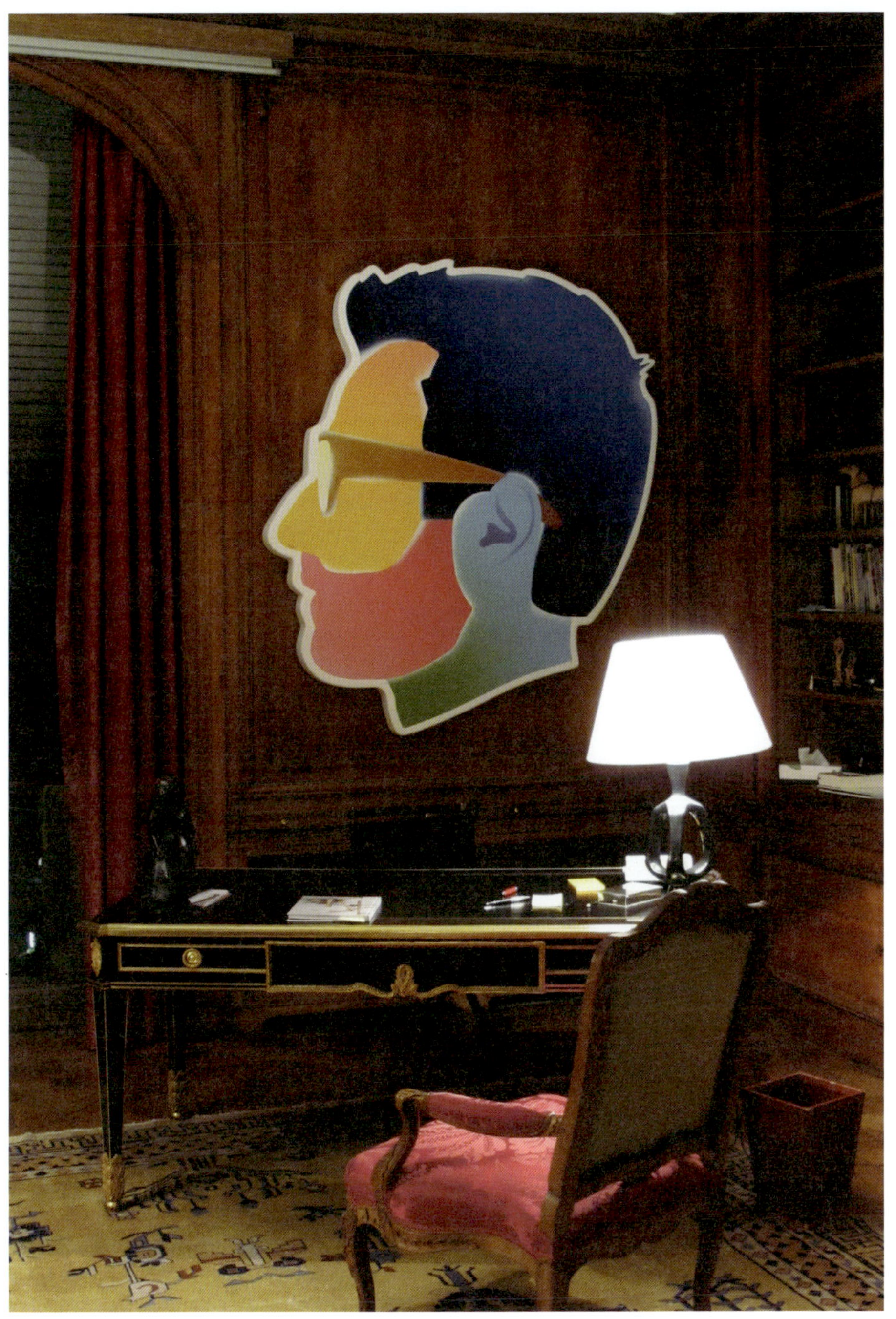

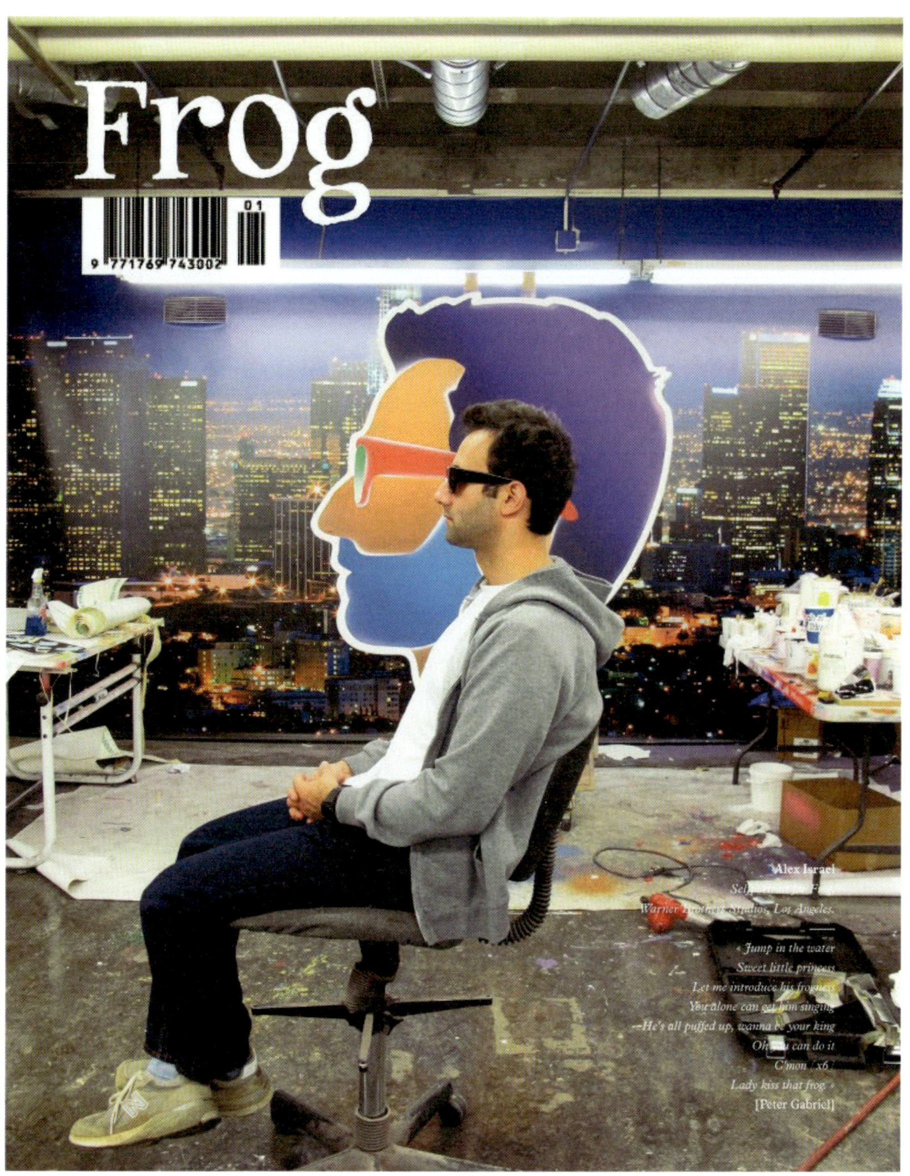

Alex Israel
Self-Portrait (Frog)
Warner Brothers Studios, Los Angeles.

Jump in the water
Sweet little princess
Let me introduce his frogness
You alone can get him singing
—He's all puffed up, wanna be your king
Oh you can do it
C'mon (x6)
Lady kiss that frog.
[Peter Gabriel]

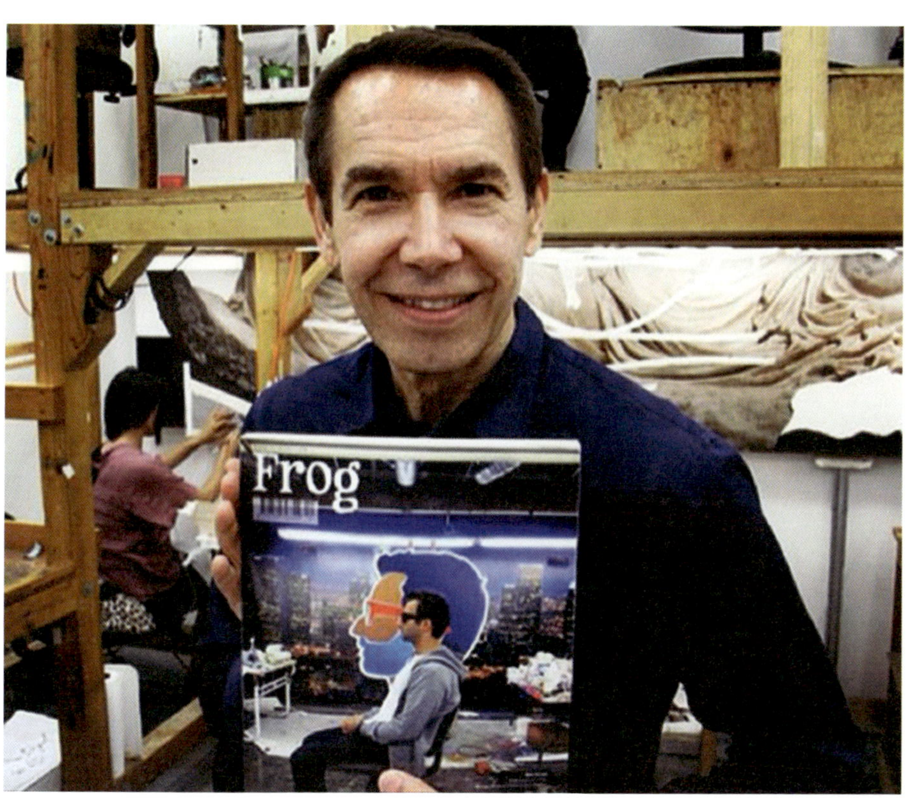

Frog

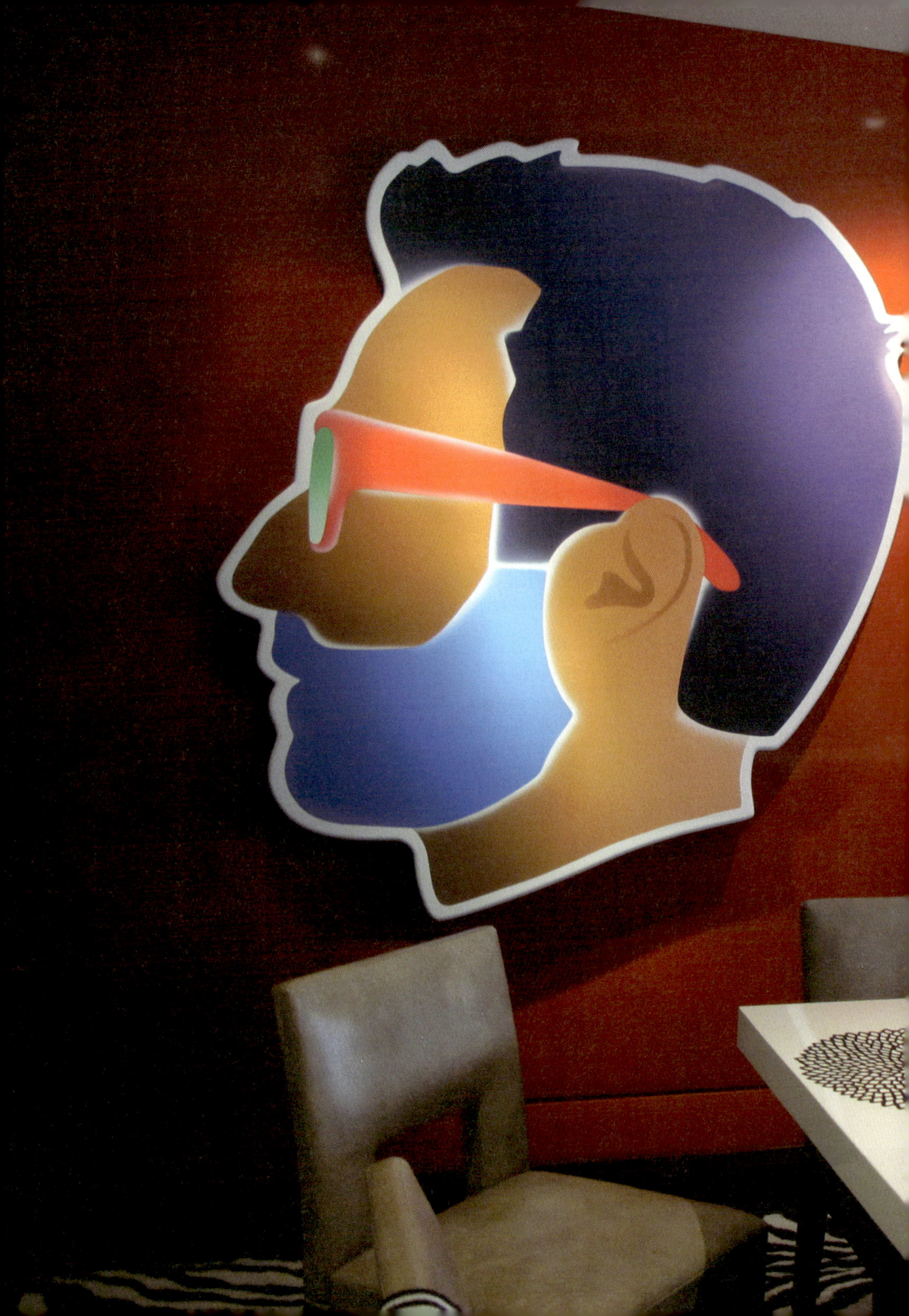

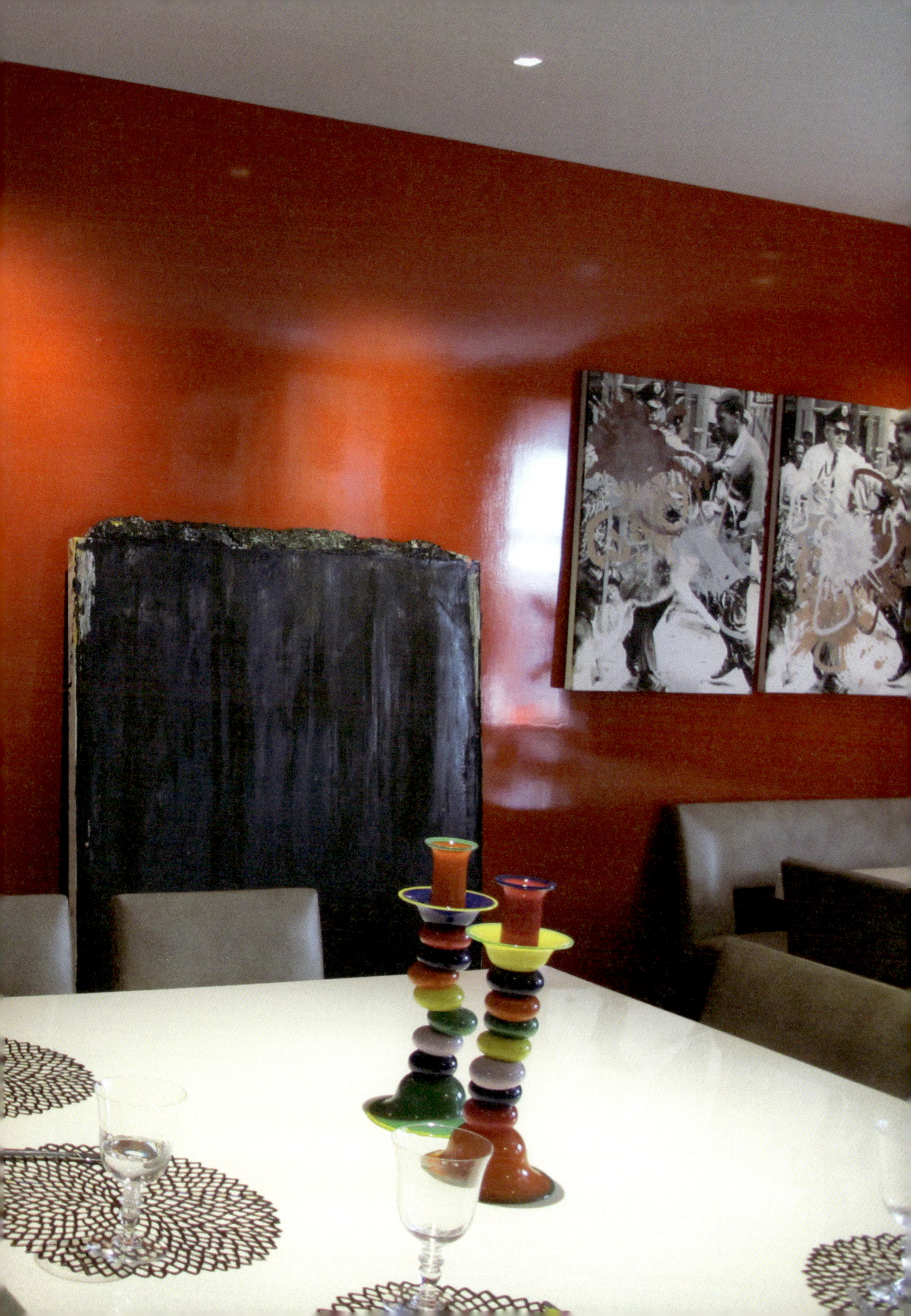

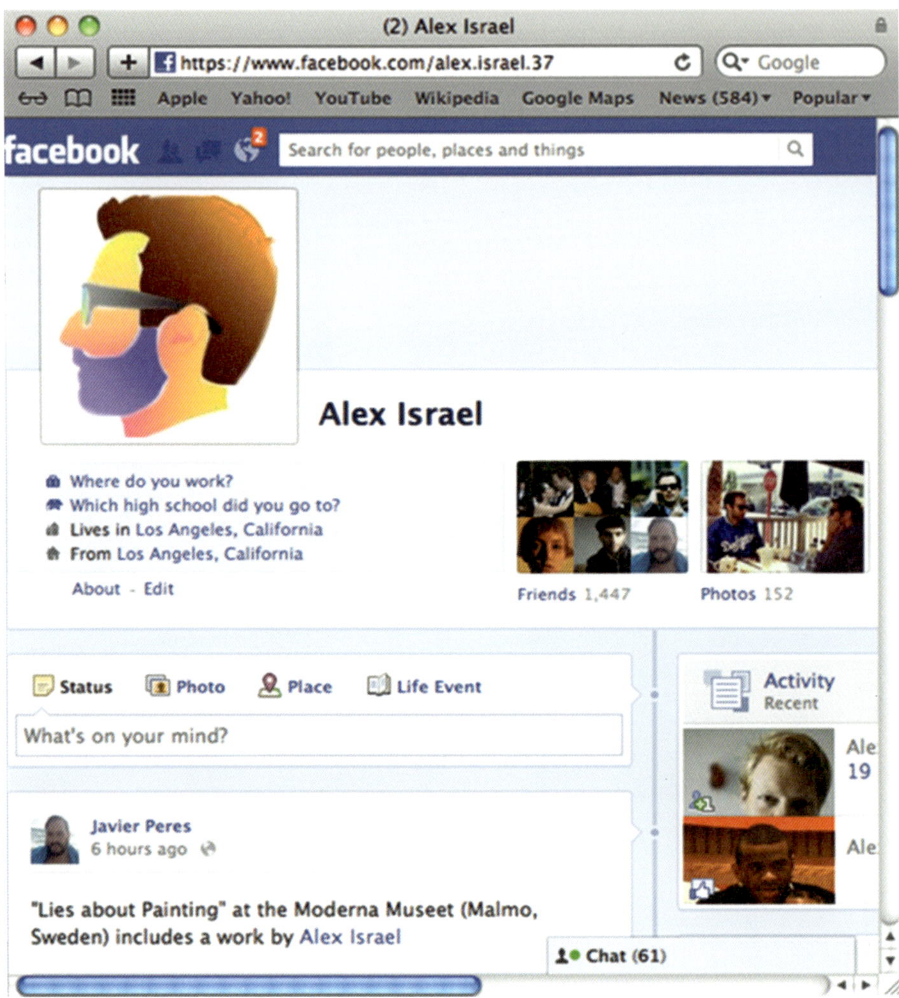

(2) Alex Israel
https://www.facebook.com/alex.israel.37
Google
Apple   Yahoo!   YouTube   Wikipedia   Google Maps   News (584)   Popular
facebook
Search for people, places and things
Alex Israel
Where do you work?
Which high school did you go to?
Lives in Los Angeles, California
From Los Angeles, California
About - Edit
Friends 1,447
Photos 152
Status   Photo   Place   Life Event
What's on your mind?
Javier Peres
6 hours ago
"Lies about Painting" at the Moderna Museet (Malmo,
Sweden) includes a work by Alex Israel
Activity
Recent
Ale
19
Ale
Chat (61)

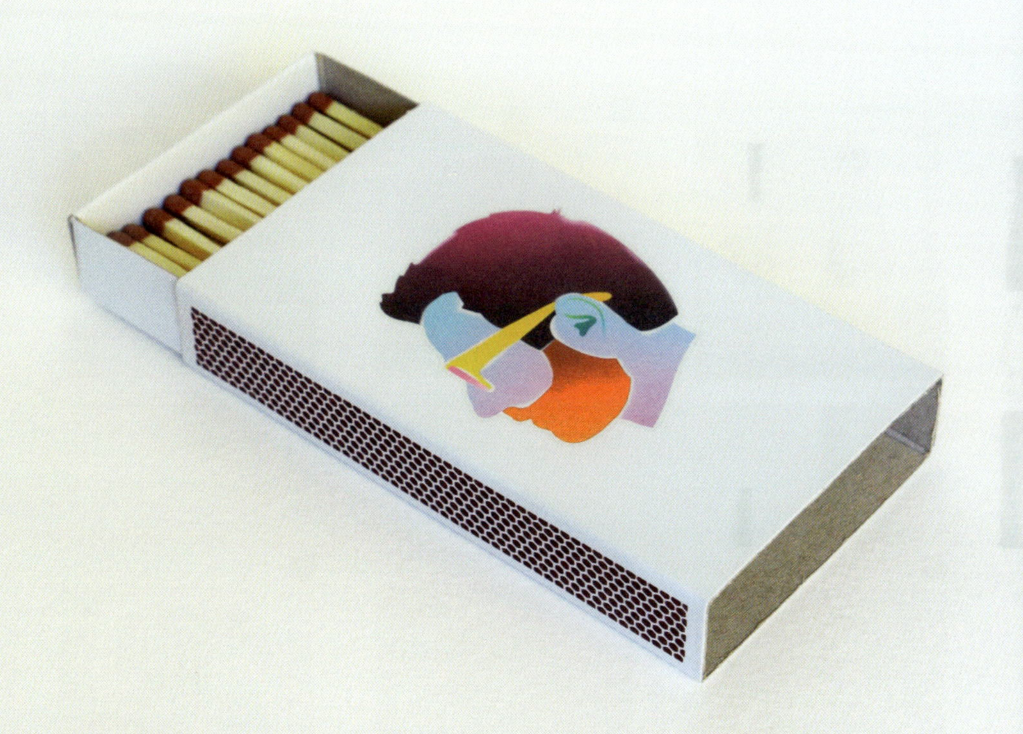

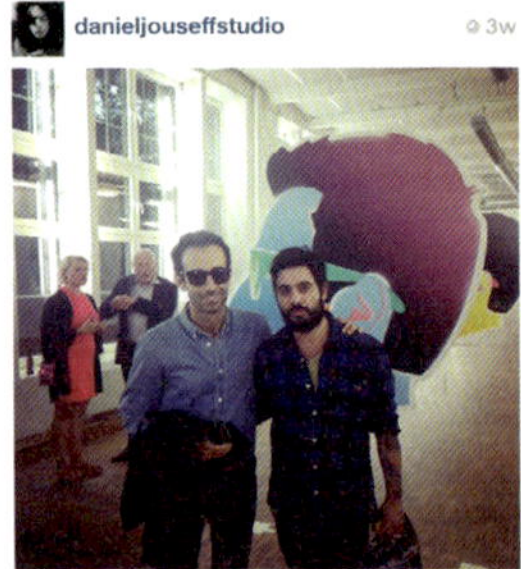

15 likes
danieljouseffstudio #alexisrael #danieljouseff
Like   Comment

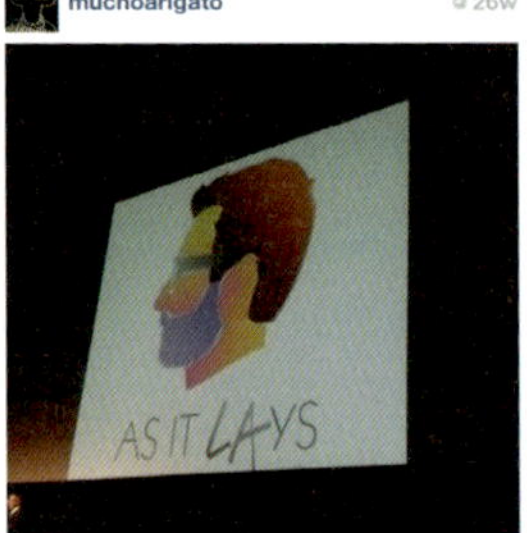

muchoarigato, china_chow, benjaminalejandro, semipermanent
muchoarigato #Alexisrael #moca #spla #semiglobal

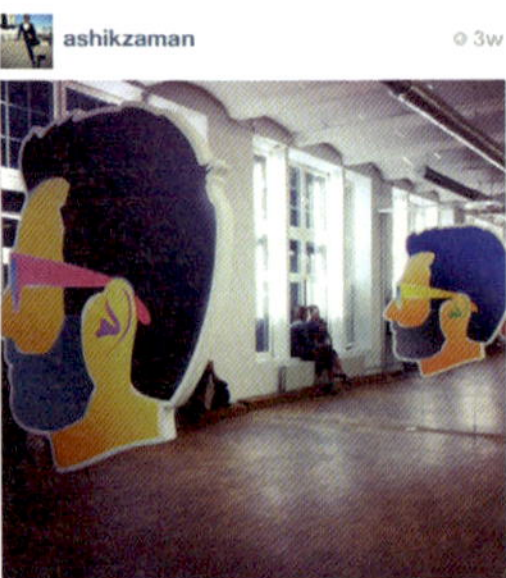

24 likes
ashikzaman Opening for artist Alex Israel #alexisrael #art #face
Like   Comment

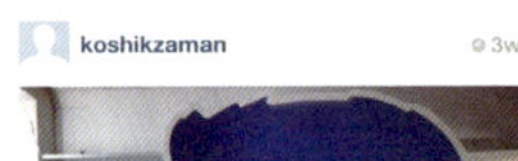

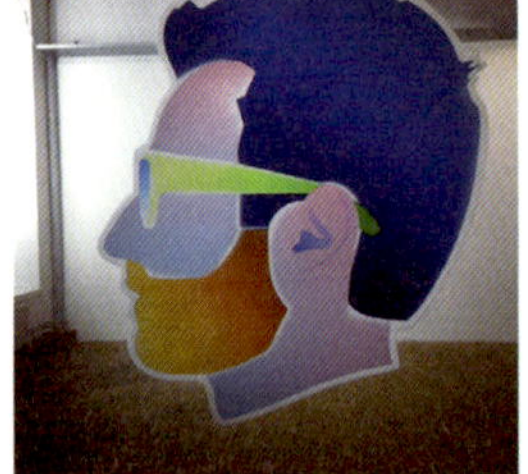

21 likes
koshikzaman Alex Israel presentation on Igeldammsgatan.
koshikzaman #art #alexisrael #spray on #fiber #glass

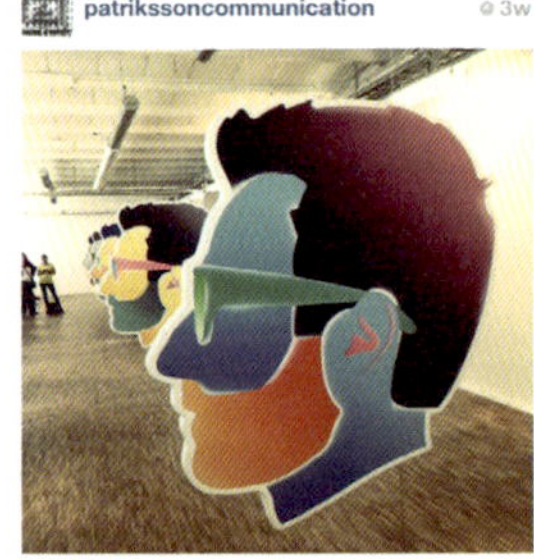

45 likes
patrikssoncommunication Preview tonight of the Alex Israel exhibition at Isbrytaren, Igeldammsgatan 22. Don't miss this! #alexisrael #kostyal

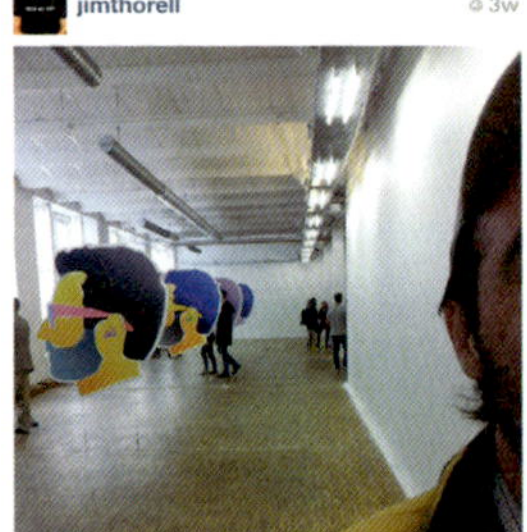

lovekarlzone, maxronnersjo
jimthorell #alexisrael #isbrytaren #kostyal #peresprojects
Like   Comment

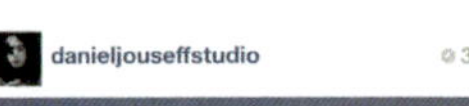

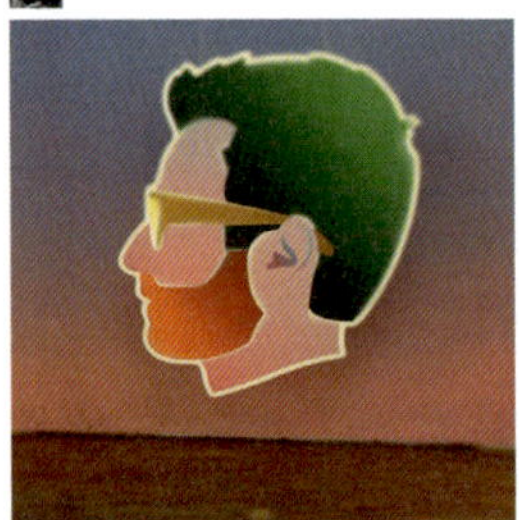

62atelier, mattekj, mackanlindstrom, idawal, dtih, adryvelez_, benjaminsjoberg, paulreinswe
danieljouseffstudio #alexisrael sthlm! #badassart

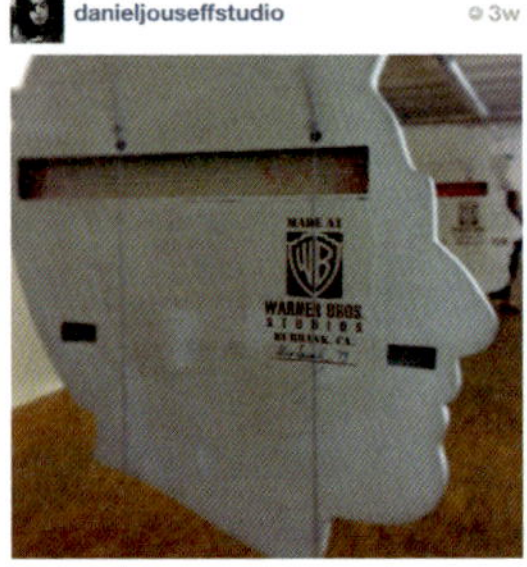

imilk, kristofer_hedlund, chrisumore, 62atelier, _andyberner_, jonakopy, micheldida
danieljouseffstudio The backside of #alexisrael

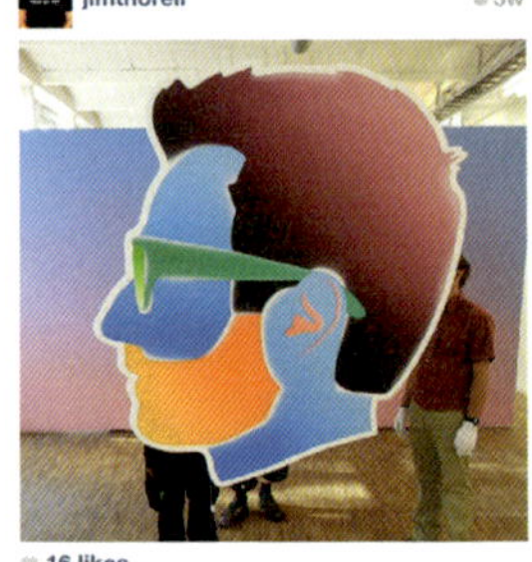

16 likes
jimthorell #alexisrael #isbrytaren #kostyal #peresprojects #la #la #berlin #stockholm
Like   Comment

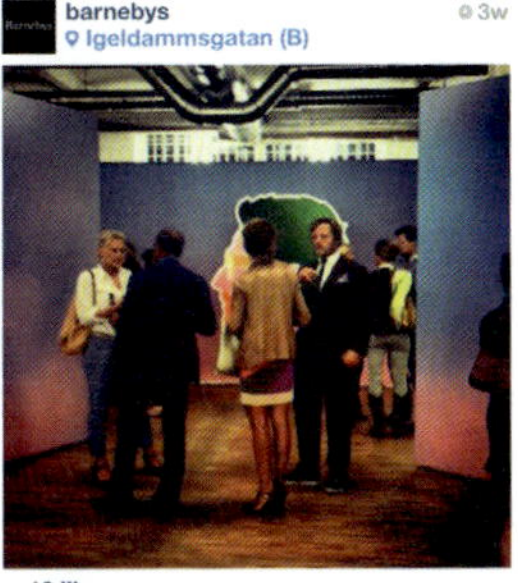

barnebys
♀ Igeldammsgatan (B)   ◷ 3w

♡ **12 likes**

barnebys Barnebys at Alex Israel Opening
Party #kostyal #alexisrael #isbrytaren
#barbebys #vernissage

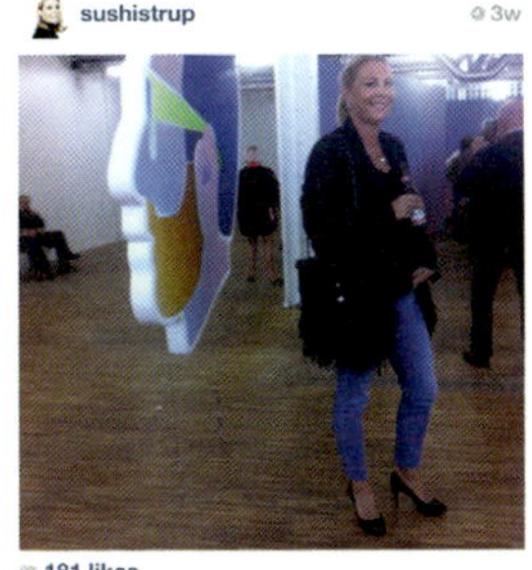

sushistrup   ◷ 3w

♡ **181 likes**

sushistrup At Alex Israel 👌 #alexisrael
view all 12 comments
savene 😍 👌 ✨

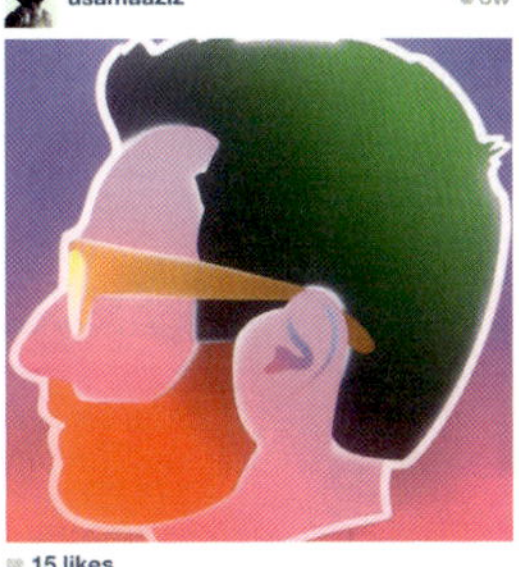

usamaaziz   ◷ 3w

♡ **15 likes**

usamaaziz Konstutställning #AlexIsrael

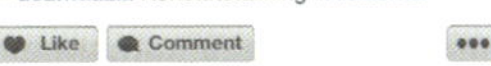

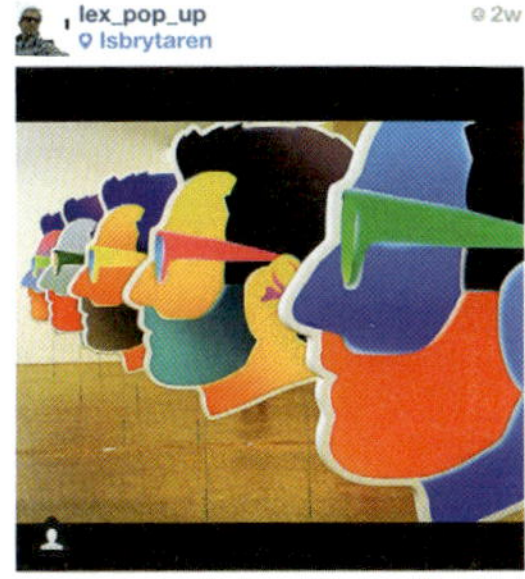

lex_pop_up
♀ Isbrytaren   ◷ 2w

♡ **35 likes**

lex_pop_up Facing left
lex_pop_up Selfies of Alex Israel @ his
Stocholm exhibition opening preview
lex_pop_up #alexisrael #selfie #heads

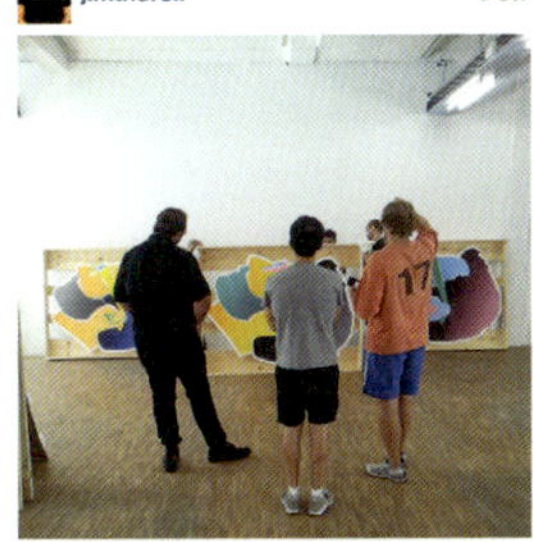

jimthorell   ◷ 3w

♡ **15 likes**

jimthorell #alexisrael #isbrytaren #kostyal
#peresprojects#la#berlin #stockholm
fannywalla är detta nu? vernissage på
lördag? #somanyquestions

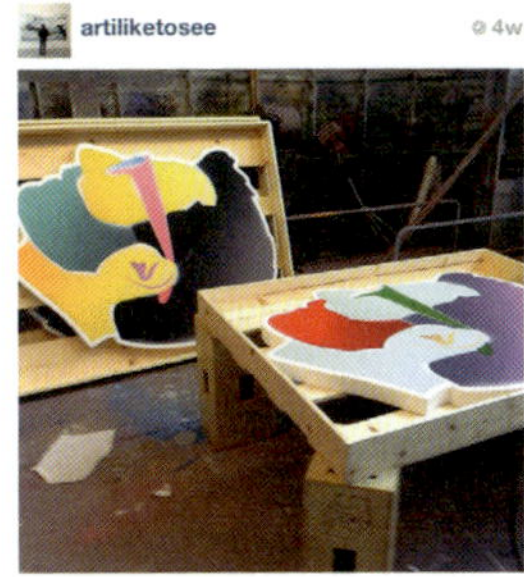

artiliketosee   ◷ 4w

♡ **25 likes**

artiliketosee Recent studio visit with Alex
Israel. #alexisrael

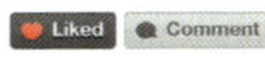

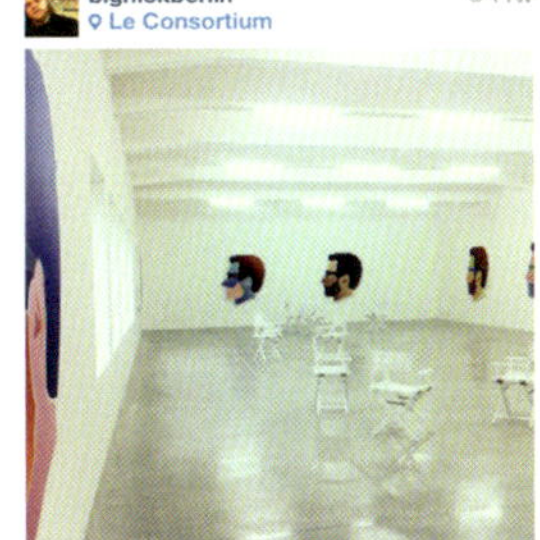

bignickberlin
♀ Le Consortium   ◷ 11w

♡ **16 likes**

bignickberlin Self Portraits by #alexisrael
from his 2013 solo show at @peresprojects
Berlin. On view at Le Consortium in Dijon, FR
bignickberlin #major

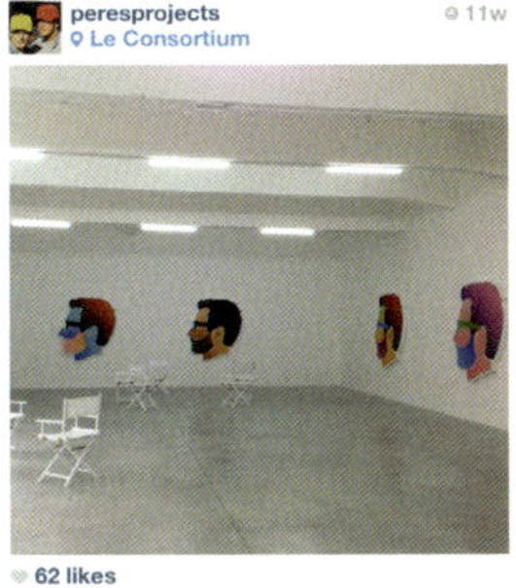

peresprojects
♀ Le Consortium   ◷ 11w

♡ **62 likes**

peresprojects #alexisrael #leconsortium
#peresprojects

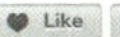

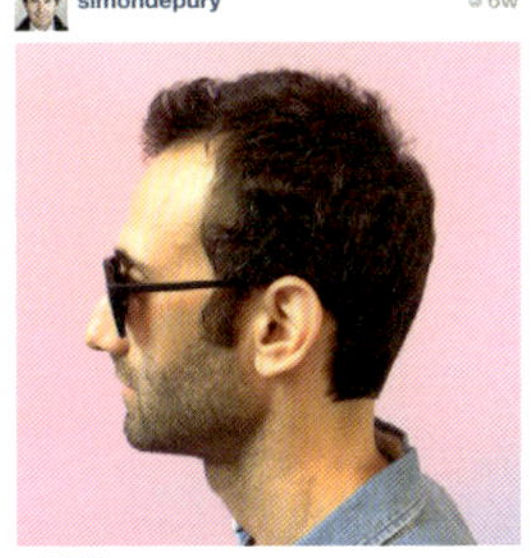

simondepury   ◷ 6w

♡ **172 likes**

simondepury @alexisrael #alexisrael
#peresprojects #alminerech
view all 7 comments
china_chow My baby daddy!!! ❤️

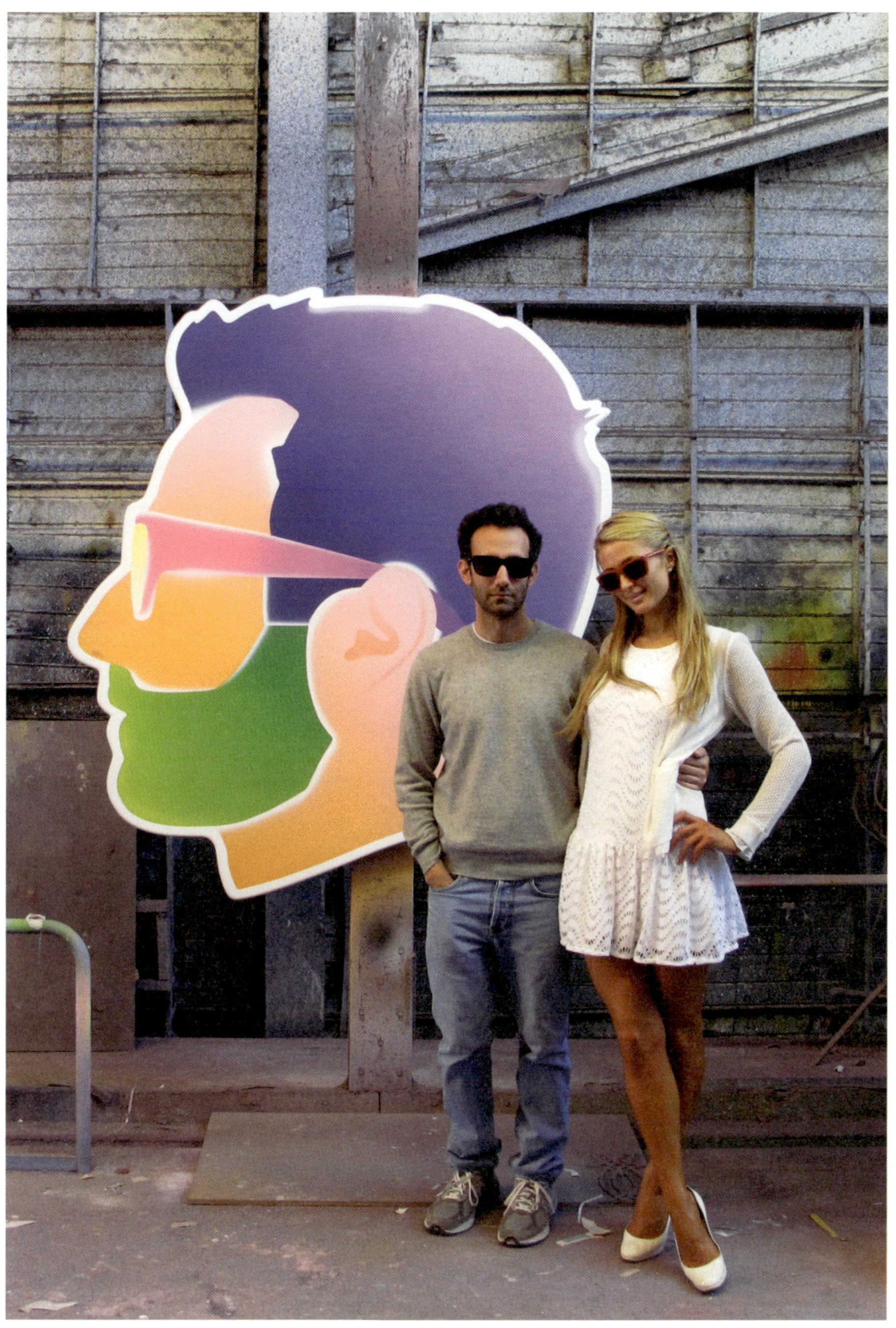

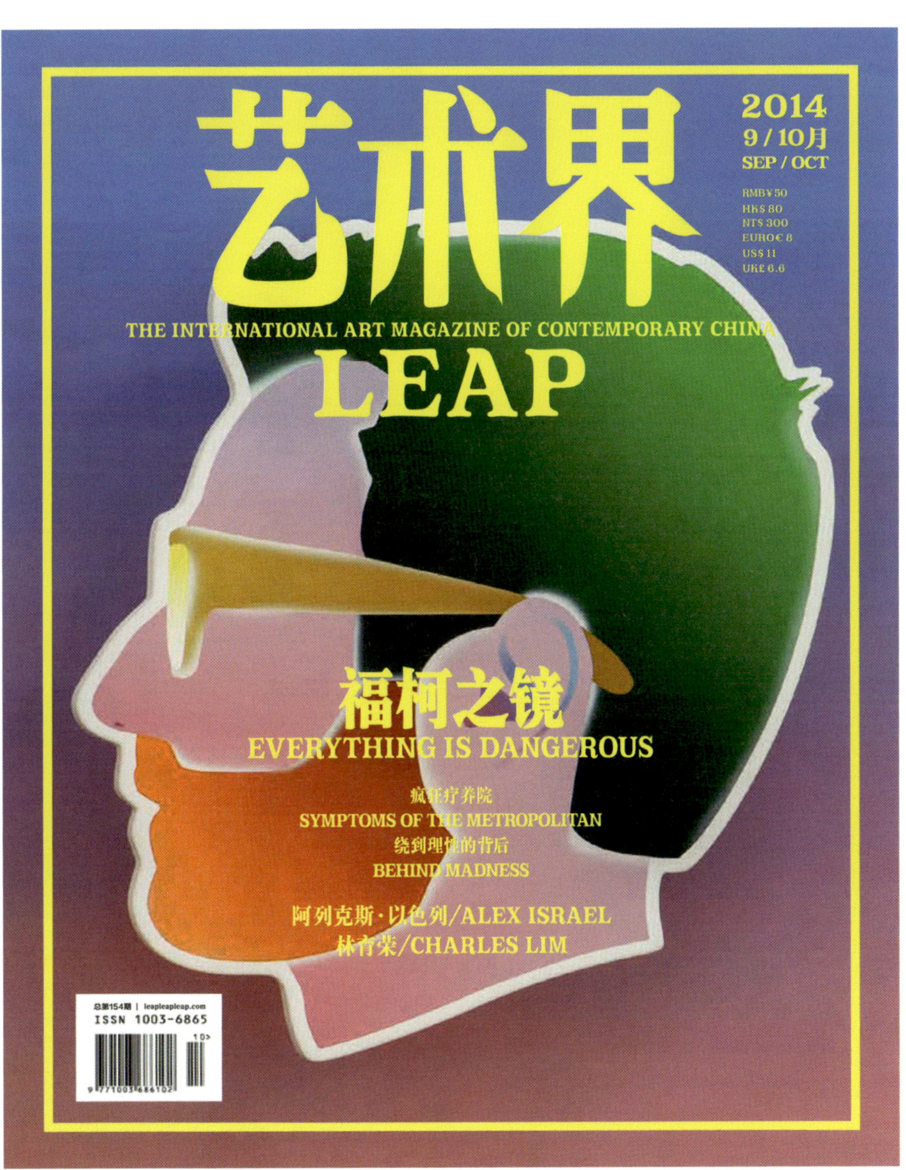

2014
9 / 10月
SEP / OCT
RMB¥50
HK$ 80
NT$ 300
EURO€ 8
US$ 11
UK£ 6.6
艺术界
THE INTERNATIONAL ART MAGAZINE OF CONTEMPORARY CHINA
LEAP
福柯之镜
EVERYTHING IS DANGEROUS
疯狂疗养院
SYMPTOMS OF THE METROPOLITAN
绕到理性的背后
BEHIND MADNESS
阿列克斯·以色列/ALEX ISRAEL
林育荣/CHARLES LIM
总第154期 | leapleapleap.com
ISSN 1003-6865

DER TAG

DER TAG

Wenn aus Feinden Freunde werden: **Alliierte Spuren** in Berlin – *Seiten 12 + 29*

Mitmach-F Zuschauer das Social

BERLIN, DONNERSTAG, 25. APRIL 2013 / 69. JAHRGANG / NR. 21 670 *

Linksliberaler soll Italien regieren

ROM - Italiens Staatspräsident Giorgio Napolitano hat am Mittwoch den linksliberalen Politiker Enrico Letta (46) eingesetzt, als designierter Ministerpräsident eine neue Regierung zu bilden. Der Vize-Chef der Demokratischen Partei (PD) soll sich die Unterstützung einer großen Koalition sichern, um die nach den Parlamentswahlen vor zwei Monaten entstandene Regierungskrise zu lösen. Er muss sich dann dem Vertrauensvotum des Parlaments stellen. Er habe diesen Auftrag unter Vorbehalt angenommen, wolle jetzt sofort mit allen politischen Kräften über eine Unterstützung sprechen und dann „so schnell wie möglich" Napolitano berichten, erklärte der designierte neue Regierungschef. Der Nachfolger des noch kommissarisch regierenden Monti steht vor einem Berg von Aufgaben. Das Land braucht dringend Wachstum. *dpa*

— *Seite 3 und Meinungsseite*

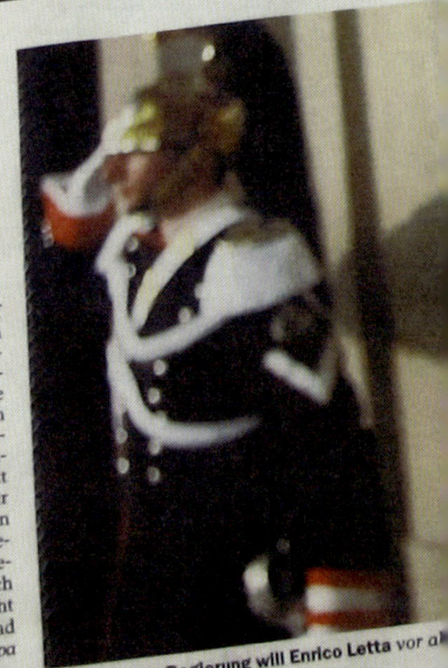

Als Chef einer Regierung will Enrico Letta vor a

Anti-Terror

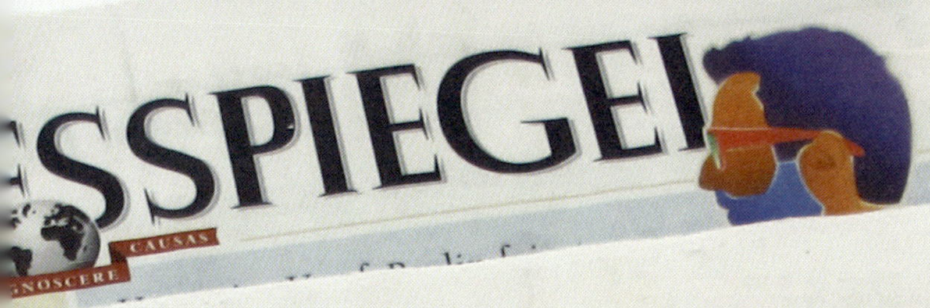

ESSPIEGEL

IM COGNOSCERE CAUSAS

Kunst im Kopf: Berlin feiert das **Gallery Weekend** und lockt Sammler aus aller Welt – Seiten 25 + 26

ehen:
ecken
– Seite 31

BERLIN / BRANDENBURG 1,10 €, AUSWÄRTS 1,40 €, AUSLAND 1,60 €

WWW.TAGESSPIEGEL.DE

Politischer Einspruch

Von Stephan-Andreas Casdorff

Andreas Voßkuhle - dieser Name wird zum Streitfall und zum Synonym: für das, was die Politik a Bundesverfassungsgericht stört, ja me noch, geradezu ärgert. Der Präside Voßkuhle also, erscheint in den Au nicht nur des Bundesinnenministe maßend. Ein harsches Wort, das sti aber es trifft die Gemütslage der rung. Denn Voßkuhle reizt mit s Widerspruch inzwischen zu instit lem Widerspruch.

Dass er, zum Beispiel, Inner Hans-Peter Friedrich nach dem von Boston doch ziemlich dire sonnenheit auffordert, bedeu ihm damit gewissermaßen nicht besonnen genug zu rea das, weil der Innenminister die Ermittlungen in den US weitete Videoüberwachun muss man kein Freund di sein; es kann einen du nehm berühren. Zumal die deutsch-deutsche kann man da sensibel s

Aber es ist anderer Der Bundesinnenmin dige für die Innere S der im Zweifelsfall, i verantwortlich ge nicht alles Möglic worden sein sollte tung nämlich auch geht also quasi u

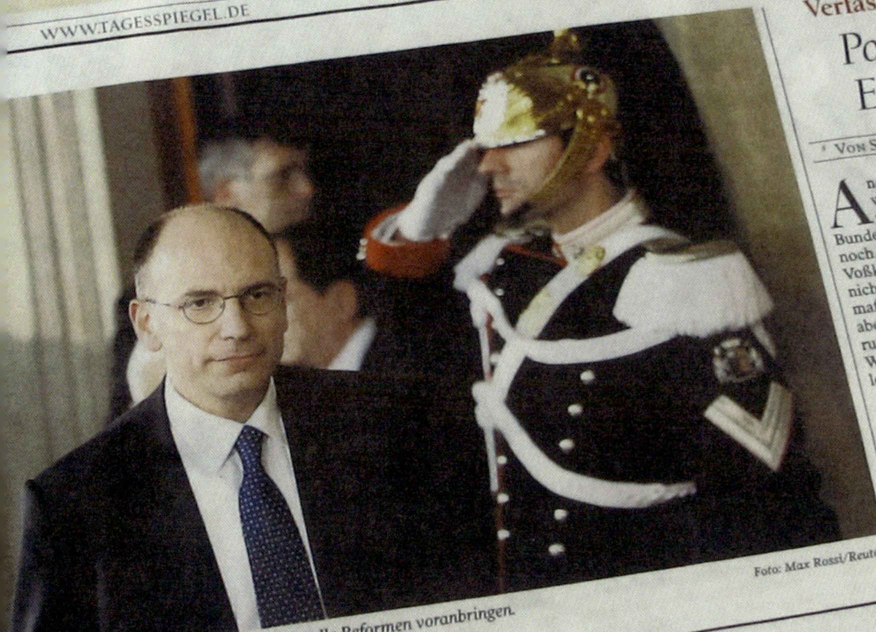

Foto: Max Rossi/Reuters

ne Arbeitslosigkeit angehen und institutionelle Reformen voranbringen.

Datei muss korrigiert werden

ismusbekämpfung rechtfertigt Austausch von Informationen

here Hürden bei

Siegfried Kauder (CDU), Vorsitzender des Rechtsausschusses des Deutschen begrüßte das Urteil eben-

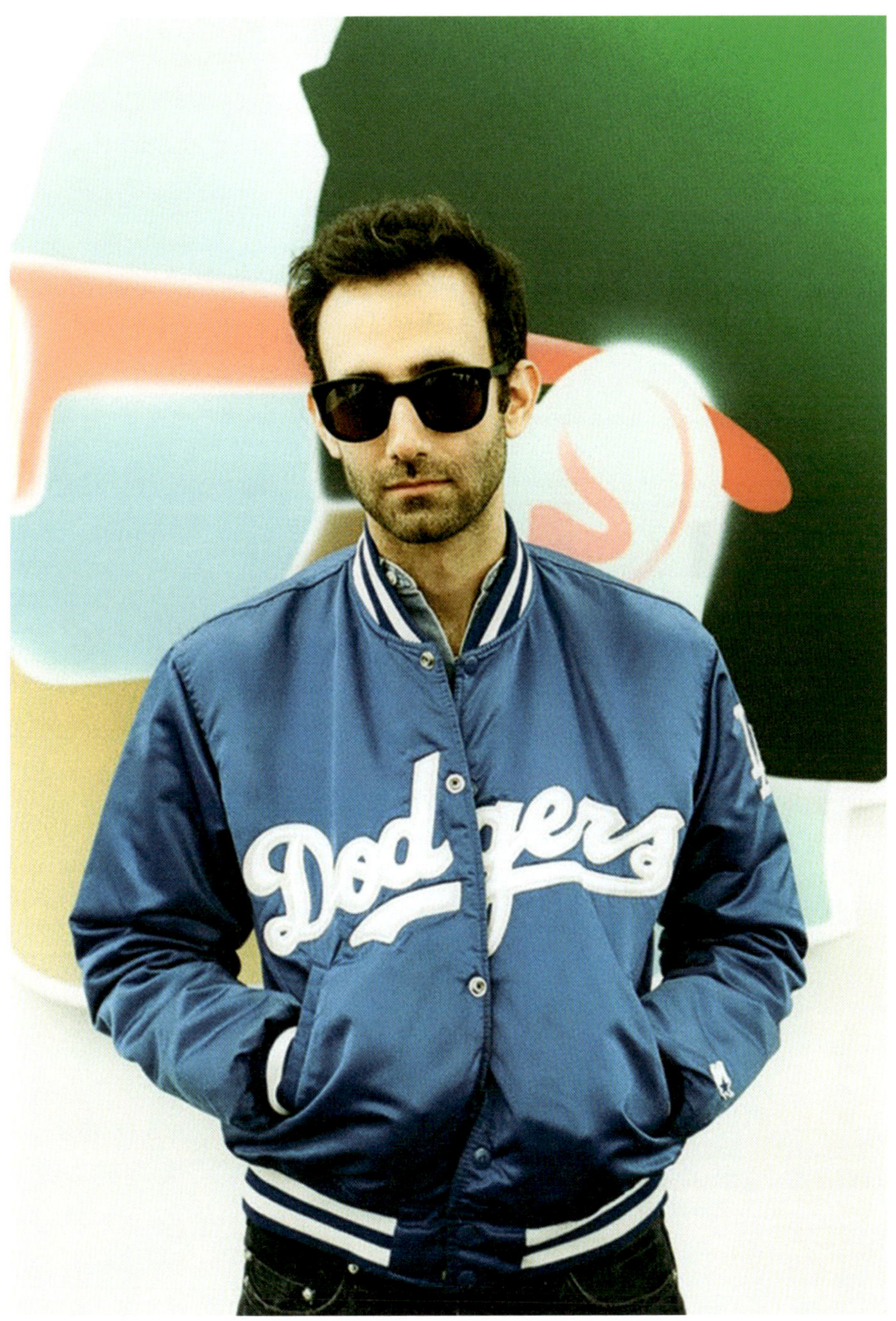

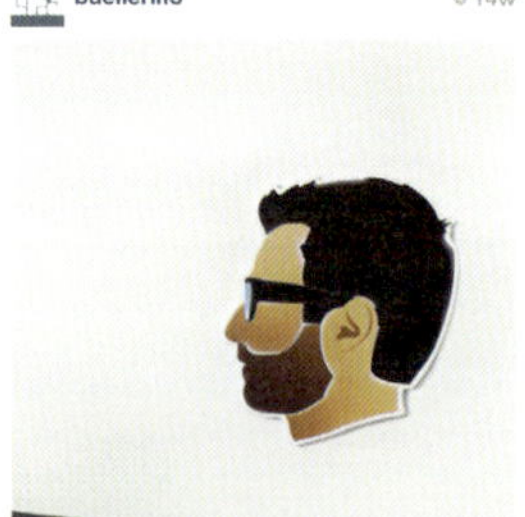

buellerlif3   14w

♡ victoriaptrsen, thedmdoodles, trent_on, kellirenae, callme_squirtle, osnuflaz, ry1c, cinc_cpac_, dylanlacey

buellerlif3 Alex Israel 'Self-Portraits' (Peres Projects) #alexisrael #peresprojects

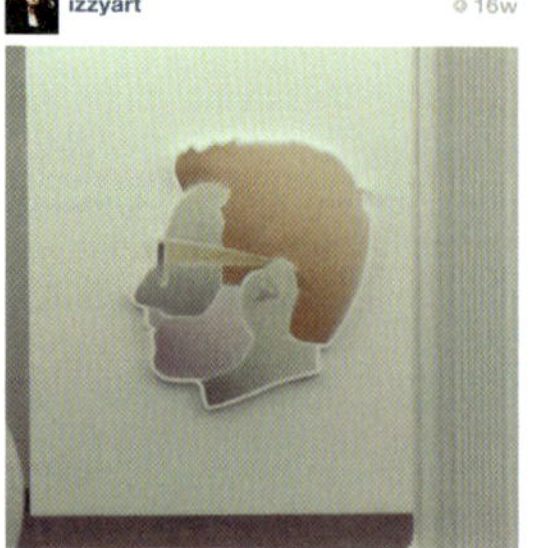

izzyart   16w

♡ 11 likes

izzyart #alexisrael #popart #berlin

♥ Like   💬 Comment   •••

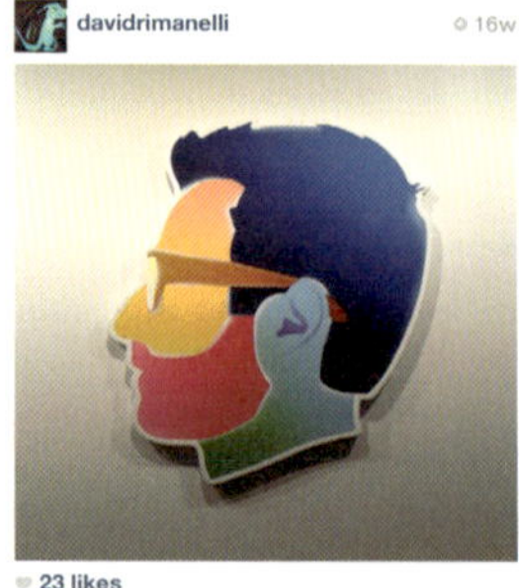
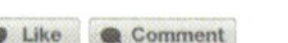

davidrimanelli   16w

♡ 23 likes

davidrimanelli #alexisrael

♥ Like   💬 Comment   •••

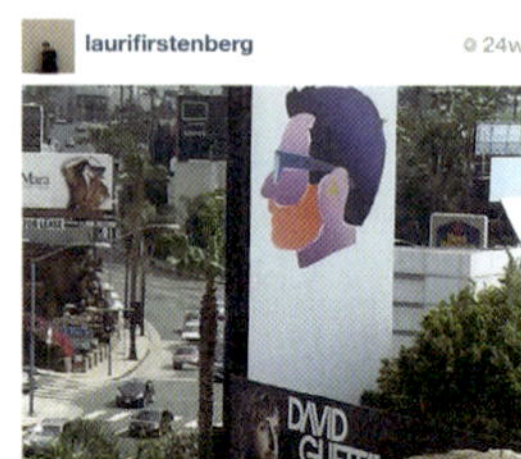

laurifirstenberg   24w

♡ 24 likes

laurifirstenberg #LAXART and #Art Production Fund present #Alex Israel #billboard on #sunset boulevard in #west Hollywood

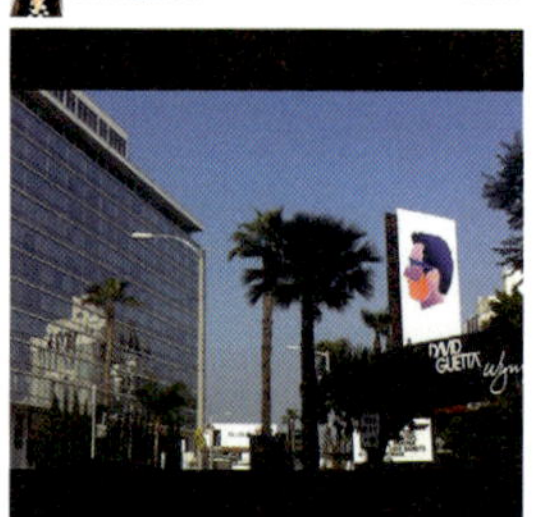

china_chow   23w

♡ 144 likes

china_chow I spy Alex Israel's self-portrait on Sunset Strip! Made possible by @laxart @foryourart @artproductionny #publicart

view all 6 comments

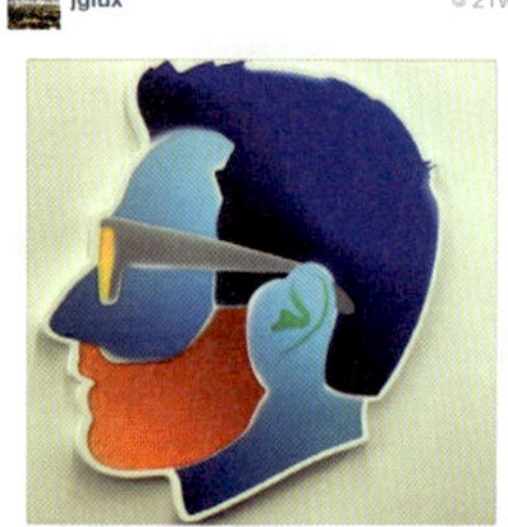

jglux   21w

♡ 17 likes

jglux #alexisrael

♥ Like   💬 Comment   •••

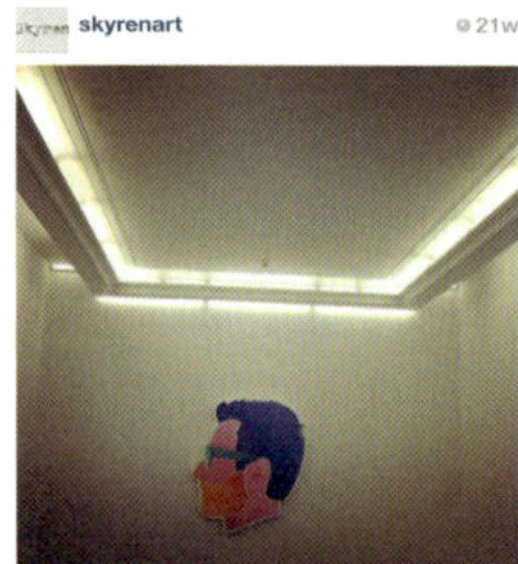

skyrenart   21w

♡ llivblog, dbolu, alexandralichtenberg, alnasser_art, ualtunkas, halloherbert, yvo___, jadetantillo

skyrenart #galleryweekend#alexisrael#berlin#selfportrait

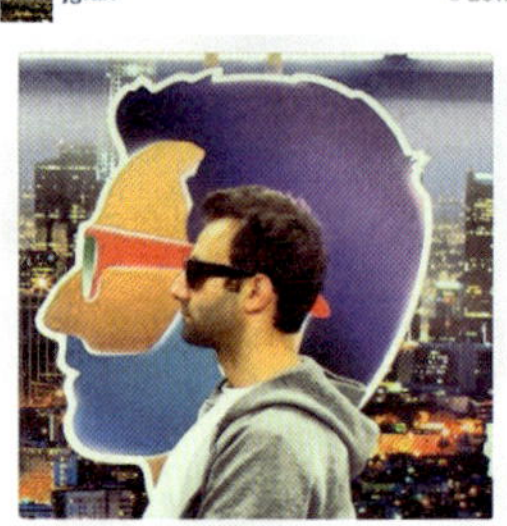

jglux   26w

♡ 23 likes

jglux 😎 🍺 📼

andisrael 🍺 🏄 ⛵

jglux #alexisrael

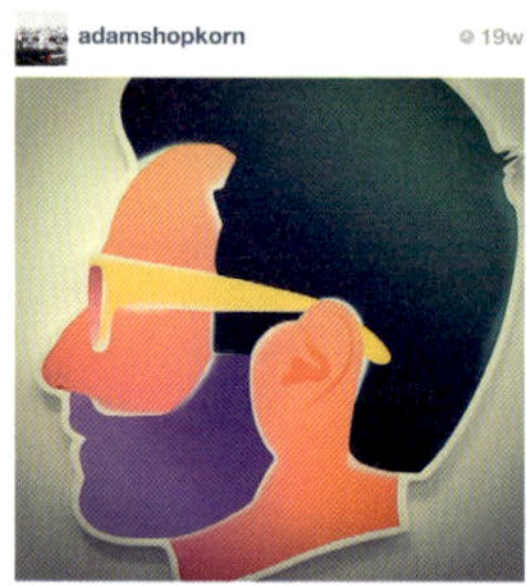

adamshopkorn   19w

♡ meenalmistry, rasnabhasin, carolyntangel, bettinakorek, jordanmatthewwolfson, ericablumenthal

adamshopkorn Homie @alexisrael at Frieze Art Fair Randall's Island #alexisrael

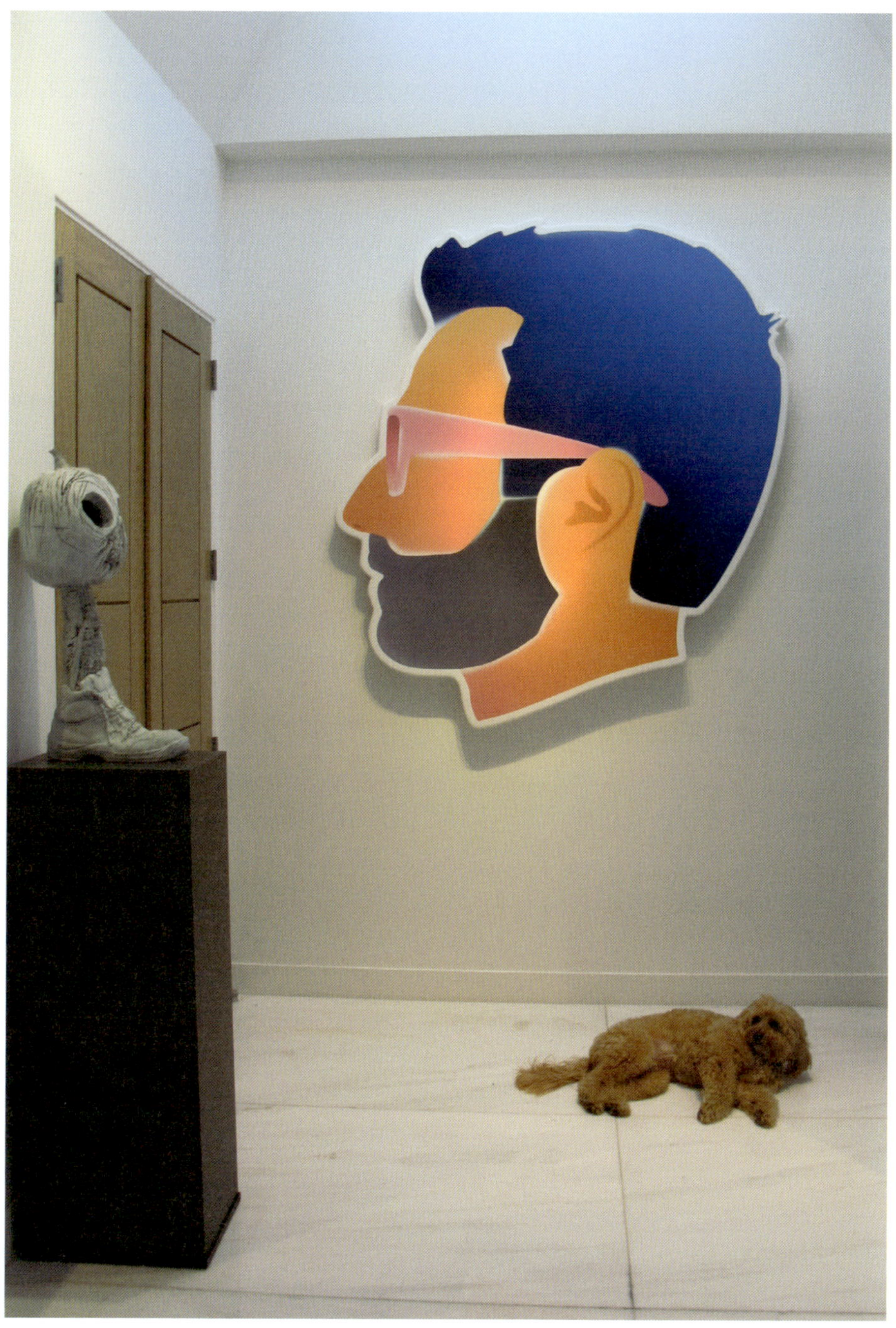

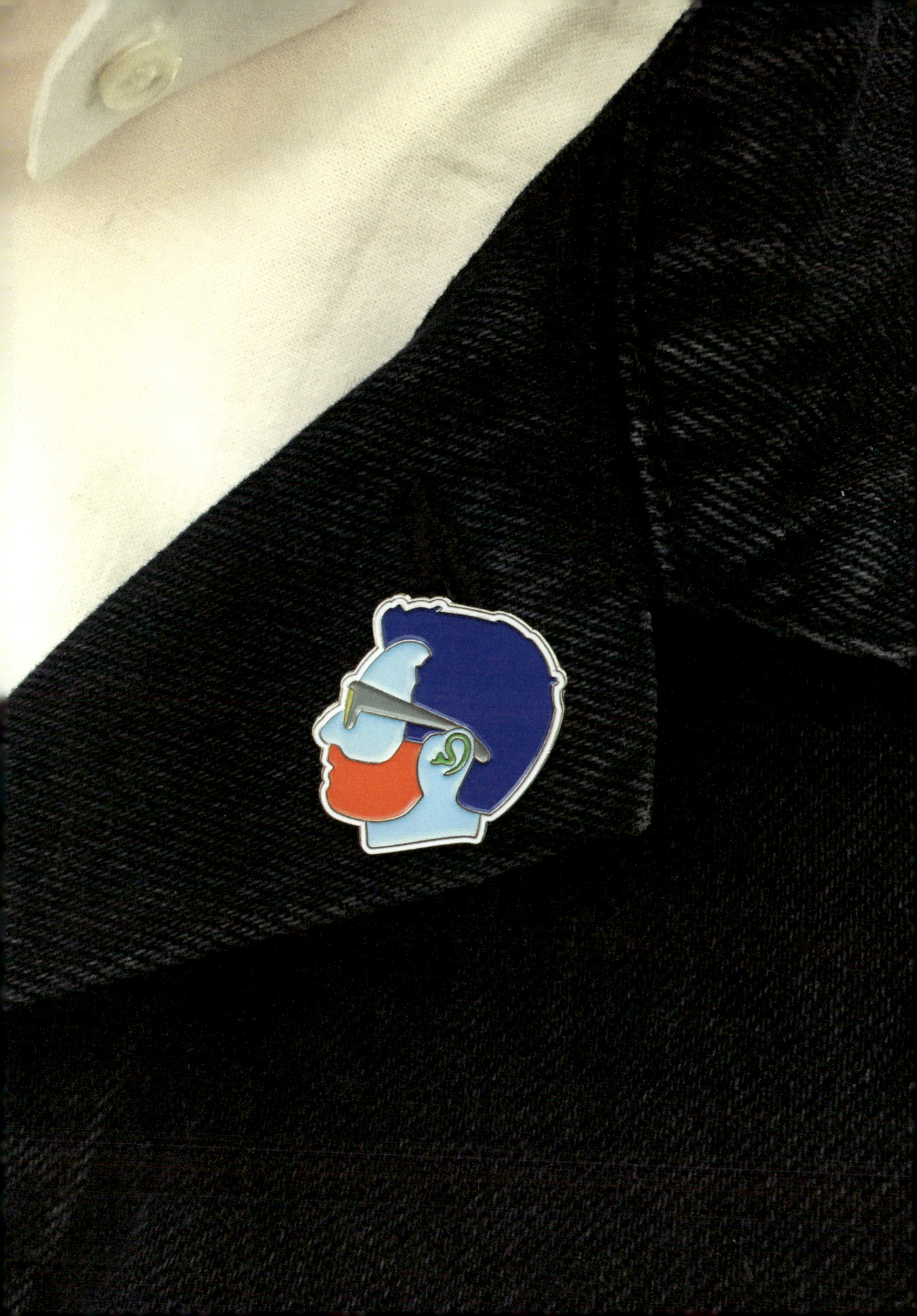

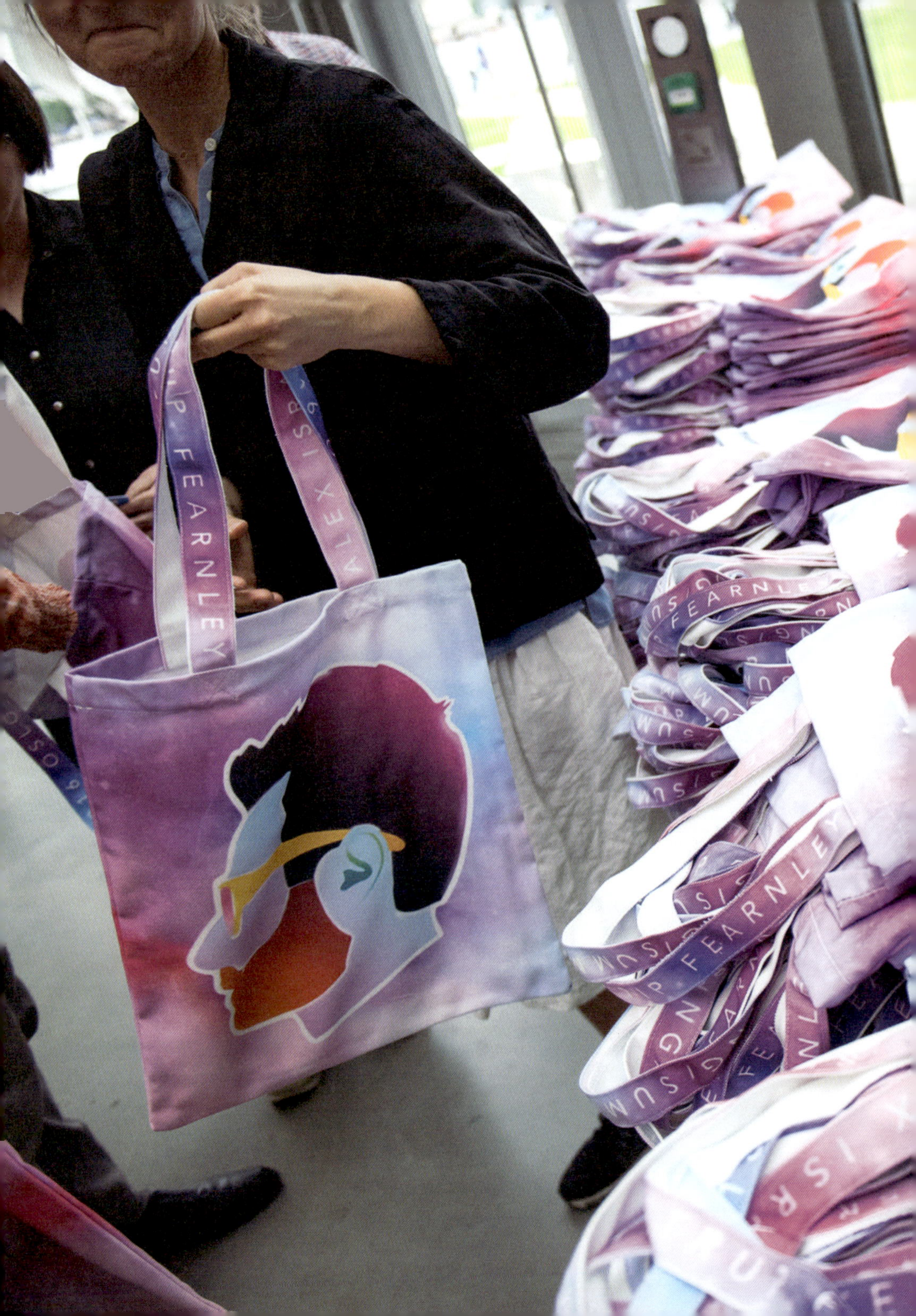

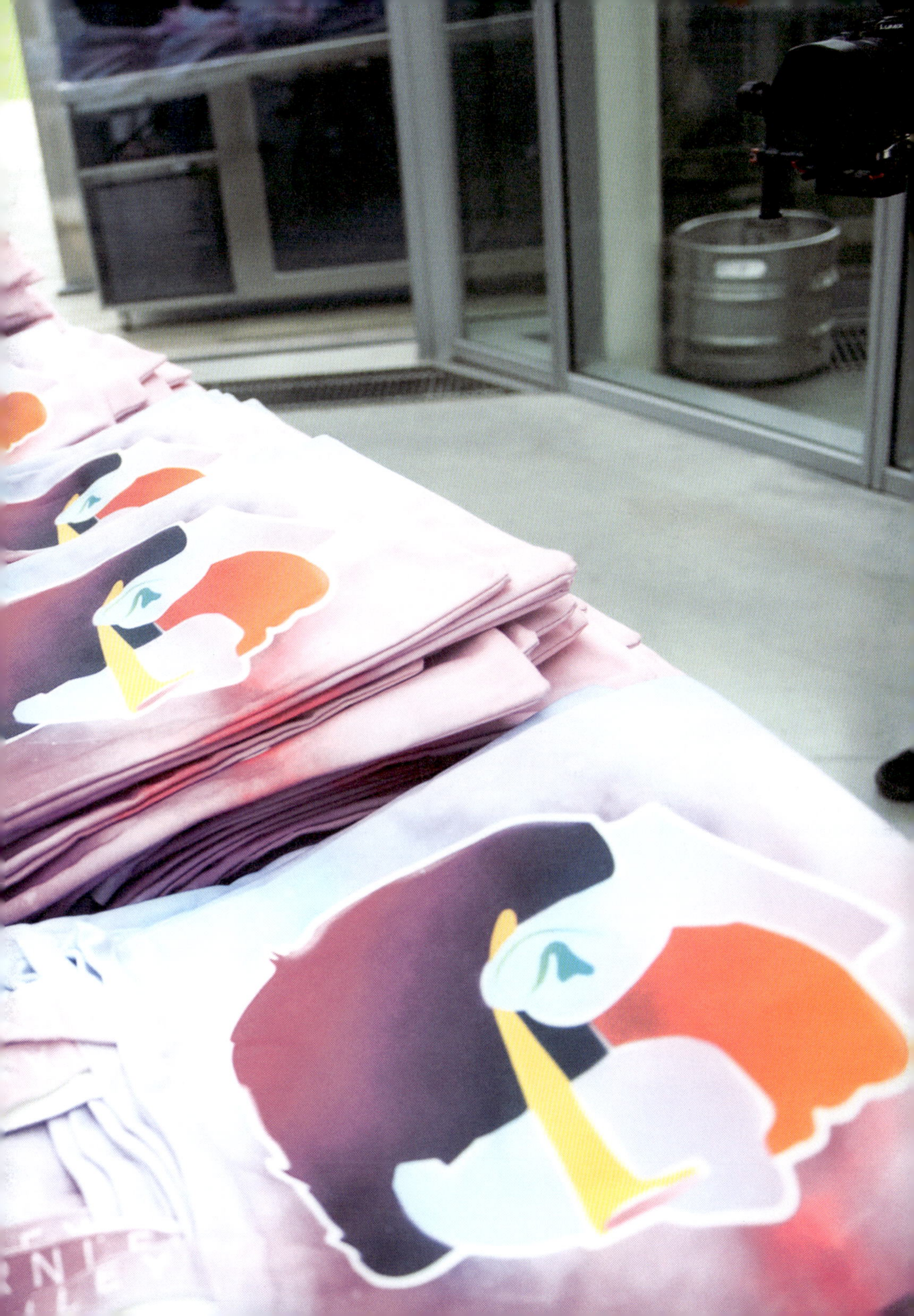

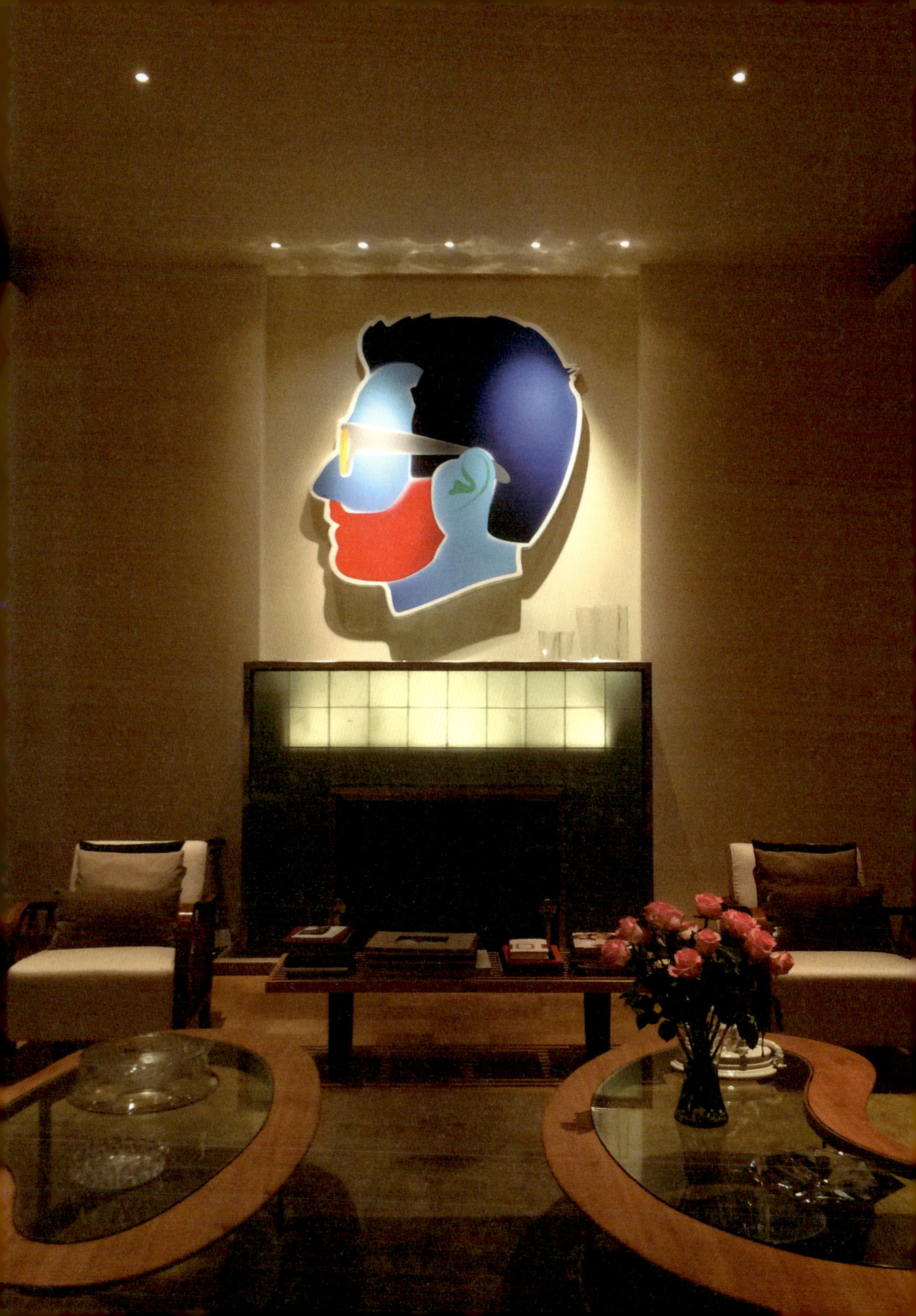

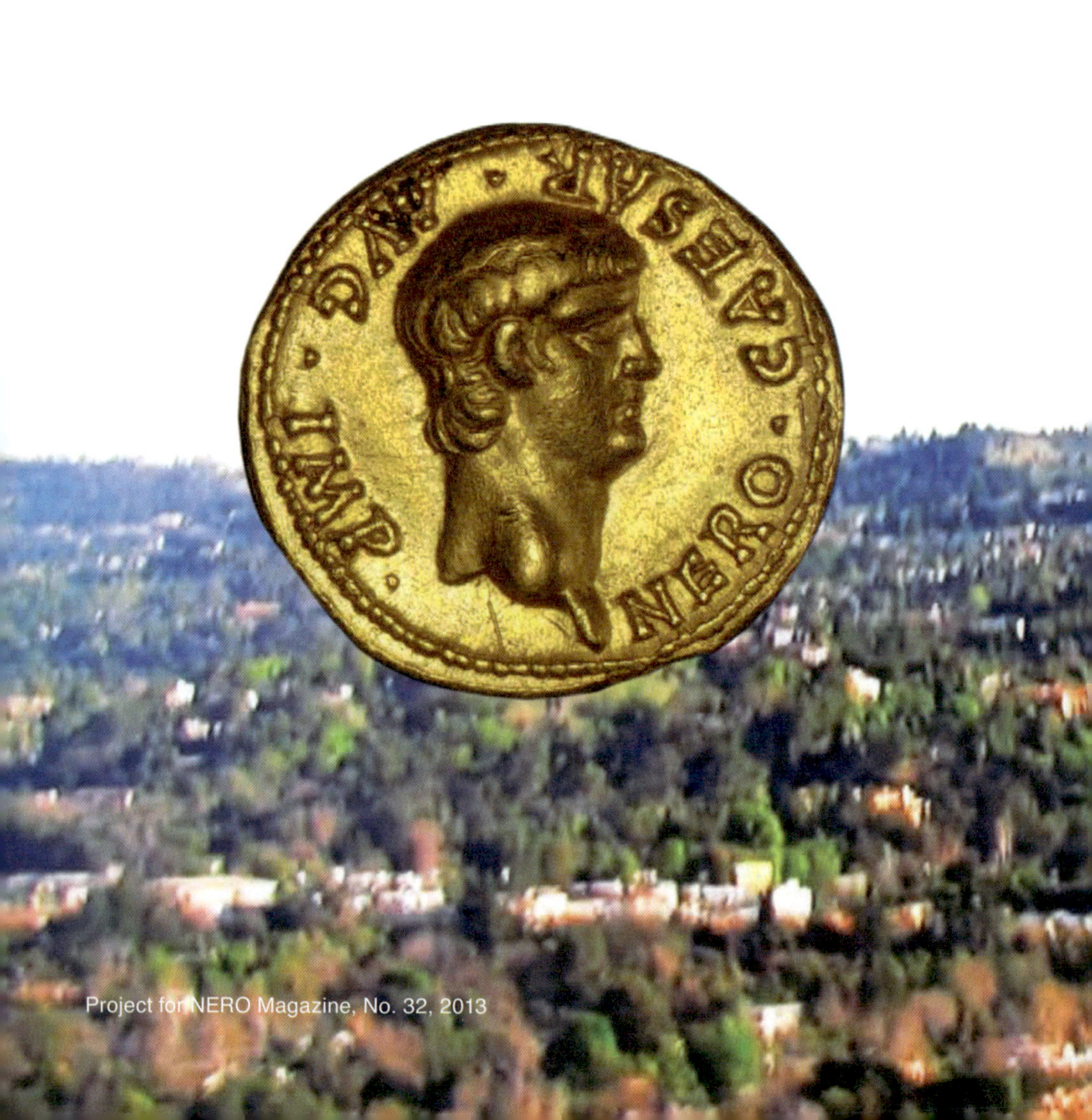

Project for NERO Magazine, No. 32, 2013

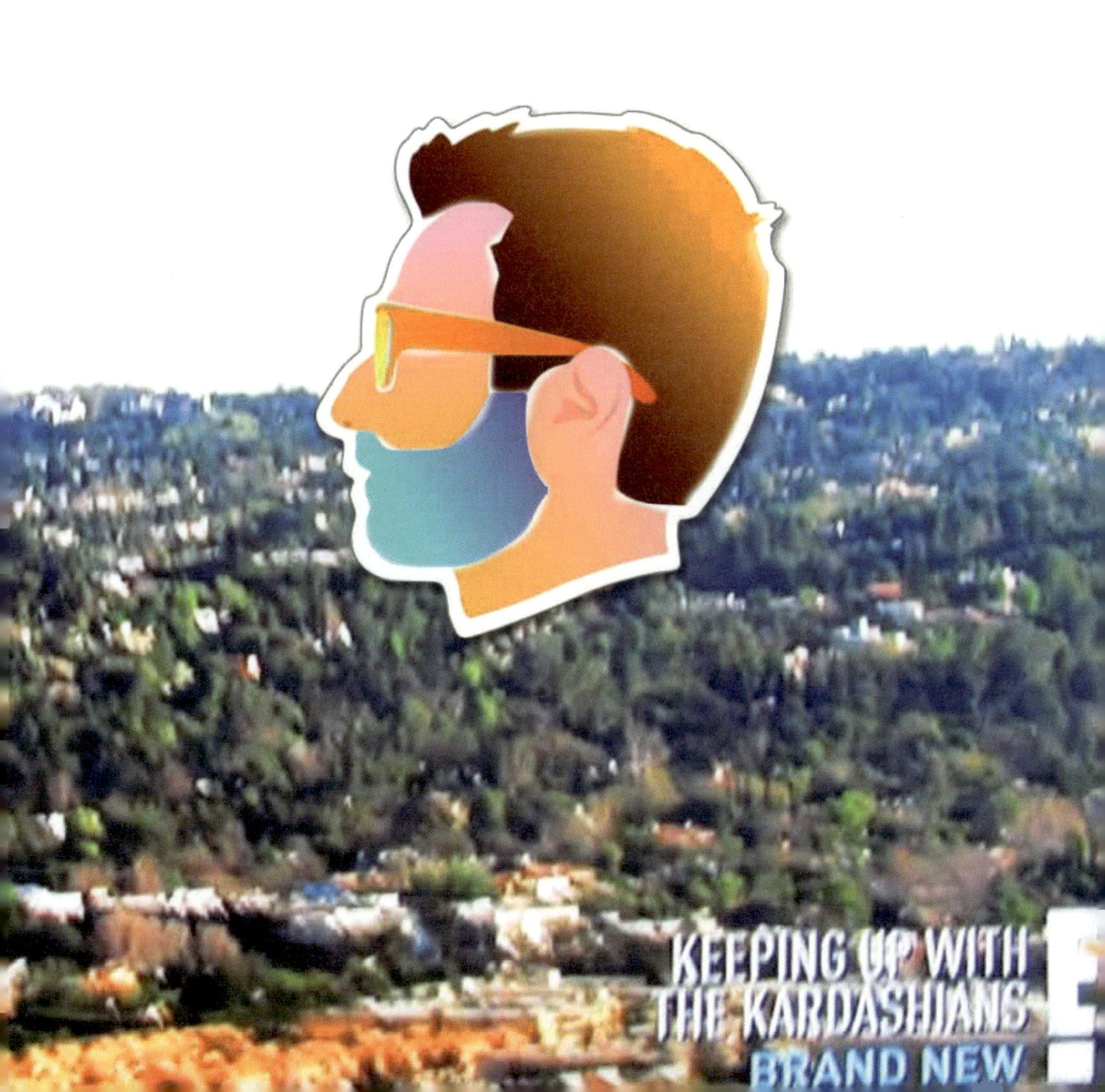

KEEPING UP WITH THE KARDASHIANS
BRAND NEW

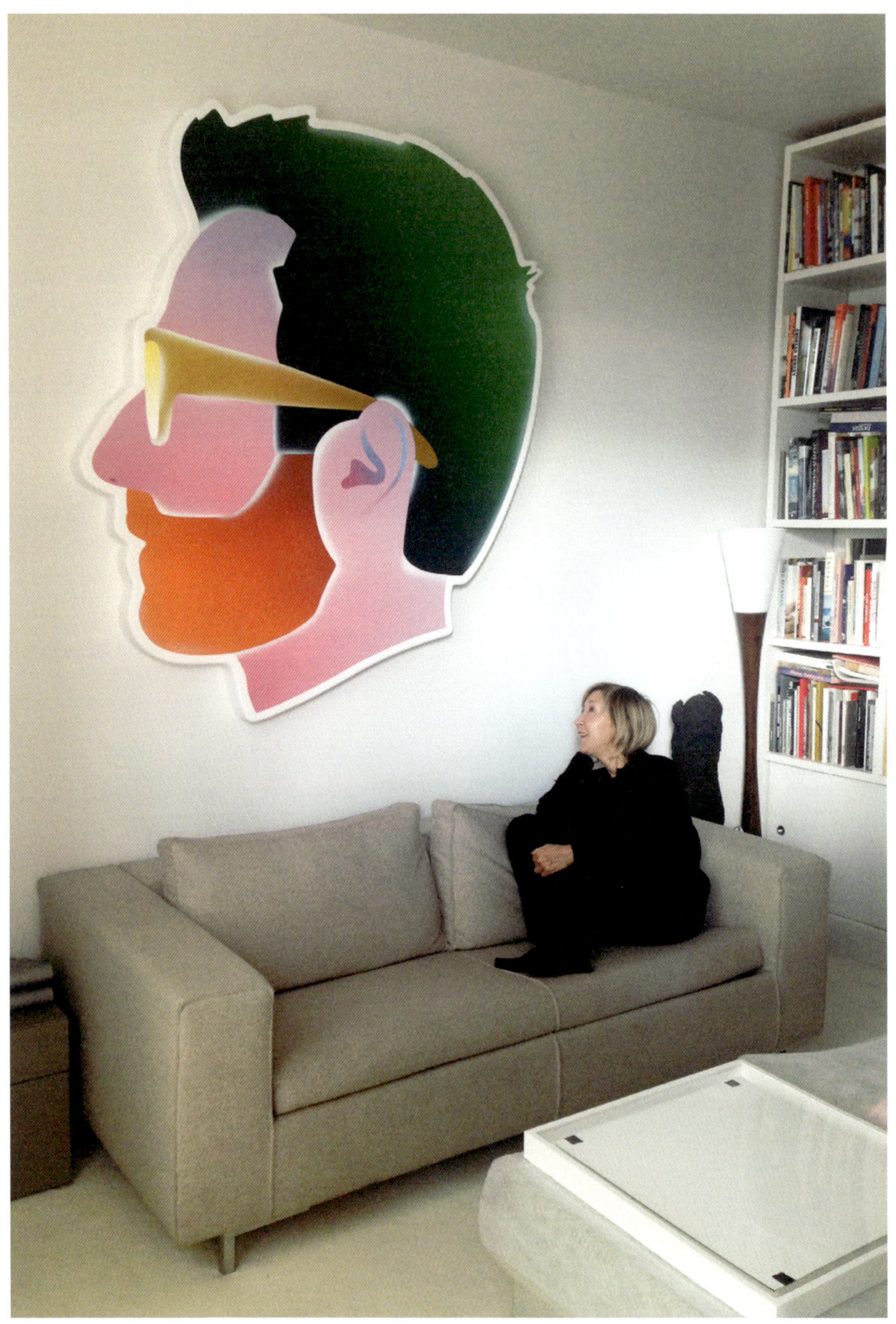

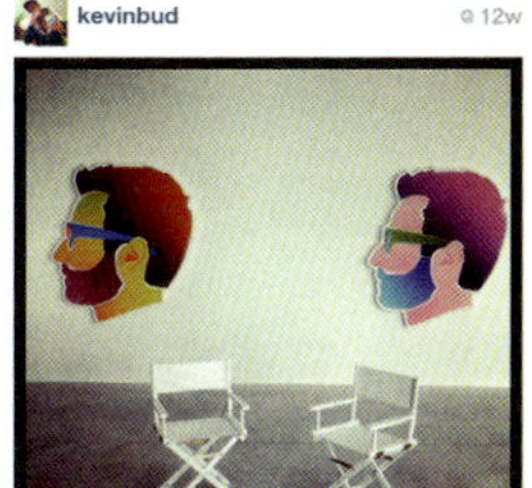

nathalielaloum, n_bertrand, cassandreperroud, adihoc
kevinbud #consortium #alexisrael #egotrip #galere

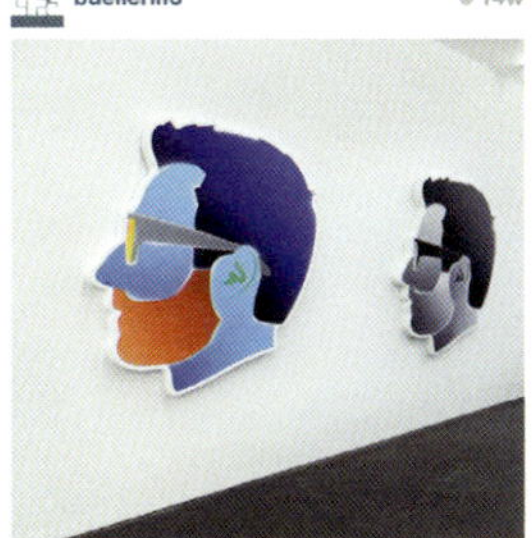

nathalielaloum, ry1c, tartofgold, johnsonc1975, kellirenae
buellerlif3 Alex Israel 'Self-Portraits' (Peres Projects) #alexisrael #peresprojects

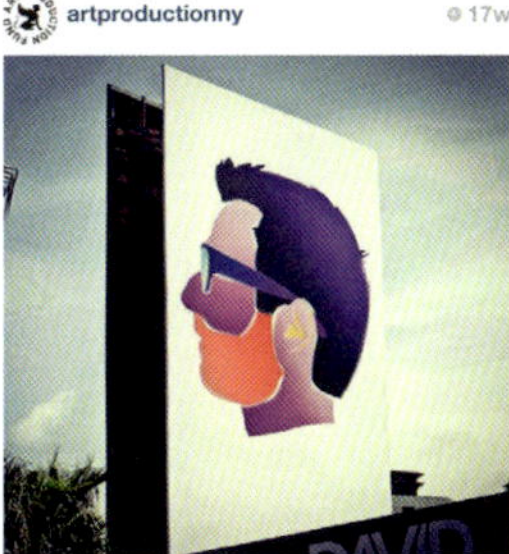

88 likes
artproductionny APF takes LA this week! Our first stop? #SunsetBoulevard to see the @alexisrael public billboard produced by APF,

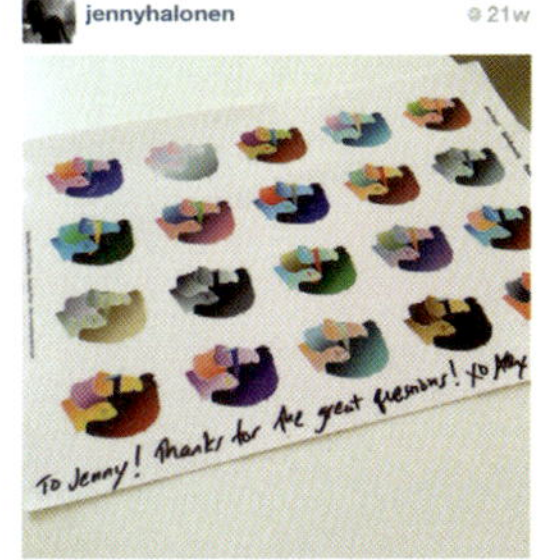

henist, heykiddolifesnotthatbad, campgabby, matsjernberg, sandhya_f, nathalielaloum, anneli56, charleslibeert, gianlucasoldi
jennyhalonen thank you #alexisrael

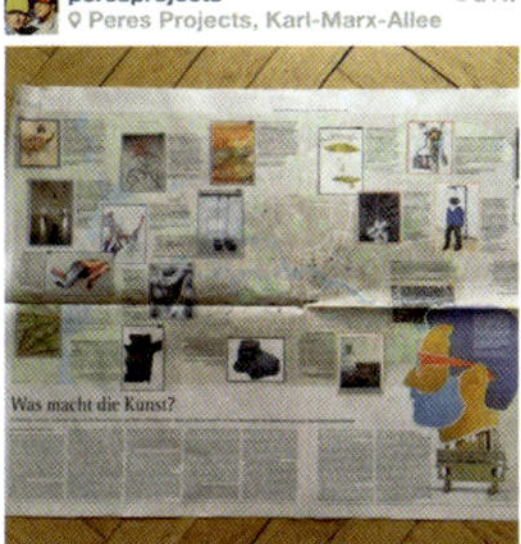

22 likes
peresprojects In today's Berliner Morgen Post #AlexIsrael #SelfPortraits #Peres

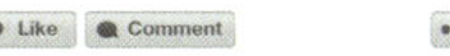

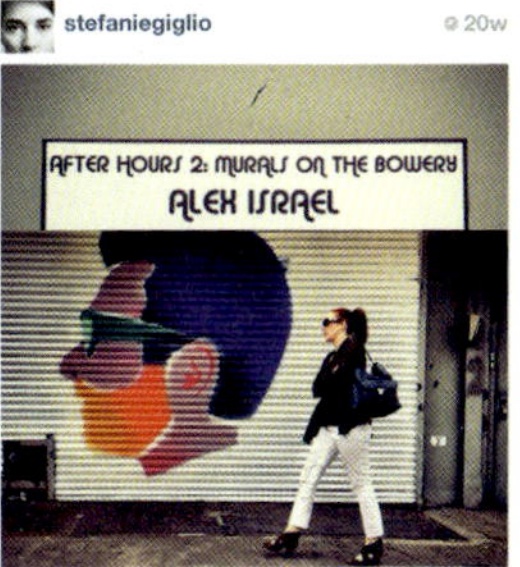

36 likes
stefaniegiglio Thanks to the Art Production Fund and the Murals on the Bowery project, my daily commutes are much more interesting.

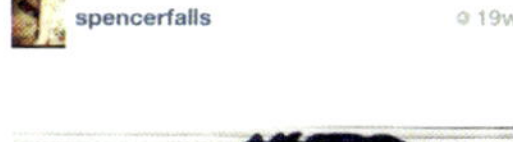

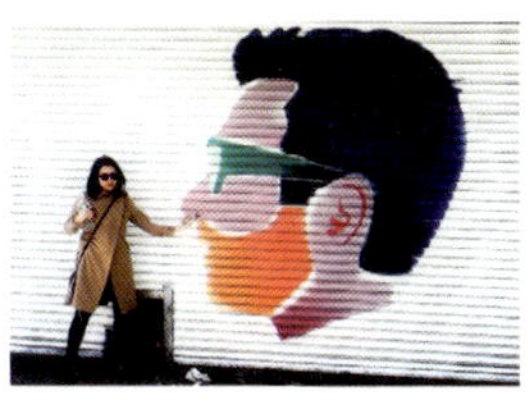

27 likes
spencerfalls A nose that big must be picked. @bones_and_feathers digging deep on Bowery. #AlexIsrael

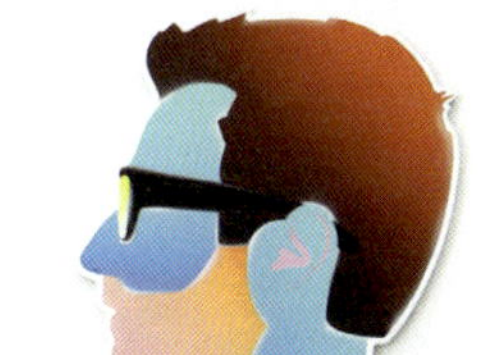

klightbox, millsmoran, bmedan, heathermhubbs, nielskantor, simmyswinder, mrgodsill, ireneneuwirth
ninomier Why I like these is beyond me. I seriously don't understand why I like these but I sort of do. But why? #alexisrael

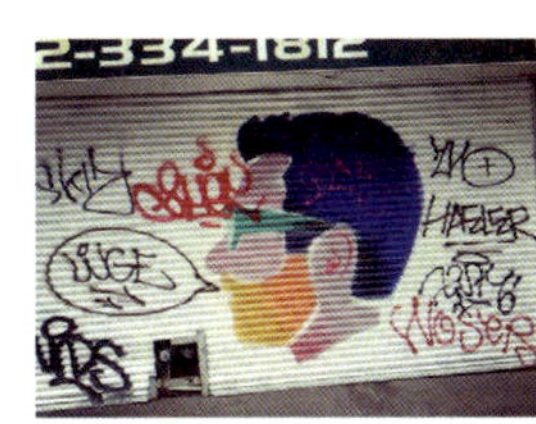

127 likes
thejournalinc @alexisrael
thejournalinc #AlexIsrael on The Bowery

HOME | ABOUT | VIDEOS

Details

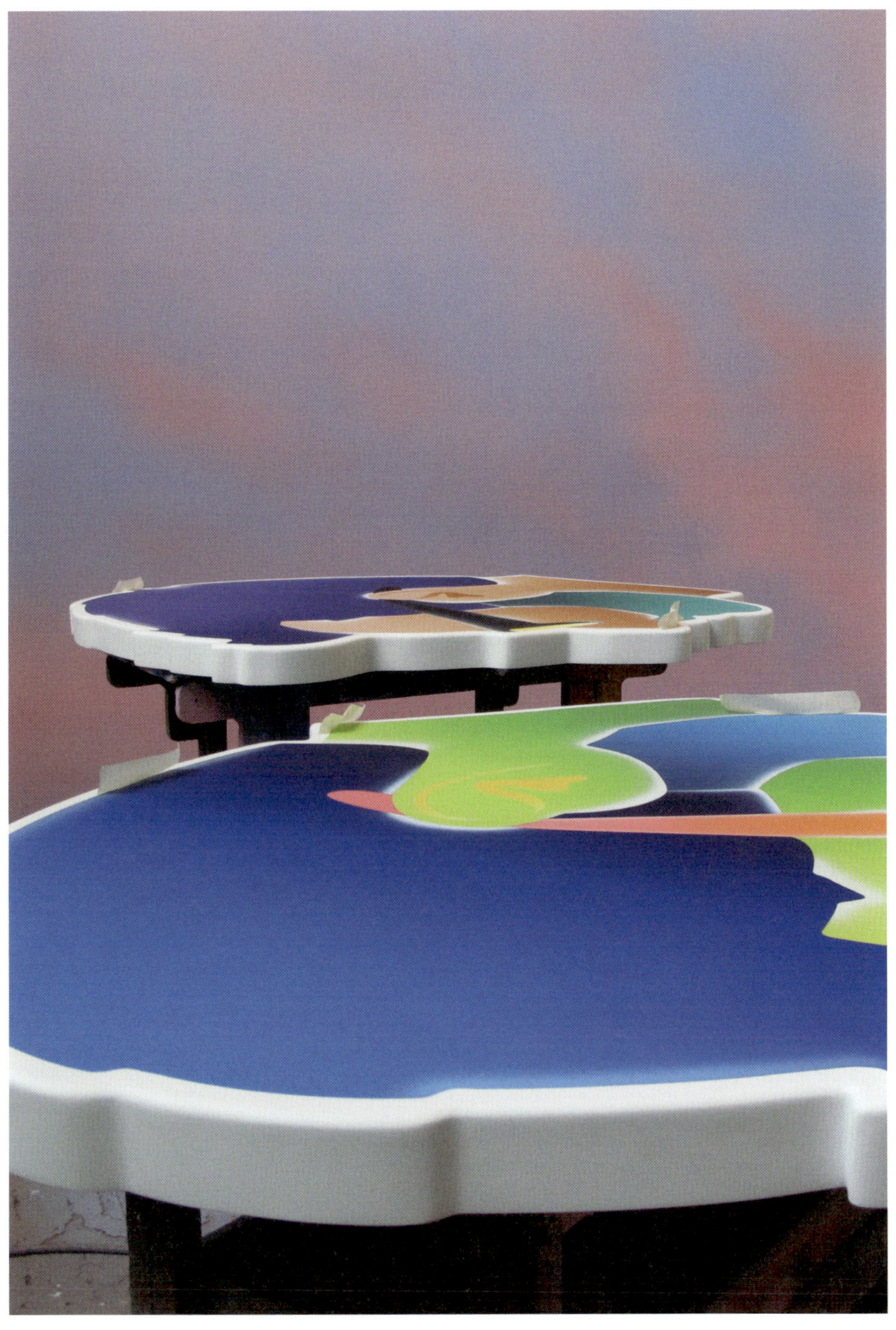

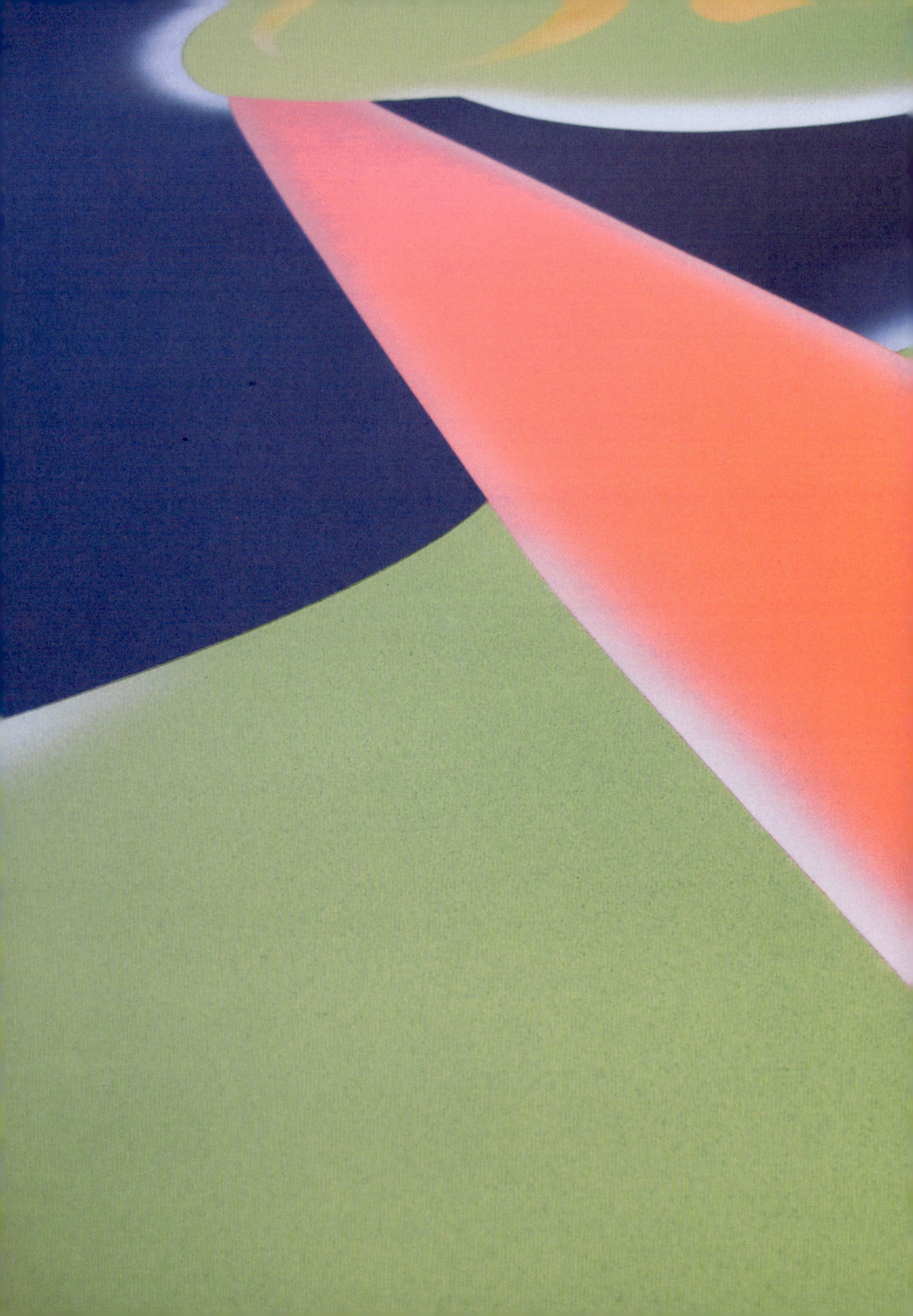

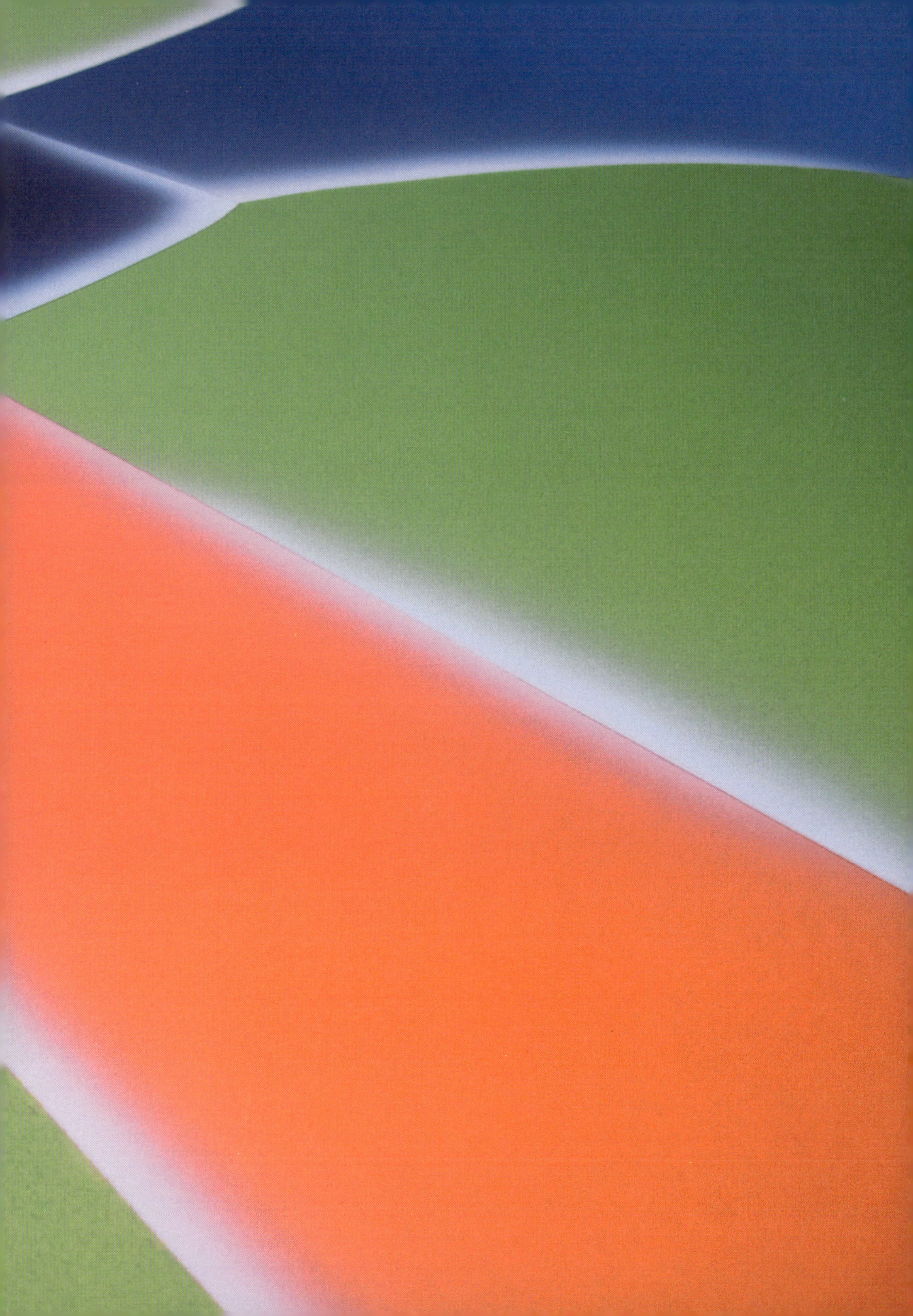

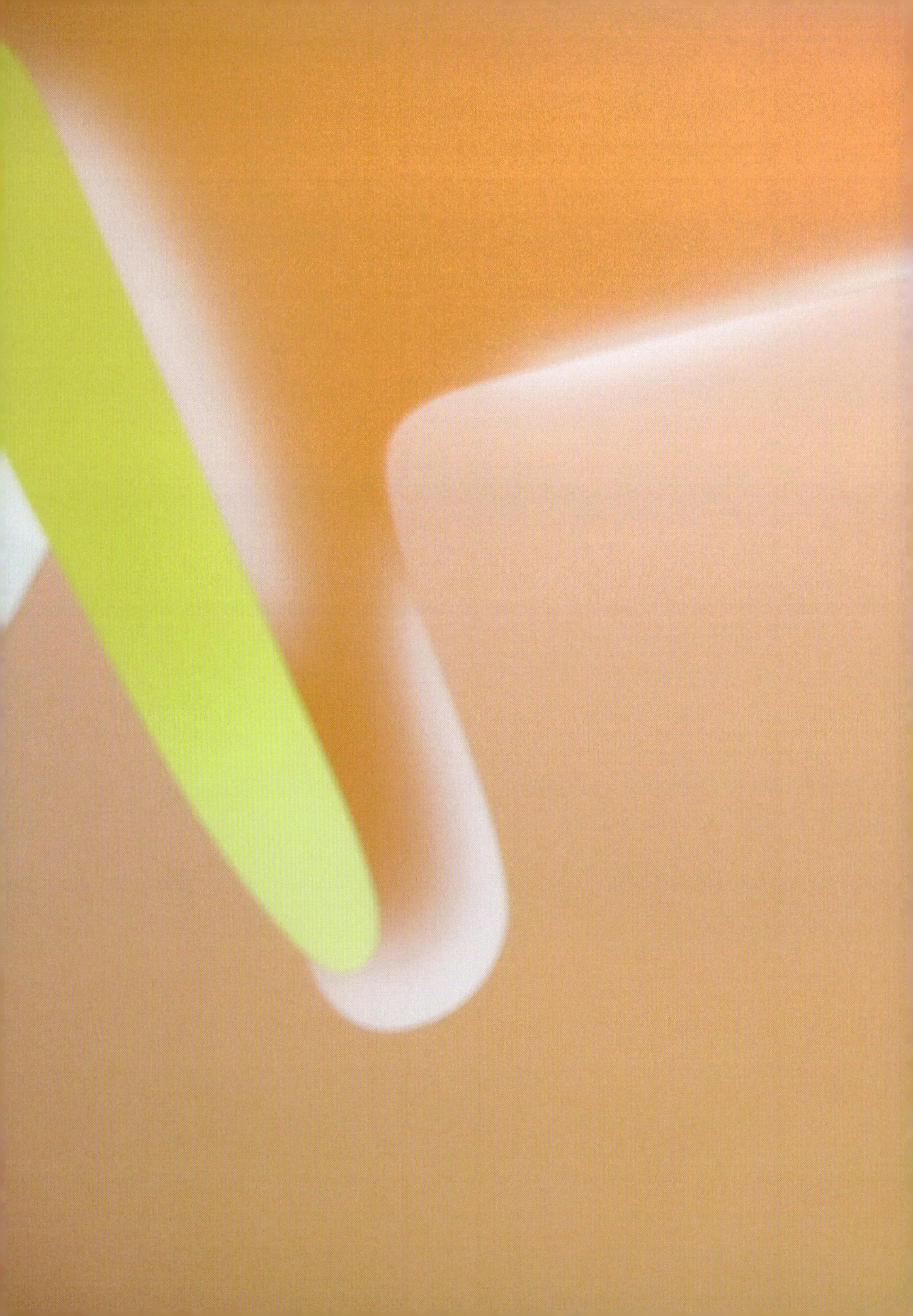

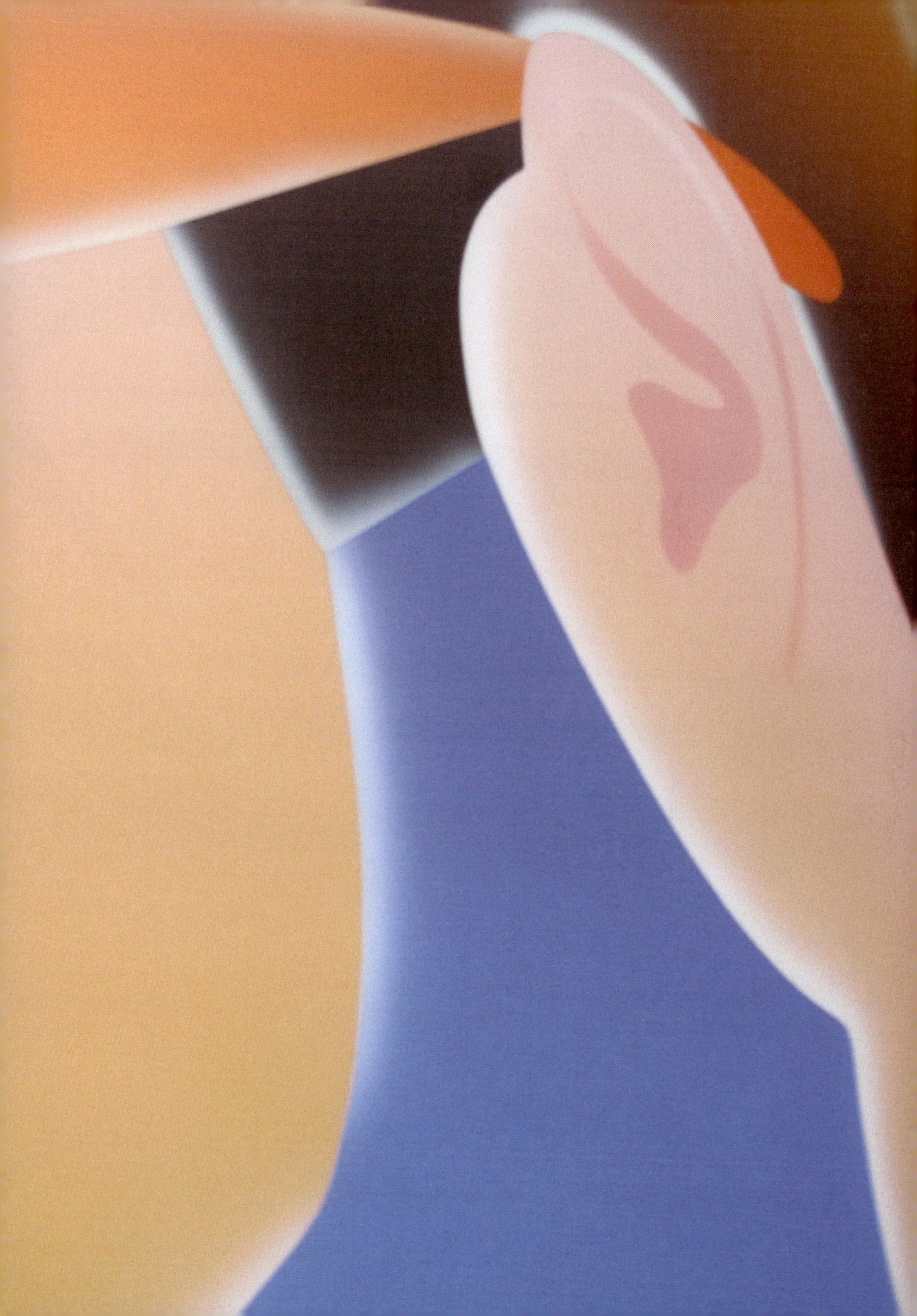

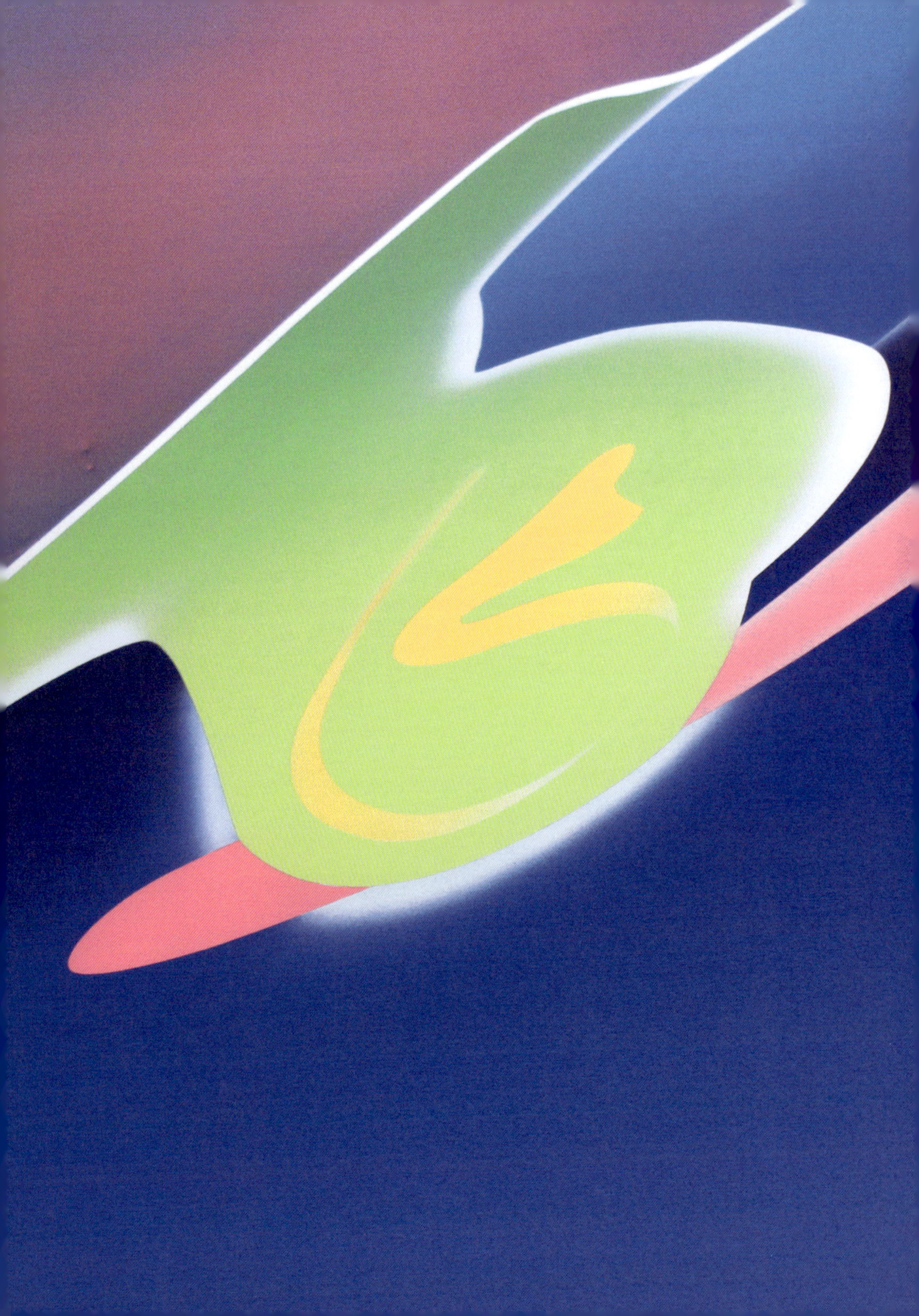

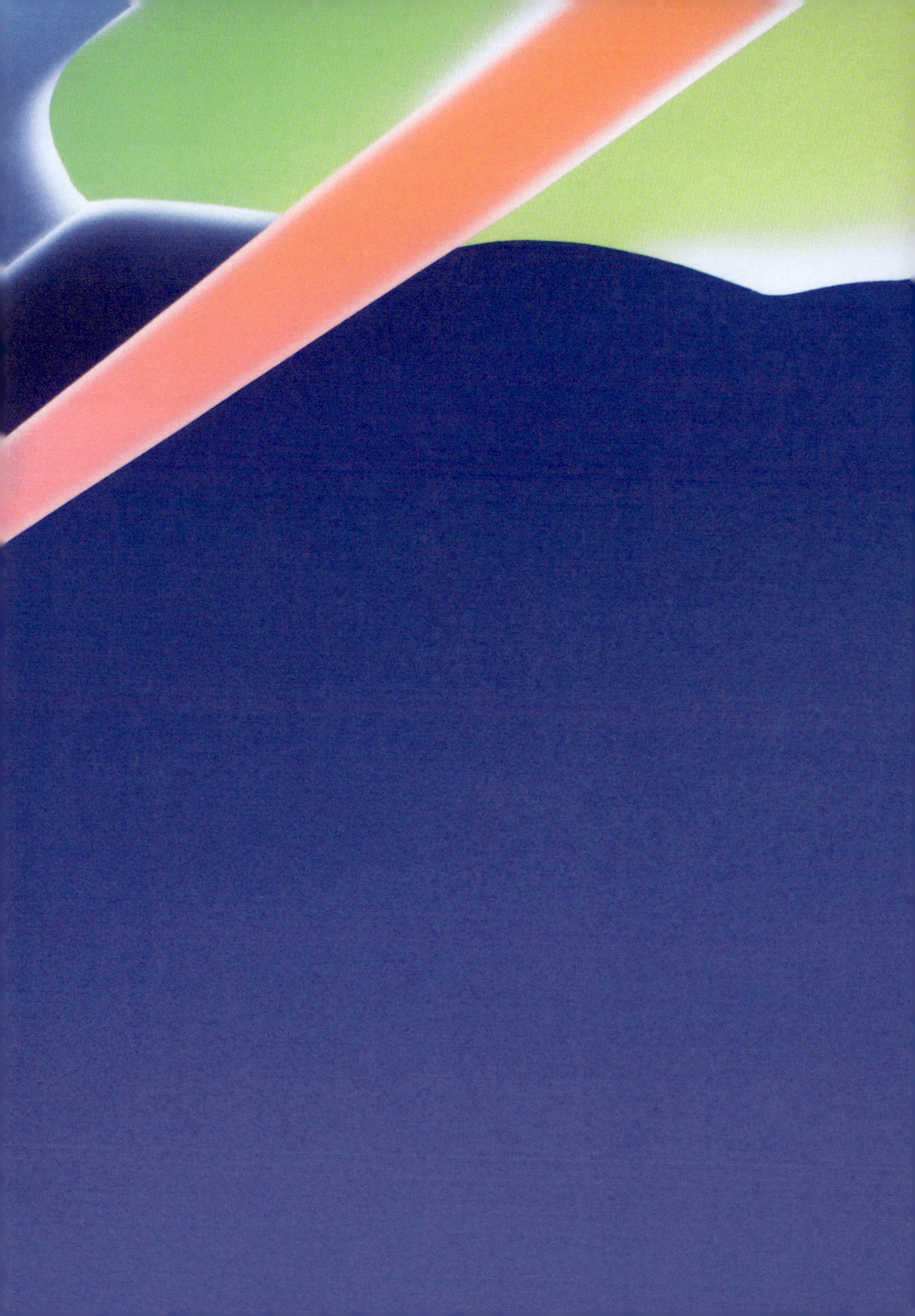

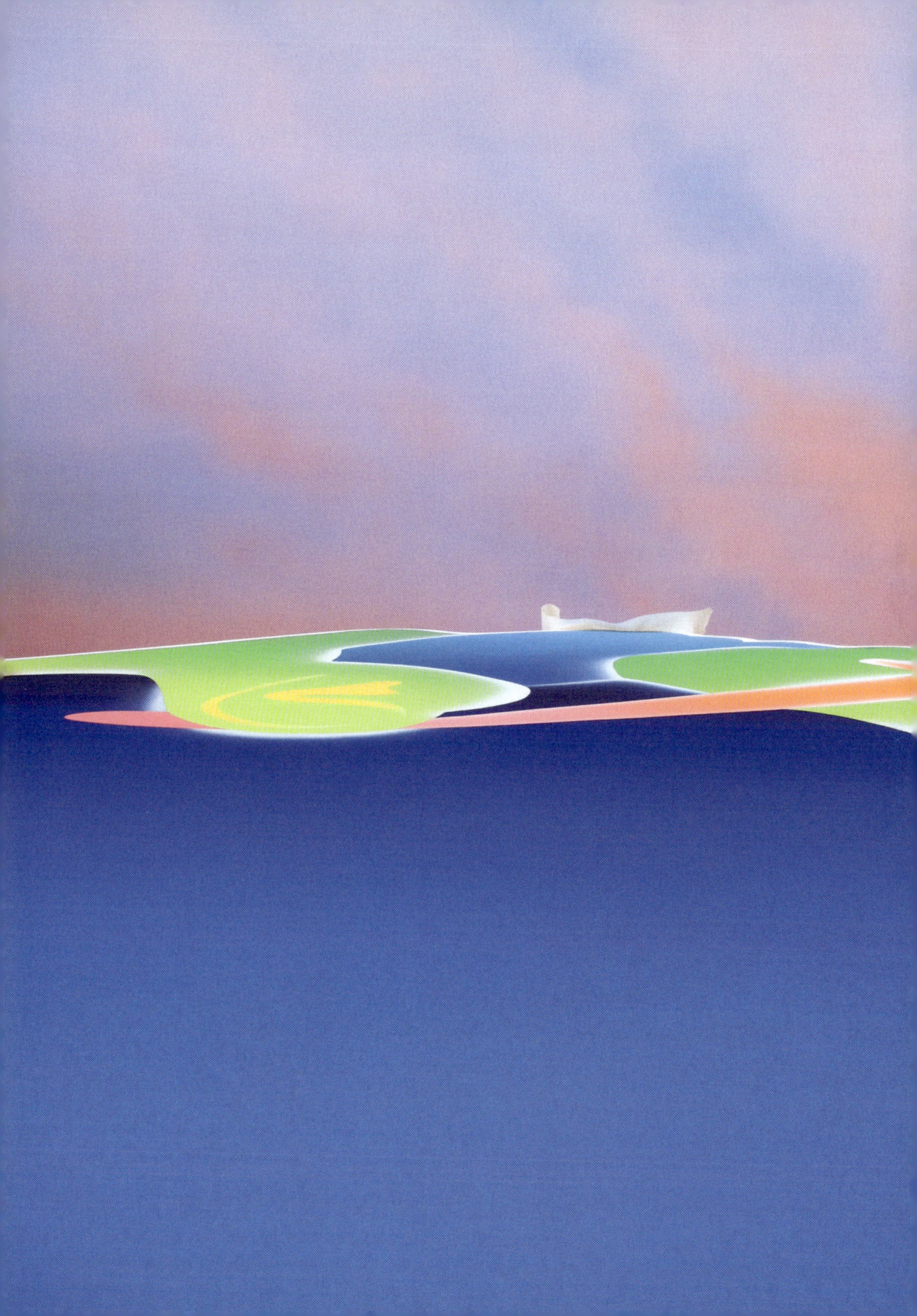

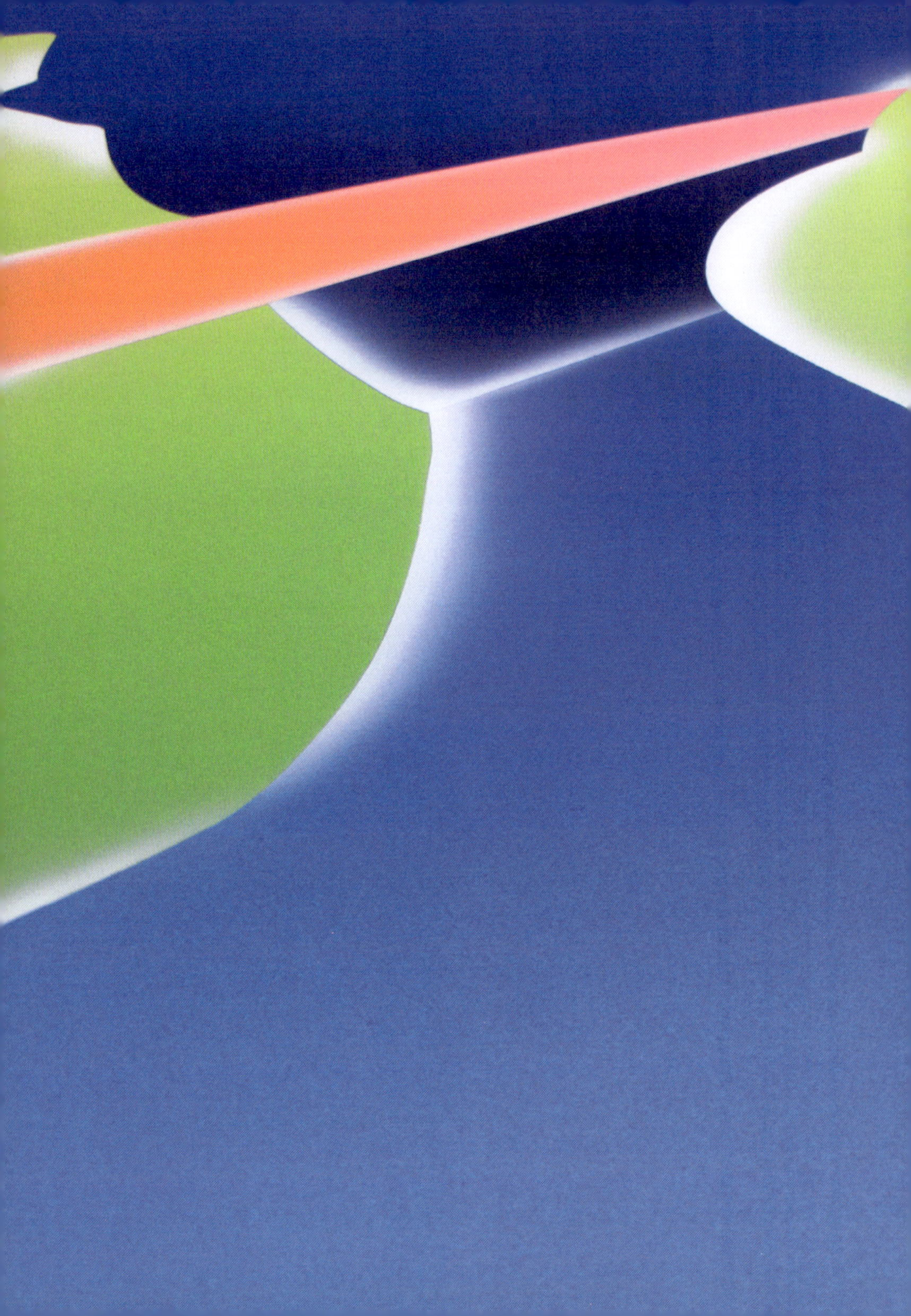

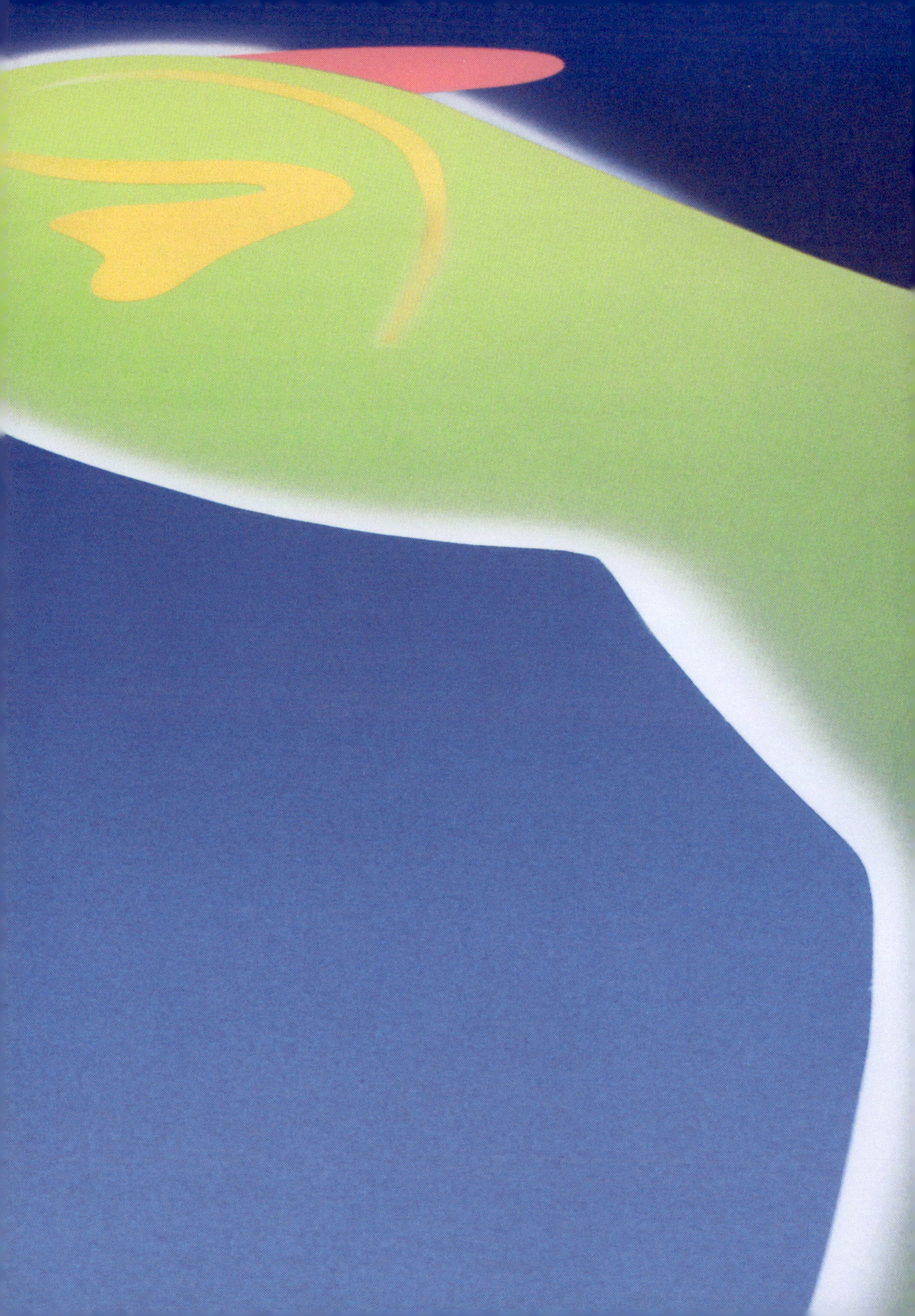

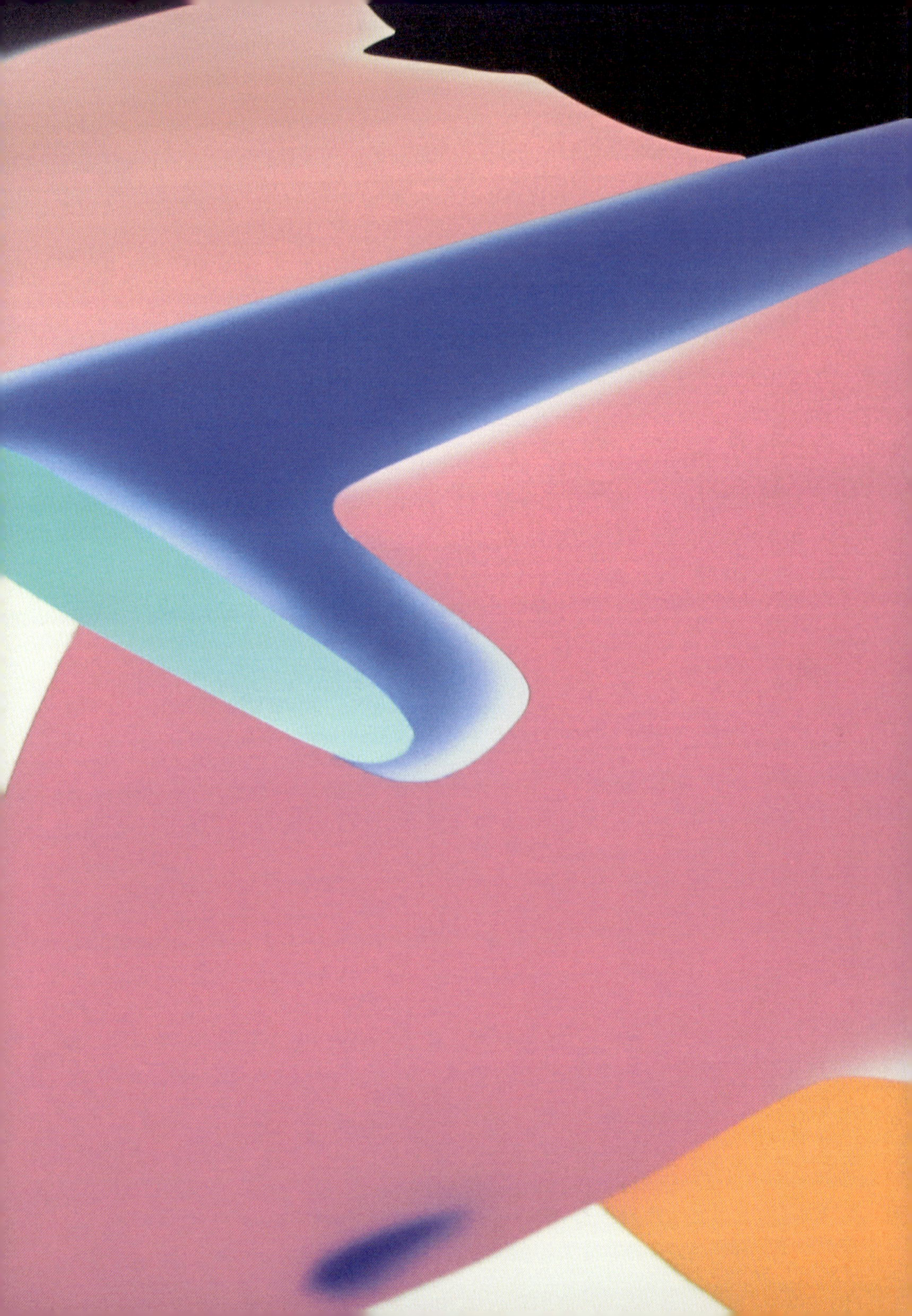

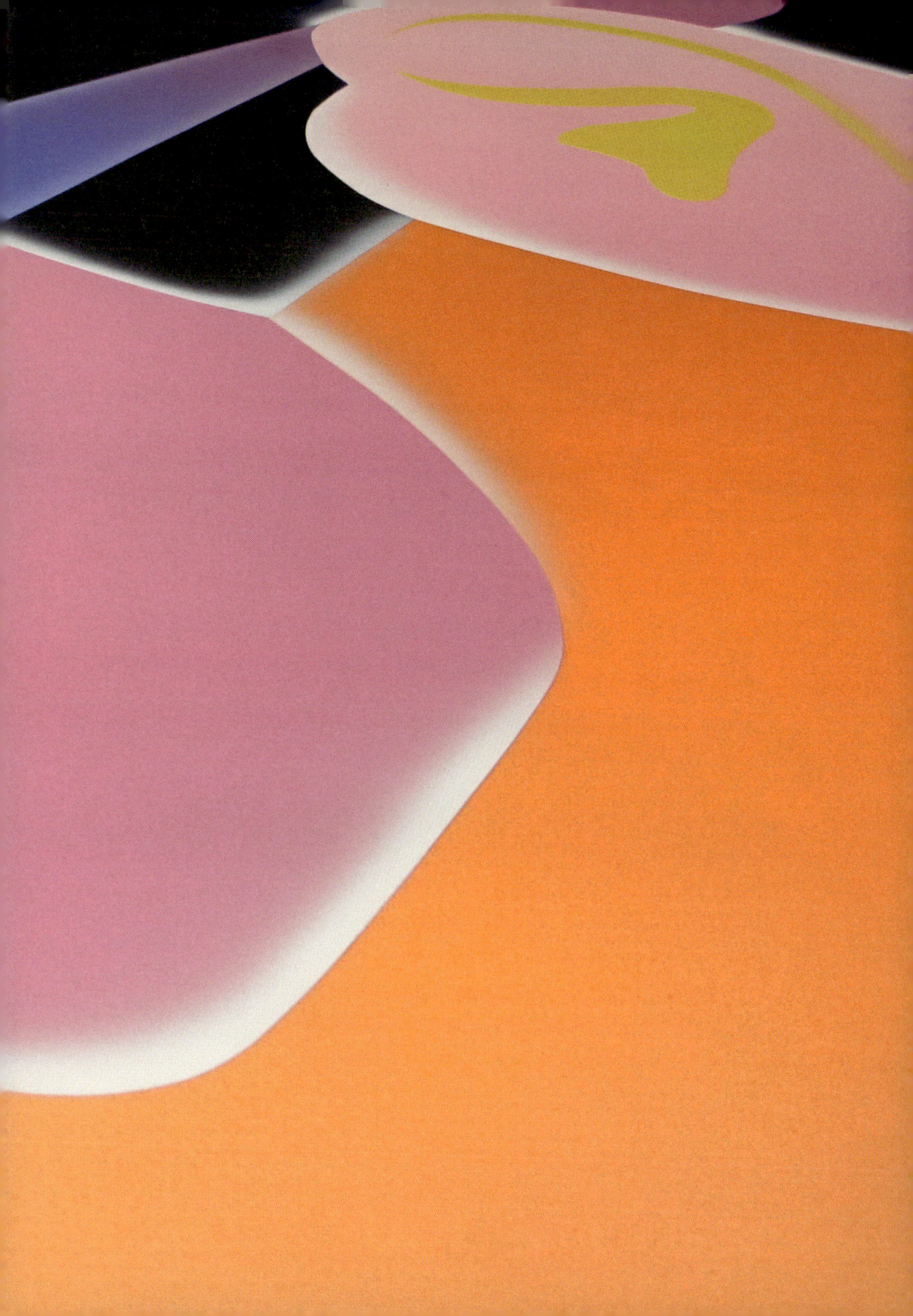

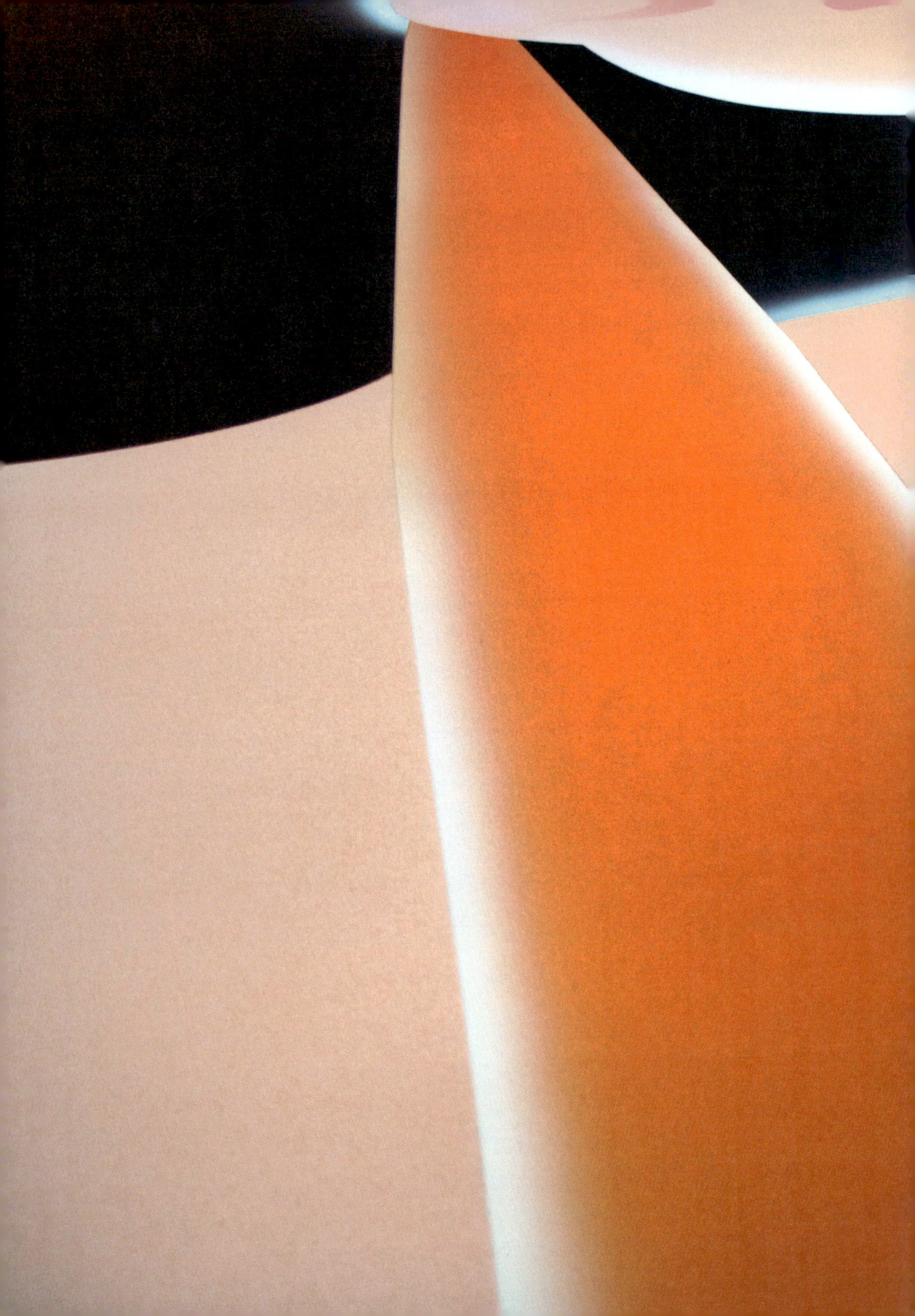

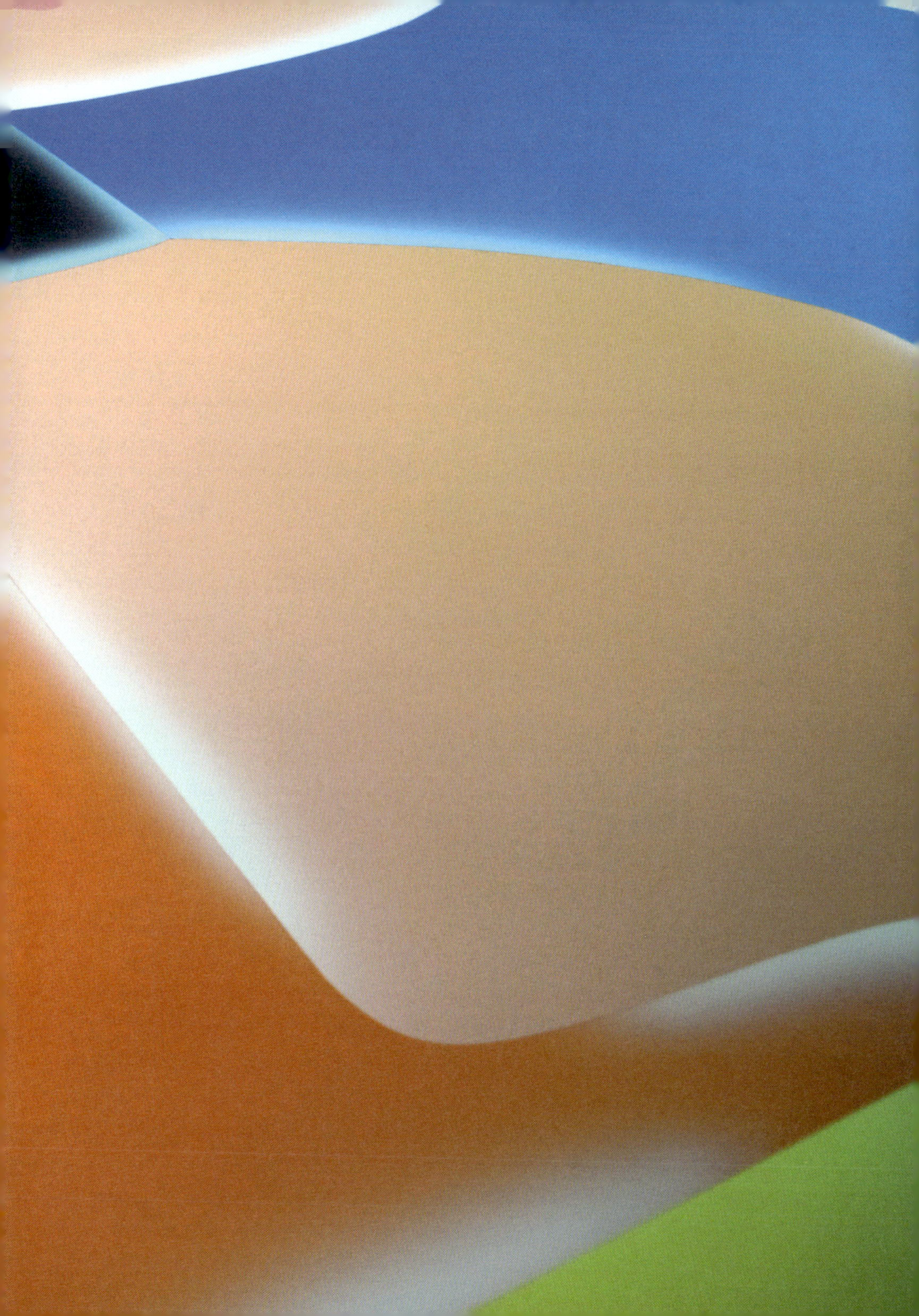

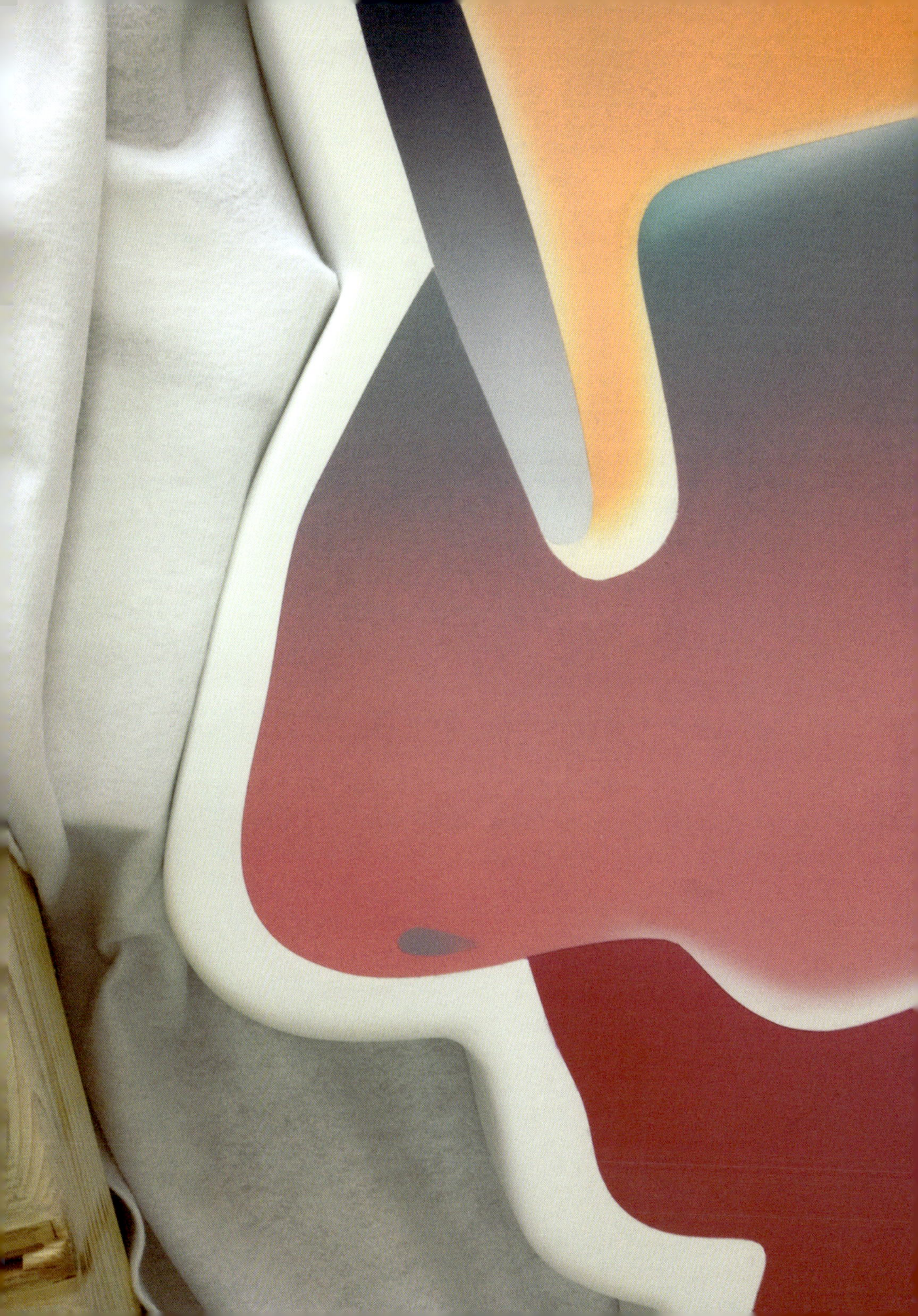